Urban Patronage in Early Modern England

Urban Patronage in Early Modern England

CORPORATE BOROUGHS,
THE LANDED ELITE, AND
THE CROWN, 1580-1640

Catherine F. Patterson

Stanford University Press
Stanford, California
1999

Stanford University Press
Stanford, California
© 1999 by the Board of Trustees of the
Leland Stanford Junior University
Printed in the United States of America
CIP data appear at the end of the book

For Charles Duane Patterson
and Joy Forster Patterson

Acknowledgments

A person who studies patronage knows better than anyone the significance of the assistance of others and the importance of returning thanks. My debts are many. Any scholarly endeavor, especially one involving research on two continents, requires a great deal of support, both financial and otherwise. Anyone who has done research in England's many county and city record offices knows the pleasures and frustrations of learning a local archive. I would like to thank the many archivists who have helped guide me through the intricacies of their collections. My bibliography spells out the debt I owe. I would also like to thank the librarians at the Regenstein Library at the University of Chicago, the Widener Library at Harvard University, and the M. D. Anderson Library at the University of Houston. The Interlibrary Loan staff at Anderson Library never quailed before my requests for obscure nineteenth-century town histories and dissertations from English universities. This book could not have been completed without the financial support I have received from the University of Chicago, Harvard University, and the University of Houston. In particular, I would like to acknowledge the assistance of a Research Initiation Grant and a Limited Grant-in-Aid from the University of Houston, which funded research trips to England, and a Junior Faculty Support Grant from the College of Humanities, Fine Arts, and Communication, which gave me a semester's leave from teaching to complete the writing of the book. I would also like to thank the Huntington Library in San Marino, California, for a Mellon Fellowship, which allowed me to use their tremendous collection.

Parts of this book have appeared in other form elsewhere. Parts of Chapter 3 appear as "Conflict Resolution and Patronage in Provincial Towns, 1590–1640," *Journal of British Studies* 37 (1998): 1–25 (©1998 by the North American Conference on British Studies; all rights reserved). I would like to thank the University of Chicago Press for permission to use this material in the present work. I am also pleased to acknowledge that parts of Chapter 6 appear as "Leicester and Lord Huntingdon: Urban Patronage in Early Modern England," *Midland History* 16 (1991): 45–62.

Many friends and colleagues have helped me greatly along the way. Dale Hoak helped spark my first interest in studying early modern England. Ted Cook and Charles Gray generously offered guidance at the early stages of this project. Betsy Wiltshire, Jeff Chamberlain, Dan Beaver, Joe Ward, Mary Bilder, Susan Lively, David Hancock, and Landon Storrs have offered both friendship and the challenge of scholarly discussion over the years. The support of my colleagues in the history department at the University of Houston has been a great help as I have worked to complete this project. I would also like to thank Jo and Mike Edwards and other friends from St. Stephens in Leicester for their hospitality and friendship during my sojourns in England. Several people have read all or parts of this work at various stages. Tom Cogswell, Richard Cust, Paul Halliday, Mark Kishlansky, John Morrill, Bob Palmer, and Bob Tittler have all offered insightful comments and useful advice that have greatly improved the final product, though remaining infelicities are entirely my own. Bob Tittler has been especially generous with his broad knowledge of early modern towns. I regret that his most recent book, *The Reformation and the Towns in England: Politics and Political Culture, c. 1540–1640* (Oxford, 1998), appeared too late to be integrated into the present work. Norris Pope and John Feneron of Stanford University Press deserve many thanks for making this project a reality. To several people I owe a special debt of gratitude. Mark Kishlansky's enthusiasm for history and his guidance and influence as a mentor have been critical to my development as a scholar. Paul Halliday has generously offered his time, ideas, and support over many years. His friendship and our ongoing conversation about the nature of early modern politics and society have made my studies in the field all the more enjoyable. My husband David deserves special credit for his good humor, love, and patience as this book took shape. To my family, especially my parents, I owe my greatest debt. They have been unfailingly supportive, and if they found it odd that a young woman from a small town in the Midwest wanted to study the arcana of early modern English history, they never let on. The dedication is a small token of gratitude for everything they have given me.

C.F.P.

Contents

Urban Patronage in Early Modern England

Introduction

Right honorable and most noble lord: We cannot but with all thankfulness
acknowledge those many noble favors cast upon our poor incorporation by
your Lop's hands for all which we stand forever obliged, so more especially
for this undeserved respect intimated unto us in your Honor's late letters, by
vouchsafing the acceptance of the burthen whereof we were bold in all humility to make the tender. For ourselves we presume that we shall have cause
to bless God for this so honorable a patronage. Our hope is and our care
shall forever be that your honor may never be ashamed of the owning of us.[1]

So wrote the bailiffs of Great Yarmouth to Edward Sackville, earl of
Dorset, in January 1630. The corporation, riven by factional strife,
threatened with the loss of chartered privileges, and abiding in the gloom
of royal displeasure, had sent out a cry for help. They called on a man who
was both king's councilor and borough officer to save the day. Dorset's
patronage, they believed, would rescue them, and, indeed, they were right.
The earl's well-placed words in Westminster and Yarmouth staved off a
meltdown of civic government.[2] Conflict did not disappear, but government worked.

Historians like to dwell on breakdown. It is flashier and more exciting
than the quotidian workings of business. The late sixteenth and early seventeenth centuries offer a variety of tensions on which to focus: rising
populations, social mobility, economic change, religious division, and political unrest.[3] A nation whose political and social prescriptions demanded
unity and order descended into civil war and revolution, the ultimate disorder. These agents of turmoil deserve close attention. But in focusing exclusively upon breakdown, we risk ignoring some critical questions. How
did Elizabethan and early Stuart government actually work? How did
central and local governments interact to preserve peace and take care of
the business of the realm? How did the leaders of this society try to create
order in the face of difference? For much of this period, a reasonably stable and increasingly integrated royal government ruled over the English

people. It is the goal of this book to explore an important part of what made government work: patronage.

Much has been written on the Tudors' consolidation of royal government and the Stuarts' attempt to secure it. Curbing authorities outside royal control and enforcing the loyalty of the peerage and gentry through coercion and favor, the Tudors transformed the nature of the government which they in turn bequeathed to the Stuarts.[4] Consolidating their position as sole focus of authority in the realm, English monarchs became increasingly adept at gaining the loyalty of the elite by offering the benefits of office and favor to those peers and gentlemen who provided the best service. By distributing the vast amount of favor within their patronage to high-born amateurs, rather than by creating a systematic professional bureaucracy (as occurred in France and Spain), English monarchs saw to the governance of their realm, from center to localities.

For early modern monarchs, patronage proved necessary to stable governance. It is a powerful tool. Historians, sociologists, and anthropologists have charted the presence of patron-client relations and the power of patronage as a system of exchange throughout history and throughout the world. Although scholars do not agree on a single definition, patronage is generally held to be a relationship of exchange that provides mutual benefits to both parties, but in which one partner is clearly superior to the other. A patron offers tangible benefits to his clients, such as economic aid and protection. In return, clients make offerings of a less tangible sort—honor, prestige, and loyalty—as well as of practical benefits like military service or political support. Relationships are based on affinity of family, place, or connection, and sometimes on a strong affective tie as well.[5] Patronage is hierarchical, reciprocal, and flexible. Patrons and clients need each other, and both partners must be satisfied in order for the relationship to prosper.[6] People seeking out patrons can cultivate multiple ties and move from one patron to another, locating the most effective aid.[7] Assisting in the process are intermediate actors, usually called brokers, who serve to link those in need with those who have. "Brokers introduce men with power to men seeking its use who are willing to give favors in return for it, then they arrange an exchange."[8] Patrons, brokers, and clients together form a network of personal relationships which in less complex societies can take the place of government, but which in Tudor and early Stuart England overlay the institutions of government.

The actions of the Tudor monarchs did much to ensure the interplay of patronage with their government. Historians of state-building have sometimes seen a linear progression from the growth of the centralized state to the decline of the authority of patrons, and thus the importance of patronage.[9] Henry VII and Henry VIII tried to curb the great landed magnates, stripping them of independent power and attempting to bring all English subjects under the direct control of the state. But rather than destroying patronage, the strengthening of the state under the Tudors and early Stuarts created new and different opportunities for its operation. Victor Morgan labels this "patrimonial" patronage.[10] In Morgan's formulation, members of the elite gladly became servants of the state (or more properly the crown) as JPs, DLs, and so forth, not simply for direct material rewards, but also for the prestige and influence that those offices conveyed. The operations of patronage were critical to the effectiveness of government because of the multiplicity of functions that both crown and clients expected officeholders to perform. Officeholders were expected to carry out the manifest duties of their position: an Exchequer clerk disbursed funds, a lord lieutenant exercised his county militia, a privy councilor gave advice to the monarch. But they were also expected to provide favor to others, assisting in administrative procedure and putting suitors on the way toward office or favor or benefit from the crown. Through this practice, clients received benefits they desired, while "the larger ends of the Crown were met insofar as they created a vested interest in the stability of the regime."[11] Patronage strengthened royal government by providing a means by which both official administration and the more informal grant of favor could occur. Simultaneously, Tudor and early Stuart government created new opportunities for patronage to work.

We know a great deal about the operations of patronage at Court and the ways that landed gentlemen were drawn into the nexus of connection that reinforced the crown's ability to govern. Scholars like Wallace MacCaffrey and Linda Levy Peck have detailed the distribution of favor by Tudor and Stuart monarchs.[12] MacCaffrey, in his seminal article on patronage in Elizabethan politics, showed how the English monarchy relied on the goodwill of the political elite—gentry and nobility—to keep the peace and govern the country. They maintained this loyalty by distributing crown favors, aiming "not at the adherence of a party or faction but at the good will of a whole class."[13] A part of this "class" entered royal service, operating the administration at Court. But most served the monarch as volunteers in the localities, carrying out royal government in the communities in which they lived. Armed with commissions granted by the crown, lord lieutenants, deputy lieutenants, and justices of the peace had the birthright of prestige and status, as well as royal backing, to command authority among the populace. These men used their positions both to

build up their own networks of personal connection and to act as mediators between central government and the localities. Other historians, like
Clive Holmes and Ann Hughes, have looked at the problem from the other
end. They investigated the ways that gentlemen responded to the pulls of
patronage, which drew members of the elite ever closer to the crown.[14]
The story of patronage as a tool for state-building seems to end there. But
what of the rest of the nation? What about the hundreds of local communities that spread out into the peripheries of the realm? The developments
of the sixteenth and early seventeenth centuries involved more than just
monarchs and their most prominent subjects. Local governments experienced the stresses of change as well. The story of patronage can be extended deep into the provinces, and there traced to investigate its role in
the early modern state.

Changes at the center deeply affected the government of communities
at the peripheries of the realm, and none more so than that of the many
boroughs that dotted the English countryside. These urban places had acquired franchises and privileges over the centuries that allowed them
varying degrees of self-government. For the men of these towns, the
changes of the late fifteenth through the early seventeenth centuries had a
direct impact.[15] Increasing numbers of provincial boroughs sought to free
themselves of seigneurial control and to establish administrative structures and courts over which civic leaders themselves presided. Requesting
charters of incorporation from the crown, the leading men of boroughs
wished to consolidate their authority over the inhabitants and remove
themselves from the jurisdiction of their former manorial overlords. The
crown happily complied in this process. It strengthened royal control over
boroughs by specifically defining the rights of town governments and by
making the chief officer of a corporation (usually the mayor) a royal officer.[16] The transition to greater self-governance for a growing number of
boroughs reflected the changes in the English state as much as did events
at Court.

Interpretations of this shift have often stressed ideas of "borough independence" and localism, divorcing corporations from the network of
connection that linked court and country. The historiography of borough
independence goes back to the nineteenth century, when both local historians and specialists in manorial tenures concentrated on the shift away
from feudal lordship among manorial boroughs. Both groups fit into a
tradition that stressed the casting off of lordly control by a rising middle
class. Feudal tenures gave way to municipal incorporation in boroughs as
industrious townsmen purchased manors in their corporate capacity, con-

trolling their own destiny and excluding as much external control as possible. Local historians emphasized the attempts of their civic predecessors to become independent, choosing their own fellows rather than gentlemen as MPs or refusing to capitulate to aristocratic influence. Boroughs became more "modern" as they jettisoned medieval forms and governed themselves with the aid of a royal charter.[17]

For much of the twentieth century, historians have accepted some of that picture as they struggled to understand how towns fit into the larger polity. For many, patronage with reference to townsmen meant only parliamentary patronage, which resulted in one of two things for civic officials. Either they suffered "borough invasion," allowing patrons to force their will on the locality, or they declared "independence," keeping the landed elite completely out of civic business. The influential Tudor historian, Sir John Neale, portrayed these struggles over patronage in the dramatic religious language of sin and repentance, good and evil. York is declared to have fallen from the "roll of the impeccable" because of its "one lapse from grace" for having accepted an outsider as MP in 1601. The record of Elizabethan Cambridge was "not unspotted" because townsmen chose John North, esq., son of their high steward, in a by-election of 1581. This "did not seem a heinous sin," however, since North had been made a burgess and alderman of the town. Neale lauds Shrewsbury for its independent spirit in the early years of the queen's reign, but assigns demerits when voters accept the nominees of the earl of Essex later on. He notes that "repentance did at last come to town authorities" in 1604, when the leaders of Shrewsbury vowed to choose two resident townsmen as MPs.[18] Neale, valuing parliament above all other aspects of government, assumed that any patronage relationship was forced on corporations by would-be parliamentary power-brokers and necessarily met with antagonism on the part of civic leaders.

Other historians have reinforced this antagonistic view of relations between urban government and the outside world. In some of the most formative work on English towns in the last quarter century, Peter Clark and Paul Slack have assessed this relationship, concluding that most towns did not fare well between 1500 and 1700. "Basic to the critical difficulties faced by English towns in our period was the vulnerability of urban communities to forces outside their control. Towns were not their own masters in early modern England and were less so at the end of our period than at the beginning." Damaged by urban decline and susceptible to "forces outside their control," towns became "dependent" on royal favor and "increasingly suffered both royal and gentry involvement in their affairs."[19] Local historians like W. G. Hoskins and Alan Dyer also stressed the essentially inward-looking nature of most early modern towns. Much of the work of urban historians concerned itself with the borough economy, which, according to economic historians, stagnated in many towns during the sixteenth and seventeenth centuries. Merchants and tradesmen concentrated on their own troubles and tried to avoid potentially damaging interaction with extramural authorities as much as possible.[20] Wallace MacCaffrey's fine book on Exeter provides a good example of this work. It situates the city in the larger polity and goes well beyond narrow economic questions, but the book still highlights the desire of Exeter's leaders to exclude authority not their own. MacCaffrey catalogs the ways in which the Exeter Assembly worked to consolidate its own power while resisting the inroads of the local gentry, cathedral clergy, and royal officers alike. For MacCaffrey's townsmen, little of importance occurred outside the city walls.[21]

This interpretation of the urban community fits nicely with the localist arguments for county politics of the same period. Alan Everitt and others argued for the existence of a deep and growing gulf between the center and the provinces over the course of the sixteenth and seventeenth centuries, a gulf that ultimately contributed to, if not caused, the English Civil War. With little or no sense of national purpose, but rather a strong loyalty to one's county community, gentlemen rejected the dictates of the king and defended the rights of their localities. Similarly, urban communities, more concerned with their economic well-being and political autonomy, became alienated from the center and stepped more easily into rebellion.[22]

While rhetorically powerful, this black-and-white world of independence and dependence, of localism and isolation, did not really exist. Localism provided a useful explanation for the breakdown at midcentury, but its validity has been questioned by scholars who have noted the complex loyalties and interests of the leaders of English society.[23] This notion of the interactive nature of central and local relations has been applied to civic governments as well as to landed gentry. David Harris Sacks has worked extensively on the city of Bristol in the late medieval and early modern periods, drawing a strong case for the widening vision of that urban community. He argues that the early modern period saw the leading men of Bristol leaving behind the internal, communal focus of the Middle Ages and expanding their horizons to London and beyond.[24] Others have echoed this argument. Richard Cust in his work on the town of Great Yarmouth shows the high degree of both political awareness and integration with the center exhibited by the town's governors. A battle over who would govern Great Yarmouth in the late 1620's was waged jointly in the Town Hall and in Whitehall, with local men attaching themselves to people at the center who represented differing interests. Cust's findings clearly show the level of interpenetration between center and locality and the role of patrons in facilitating that connection.[25]

This book moves beyond the individual local study to investigate the wider workings of patronage that affected all towns. The town fathers of England's incorporated boroughs sought out connections as a means to strengthen their own position by gaining access to the center. Not simply pawns in the game of central and local relations, civic governors took an active part in shaping those interactions. Integration between the center and the locality, the extensive and the particular, was crucial to the survival of both. The quest of civic leaders for the favor of the powerful did not originate with the reign of Elizabeth. One historian of late medieval England has said that political and economic circumstances forced towns to find influential friends who could press local claims at Court, leading to an almost "obsessive search for lordship."[26] But the increased strength of the early modern state and the growing demands the state placed on local governors like mayors and aldermen made the drive to find patrons all the more compelling. Civic leaders carefully crafted connections with the powerful men who ruled England, enlisting aid to serve the purposes of themselves and their communities. While adamantly resisting elite control over urban government, townsmen found ways to elicit help from their more powerful neighbors and friends and to reinforce their own authority at the same time. They used traditional forms of exchange—deference and honor, gift-giving and hospitality—as well as local office and parliamentary seats, to cultivate the favor of the powerful. These building blocks of patronage and clientage depended little on ideological connection. Townsmen were not ideologically naive provincials, nor were they averse to seeking out the favor of those with whom they shared common beliefs, particularly in religion. Yet ideology took a secondary place to pragmatic considerations of individual and community interest as well as traditional social bonds of good lordship and neighborhood. Corporations all over the realm sought links to those great men most likely to provide the advantages of local power and royal connection.

Corporations and their patrons entered into these relations for their own benefits and interests. A national consciousness, or an intentional drive to state-building, played little part. Yet the result was the increased strength and integration of royal government. Men in the provinces identified the crown as the fount of favor, and they worked to gain access to the channels that flowed from that fountain. This created an infrastructure of personal connection that reinforced the crown's authority. Institutions, such as the central courts, the Privy Council, and the Assizes, provided a backbone for government, but it was this network of personal connection that made government work. The strength of the early modern English state depended heavily on the willingness of those who governed to cooperate with and give support to it. To a large degree, its growth depended not on the crown's ability to coerce, but rather on the actions of local leaders to knit their localities to the center. One scholar has recently suggested that the power of the state in fact grew during the seventeenth century not because of any institutional innovation, but simply because the elites who governed willingly participated in it.[27] Patronage was a critical factor in developing the state's strength.

Institutions always remained building blocks of the English state. But if institutions provided "points of contact," as G. R. Elton suggested, it was people rather than structures that served as the glue that held the realm together, that made governance succeed or fail.[28] The bonds of patronage and connection between individuals and communities made politics and administration work in a country that lacked both a standing army and an elaborate professional bureaucracy to coerce compliance with the center's needs. The integration of the state occurred because local leaders, like the mayors and aldermen of corporate boroughs, acted to engage themselves with the crown's government, not simply because the central government worked to rope them into its fold.

SOURCES, METHODS, AND APPROACH

In looking at the integration of the English state from the perspective of provincial corporate boroughs, this study offers a fresh angle from which to view governance in the late sixteenth and early seventeenth centuries. Previous discussions of government have tended to focus heavily on the counties, with little reference to urban communities.[29] While county studies provide critical insights into early modern society and politics, the lack of systematic attention to borough corporations conceals a source of great value for understanding this period. Each of England's over 150 incorporated boroughs had its own constitution and slate of local governors who met with each other on an almost daily basis to make decisions for their locality. Spread all over the country and ranging in size and importance, corporate boroughs provide a detailed set of records of local government and a platform for comparison of activities and attitudes around the realm. A number of important individual town studies have addressed the themes of order, connection, and integration,[30] but it is hoped that this book will provide a broad vision of the English state. The nature of the records, as well as the nature of the subject, places focus on the thoughts and actions of the magistrates of England's corporate boroughs. The voice of civic governors, rather than the urban populace in general, predominates.

This study is based largely on the records of provincial borough corporations across England. The core of evidence comes from the manuscript archives of a number of incorporated towns: Chester, Dover, Exeter, Ipswich, Leicester, and Great Yarmouth, as well as Coventry, Worcester, Barnstaple, and Winchester. They range from modest county towns to important provincial capitals; the greatest cities—London, Norwich, Bristol—are not central to the work. They all had populations in the middle range, between about 3,000 and 10,000, with Leicester and Barnstaple at the smaller end of the scale and Exeter and Chester at the other. These towns are also geographically disparate, providing a varied base from which to draw conclusions. Finally, all of these towns have excellent archives, with voluminous extant records from the sixteenth and seventeenth centuries, including Common Hall or Assembly minutes, correspondence, and civic accounts. An intensive investigation of the records of these corporations brought to light the patterns of urban patronage that form the basis of this study. These patterns, once established, were then traced through the manuscript archives and printed records of over 40 other boroughs in order to make a broader argument concerning towns and patrons. Wherever possible, the letters and papers of the patrons of particular corporations were consulted as well, in order to present both sides of the story. The records of central government, principally State Papers and Privy Council records in the Public Record Office, provided a source for investigating the crown's perspective on the issue of urban governance. Spelling and punctuation in quotations from these manuscript sources have been modernized. Dates are in old style, but the year has been taken to begin on 1 January.

Royal responses to urban government were not uniform throughout the period, nor did all corporate boroughs react the same way to their circumstances. Strain and conflict, as well as cooperation and advantage, could characterize relations between corporations, their patrons, and the crown. Size, location, economic circumstances, and historic connections to neighboring landed families could have a defining effect on the way a particular borough dealt with other authorities. The focus is on provincial towns; London does not feature significantly in this study, except for reasons of comparison. The distinguishing feature of all the towns considered here is that they had or gained charters of incorporation from the crown in this period. Charters guaranteed their rights and privileges, setting them off from the more numerous market towns that were also more susceptible to control by nontownsmen. While different towns had differing abilities to handle the demands of government by personal connection, the common themes ring through clearly. The goal here is not to create a single model that describes the action of every corporate borough, but rather to show the broad outlines of the framework of patronage and the various ways that urban government worked within it. This book also attempts to show the strains and conflicts, as well as the benefits, that could arise out of a system based on personal connection.

This study takes as its time frame roughly 1580 to 1640, terminal dates that are, like most, rather artificial. Yet they offer convenient bookends for the subject of urban patronage. The instability and experimentation of the earlier sixteenth century had substantially subsided. For boroughs, the great wave of incorporation had passed; the majority of those that were to be incorporated in the sixteenth century had been by 1580. The office of high steward, which (as will be seen below) was an important element in urban patronage, became increasingly common in corporations after this date. On a broader scale, patterns of government, both at the center and in the localities, had by 1580 begun to settle into the routines that have sometimes been referred to as the "Elizabethan constitution."[31] Much of the political and administrative activity of the period (including patronage) attempted to keep this constitution running. By our ending date of 1640, the consensus that characterized the previous 60 years was no longer quite so sound. The meeting of the Long Parliament and the events that ensued altered the relationship between king and parliament, center and localities. The present work, aiming to illuminate the way government worked, does not ignore the fact that war was to come, but nevertheless seeks to avoid overemphasis on later divisions.

The investigation of urban patronage and early modern government is presented here in six chapters, five thematic and one a longer case study. They are arranged like concentric rings, beginning at the local level and emanating out in larger circles as the locality met the larger realm. Chapter 1 reconstructs the basic building-blocks of urban patronage, showing the methods corporations used to solicit favor and the reasons potential patrons responded. Chapter 2 details the particular ways that patrons participated in borough life, while Chapter 3 demonstrates how patrons helped to maintain order in the local community. Chapters 4 and 5 move out beyond the locality, investigating the ways that patronage worked to mediate between civic corporations and the rest of the realm, from county government to regional courts to the crown. Chapter 6 then brings all these parts together by showing how urban patronage worked over time in an ongoing relationship, that between the borough of Leicester and the earls of Huntingdon. Together, these chapters intend to reconstruct the multilayered relationships that made government work.

That government did generally work is at times obscured by our fascination with locating the origins of civil war and revolution. By its very nature, that endeavor brings to light alienation and fragmentation. The seriousness and impact of that conflict cannot be underestimated. But directing our gaze away from the breakdown at midcentury allows us to begin to understand the practical workings of government and authority in this period. A complex picture of connection emerges. The motivation for this linkage came from both directions—a centralizing royal government trying to gain a firmer grasp on the realm, and local leaders who saw that their best chance for continued authority and prosperity came from the crown. The pages below demonstrate how the leaders of corporate towns regularly reached out to engage with the rest of government. Operating with complex notions of honor, deference, responsibility, and self-interest, they made connections with the leaders of landed society to ensure their links to the crown. By this they secured their own authority. Just like gentlemen, the fictive individuals called corporations reaped benefits by crafting channels of access to the center. They manipulated the network of patronage so as to achieve their own ends and to do the crown's bidding.

Such relationships were by no means unproblematic. Serious friction at times existed between patron and client, between center and peripheries. Local authorities could not and did not solve all their problems by appealing to patronage. The traditional social exchange that grounded patronage had difficulty accommodating deeply held opinions, and might break under the stress of being unable to provide real remedies. Nevertheless, even during times of great stress, corporations continued to try to work through the traditional means of patronage and connection to the crown to solve the knotty political and religious problems that confronted them. Patronage offered a vital tool. It suited both local needs and royal will, varying with the vagaries of royal policy. An understanding of the effectiveness of governance by personal connection illuminates both the increasing cohesiveness of the English state and the severity of the problems that underlay the civil war.

ONE

Corporations and Patronage

Making Connections

Whereas we of the Town of Barnstaple do find by daily experience that through the envy of others maligning the prosperity of this town we have many heavy burdens laid upon us, under pressure whereof we have a long time groaned & are yet to be without remedy unless we may procure the assistance of some great man who is powerful at the Court and Council Board. . . . And forasmuch as the right honorable the earl of Dorset hath lately declared himself to be a noble friend unto this town, both before the Council Board and elsewhere, and hath vindicated the wrongs which have lately been offered unto the Mayor and others of this Town . . . , and he being a Privy Councilor and a man greatly in grace with the King's Majesty, we therefore think it fitting and do consent and agree that a patent of High Stewardship be forthwith drawn up for the earl of Dorset and to be with all expedition sent up to London under the Town Seal . . . together with a piece of plate or some such thing as a present.[1]

The corporators of Barnstaple felt oppressed. Although the modest seaport in North Devon held its own and even thrived in the unstable years of the sixteenth and early seventeenth centuries, it could not remain immune from the social, economic, and political vagaries of the day. Throughout the early seventeenth century, Barnstaple's active trade with France burgeoned and the city prospered. But in the late 1630's, rival West Country ports and the monopolizing London and Bristol merchants threatened this prosperity. The merchant elite of the town complained of the "patentees and pursuivants" who interfered with their business. Simultaneously, the townsmen suffered under the increasingly onerous burden of Ship Money, the unpopular levy imposed by Charles I. These problems in turn stirred internal strife. The "common burgesses" complained that the magistrates had begun creating freemen against local ordinance, giving the liberty to men who had done no apprenticeship, so that (it was said) the corporation could rate them for the "King's service."

The burgesses alleged that the magistrates created the extra freemen in order to collect more Ship Money than necessary, then used the "overplus" to maintain their private quarrels, thus impoverishing the town.[2] Civic leaders knew that they must take action to battle back against the forces aligned against them. In 1637, the corporation of Barnstaple did what so many other borough governments did during this period: they sought a patron.

Corporators assessed their situation carefully. In their statement, they acknowledged their need for assistance from "some great man," someone with authority far greater than theirs who could defend them against the jealous maligners and lift them out from under the pressure of their burdens. They also saw that they required an advocate who was not simply strong, but who had a particular type of strength: a "man who is powerful at the Court and Council Board." Court and Privy Council would be the places that the men of Barnstaple would find remedy. Their advocate must have authority there. Next, they described their reasons for choosing a particular great man. Several peers would certainly have qualified for the office, but the earl of Dorset had several advantages. He not only sat on the Privy Council, but he was "greatly in grace" with King Charles. He had the ear of the king. Also important from the town's point of view was the fact that Dorset had recently shown a personal, beneficial interest in the town. He "declared himself to be a noble friend" of Barnstaple, overtly acknowledging his benevolence toward the city. He made these motions of friendship not only at Court, but elsewhere, as well. And, most importantly for the practical needs of the corporators, he took action on the civic leaders' behalf, vindicating the mayor and others of the charges laid against them. It was this sort of friendship that the corporators needed.

The city fathers took careful steps to cement that friendship. A onetime act of favor by the earl helped, but an ongoing relationship with Dorset would profit the corporation in the future. They decided to formalize their relationship with Dorset, establishing him as a patron by making him an officer of the corporation. As high steward, Dorset would have an official connection to Barnstaple. This would oblige him to look out for the town's interests, and it would also provide townsmen with a direct link to the halls of power in London. They sent their recorder to deliver a patent of office personally to the earl, to express their duty and goodwill. But the patent of office served as only one sign of connection between borough and lord. The townsmen also wished to bestow on the earl a valuable gift, a piece of plate, to symbolize the personal, affective element that they understood to be part of their relationship with him. Not just an office, but mutual obligation, stood at the foundation of this connection. With gifts and patents, Barnstaple's civic leaders successfully engaged the interest of the fourth earl of Dorset. He accepted the office of high stewardship and continued to serve in that place until at least 1643.[3]

This "Order for Choosing a High Steward" provides an explicit statement of a corporation's need for patronage and the specific steps taken to acquire it. Barnstaple's case is instructive. The distribution of favor and the manipulation of patronage have long been acknowledged by historians as key ways in which the central government of early modern England ruled. The crown possessed offices and benefits that it doled out to the gentry and nobility, who in turn secured the order and safety of the nation. This was one of the most important ways that the Tudors and Stuarts built up the power of the state. Yet this document from Barnstaple suggests that the use of patronage and connection went far beyond the crown and the aristocracy alone. Local leaders, too, undertook to navigate the channels of favor and benefit. Cultivating links of patronage and friendship with England's elite, the governors of localities in the provincial hinterlands advanced their own authority by connecting themselves with the center.

I

Patronage permeated early modern society. From the Court to the counties to the towns and villages of sixteenth- and early seventeenth-century England, power-brokers and favor-seekers engaged in the rituals of gift-giving, hospitality, and the language of love. These both elaborated social conventions and supported government policy. Associations that would now be considered political manifested themselves in social display. Historians studying patronage have tended to focus more attention on the pragmatic benefits of these relations—office, favor, parliamentary seats. For early modern Englishmen, however, these benefits formed only part of a proper relationship. The ceremonial side of patronage was critically important to the cultivation and maintenance of connection between those who had and those who needed. Such displays reinforced the dominant ideas of social hierarchy of the time. Those of high social and political standing were expected to offer service, protection, and largesse; in return they received deference, obligation, and honor. The connections that formed between patrons and clients in general, and specifically between corporations and their patrons, depended on a reciprocal exchange of both political and social goods. These relationships combined elements of symbolism with pragmatic, material benefits. Urban patronage cannot be understood without acknowledging the significance of social exchange in political connection.

The language of patronage and clientage reflected and amplified the hierarchical nature of the relationship. Those seeking the favor of the powerful used the language of supplication in almost ritualistic ways, trying to create obligation in their hearers. Indeed, books of instruction existed, telling letter-writers exactly how to address their social superiors and how to word their letters for specific circumstances and requests.[4] Early modern townsmen, while not at the centers of power, used the language of patronage frequently and knew what practices it encompassed. The word "patron" was certainly part of their regular vocabulary, although "good lord" frequently served as a substitute. When Chester's mayor and aldermen wrote to the earl of Derby to ask a favor, they addressed him as "our very good lord," but also called him "our chief patron on whom we only depend, under his Majesty."[5] Similarly, the mayor of Oxford referred to William Lord Knollys as the "patron" of the city of Oxford, and worried that if the city alienated Knollys, they would be "unreceived into patronage" by other noblemen, as well.[6] The word "client," on the other hand, was less common in contemporary usage. "Suitor," "servant," and "follower" saw more frequent use. "Broker" is also a modern coinage; early modern people used parallel words like "friend," "mediator," or "means." Regardless of the words they used, the officers of corporate boroughs knew their position in the network of patronage and worked to become effective suitors to the men in power. Reciprocity and mutual obligation infused the language of patronage. They underlay social and political interaction.

The exchange of gifts and hospitality, a critical element of patronage, offered a basic means of expressing political connection. While we would now generally associate them with private life—things offered to close friends and family—early modern society considered presents and shared meals part of public life. They symbolized the respect of the giver toward the recipient, as well as the acceptance by the recipient of the obligation it conveyed.[7] Texts from classical antiquity, much in vogue in this period, clearly informed contemporary notions of benefits and obligations. Seneca's *De Beneficiis* (Of Benefits) went through three English editions between the 1570's and the 1620's.[8] This treatise captured the complex nature of exchange, which combined freely given honor and favor with the less altruistic motivation of personal gain. On the one hand, the giver of a benefit should never expect return; it is indeed more virtuous to give where no requital is expected. On the other hand, the recipient of a benefit is clearly expected to make some return. "He who requiteth not a favour done him, sinneth more."[9] Giving assumes mutual obligation. But the obligation rests not on the exchange of things in and of themselves. The relationship symbolized in the benefit or gift holds greater importance. "A benefit therefore consisteth not in that which is eyther done or given, but in the mind of him that eyther giveth or doeth the pleasure."[10] Gifts also bestowed something of great importance in early modern society: status. According to Seneca, benefiting bore three fruits—contentment for having done a thing well, reciprocity, and reputation.[11] Participation in the exchange provided honor to both parties. Giving a gift showed respect to the recipient. It also signaled that the giver deserved the same. A gift simply stood as a marker, an external expression of an intangible bond of respect and honor.

Civic leaders, well aware of the potential power of gift-giving, made sophisticated use of it to benefit themselves and their localities. Gift and exchange constituted a fundamental part of political practice. In a system where hierarchy and deference ruled social and political relations, the giving of gifts provided a way to ensure that the more powerful would be kept in mind of the less powerful. Queen Elizabeth clearly expected gifts during the holiday season, and nobles agonized over what would be the appropriate item to express loyalty and remind the monarch of the giver. Christmas and, especially, New Year marked the traditional season of gift-giving among the elite, providing a specific occasion for clients to remind patrons of their existence and their service.[12] Never shy to grab the main chance, however, clients also gave patrons gifts anytime they required a particular favor. While this might smack of bribery or corruption, it was not seen as such in early modern England. Bribery existed, but within narrow parameters. "Gift" covered a wide range of exchange and formed a legitimate and important part of political and social activity. The monarch, like a fountain, stood as the ultimate well-spring of favor that flowed down to all his subjects. Subjects made return by providing loyalty, service, and obedience.[13] Similar relations existed between patrons and clients all up and down the social scale, and the giving of gifts offered one manifestation of this connection.

Corporations made extensive use of gift-giving and hospitality in crafting connections to noblemen and gentlemen.[14] Civic financial accounts reveal regular expenditures on gifts and hospitality, suggesting that local leaders saw this as an important use of public funds. Many corporations operated on (or over) the threshold of insolvency, but nevertheless continued to lay out money to court the powerful. Typically, 3 or 4 percent of the annual outlay went for gifts and hospitality, although it might be higher or lower depending on circumstances.[15] Some of these civic accounts are extraordinarily detailed, not only stating various expenditures but also explaining the reasons for the outlay. Leicester's accounts provide such running commentary: "Item the xiiith day of June [1611] paid for wine sugar and cherries given to Mr. Walter Hastings at London who went to the Judges to move them to hold the Assizes at Leicester notwithstanding the sickness of the plague being then in several places in Leicester, 3s. 4d."[16] Even those accounts that offer only the barest of reckonings reveal the importance of gifts and hospitality in tying corporations to the larger realm.

Gift-giving was fundamental to urban patronage. Gifts could signify different things, either long-term commitment to a particular patron or a more ephemeral act of deference to a passing dignitary. Visits by a monarch to a town brought forth the most lavish gifts and rituals of hospitality. This usually included presenting the monarch with silver or gold and greeting him with fanfares and Latin orations, while the members of the corporation presided over the proceedings wearing their finest scarlet robes. On these occasions, infrequent as they were, townsmen expected to spend significant sums both to honor the royal visitor and to demonstrate the loyalty and dignity of the town and its leadership. When King James I and Prince Henry came to Leicester in August 1612, the corporation spent nearly £40 for gifts to the monarch and his son, as well as about £60 in other charges for the sojourn, such as repair of the roads and fees to officers in the king's train. The town typically spent between £400 and £600 *per annum* in total, so this £100 made up a significant sum. The members of Leicester corporation clearly hoped to uphold their reputation through these activities, as they sent the town clerk to Newark-upon-Trent and Nottingham, other stops on the king's route, "to see how they [*sic*] Townsmen entertained the King and Prince thither."[17] In honor of King Charles's stay in Dover in May 1625, when he went to greet his new bride Henrietta Maria, the Dover corporation agreed to furnish "two fair double gilt cups of 100 marks price" for the royal couple. They also sent one of their members off to see the cups that Canterbury gave the monarchs so they could compare them and ensure the propriety of Dover's gift.[18] The reputation of the town rested on these presents; providing an inferior one would reflect badly on the corporation and might lead to a loss of favor. Such ceremonial moments solidified connections between center and locality and allowed local governors to prove their authority.

Royal visits were rare, but most corporate boroughs saw a steady stream of lesser dignitaries passing through their gates. Whether traveling on royal business or simply for personal pleasure, prominent visitors offered civic leaders opportunities to gain benefits for their towns. By presenting gifts, corporators hoped to secure the benevolence of their guests. Civic accounts from most boroughs record that judges, privy councilors, local magnates, visiting gentlemen, and other figures of authority received "gratuities" during their sojourns in towns. Wine and sugar served as the gift of choice for most corporations, but regional specialties—salmon pie or cheeses—might also make their way into the hands of visiting dignitaries.[19] In 1605–6, for example, the chamberlain of Ipswich laid out money for wine and sack for "Mr. Chancellor," a marchpane and "Ipocras" for Sir Michael Stanhope and his lady, and red and white wine and claret for the king of Denmark's secretary. In 1613–14, Chester's corporation gave wine and sugar to Sir Thomas Wilbraham as he returned from Ireland, entertained Judge Warburton with "meath, aquavite, and other appurtenances," held a lavish banquet for the lord deputy of Ireland, sent wine and a sugar loaf to the countess of Derby, and presented sack and claret to the bishop of Chester when he returned from Parliament.[20] When Assizes met in a town, the judges typically received gifts and hospitality, not necessarily to influence particular judicial decisions, but to show respect for and gain the goodwill of these important figures.[21] For particularly consequential visitors, a corporation might go out of its way to treat them well, as the city fathers of Exeter did for the earl of Essex in 1596–97. The corporation sent sugar loaves to him on various occasions, gave him a salmon, sent messengers to him at Plymouth, and had the earl's arms painted for the city, all at their own expense.[22] In this way, the corporation honored a great lord and showed itself to be deserving of his friendship and aid. Such powerful figures may not have had any long-term connection to the locality. But out of customary deference for men of high status, as well as for the benefits in reputation and service that might accrue to the town, corporations continued to lavish attention on passing dignitaries.

Gifts, or the absence thereof, could have serious consequences for borough corporations. Presents came to be seen as an integral part of the deference that townsmen owed their betters, and the meaning of gifts could become politicized. Dover corporation apparently felt shame over the inferiority of the wine sent to the lieutenant of Dover Castle in 1618, for they paid a carrier "for carrying one hogshead of wine to the Castle, and for bringing down the same again and for carrying up a better hogshead of wine instead of the former."[23] An inferior gift could be taken as a sign of disrespect and reflected badly on the reputation of the town. Townsmen understood that while gifts could have an important positive meaning in attracting patronage, undelivered or unfit gifts could also send a negative message. Tym Tourneur, Shrewsbury's recorder, noted this when he chastised the members of the corporation for not treating the Assize judges properly in 1639. Among other things, the townsmen had failed to present the judges with velvet coats, which Tourneur said made the judges censure the town fathers with pride. "The things to be done are neither chargeable nor troublesome. The displeasure that may increase by the neglect may be very prejudicial to our town." Shrewsbury's problem with the judges occurred in the midst of a period of domestic disorder and the city's failure to collect Ship Money properly. If ever the corporation needed to be on its best behavior, it was then—as the recorder clearly knew.[24] The failure to present an appropriate gift, combined with other perceived faults, jeopardized the corporation at a sensitive moment when Shrewsbury's chartered privileges were already under fire. As the recorder of Shrewsbury said, "It is unsafe and indiscreet for us to contend with judges."[25] Great care had to be taken to prevent offense and to engage the benevolent interest of the elite.

While such ad hoc exchanges benefited local authority, a more important use of gifts was the cultivation of continuing relations with particular patrons. These relationships can be distinguished by longevity, intensity, and mutuality. First, a consistent pattern of gift-giving over a period of years usually signaled a patronage relationship. Some towns, like many members of the landed elite, had regularized their gift-giving by offering annual New Year's presents. Lord Wotton and the Fane family, local landowners and "friends" of the town of Maidstone, received fairly regular presents of wine, fish, and sugar from the corporation in James's reign.[26] Similarly Dover, while not invariably remembering the lord warden at the New Year, did annually send a present to the lieutenant of Dover Castle: "24 December [1601] Paid for a pottel of sack and another pottel of claret wine to be sent tomorrow in the morning to the Castle to Sir Tho. Fane according to custom here used . . . 5s. 10d."[27] The town of Leicester routinely presented wine and sugar to the earls of Huntingdon throughout the sixteenth and seventeenth centuries: on 31 December, 1607, they sent him 10½ gallons of muscadine, 6 gallons of sack, 3 quarts Ipocras, and a 9-pound sugar loaf at a total cost of £4 16s. 3d. Town leaders had a particular reason to impress the earl that year. But the expense did not far exceed the usual amount Leicester spent toward New Year's gifts to Huntingdon's household in the early seventeenth century.[28] This annual recognition of mutual obligation held particular importance in cases where a town had an ongoing and long-standing relationship with a patron.

Second, when a corporation went out of its way to gratify someone—for instance taking the time and expense to send a gift out of the town to a lord's residence—it usually connoted that the townsmen considered him a patron. The corporation of Nottingham sent a gift of "a veal, a mutton, a lamb, a dozen of chickens, 2 dozen of rabbits, 2 dozen of pigeons, 4 capons, wine and sugar" to the earl of Shrewsbury, when courting his patronage in 1605. The earl of Rutland received numerous gifts of food and drink at his home at Belvoir Castle from the aldermen of the small town of Grantham, who considered the earl their "good lord."[29] The townsmen of Tewkesbury, in special thanks to the earl of Leicester for obtaining their charter in 1574, sent him a silver cup worth about £16, and later an ox worth £14. These gifts represented a significant outlay for a small town like Tewkesbury. The charter meant new life for the town, and only a gift befitting the favor could be given to the one who procured it. The Cinque Ports, by custom, presented a purse full of gold to each new lord warden when he swore his oath of office. Dover itself also presented the warden with its own gift, usually a cup of silver or gold. This both signified the duty the town owed to the person and office of the lord warden and held out hope for future favors the new warden would grant.[30]

Mutuality of gift-giving provides a third clue that a patronage relationship existed. Patronage implied reciprocal obligation. Signs of respect traveled in both directions. Some corporations received presents of venison from patrons and held civic feasts to honor the giver. Lord Wotton gave gifts, usually of venison, to the corporation of Maidstone annually in the early years of the seventeenth century. The earl of Huntingdon on several occasions sent bucks to the corporation of Leicester, as did other area magnates, Lord Grey and the earl of Devon. Lord Keeper Coventry, recorder of Worcester, sent bucks to the corporation several times throughout his tenure as an officer of that city.[31] Other examples of this can be seen in Southampton, Reading, Plymouth, Barnstaple, and Grantham.[32] Although gift-giving most frequently went in the direction of town to patron, the opposite clearly signified mutual recognition of obligation. Gifts made patronage manifest.

Hospitality also reinforced connection. The symbolism of the shared meal, the offered room, resonated strongly with early modern Englishmen. It served to acknowledge and cement feelings of mutual respect and interest. Felicity Heal, in her monograph *Hospitality in Early Modern*

England, shows that the offer of hospitality formed a key element of early modern conceptions of honor and obligation. Although writers rhetorically presented hospitality as a free benefit, contrasting it with the greed of the market, in practice "the English acknowledged a system which traded in the less tangible assets of honour, loyalty, alliance, and beneficence."[33] Hospitality meant more than simply "calculated reciprocity." Like a gift, hospitality served as a sign of the honor of both the recipient and the host. Being hospitable, showing generosity at the table, offering to friends—and strangers—liberality in food and drink and lodging all added to a host's honorable reputation. Among the English elite, keeping a good house was necessary to prove one's membership in the group. Heal argues that an elite ethos existed in which "honour accrued to acts of beneficence and shame to forms of avarice;" the early modern social system was one in which "gift-exchange transactions had not been wholly superseded by commodity-exchange."[34]

Although urban governors did not fit easily into the honor community of the landed elite, they nevertheless operated with many of the same notions of hospitality as did the aristocracy. Ritual celebration and feasting had long been parts of urban identity, expressing the solidarity and honor of the community, or at least its leadership. Town leaders evinced the same concern for reputation and honor as did gentlemen, and used hospitality, both corporate and individual, to enhance their public image.[35] Corporations made the entertainment of patrons and other dignitaries an aspect of the round of civic feasting that occurred in most towns. This had the double function of expressing honor for the guest while placing a sense of obligation on him and of drawing attention to the honor and reputation of the corporation through the display of liberal hospitality. When Lord Keeper Coventry came to Ipswich in August 1634, the portmen agreed that "he shall be entertained with a dinner at the moot hall, and shall be met at his coming with the Twelve and Twenty-four and Chief Inhabitants, and the trained band also." Sometimes a corporation's desire to impress a visiting dignitary could appear blatant indeed. The Boston Assembly, in 1605, "agreed that Sir Julius Caesar, being a man that may stand this corporation in great stead, who is now forth with his Lady, children, and friends to come to the town, shall be kindly received, entertained, and welcomed at the charges of the corporation in such sort as the Mayor and the Ancient Justices shall think fit."[36] Important events or meetings also served as occasions for extending corporate hospitality. Assizes, Quarter Sessions, and subsidy commissions frequently ended with a civic dinner, providing entertainment for the gentlemen who carried out the business.[37]

A feast in Leicester to celebrate the accession of King Charles, attended by citizens, gentlemen, and noblemen, cost the corporation £17 9s. 2d.[38] In return, patrons sometimes reciprocated this hospitality as an acknowledgment of their connection to a corporation. The earl of Bath treated the aldermen of Barnstaple to dinner at his great house at Tawstock and the mayor and aldermen of Leicester dined at the hospitality of the earl of Huntingdon and of Lord Grey.[39] Although articulated through a different set of institutions, urban ideals of hospitality paralleled those of the landed elite and tied urban leaders more closely into the culture of the ruling orders of early modern England.[40]

Feasting and hospitality, although often costly for the corporators, performed an important integrative service for urban elites. They brought the landed gentry into the town, allowing the corporation to exhibit honor and liberality and to underscore the similarities between guests and hosts. When the duchess of Tremoille, the mother-in-law of Lord Strange (heir to the earl of Derby) came to Chester in 1630, both the county and the city put on a grand show. The artillery company stationed in Chester met the duchess outside the walls. Clothed in "great white and blue feathers," they saluted her with three volleys of shot. Not to be outdone, the mayor and aldermen met the duchess and her train at the Eastgate, where they greeted her in their "best gowns and apparel." They attended divine service with her at the cathedral, then entertained her and her party with a banquet at the Pentice. According to one observer, "so many knights, esquires, and gentlemen never were in Chester together, no, not to meet King James when he came to Chester."[41] This gathering may have had a subtle political meaning: the heroism of the Huguenot Tremoille family at La Rochelle stood in sharp contrast to the ineffectuality of Caroline leadership in the war. The lavish display in Chester both reinforced the city leaders' connection to the important Stanley family and accentuated their common interests—political and social—with the gentlemen of Cheshire.[42] A feast served as common ground for citizens and gentry. It could also symbolize the unity, strength, and dignity of a corporation. As Felicity Heal has pointed out, "Since the status of the town was less secure than that of the landed magnate it may even be that reputation-enhancing gestures were even more mandatory in the civic context than in the countryside."[43] If indeed town leaders attempted to integrate themselves into the governing elite of England, the honor and reputation they gained through their hospitality may have assisted them in attaining their goal.

It has been argued that money superseded gift and that the marketplace invaded hospitality in early modern England.[44] It is certainly the case that monetary transactions were often necessary for accomplishing business. Borough accounts abound with fees to clerks, servants, officials, and middlemen who had to be "gratified" in order to complete a transaction. Even those in the upper echelons of power at times demanded gratification of this sort. Sir Thomas Lake, when solicited by the city of Coventry to assist in some legal business over civic charters, refused the corporation's offer of £20 and demanded no less than £100, saying that "the matters were tedious and the world had changed."[45] The world was changing, but both the powerful and the favor-seekers clung to some older notions of exchange, continuing to believe in the efficacy of gifts and hospitality. The wine that Ipswich gave the chief justice or the feast that Chester held for the earl of Derby established a pattern of mutual obligation those towns could rely on for future favor. These symbols of connection and reciprocity supported the business of government—administration, taxation, law—by offering a basic medium of communication and action among different parts of society.

II

Gifts and hospitality offered a social matrix through which connections could be made and nurtured. Corporations used them in a general way, to court the favor of any dignitary who passed through town. But townsmen also used them in a much more specific way, to build long-term relationships with particular members of the elite. The increasing burdens that Elizabethan and early Stuart government put on local leaders, and the increasing need of localities to gain favor from the crown, made connections between central and local governments critical. For borough corporations, finding an individual to provide that link through patronage protected local interests and helped local voices to be heard at Whitehall. It is to the practicalities of finding patrons and the logic of choice that we turn next.

For all borough corporations, the need to reinforce their own authority stood at the heart of patronage. Ensuring good government (which to civic leaders meant government by themselves and not by the majority of the citizens) dominated their choices about patrons. But the circumstances among towns, and hence their response, could vary widely. Many considerations could have an effect: size, economic prosperity or decline, location in the county or the realm, links to neighboring gentlemen or peers, or simply the customs of the particular town.[46] London stood in a class by itself, huge and ever-growing, able to speak for itself before the crown. An important regional capital like Chester or Exeter had considerable leverage in defining how a patron would interact with the corporation and was less likely to become beholden to an overbearing "friend." Towns suffering from decline in prosperity might be more aggressive in pursuing patronage and more willing to gratify patrons for financial reasons. A port town with a silted-up harbor, like Rye, or a city like Boston seeking support for fen drainage fit this category.[47] Smaller market towns like Evesham or Abingdon often had close relations with neighboring gentry or nobility and sometimes struggled to maintain autonomy while also cultivating patronage.[48] Despite these differences, nearly all corporations sought to gain the patronage of powerful men at some point in this period.

Corporations chose to have patrons for the same general reasons and out of the same essential need, yet the basis of patronage links varied. It could be an informal connection, a purely customary agreement between a borough and a prominent man who had some interest in the town, through proximity or other historical ties with the locality. It could also be a more formal arrangement, institutionalized in some way either through central government decree or by order of the borough itself. Local or regional circumstances usually dictated the sort of connection that existed between borough and patron. For instance, in the northwest of England, the house of Stanley had long-standing ties to several towns. The corporations of those towns naturally turned to the earls of Derby in times of need, even when the Stanleys held no particular office in the borough.[49] In contrast, the town of Dover and the other members of the Cinque Ports essentially had a patron determined for them by the monarch. The lord warden of the Cinque Ports both by law and tradition served as the ports' peacekeeper and advocate with the crown. But townsmen also called on the lord warden for favors that fell outside his official duties.[50] Finally, a growing number of towns created an office in their corporate government—the high stewardship—in order to formalize relations with a patron of the corporation's choosing. All three types served roughly the same purpose, although the intensity of feeling between townsmen and patron might well differ from case to case.

The first category rested on an informal basis, in that the patron in question had no official capacity in the borough. Informality should not suggest weakness, however. These relationships often had deeper roots and longer life than others. The connection usually rested upon long-term ties between a town and a local magnate's family living in close proximity, such as the Fane family (earls of Westmorland) in Maidstone, the Manners family (earls of Rutland) in Grantham, or the Hastings family (earls of Huntingdon) in Leicester.[51] These relationships often continued an older tradition of good lordship, with a high level of interaction between lord and town through gifts, hospitality, and symbolic gestures. As noted above, the influence of the earls of Derby in Lancashire and Cheshire made them the clear choice as patron for many of the towns in the region. From a major provincial capital like Chester to small boroughs like Liverpool or Preston, townsmen acknowledged the power of the Stanleys, depending on them both to settle internal differences and to act as mediator between locality and the center. Indeed, it was an earl of Derby who procured for Liverpool its incorporated status. Similar to these were cases where the connection was based on long family ties, such as in Boston (earls of Lincoln), Doncaster (earls of Shrewsbury in the sixteenth century), Barnstaple (earls of Bath), and East Retford (earls of Rutland).[52] Some of these relationships were "official" in the sense that the noblemen held the office of high steward in the corporation, but the link emerged out of traditional ties between the family and the locality. Generations of Talbots served as high stewards of Doncaster, as did generations of Savages in Macclesfield and Cecils in Stamford.[53] Although such relationships can be found all over the country, they appear to have been more prevalent in the midlands and the northwest.

Possibly the best-documented connection between town and patron existed between Leicester and the Hastings family, earls of Huntingdon. The earls of Huntingdon held the premier place in Leicestershire's social and political hierarchy and were acknowledged throughout the sixteenth and seventeenth centuries as the "good lords" of the town of Leicester. Although the townsmen of Leicester occasionally solicited the assistance of other powerful figures, both the corporation and the central government viewed the earls of Huntingdon as patrons of the town.[54] Patrons of this sort expected a great deal of deference and obedience from the corporate government to which they were attached. Possibly for this reason, patronage connections like this resulted in a good deal of friction as well as cooperation. As will be seen, corporations tended to move away from this type of connection toward one in which they had greater latitude. Nevertheless, for towns of this sort, the choice for patronage was obvious. Influential magnates living near the town and with historical ties to it had links to the center that corporations needed, as well as the respect of local gentry and townsmen.

A number of towns, though a steadily decreasing one, still depended on a manorial lord to provide the services that other towns sought from patrons. Smaller towns tended to fall into this category, although a city as prominent as Lincoln still had an active manor lord during the reign of Elizabeth. This meant that, technically, at least, townsmen owed service to the lord of the manor, while expecting his "good lordship" in return. Such an arrangement could be advantageous to a borough, especially when its owner was a prominent peer or gentleman. During the reign of Elizabeth, Sir William Cecil held the borough lordship of Stamford. As the queen's premier councilor, Cecil was well placed to assist the town in its business. But while this type of link could be useful to a borough, it was also the case that the manor lord could have extraordinary authority over the town's internal government. The interests of the townsmen and those of the lord of the manor might well diverge, and it would have been difficult for a town in this situation to go looking elsewhere for patronage. Indeed, over the course of the sixteenth and seventeenth centuries, manorial boroughs attempted to free themselves of these legal obligations by gaining incorporated status or at least by purchasing the fee farm to their lands to expand their own authority in the borough. Walsall, Staffordshire, displays a particularly interesting case of this phenomenon. After several years of conflict with the lord of the manor, Sir Richard Wilbraham, the town governors worked for and obtained a charter of incorporation for Walsall in 1627.[55] Yet even towns that bought themselves out of gentry control of their manors looked to find new ways to relate to their elite neighbors.

Patronage based on traditional connections remained very important in those areas that had powerful resident magnates. There seems to have been a regional element to it, as well: as suggested above, it occurred more commonly in the midlands and the north and west. The tradition of regional magnates remained more resilient there than in the southeast, as the Tudors and Stuarts solidified their rule.[56] It was here that some of the greatest noble families—Clifford, Talbot, Hastings, Manners, Stanley—clung to their traditional holdings. But even in those areas where these ties of lordship were the strongest, another pattern, one of change over time, is clear. Close connection to local magnates as a primary source of patronage for corporations became less common during the period under study. While social ties to these families might remain, corporations increasingly looked to more Court-oriented peers for aid in accomplishing their business. Townsmen knew that they needed connections to the center in order to prosper, so they looked to those men who could offer what they needed. In many cases, local magnates lacked the importance at Court that corporators came to view as necessary. Corporations like Barnstaple, Leicester, and Chester, which had each been associated with a powerful local family in the reigns of Elizabeth and James, gradually turned to Court peers for patronage in the reign of Charles I.[57] A few retained their authority, but did so at least in part because they combined court ties with regional ones. The earl of Banbury, for instance, was a great regional magnate in the Cotswolds, but he also sat on the Privy Council and served as chamberlain of the royal household.[58] As the Stuart state increasingly made demands on the localities and offered more benefits to them, borough corporations responded by seeking out patrons who could best mediate the exchange between center and locality. Those men were Court peers.

Another group of civic patrons had both regional and central connections, but their local authority rested on their official status rather than land ownership. Into this category would fall royal servants such as the lord president of the Council of the North, centered at York, and the lord president of the Marches of Wales, resident in Ludlow, Shropshire. For most of the period under study, the city of York and the lord president of the Council of the North engaged in a regular round of hospitality and gift-giving, although at times relations between city and council became less friendly, when city leaders perceived their jurisdiction to be threatened.[59] The town fathers of Ludlow cultivated the goodwill of the officials who came to serve in the Council of the Marches of Wales. The corporation of Worcester also had a cordial relationship with various lord presidents, although they came to Worcester much less frequently than they sat at Ludlow.[60] Ecclesiastical officials, too, could serve as patrons. Bishops might provide assistance to any corporate town within their dioceses. Both Reading and Evesham obtained royal charters with the assistance of ecclesiastical patrons, while the corporation of Kingston-upon-Hull chose Archbishop George Abbott as high steward.[61] Bishops often wielded particular influence in their cathedral cities. As a resident holder of high royal office, a bishop was well-placed to provide aid to a corporation. But civic and ecclesiastical authorities in cathedral cities often had ambiguous, even strained relations, making strong patronage links problematic. Cities like Chester, Exeter, and Worcester had periods of cordiality as well as periods of strife with their bishops.[62] The potential existed for a corporation to seek ecclesiastical patrons, but not all chose to do so. All of these offices, secular and ecclesiastical, had a permanent place in the community as well as clear and direct links to the center, giving them (if not the individuals holding them) the two elements most important for effective patronage.

The cities of the Cinque Ports, which fell under the direct purview of a royal appointee, were probably in the most unusual position regarding patronage, and yet their experience was in most ways similar to other towns. The lord warden of the Cinque Ports fits roughly into the category of central government official as patron, but his authority over the towns involved was direct rather than by virtue of proximity. For the five ports, two ancient towns, and their members, the lord warden had for centuries served as their chief officer and main link to the monarchy. The warden also had judicial duties, and his high court at Shepway served as the final court of appeal for the ports. The military and judicial importance of the wardenship had waned by the seventeenth century, but the ceremonial aspects, including the giving of gifts, continued throughout the period.[63] The ports relied heavily on the connections forged with the center through the wardenship, and both the warden and his subordinates had a high level of interaction with the members of the ports' corporations. The institutionalization of the connection gave it unique qualities. The lord warden had very specific jurisdiction over the ports, so member corporations might regularly appeal to him in his official capacity. But townsmen also solicited him in a more informal manner, asking for favors from the crown to gain local benefits. The corporations of the Cinque Ports had little latitude in seeking patronage, but they relied on their lord warden to provide the connections that other corporations gained through free choice.[64]

Few towns had as clearly defined a connection to a particular peer. For most corporations that desired to cultivate patronage relations, the matter of choice involved a much higher degree of calculation and of complexity. They had neither a great magnate family with traditional links to the town nor a high official specifically assigned to their locality. These corporations actively sought out patrons, calculating who might best serve local needs. Corporations took a wide variety of factors into consideration in making these overtures. First, a patron needed to have the power and authority to provide for the needs of the town. This involved several different layers—mediation with the crown, mediation with other local or regional authorities, and participation in corporate life and business. Of these, mediation with the center stood out as the most important, although often the least frequently transacted. This being the case, a potential patron's connections to the center and influence with the crown formed one of the key criteria in a town's choice. Other considerations, such as historic connections of the potential patron to a locality or region, or the patron's record in the past of showing favor to towns in general or to the particular town, also carried weight. As will be shown, a complex calculus of all of these factors went into the choice of patrons, and a particular corporation's circumstances might cause them to weigh one factor more heavily than the others.

Urban patronage is most often associated with the office of high steward. The high stewardship, an office of considerable honor but few specific duties in civic government, became increasingly common in corporations in the late sixteenth and early seventeenth centuries. The holder of the office, while generally remaining aloof from the day-to-day workings of local administration, provided the corporation with links to the center and promised protection and support for the town and its inhabitants. The origins of this office are vague. Bristol appears to have instituted the position very early; Thomas Cromwell served as recorder (an office that usually required legal knowledge and skills) in the reign of Henry VIII. Upon his fall, the city leaders created a new office, that of the lord high steward, which they proceeded to confer upon Lord Protector Somerset. The new office fulfilled the same functions as Cromwell's recordership, but disentangled it from the legal responsibilities generally associated with the recorder. The terminology of the office could be confusing. Some towns never had a high steward, but instead, like Bristol earlier, appointed recorders of the highest social rank, who clearly functioned as high stewards did elsewhere. The earl of Bath served as Barnstaple's recorder for nearly 30 years, while the earl of Salisbury served as recorder of Colchester in the early seventeenth century. Both towns later instituted the office of high stewardship and maintained a lawyer as recorder. Cambridge apparently had a high steward beginning in the reign of Henry VIII, Gloucester by the reign of Queen Mary, and Great Yarmouth at least by the time of Edward VI.[65] Not all towns adopted the office this early, but by the reign of Elizabeth it became more common. As civic governments felt a compelling need to connect themselves to the center and to gain patronage in order to effect civic business, they increasingly used the office of high steward to accomplish these goals.

As it evolved, the high stewardship gradually formalized. In some towns, the office began as a customary one, not specified by charter. But increasing numbers of corporations had the high stewardship written into the civic constitution, in some cases recognizing customary practice, and in some cases creating an entirely new office.[66] Other corporations, having let the office lapse or lie vacant for a time, reestablished the office by corporate order.[67] Corporations considered the high steward a member of the body and an honorary citizen of the town, although he typically had no voting voice in corporate business or elections. Invariably, the holder of the office came from the highest social ranks, most frequently the titled nobility. Some corporate charters actually defined this status requirement. According to the charter of Banbury, the high steward was to be "one honorable man that shall and may be a Baron of this our Realm, or at least a knight." Hertford's was to be "one right noble and discreet man."[68] Charles I, characterizing the office in 1628, said it was "rather titulary than of substance to him that shall be chosen."[69] While the position was honorary, corporators certainly did not see it as without substance. The purpose of the office, from the locality's point of view, was to protect the borough's liberties and to provide an advocate for the corporation with the crown or any other authority with which the corporation had dealings. As the charter of Colchester put it, their high steward was "to advise and direct the Mayor and commonalty of the same borough in the chief business touching that borough."[70] High stewards made ideal patrons. They offered assistance to local governors—but at a safe distance.

The initiative for choosing stewards, and for including this office in corporate charters, came from the localities themselves. This gave townsmen wide latitude in selection and use of the stewardship. Records of the selection process—and even votes—for high stewards exist in many corporations' archives.[71] It does not seem that, under Elizabeth, James I, or Charles I, central government made a regular practice of imposing particular men on corporations to be their high stewards. Only two clear examples of royal initiative have been found. In 1611, King James wrote to the corporation of Barnstaple, commanding them to retain the earl of Bath (who had held the office since the 1580's) as their recorder when they obtained a renewal of their charter. In 1628, King Charles wrote to the corporation of Doncaster, Yorkshire, to make his cousin William Crichton, Viscount Ayr, high steward. Charles recommended him for his loyalty to the king's service and the good affection he bore for the town as a local landowner, as well as "the means which he may have to advance and further the common good and profit" of the town. It took two requests, but the corporation ultimately accepted Ayr as high steward.[72] These rare exceptions reinforce the fact that corporations had authority to choose their own high stewards. It also seems clear that the crown agreed with this local initiative, since successive lord chancellors allowed this innovation to enter into charters and supported the choices of stewards that corporations made.

An analysis of the men corporations selected to fill the office of high steward illuminates the patterns of patronage. Although these choices varied as to specific persons, one common theme stands out: Court figures, rather than simply local magnates, most frequently became high stewards. The reasons for this are not hard to imagine, and they follow the pattern of political power in England in general. As Tudor and Stuart monarchs centralized authority upon themselves, the men that forged the closest ties to the crown and procured offices at Court maintained and gained personal power. Local leaders simply followed the lines of power. During the reign of Elizabeth her most powerful councilors, Lord Burghley, the earl of Leicester, and the earl of Essex, each accumulated the high stewardships of several towns. As those having most access to the queen, they offered logical outlets for towns that wished to connect themselves more closely with the center. In some cases, the stewardship resulted from one of these lords procuring parliamentary representation for a borough from the monarch and Parliament, which often meant that the town gave its patron the nomination of at least one of those representatives.[73] This trend toward increased connection with central government figures continued throughout the late sixteenth and early seventeenth centuries, as boroughs increasingly had the high stewardship written into their charters and chose privy councilors over local magnates.[74]

In the period under study, at least 52 corporate boroughs selected high stewards (or in some cases noble recorders), giving formal structure to the patronage connection (see Appendix). These towns tended to be larger, more sophisticated ones, although exceptions existed in both directions. Neither London nor Norwich maintained a high steward, but the tiny towns of Chipping Wycombe and Woodstock did. Bristol, Exeter, York, Ipswich, and Salisbury all elected high stewards, typically choosing members of the Privy Council or other high officers of state. Across the board, those who wielded greatest power at Court received the most nominations to the stewardship by towns.[75] Burghley, Leicester, and Essex dominated the high stewardships in Elizabeth's reign.[76] Under James I and Charles I, the wealth spread out a bit more broadly, but royal favor and central authority still counted heavily. Because the lord chancellor held final power (under the monarch) over the charters and patents that ruled corporations, those who served in that office often received nominations for the stewardship from several towns. Lord Chancellor Ellesmere occupied multiple stewardships: Cambridge, Canterbury, Hull, King's Lynn, Oxford, and St. Albans.[77] Lord Keeper Coventry held the stewardship or recordership of eight towns: Boston ("chief recorder"), Cambridge, Coventry (recorder), Evesham, Hull, St. Albans, Worcester (recorder), and York.[78] The lord chancellorship was not the only source of power at Court, however. One courtier who had a great multiplicity of stewardships was not a lord chancellor at all, but Robert Cecil, earl of Salisbury, lord privy seal and principal secretary of state. He held twelve stewardships in his lifetime: Bristol, Colchester (recorder), Dartmouth, Doncaster, Exeter, Hertford, Hull, Plymouth, Totnes, Westminster, Winchester, and

York. He acquired all but one of these during his years as principal secretary, between 1598 and 1612.[79] Clearly, power at Court weighed heavily in a corporation's decision to cultivate ties with a particular patron. Association with such important men redounded to a corporation's honor and provided the best potential access to the crown.

Status as a courtier alone did not persuade townsmen to choose a particular patron. They seem also to have put some importance on the connection a lord had to the locality, by residence, past assistance to the community, or even more nominal links. Ipswich, for instance, offered the stewardship to the successive earls of Suffolk, while the successive earls of Pembroke served at Bristol, Exeter, and Salisbury, reflecting their West Country origins.[80] Sir William Knollys, earl of Banbury, served as high steward of Banbury as well as of several other Cotswolds towns.[81] Both Great Yarmouth and Barnstaple offered their high stewardships to the earl of Dorset in Charles I's reign, explicitly recognizing his previous assistance to their respective towns.[82] Local ties made an obvious connection to which towns could appeal when they courted patrons. Although not averse to calling on figures who had no apparent link to the locality, townsmen seem to have been more confident of success when dealing with locally known quantities.

This complex mixture of influence at the center and connection to the locality seems to be borne out in the case of Sir George Villiers, the duke of Buckingham. If Court power formed the sole component of choice, surely Buckingham would have been the quintessential high steward. Because of his closeness to both King James I and King Charles I, he wielded unmatched power after the monarch.[83] In practice, however, his paramountcy at Court did not make him the beneficiary of a broad range of high stewardships. He did hold four, a relatively large number. Yet a look at the specific localities shows the narrowness of his reach. Westminster, Winchester, Windsor, and Rochester all lay in relatively close proximity to the Court in London, and two had some fairly direct connection with the monarchy. Rochester was also closely connected with the navy, of which Buckingham was lord admiral.[84] Despite his power, few provincial towns selected him as high steward. One reason for this may have been that townsmen perceived him to be too occupied with the business of state to deal with local requests. Townsmen understood the wisdom of Sir Francis Bacon's advice on making suits: "Let a man, in the choice of his mean, rather choose the Fittest Mean, than the Greatest Mean: And rather them that deal in Certain Things, than those that are General."[85] Buckingham may have been the "greatest mean," but he was rarely the "fittest."

A second possible reason is more political. It is difficult to argue from negative evidence, but provincial townsmen may have perceived the duke as too much a Court figure to serve them well. He lacked the local ties that might sensitize him to the needs of a provincial town. Certainly, he was not an overwhelmingly popular figure among either the landed gentry or the urban population. Even in places where he held authority, he could not always use his influence effectively. It has been shown by John Gruenfelder that Buckingham, as lord warden of the Cinque Ports, failed signally in his attempt to control the parliamentary patronage of the ports in the elections of 1626 and 1628.[86] A similar mistrust of the duke on the part of authorities in other communities might have influenced them not to attach their towns to him through the stewardship. Even the town of Leicester, county town of the shire in which Buckingham had been born and raised, only made one approach to the duke concerning town business in the entire period of his ascendancy.[87] Buckingham, so closely identified with the center, never acquired a broad or enthusiastic following in the provinces. The combination of central authority and local roots, which the duke lacked, seems to have been the key to the development of a good relationship between town and patron.

Buckingham's anomalous case appears to prove the rule that corporations chose high stewards who could provide central authority and local sympathy. Other patterns of choice can also be discerned. An analysis of holders of high stewardships between the mid-sixteenth and mid-seventeenth centuries indicates that the office became increasingly noble. Whereas late in the reign of Elizabeth and early in that of James, towns sometimes nominated knights for the stewardship, after 1603 this was increasingly rare. Sir Edward Coke served as Gloucester's high steward in the early years of James's reign, but the corporation later chose the earl of Northampton to fill the place. Similarly, Hereford chose Sir John Scudamore as high steward in 1601, but selected the earl of Pembroke for the office after Scudamore's death. During King Charles's reign, only small towns like Maldon and Leominster maintained gentlemen in the office.[88] Gentlemen often served as town recorders, the legal officers of a locality, but the stewardship went to men of higher rank and presumably greater authority. Several corporations that had the office of recorder, but not that of high steward, in their charter began to choose noblemen as recorders, while selecting a trained lawyer to carry out regular legal business.[89] This trend toward nobility seems part of a larger pattern in office-holding, as the lord lieutenancy also became more limited to the peerage during this same period.[90]

Second, it seems that high office-holders and privy councilors were most likely to receive patents of high stewardship. This trend is not directly linear. Under Elizabeth, a few leading councilors—Leicester, Burghley, and Essex—amassed the majority of all high stewardships.[91] During James's reign, privy councilors still predominated, but a larger number of them shared the offices. In this period, men who were not in the king's inner circle could and did receive nominations for high stewardships. Although prominent figures like the first earl of Salisbury and the earl of Northampton held the most stewardships, less well-connected lords—like Lord Harrington, the earl of Shrewsbury, or the second earl of Salisbury—also obtained stewardships in this period.[92] After James's death, a trend toward somewhat greater exclusivity began. King Charles's friends and supporters—the earl of Portland, the earl of Holland, Lord Coventry—all received patents of stewardship from towns during the late 1620's and 1630's. Other peers who had less access to the inner circles of power—for instance, the second earl of Salisbury—received no nominations to the office in that period.[93] With the increasing importance of Court-centered politics in this period, especially during the eleven years between parliaments, links forged to the center through the office of the high steward became even more crucial to the life of a provincial town. Townsmen knew that these men were the ones who mattered.

This movement toward the Court shows up clearly in the case of Barnstaple. From about 1585 until his death in 1623, William earl of Bath served as the recorder of the town. A local figure, Bath had married the daughter of the regionally powerful earl of Bedford. With his main seat of Tawstock only two miles from the town, Bath viewed the town as his, and the people of Barnstaple looked to him for aid and advice. However, he never found particular favor at Court and had a reputation of being peevish and somewhat dull-witted. During his lifetime, he held the corporate office of recorder, but in times of real need the corporation sometimes went around him and appealed directly to figures at Court. In particular, they sought the aid of Sir Robert Cecil, earl of Salisbury, of whom one of the leading aldermen was a client.[94] Because of their connection to Salisbury, the corporators apparently felt they could shift patrons. In 1611, when the corporation received a new charter, James I wrote a stern letter to the mayor and burgesses, requiring that they choose the earl of Bath as their recorder again. Presumably, the king would have seen no need to do this unless the townsmen indeed planned not to select Bath under their new charter.[95] The corporation selected Bath again and continued to deal with him, but the connection had weakened.

Upon the earl's death in 1623, his son Edward succeeded him to the title, but the new earl apparently never held the office of recorder of Barnstaple. Unlike his father, earl Edward spent most of his time in London and little at home at Tawstock. When he died in March 1637, the earldom passed to his cousin, Sir Henry Bourchier, an Irish gentleman.[96] Neither of these men had strong ties with the locality or strong connections at Court. After old earl William's passing, Barnstaple maintained ties of gift-giving with his successors, yet remained without a clear patron for several years. When the town leadership again sought out a patron of high rank, they turned their attention to cultivating a different sort of person, one with fewer ties to the locality but a strong position at Court.[97] In 1637, despite the fact that the new earl of Bath was in residence at Tawstock, the corporation selected the earl of Dorset, who as a privy councilor and lord chamberlain of the queen's household had access to the royal couple and the council.[98] Dorset had no particular local connection to Barnstaple, but as noted above he had advocated for the corporation before the board. Barnstaple's town governors shifted their focus of patronage as their needs drove them to seek stronger connections with the source of power, the crown. Townsmen as well as gentlemen knew the significance of having the ear of the king and turned increasingly to those figures known to be powerful at Court.

Once corporators decided whom they wished to become their patron, they had to find ways to solicit that person's interest. Townsmen typically wrote to their nominee in deferential terms, recognizing his status and thanking him for the marks of favor he had shown to the community in the past. They also tried to market the advantages of their town. The corporators of Totnes pointed out their town's active seagoing trade and the customs revenues received by the king from them as attractions of their locality. Their letter to the earl of Northampton in 1612 is worth quoting in full:

> Right Honorable, our humble duties remembered. We the Mayor and Masters of the Town of Totnes in the behalf of the whole corporation with the advice and consent of Sir George Carey our Recorder do humbly entreat your good Lo: that you will be pleased to be our Chief Steward to protect us in all our just and lawful actions. And although the fee or annuity be but small, being only 5 li. per annum, as was formerly paid unto the late Lord Treasurer of England for many years before his death, yet we pray your good Lo: to accept thereof. May it also please your good Lo: to understand that our town of Totnes is an Ancient Town and Corporation, chiefly depending upon the trade of merchandise beyond the seas with our neighbor

countries France and Spain, by reason whereof his Majesty receiveth yearly great sums of money due for His Highness customs. Your Lo: patent and fee we have entreated this bearer to present unto your good Lop. And so relying upon your Lo: favorable acceptance, and craving pardon for our boldness in the premises, we humbly take our leave.[99]

Like Totnes, corporations offering a high stewardship invariably sent the nominee a decorative patent of office, often in an ornate box, that a member of the corporation carried personally to the lord. Most towns also offered gifts and hospitality as signs that they wished to engage in a mutually beneficial relationship. High stewards, as officers of the corporation, usually received an annual monetary fee as well, often £5 but sometimes as much as £10.[100] On rare occasions, the nominee might make a personal appearance in town to be instated into office, as Lord Knollys did with much pomp and circumstance in Oxford in 1611.[101] More typically, corporations simply presented patents of office to nominees in London or at their country estates. These overtures did not invariably succeed. The earl of Salisbury turned down an offer of the high stewardship of Ipswich in 1608, "for certain causes him moving." Others resigned their places voluntarily before their deaths.[102] These were the exceptions that prove the rule; in most cases, high stewards and corporations entered happily into and stayed in the relationship.

While most towns found it useful to cultivate a relationship with one particular patron, this did not necessarily mean rigidity or exclusivity. Rather, town leaders might appeal to a variety of influential people if the particular circumstances warranted it, sometimes calling in obligations created through the practice of gift-giving and hospitality. If an established patron proved unable or unwilling to provide aid, civic leaders regularly sought out more effectual help. For instance, when the civic leadership of Salisbury attempted to procure a royal charter of incorporation in 1590, the town council authorized solicitors to offer an annuity of £3 6s. 8d. to Attorney General John Popham. The city retained Sir Christopher Hatton as high steward, but in this particular situation the town leaders considered Popham's legal skills and connections necessary insurance for obtaining their charter. While this might in part have been a fee for service to the attorney general, the fact that they offered Popham an annuity suggests the townsmen's desire to retain his interest in the longer term.[103] Similarly, in 1628, when Salisbury's corporation tried to renew the civic charter, the town's attorneys did not work directly with the high steward, the earl of Pembroke, whose gall stones had incapacitated him. Unavailability meant ineffectuality. To get around the problem, the attorneys sought out others who showed sympathy—Lord Gorges, "whom we find very kind and ready to help us in any thing," and Philip earl of Montgomery, younger brother of the ailing earl of Pembroke.[104] Corporations pursued several courses, hoping that at least one would prove effective.

Such maneuvering did not always please established patrons. When the town fathers of Barnstaple went around the recorder, the earl of Bath, and dealt directly with the earl of Salisbury in a bit of civic business in 1611, Bath felt slighted and complained of his treatment to Salisbury. Despite such complaints, however, the rules of patronage allowed clients such latitude. If a patron could or would not perform, a client might properly look elsewhere for assistance.[105] Borough leaders had to be mindful of permanently antagonizing their patrons, but the integrity of the town counted as much as or more than the happiness of the patron. Patronage constituted a flexible enough connection that this usually caused little difficulty for most towns. Because of the way early modern government worked, suitors needed to exploit multiple sources of patronage in order to gain their ends. Just like gentlemen looking for preferment, town leaders learned to operate effectively within this system.

Exeter's corporation tested the possibility of switching patrons in the 1620's. The city fathers knew well how important it was to have a potent patron in London looking out for the city's interests at the Privy Council. They believed they made a wise decision when in 1615 they chose Thomas earl of Suffolk to replace his uncle, the earl of Northampton, as high steward. A prominent privy councilor and father-in-law of royal favorite the earl of Somerset, Suffolk also served as lord treasurer of England. He seemed like the ideal patron for Exeter, which traditionally chose high Court officials as high stewards. Suffolk's predecessor Northampton had succeeded the earl of Salisbury. Exeter's main concern was to have a friend on the Privy Council to forward local business. Given these needs and assumptions, Suffolk made an excellent choice. He had the ear of the king, he boasted of kinship ties with many of the most prominent families in England, and he traversed the halls of power. The corporation happily sent him his fee of £10 annually to cement the bond.[106]

The chance winds of Court politics, however, brought a dark cloud to the provincial city. In what amounted to a palace coup, the earl of Somerset and his Howard in-laws lost their privileged position to the attractive new favorite, George Villiers. By 1615, Somerset and his wife had been implicated in the murder of Sir Thomas Overbury, bringing scandal on themselves and their Howard connections. Then, in 1618, the earl of Suffolk suffered the personal disgrace of being tried for financial corruption in his office as lord treasurer. After a guilty verdict, Suffolk and his wife found themselves committed to the Tower and fined £30,000. Suffolk's dramatic fall forced his withdrawal from public business. Although he managed to climb back into the king's good graces by late 1620, he never regained his former status. His credit at Court shattered, Suffolk surrendered his place as lord treasurer and ceased to take part in council business altogether by the summer of 1622.[107] All of this left the corporators of Exeter in a vexed position. Having granted Suffolk a patent for life, they could not appoint a new high steward. The corporators of Ipswich had stripped the earl of Essex of high stewardship after his rebellion and treason in 1601, but this did not serve as much of a precedent.[108] At the same time, Exeter could expect no help from Suffolk at the Privy Council. As one of the city solicitors put it, "I wish in case of assistance you had another Steward at the Council Board where the Lord of Suffolk comes not."[109] Faced with this quandary, solicitors for the city repeatedly attempted to convince the earl to give up his patent voluntarily in return for a settlement.

Unfortunately for Exeter, the earl of Suffolk persistently refused to surrender his office.[110] Solicitors for the city spent much of 1621 to 1623 in London trying to divest themselves of Suffolk, and at the same time fighting off the attempts of the bishop of Exeter to invade borough liberties. The city needed strong friends at that particular moment. According to the city's agent, William Prowse, the bishop was "potent and hath many eminent friends to back his enterprises, wherein he hath the advantage of you (your Chamber standing upon bare feet and is without a pillar to lean unto in this day of need)." Prowse continued to ask Suffolk to give up the stewardship voluntarily, but suggested that the corporation choose an assistant high steward to fill the gap. "It is now high time for your worships to look about you and speedily to consult and resolve to strengthen your chamber with an Assistant Lord Steward that may in this time of need stand by and back you." Prowse identified Lord Treasurer Cranfield as the appropriate choice.[111] Cranfield accepted the position and "nobly promised to stand for us and for our petition, and to speak with his Majesty hand to hand for the furtherance of our suit."[112] Only by using this expedient could Exeter accomplish its business. With Suffolk a nonentity at the council, the men of Exeter saw it as perfectly within their rights to pursue the patronage of those who could really help them. Indeed, they considered Suffolk to be in the wrong for refusing to give up his patent of high stewardship once he lost his power at Court, even though he held the office for life. As it happened, Cranfield (by then the earl of Middlesex) proved an equally ill-advised choice, as he fell from grace and office in 1624. Fortunately for Exeter, the crisis with the bishop had passed by that time, and the earl of Suffolk finally resigned his place in 1625.[113] Towns like Exeter had a critical need for patronage, as the impassioned letters of William Prowse show. But they also felt they had a right to have effective assistance, and the protean boundaries of urban patronage allowed them to forge new connections.

The informal, nonbureaucratic nature of patronage ties allowed for flexibility in the way towns interacted with patrons and for variations in the level of interaction a patron had with his client town. This depended partly on the patron's inclinations and partly on the borough's interests and desires. For example, William earl of Pembroke served as the high steward of Bristol, Salisbury, and Totnes in the 1610's and 1620's. Bristol, as a major city second only to London, enjoyed a high degree of influence in its own right. The corporation had solicitors to watch out for civic interests in London, and hence it had less need for constant attention by a patron. It offered the high stewardship to Pembroke as an honor to him, but the city fathers expected little from him beyond general goodwill. He did aid the corporation in a few matters that came before central authorities, and he received gifts in return. But direct contact between city and steward remained uncommon. Pembroke had little influence over the corporation itself, as the aldermen never offered him nominations to parliament or to local office.[114] Bristol differed from Salisbury, where Pembroke had greater influence, although again little electoral patronage. He helped the city governors obtain their charter and watched out for their interests in London. When Salisbury's problem with poverty reached drastic proportions in the mid-1620's, it was to Pembroke that the corporation sent their petition for redress from the crown.[115] Pembroke also served as high steward of Totnes, a small but bustling port in Devonshire. Here, the earl served as a semiregular participant in corporate business. Although he may never have actually visited Totnes, the corporation consistently wrote to him for favor or advice. While there is no extant evidence to indicate that Pembroke took part in nominating clients to local or parliamentary offices for Totnes, it is certainly the case that both his predecessors and successors in the high stewardship did.[116] Clearly, different localities had differing ideas about the role of a patron in town business. Town governors had a certain amount of leverage in determining what that relationship was to be.

In the end, civic leaders acted in ways that would be most beneficial to the health of the corporation. This meant gaining specific economic and political ends, but these could not be separated from the social needs of the community. Establishing patronage connections provided an effective way for corporators to work at preserving their place in the commonwealth, protecting the livelihoods of the inhabitants, and, importantly, enhancing the dignity and honor of the corporation. Patrons of towns in the north and west generally had more frequent and active interaction with their client corporations than those in the south. The north seemed to cling to some of the older traditions of good lordship involved in patronage, while the south saw earlier moves toward more formal, less intimate connections. The patterns of choice highlight the dual need for practical benefits and social benefits in early modern society. The ongoing transactions of patronage similarly point to this complex combination of motivations. Because of the fluidity of patronage, the precise expectations of patrons and client towns transcend easy definition. Nevertheless, these versatile relationships contributed considerably to effecting the business of government.

III

The bulk of this chapter has treated the subject of patronage from the town's point of view. Indeed, the majority of the evidence for urban patronage comes from corporation sources. This view alone, however, would create a skewed picture of patron-client relations. While corporations reaped clear benefits by tapping into the patronage network and attaching themselves to men with authority at both center and locality, one might well ask why men of high status and power would bother to stand sponsor to provincial towns. Being an urban patron required the performance of occasionally burdensome duties. It also meant dealing at length with a group of people who, unlike the landed gentry, did not have the advantages of status or social rank that might redound to the honor of the patron. Why did urban patronage work, from the patron's point of view?

To some degree, it had to do with the prevailing sense of duty and authority of the time. In the hierarchical social system of early modern England, those at the top enjoyed prestige, wealth, and political power, while recognizing their responsibility to maintain the well-being of their inferiors. Urban patrons, as other men in positions of high authority, believed it their duty both as gentlemen and as Christians to assist the less powerful. According to one contemporary commentator, "we may conjecture, that to be liberal is a signe of an excellent mind. The property of bestowing, is a commendation in noble persons: for in liberal giving and beneficial doing, are Princes compared unto God. . . . O liberal hart, O passing policy, O happy estate, and glorious stay of such a Commonwealth wherein like liberality . . . is found."[117] Paternalism prevailed as an ideal. Yet reality as much as the ideal motivated men to become urban patrons: they could raise their stock with the crown by serving as mediators to corporations.

The reigns of Elizabeth, James, and Charles saw an increasing amount of crown intervention in the provinces. To rule, central government needed the assistance of those with influence in the localities as well as at the center to enforce royal policy.[118] Communication of royal policy to towns often occurred through lords known to have special relationships with them. Commissions of the peace and gaol delivery issued to towns show that the crown was aware of connections between boroughs and patrons. High stewards appear at or near the top of these commissions.[119] They appear on other sorts of commissions as well. When assessing Privy Seals or other sorts of loans, the crown might place a town's high steward or unofficial patron on the assessment commission there. The earl of Banbury headed the commissioners for the Forced Loan in Reading, Wallingford, and Abingdon, while the earl of Huntingdon assessed Privy Seal loans for Leicester.[120] Privy councilors especially associated with a town often took charge of council orders directed to that place. The earl of Pembroke, when high steward of Exeter, signed and sent letters to Exeter corporation concerning a problem in city government, among other things.[121] Specific information from the crown to a borough also passed through patrons. The king's order concerning the making of saltpeter reached the town of Reading through privy councilor the earl of Banbury, also Reading's high steward. King Charles communicated his ire with the corporation of Great Yarmouth for religious and political wrangling through the earl of Dorset, a privy councilor and high steward of Yarmouth, because of Dorset's direct and personal relationship with the town.[122] The crown doled out offices, honors, and favors to these privileged men, who in turn used this authority to govern the provinces and bring local matters to the attention of the center. They could use both their official and unofficial roles to the benefit of the crown. This enhanced their prestige in the eyes of the Court and increased their influence in the locality.

While the advantages of royal approbation probably moved urban patrons most strongly, the local rewards and benefits made an impact as well. The gifts and hospitality bestowed by corporations upon their patrons had real significance to both parties, and their importance should not be diminished. They provided a medium of exchange for the intangible benefits so crucial for this society: honor, recognition, "worship," deference, and mutual obligation. Beyond these symbolic rewards, patrons also received more tangible benefits, like civic office for themselves or their dependents. Patrons had their own networks of individual clients whom they had to gratify, and gaining access to civic offices could help them fulfill their responsibilities to these individuals. Borough corporations had many appointed offices as well as the freedom of the borough to grant. A patron could strengthen his own position by gaining influence over local offices. Just as significant might be the nomination of parliamentary burgesses, which some corporations offered to their patrons almost by right. Patrons prized such nominations highly. They could offer them to their own family members or friends, building up their personal prestige (if not a principled voting block) in the process.[123]

Some historians have intimated that this was the primary, if not the only, aspect of the relationship of any importance to the elite. This, however, does not explain why a nonparliamentary borough, such as Doncaster in Yorkshire, saw a battle between two prominent peers who both wanted to be the high steward of the town. Doncaster had no seat in Parliament until the nineteenth century, despite its growing population. Nevertheless, two great lords, the earl of Shrewsbury and Lord Hunsdon, contended with each other for the stewardship of the town. The earls of Shrewsbury, great landowners in the area, saw it as a perquisite of their status and place, while Lord Hunsdon, also a local landowner, served Queen Elizabeth as her lord chamberlain. When George earl of Shrewsbury died in 1590 and the borough chose Lord Hunsdon rather than the Shrewsbury heir as their next high steward, the new earl expressed anger and dismay. He sent a client to Lord Hunsdon to see if the lord chamberlain planned to accept the patent of office. The client, Dorothy Edmund, found Lord Hunsdon "very resolute to deal with them that had chosen him," saying "that he would accept the patent they gave him and that he would do all he could for them and that he had land near the town and he would hold their good neighbors."[124] The honor of the place itself and the desire to be a "good neighbor" to an important local hub made both men desire the stewardship, although Shrewsbury had the added incentive of tradition. None of this had anything to do with parliamentary patronage. Honor and status motivated the contenders.

Increasing their honor and authority seems to have been a major impetus for urban patrons. It enhanced a patron's prestige to appear as the "good lord" of a town, especially of an important corporation. The earl of

Northampton conveyed this when he thanked Exeter's corporation in ful-
some terms for having chosen him as high steward.

> Let me crave your pardon, worthy Mr. Mayor and the rest of your reverend
> society for deferring my thanks thus long for the greatest demonstration any
> man alive could expect of your true love without any precedent merit of
> mine. But my care both must and shall be if it be possible to overtake you in
> the race of your affection and so supply by industry what you may justly
> claim by prevention. I know very well that it was in your choice to have
> made election of many better able to assist your causes than myself, but that
> none shall exceed me in desire and care, experience shall testify. . . . Wishing
> the preservation and happiness of your worthy corporation to which your
> confidence and love hath bound me to be a constant servant.[125]

This letter holds particular interest, since it lays out some of the assumptions with which patrons—not just corporations—operated. First, Northampton suggests that a patronage relationship should be based on "true
love" and "affection." In reality, little affective connection existed between Exeter and the earl, yet the fiction of feeling was important. Second,
he acknowledged that the choice lay completely in the hands of the locality, and that the corporation might well have selected somebody other
than him. Certainly, some of this is merely false humility on the earl's part.
Yet his statement rings true. He valued Exeter's choice of him, since it sin-
gled him out for this honor from many other peers who might have been
given the place.

Although corporations did not fit into the status hierarchy that put a
premium on land and bloodlines, they did have a degree of civic honor and
status similar to that of the gentry, allowing a great lord like Northampton to accept membership into such a body. Like gentle families, corporate
towns received coats of arms from the College of Arms. Some patrons actually sought out high stewardships and urban patronage relations. Sir
Robert Cecil actively solicited the office of high steward or recorder of at
least three towns. While an important element of this desire may well have
been the parliamentary nominations that often came with a high stewardship, the honor of the position as well as the political clout made it attractive.[126] A peer or gentleman who stood as patron to a corporation could
acquire prestige from this relationship, as he also could from acquiring a
gentle clientele.

That honor accrued to a person because of his role as patron is apparent from the comments of patrons themselves. A man staked his reputation on his clients' actions and expected loyalty and obedience. If a town
did not comply with a patron's wishes, he might feel that his reputation

had been sullied before his peers. What others thought counted heavily in the honor-based society of early modern England. Viscount Wallingford (later the earl of Banbury) expressed this sentiment when he dealt with the townsmen of Reading about the contribution for Princess Elizabeth in 1620. The town authorities assessed the contribution equally on all members of the corporation rather than according to ability, bringing in a smaller amount than Wallingford thought suitable. He declared himself "ashamed to see this penury in so weighty a cause" and cajoled them to give more, adding plaintively, "I pray you, let the world know that I have some power with you."[127] A similar concern for the external perception of the relationship was expressed by the fifth earl of Huntingdon when he declared to the leaders of Leicester corporation that "the world may see that out of fear and not out of love you respected me."[128] Both of these examples show that a negative response on the part of a town toward a patron reflected badly upon his honor. Conversely, being nominated as high steward or being obeyed and revered as an urban patron added to a man's honor and authority.

For some peers, urban patronage seems even to have been used as a prop for fading fortunes. As noted above, the earl of Suffolk refused to relinquish his patent of high stewardship of Exeter at a time when he had lost his place and his credit at Court. With his fortunes at such a low ebb, he balked at allowing yet another blow to his prestige, even one so minor in comparison to the others.[129] Lawrence Stone has argued that the aristocracy faced a crisis during the early modern period, that both their honor and their incomes diminished. For some peers, especially local magnates with less influence at the center, this appears true. But one of the ways in which they hoped to slow their slippage was to increase their prestige by acquiring more clients and making sure of the loyalty of those they already had. Some made patronage of a town within their purview a major point of their honor, any deviation from which threatened their status. The earl of Bath in Barnstaple and the earl of Huntingdon in Leicester both worked hard to preserve their positions as patrons to their respective towns in a time when they feared a loss of personal authority. The earl of Bath convinced King James to command the townsmen of Barnstaple to continue to retain Bath as recorder once they received their new charter. Bath feared a loss of face and authority if he lost his office in what was a rather small Devon town. Similarly, the fifth earl of Huntingdon used his position as patron of the town of Leicester to help preserve his dignity in the shire when his great rival, Lord Grey, tried to supplant him. Huntingdon refused to allow the mayor of the corporation to exercise an office in the civic court, which had traditionally belonged to the earl's family, as it would damage his own dignity as well as the memory of his ancestors.[130]

In the reputation-conscious society of early modern England, honor—as much as or more so than parliamentary patronage—seems to have been the motivating factor for many peers to take on the often tedious duties of local patronage. As Sir John Neale said regarding Elizabethan high stewards, "We should be guilty of a bad anachronism if we imagined that [peers' desire for high stewardships] had any connection with electioneering," for "it was the prestige and sense of power that rendered the office attractive." The same "social urge" that made members of the elite show off their wealth and power through hospitality, funeral processions, or service on the county bench made them "as ready to accept, as boroughs were to offer the office."[131] This "social urge" was not simply an outward display, but also an inward reflection of the notions of honor and service current in this era. Part of the code of honor in the early modern period involved proper service to the crown. The role of the elite was to govern, maintaining the connection between the localities and the center and ensuring the rule of the godly prince. This honorable service fortified the status of those who performed it.[132] By acting as an urban patron, a person received various material benefits, but more importantly he fulfilled his role as a member of the honor community and as a loyal servant of the crown. While urban patronage may not have been glamorous, it enhanced a patron's prestige and reinforced his position as an authority to be obeyed in the community. It increased a patron's usefulness, as well as his status, in the eyes of the crown, gave him an opportunity to gratify his individual clients with offices and favors, and provided him with the affirmation of honor and respect in the locality as well. Patronage conveyed power.

Patronage provided a basic framework for interaction in Tudor and early Stuart England. Lacking a fully formed institutional bureaucracy, the early modern state depended on the voluntary efforts of the landed elite to govern the realm. The integrity of the state depended upon the assumption that the vast majority of Englishmen would accept this voluntary system of rule, along with specific formal offices of royal government. Because English society in this period operated on a hierarchical model that put a premium on honor and reputation, gift and obligation, privilege and responsibility, the assumption of deference to social as well as political authority was a workable one. Within these general parameters of society and government, specific rules of engagement developed as a way to establish and maintain order. Local authorities engaged themselves just as much as central authorities in forging those rules for order. Using many of the traditional means of exchange, like gifts and hospitality, townsmen cultivated powerful patrons as a way to gain benefits from the crown. They also developed offices like the high stewardship in new ways in order to begin to formalize relations between towns and their noble protectors. Such relations were not ones of domination and servility, but rather reflected the social and political realities of the day. Noblemen and gentlemen wielded greater power than did townsmen, but they also had a responsibility to support and protect the less powerful. Patronage formed a pattern by which the early modern state and society could operate. Urban patronage, as one element within a larger nexus, manifested itself at both local and national levels, providing a means of integration between boroughs, the landed elite, and the crown.

TWO

Patrons in the Locality

Creating the Basis for Obligation

In the summer of 1630, the corporators of Reading sent out an impassioned plea to their high steward. The earl of Banbury, at age 83, had written to the town tendering his resignation from the office. Age and infirmity, he said, made him unable to serve as he desired; the love he had always received from the townsmen made him wish provide them with a patron that would best protect them "in the free enjoying of their just privileges and lawful immunities." While the corporators understood the old earl's reasoning, they still retained the "utmost respect and gratitude" for their high steward. They begged him to remain in office to the end of his life.[1] The men of Reading had good reason to hold their steward in such high esteem, for Banbury had been a friend of the town since the reign of Queen Elizabeth. He not only held a strong position at Court to aid Reading in dealings with the crown and Council, but he also took an active part in the life of the town itself. Banbury acted as a conduit of information and orders from the central government to the corporation of Reading, for instance serving as collector for the aid for Princess Elizabeth and as a commissioner for the Forced Loan. He involved himself in the more quotidian activities of local government and society, attending the town council in his capacity as a member of the corporation, distributing alms to the poor of the town, helping the corporation deal with the town schoolmaster, and giving advice on how properly to prepare for a visit from the queen consort. Banbury received benefits in return. His clients received the freedom of the borough, he nominated a suitor to be steward of the borough court, and he nominated his relatives—some successfully and some not—as burgesses to Parliament for Reading.[2] The earl behaved precisely as a patron should, and the townsmen responded by offering him gifts of wine and sugar as well as social and political deference. The relationship went through its stormy periods, but it worked. In the end, the pleas of the men of Reading succeeded. Banbury consented to retain the stewardship for life, taking "no small comfort" in their demonstration of love. He held the office until his death in 1632, when the corporation chose his nephew, the earl of Holland, for their new steward, as Banbury had requested.[3]

The connections between a noble patron and his client town could be broad and deep. The earl of Banbury served Reading in a range of roles, both as the main conduit to the crown and council and as a member of the corporation itself. The townsmen encouraged this local activity as a way to maintain their lord's interest in helping the town. Much of the interaction between borough corporations and their patrons occurred at the local level, as a counterweight to the actions taken by a patron in London. Patrons could fulfill their role in the hierarchy, as gentlemen and as Christians, by providing for the safety and welfare of the less powerful, as well as gaining the material benefits of an increased patronage network. Boroughs in return received assistance with social problems and administrative difficulties. They also used local offices and activities to draw patrons into a stronger identification with their town. Civic leaders walked a fine line between retaining their own firm control over local government and obtaining the benefits that elite participation could bring. In offering noblemen or gentlemen membership into the community, corporators did not give away their own authority. Rather, they attempted to create a sense of obligation that would work to the benefit of the locality. These interactions sometimes sparked conflict, but they also fueled the activities that helped provide effective governance.

A negative assessment of the relationship between urban governments and the landed elite has predominated in discussions of the subject. One historian has said that "civic independence bowed out to county fashion."[4] Corporations did fear the possibility that gentlemen or noblemen might try to dominate civic business. Townsmen understood the dangers to their authority, but they also knew that complete disengagement was neither possible nor productive.[5] The needs and safety of the borough were carefully weighed when engaging in patronage. A close look at how corporations dealt with the elite in the local context demonstrates the complexity of this balancing act. Townsmen both worked diligently to preserve and expand their own privileges, and at the same time invited noble and gentle patrons into the life of the town. Needing benefits, which ran from establishing schools and resolving local poverty problems to gaining advantages in Parliament and obtaining charters, corporators turned to the elite for aid. From the townsmen's perspective, such assistance was best if it occurred at a remove. Corporators did not wish to give their authority away to patrons. Yet patrons had to be given an interest in the client locality, and they required returns for their investment of time and favor. Corporations negotiated the level of interactions between themselves and their patrons, working to gain the greatest benefits for the locality without damaging corporate authority. As will be seen, this negotiation could lead to extensive involvement of the elite in local activities, involvement that corporations manipulated.

I

While "urban patronage" might commonly evoke images of parliamentary or political influence, in fact some of the most important aspects of relations between towns and the elite had little to do with civic government per se. Religious, social, educational, and economic institutions and interactions served as crucial connections between many towns and their patrons. Some families came to be known as benefactors of a particular locality. Often this grew out of historical ties of proximity and sometimes reflected a direct outgrowth of an older manorial connection. Elite families regularly developed a strong sense of "good lordship" over neighboring towns, even if they no longer had any legal connection through land ownership or office. Good lordship added to a man's prestige and authority in a locality, but it also provided services and favors to its recipients. The social concepts of lordship—beneficence, charity, paternal assistance, and protection—continued well into the early modern era.[6]

The precise nature of patronage and good lordship as practiced in provincial towns arose partly as a response to the Protestant Reformation. One of the marks of elite status in English society had traditionally been a lavish display of Christian giving. The fourteenth and fifteenth centuries saw gentlemen and nobles endowing chantries to the glory of God (and themselves), distributing alms to the poor, and decorating and beautifying their parish churches. The Reformation took away these opportunities for giving traditionally associated with the Roman Catholic Church.[7] Yet the belief that benefaction added to one's prestige on earth as well as one's credit in the hereafter did not die. The English elite turned to supporting Protestant or secular causes, such as schools, "puritan" lectures, and poor relief schemes, often established in corporate towns.[8] Men like the earl of Banbury in Reading, the earl of Leicester in Warwick, the earls of Huntingdon in Leicester, and the Bacon family in St. Albans could gain credit for their philanthropy, while civic leaders welcomed their participation for the public services it brought to the locality. Of course, Christian altruism alone did not motivate patrons. They gained practical benefits, as well. Most important, establishing a close connection with an urban community gave a patron inroads into the many offices and favors that a corporate borough had in its grasp. Establishing a school gave patrons some control over the choice of the schoolmaster; establishing a lectureship gave a patron the opportunity to place his own clerical clients. The reciprocity of urban patronage, the advantages it could provide to both borough and patron, can be seen most clearly at the local level, in the domestic life of the town.

Educational patronage was one of many things that manifested this reciprocal connection. Wealthy and prominent families founded many urban schools, providing land revenues or other resources to organize them.[9] Civic leaders typically oversaw day-to-day administration, but consulted the patron or his heirs when making important decisions. For instance, the Bacon family of Gorhambury, great believers in education, established schools in both Bury St. Edmunds and their neighboring town of St. Albans in the 1560's and 1570's. Sir Nicholas Bacon, the lord keeper of England and steward of St. Albans, himself had drawn up the original orders for that town's school.[10] In 1595, the master of the school fell seriously ill, and Sir Nicholas's son, Anthony Bacon, esq., took the opportunity to nominate a client for the position when the old master died. "I thought it the part of a neighbor and friend to advise you . . . by providing . . . some sufficient man for the place, and to recommend to you the bearer hereof, Mr. Thomas Stretely, Mr. of Art, well-born and sufficiently qualified for the instructing of youth, whose behavior I have found to be good and honest, and therefore am moved to request you that you would nominate and elect the said Thomas Stretely."[11] The corporation considered the matter carefully. They accepted Bacon's nominee after reflecting upon the great friendship that Bacon's father, their "late good lord," had shown for the town and their hope for ongoing friendship from Bacon himself. They decided they would "altogether rely upon your circumspect providence in this behalf, whose care toward us we ought not to doubt." Stretely took up the position in 1596.[12] The Bacons had been patrons and friends to the town since Sir Nicholas purchased Gorhambury early in Elizabeth's reign. His youngest son, Sir Francis, later served as St. Albans's special counsel, then recorder, and finally high steward. Upon his ennoblement, he took his title from that place, as Lord Verulam (the Roman name for the town) and Viscount St. Albans.[13] The close connection between the family and the town and its institutions made Bacon patronage of positions like the schoolmastership completely logical in the minds of both the members of the corporation and the members of the Bacon family.

Similar connections existed in other towns. Leicester's civic leaders consulted the fifth earl of Huntingdon about appointing officers of the free school decades after the death of his grand-uncle, the third earl, who had helped establish the school in the sixteenth century.[14] On at least two occasions, Lord Knollys (later earl of Banbury), high steward of Reading, wrote to the corporation on the behalf of Mr. Byrd, schoolmaster of the free school, to have his stipend raised and paid in a timely fashion. It is likely that Byrd obtained his position on the recommendation of Lord Knollys.[15] When the earl of Hertford recommended "Alexander Rosse, a Scottishman" as schoolmaster of the Southampton free school in 1616, the mayor and assistants immediately accepted him. Rosse had good credentials and went on to be a prolific author and eventually a royal chaplain to Charles I. Hertford had a clear patronage connection to Southampton, as he had been chosen an honorary burgess there in 1588 and remained friendly to the town afterward.[16] No firm connection between the earl and the foundation of the free school has been found, but Hertford clearly discovered a way to link his clients into the offices available in the town. Borough leaders forthrightly appealed to patrons' sense of honor and authority to gain public services. The earl of Northumberland received a petition from the leaders of the market town of Alnwick to found a grammar school there. "That your Honor (unfeignedly we wish it may be long so) *primus apud Alwicensis obtinere partes ratione dignitatis* so you may be *summus respectu benignitatis*, & worthily enjoy the name and fame of Founder of our Grammar School." The earl gave the annuity, establishing the school in 1613. Northumberland, like other patrons, added to his name and fame and also added one more office, that of schoolmaster, to the others within his sphere of influence.[17]

Religious foundations, such as civic lectureships, also offered points of linkage between boroughs and their patrons. Several zealously Protestant patrons in Elizabeth's reign wished to spread the gospel in urban areas by establishing these popular lectures and choosing the men who served in them. Sir Nicholas Bacon founded the lectureship at St. Michael's church in St. Albans and acted as patron in the naming of new lecturers. It was in this church that Francis Bacon, Viscount St. Albans, later asked to be buried.[18] In 1585, the earl of Derby used his influence to promote the removal of an "insufficient" minister of the chapel in Liverpool and his replacement by a more qualified nominee. Although opinion in the Assembly was divided, a majority of corporators accepted the earl's nominee.[19] Probably the greatest patron of the reformed ministry was Henry, third earl of Huntingdon. As lord president of the Council of the North, he had a strong influence over the towns within his jurisdiction, many of which he felt to be backward in religion. He saw a preaching ministry as a way to reform this problem, and he vowed "to get good preachers planted in the market towns of this country." He nominated Newcastle's lecturers in the 1580's and managed to convince the corporation of York, a city not overly receptive to strongly reformed religion, to establish a lecture in the city in 1580.[20] Religious foundations offered a service to a town and an opportunity for largesse to a patron.

The third earl of Huntingdon played his most active and consistent role in founding the lectureship at Leicester, near his ancestral estate. It was the third earl who put Mr. Sacheverell, longtime and much-loved town preacher, into the position and induced the corporation to provide him with a stipend of £30. The earl, a strong proponent of reformed religion, desired the townsmen to reflect his religious enthusiasm. When they failed to pay the preacher's stipend promptly, he admonished them for their laxity and implied that they did not love the gospel well enough, or they would have been more ready in their payments. He was not above using threats: "When your town had any need of the help of me and other friends, then they could promise and offer to deal both liberally and lovingly toward their preacher."[21] Corporators always took consideration of Huntingdon's nominees for lecturer and minister, a consideration also accorded his successors.[22] For the third earl—the so-called "Puritan Earl"— his ongoing support for the town was intimately wrapped up with the town's support of its ministers and reformed religion.

While few patrons felt as strongly about reformed religion as did the third earl of Huntingdon, they did see religious patronage as something within their purview.[23] Lord Zouche, the lord warden of the Cinque Ports during much of King James's reign and a firm believer in reformed religion, had helped to establish the lecture in the town of Rye, one of the ports in his authority. When a bitter dispute arose between the lecturer and the parish curate over access to the pulpit, causing division in the town, Zouche took the lecturer's part and guaranteed his right to preach. He wrote to the bishop of Chichester, requesting that the lecture be restored. This the bishop did, and even placed the lecturer, Mr. Warren, into the curacy and ejected the obstreperous former curate, Mr. Whittaker. The town leaders responded by thanking Lord Warden Zouche enthusiastically and apologizing that the disturbance had caused trouble for him.[24] At

Ipswich in 1602, the town accepted the suggestion of their high steward, Lord Treasurer Buckhurst, of one Dr. Reeves to be their town preacher.[25] In an example of female patronage, the Chamber of Exeter sought out the opinion and support of the countess of Warwick and Lady Paulett for naming the civic lecturer. The two great ladies suggested Edmund Snape, a known puritan and leader of the defunct Northampton classis, a choice likely to please the townsmen more than the bishop.[26] By maintaining an interest in the urban ministry, patrons could satisfy their own religious convictions, their clerical clients' need for positions, and often the borough's desire for a good preaching minister.

This combination of religious sensibility and the practical needs of both patron and town also appeared in the provision of poor relief and benevolence, an issue of great importance to early modern towns. Urban authorities, facing a large and growing problem of poverty, looked for effective ways to curb it. At the same time, taking responsibility for the poor formed an important part of the Christian gentleman's credo in early modern England, both for religious principles and for the preservation of good order. The intersection of the need to display good lordship and a town's need for help with this problem presented a perfect opportunity for patronage to operate. Sometimes this consisted of purely casual giving on the part of a peer to the poor of a town, which might more rightly be considered generalized almsgiving, without a specific patronage connection between lord and town. The earl of Huntingdon, on "progress" to Harveile to visit his mother-in-law, the countess of Derby, contributed a few shillings to the poor at almost every town in which he stopped—6s. at Lichfield, 4s. 6d. at Worcester. Fleeting evidence of this practice can be found elsewhere, for instance Lord Treasurer Dorset gave 40s. to the poor of Coventry in 1608.[27] While peers and gentry saw this sort of benevolence as a duty to the less fortunate in general, they both also felt a special responsibility to the places they saw as within their patronage. Upon his election as high steward of the borough of Totnes in 1632, the fourth earl of Bedford remitted his annual fee back to the town for the relief of the poor there.[28] The earl of Rutland gave nearly £60 to the poor visited people in Newarke and Grantham in the autumn of 1604, a princely sum for those two small towns. Other lords left money for the poor of their client boroughs in their wills. The earl of Bath left £10 to the poor of Barnstaple, while the earl of Lincoln left £100 in lands to be used for the poor of Boston.[29] The fifth earl of Huntingdon apparently made it a regular practice to distribute money to the poor of Leicester and the poor prisoners in the jail when he came to town. In June 1607, when he frequently visited

Leicester due to a series of enclosure disturbances, the earl distributed nearly £8 10s. to the poor and the prisoners, including lump sums of £5 to the poor of the town and £2 to the "Ospitalls" on 27 June.[30] Such largesse bolstered his image, but it also manifested his sense of responsibility to the people of a town he considered as his.

For some noblemen, this sense of responsibility to the urban poor went beyond casual almsgiving and became instead support for larger-scale schemes to relieve the poor. This both provided charity in the town and gave patrons a venue where they might place their own poor suitors.[31] In 1616, George Abbott, archbishop of Canterbury, provided for the poor of his birthplace of Guildford, Surrey, founding a small hospital there for single elderly people.[32] Likewise Lord Burghley, lord of the manor and patron of the town of Stamford, founded a hospital there in 1597.[33] Other noblemen tried to rectify urban poverty problems on an even grander scale, with large institutions for relieving the poor. Such schemes gained popularity in Elizabeth's reign particularly, when various godly peers advocated poor relief programs that combined the reformation of manners with the further reformation of religion. Robert Dudley, earl of Leicester, a leader of this group, extended his patronage to the town of Warwick in its bid to combat its poverty problem. Leicester and his brother Ambrose Dudley, earl of Warwick, had strong influence in the town in the sixteenth century. When the queen granted the earl of Leicester authority to establish a hospital for the poor at either Kenilworth or Warwick, the burgesses of Warwick petitioned aggressively to have the hospital in their town. They bungled the process and ended up granting their own guildhall for use as the hospital, but they finally established the scheme under the earl's auspices and with his financial support. The earl established the Hospital in Warwick, which to the present day still bears his name, with an endowment of £200 per annum. The effectiveness of the poor relief scheme can be questioned, but its foundation and longevity indicate the level of interaction between town and patron.[34]

Similarly, the third earl of Huntingdon gave his assistance to the corporators of Leicester in their establishment of a plan to set the able poor of the town to useful work in making cloth. The corporation drew up articles of agreement for the project under the earl's auspices, and the earl chose the first clothier who headed the workhouse. When Bradgate the clothier fell into "decay" in the mid-1580's, the corporation turned to the earl for financial assistance and advice in setting up another clothier. As at Warwick, the scheme never operated very reliably. In 1592 the corporation wrote to the earl to apologize for allowing the cloth works to decline, but forwarded a new plan to make the project more efficient. The third earl supported many godly causes during his life, but he saw Leicester as his personal laboratory, a place where his reforming projects might come to fruition. The townsmen in return consistently sought out their patron's aid and advice whenever they made decisions affecting poor relief.[35] Although the schemes at Leicester and at Warwick faltered in the end, in both cases the establishment of the project fostered bonds of obligation between patron and urban community.

Elite involvement added to the social and religious life of towns, kept patrons integrally involved in the locality, and helped strengthen their patronage networks. Reciprocal benefits could extend into the economic life of a borough as well. That the gentry and nobility increasingly resorted to towns, looking for entertainment and spending money, has long been noted. Increasing numbers of the landed elite bought town houses in provincial cities, not simply the capital. Even before the so-called "urban Renaissance," civic leaders tried to lure wealthy men into their towns by establishing genteel entertainment, such as the horse races in Chester and in Winchester or the spas at Bath or Tunbridge Wells. Winchester established a race meeting as early as 1591, and the corporation provided refreshments for gentlemen attending the race. The marquis of Winchester and the earl of Southampton both took active interest in the races. By the 1630's, noblemen not only attended the races, but competed in them. Similarly, the corporation of Chester sponsored horse races along the Dee in order to attract gentle and noble interest in the city. These two cities may have been precocious in this development, but they signaled the wave of the future.[36] Corporations benefited from such involvement both in their treasuries and by the connections they gained.

The most extensive "economic patronage" occurred in those towns with long-standing connections with local magnate families. The earl of Bedford owned a house in Exeter, the chief city in his lieutenancy. The third earl of Huntingdon purchased what came to be called "The Lord's Place" in the Swine Market of Leicester in 1569, and his descendants continued to use it until the middle of the seventeenth century as their town residence.[37] The earls of Derby owned a fortified house in Liverpool where they often stayed on their way to the Isle of Man, where they held the lordship. William, the sixth earl of Derby, bought a house on the Dee near Chester, where he retired upon his resignation of his holdings to his son James, Lord Strange, in 1637. He also invested in various parcels of land within Chester itself. One, the so-called "bowling alley," was leased by earl William around 1618, and he improved this property various times during the next twenty years. In 1619 he paid 20s. in rent to the city chamberlain, more than any other gentleman in the city.[38] On the subsidy roll of 1641–42, William earl of Derby is assessed £8 in the city, indicating the size and value of his holdings in Chester by the eve of the civil war.[39] Property in Chester offered a good investment in this period, but the purchase also shows the longer-term attachment to this particular place displayed by the earls of Derby. Rents, as well as profits gained from members of the elite obtaining goods and services in a town, could sometimes form an important and salutary part of the urban economy. Both Grantham and Leicester benefited because their patrons made use of their respective markets.[40] Civic leaders cultivated ties with the men who spent money in town, attempting to gain advantages from their proximity.

The reciprocity of such economic connections can be seen in the case of Coventry corporation and its coal mines. The corporation owned mines near the city, which they regularly leased to prominent gentlemen and noblemen. As Lawrence Stone has noted, the aristocracy were among the most important industrial entrepreneurs during the late sixteenth and early seventeenth centuries.[41] In the case of Coventry, the corporation leased its coal mines to courtier Endymion Porter and Henry Carey, earl of Dover, in 1636 for 41 years. In September 1636, Dover came to town to attend to business concerning the lease. The corporation, desirous of making their noble lessee happy, decided to make the earl a citizen of their town. Dover, "declaring his noble disposition toward this city, this House observing that his Lordship was pleased to honor this city so far that he became a freeman thereof; it was thereupon by unanimous assent of both houses agreed and ordered, that the said earl of Dover is and shall be a freeman thereof." The earl graciously accepted the position, becoming a member of the city to which he was seemingly bound only by economic ties.[42]

Patrons regularly gained advantages for themselves by these relationships, but they also used their connections to towns in order to gain advantages for clients and suitors. The urban economy offered many opportunities for small but important benefits. To a poor person, procuring a license to brew beer or ale or to "kill flesh" during Lent made a dramatic difference in their quality of life. Patrons, regaled with many requests from poor suitors, used their connections with towns to grant these favors.[43] They also might try to obtain advantageous leases of borough property for their clients. Richard and Frances Savage received a lease for life to the tolls on corn coming into Doncaster market because the corporation agreed to grant it "at the request of our very good lord the lord Darcy and in consideration of his honourable favor always shown to us."[44] The earl of Huntingdon asked the corporation of Leicester to grant leases to servants, as did Lord Harrington in Coventry.[45] When Dr. Chippingdale, who served in the archdeaconry court at Leicester, wished to renew his lease in town, the corporation received letters on his behalf from Sir Julius Caesar, Viscount Cranborne (Chippingdale's patron), and the earl of Huntingdon.[46] Acceding to such requests helped obligate a patron toward a client-corporation in a concrete way.

Townsmen only granted such favors after careful thought. Requests from patrons could be awkward and unwanted. Civic leaders considered first the condition of the town's economy and second the need to gratify their patron. When the fifth earl of Huntingdon asked the mayor of Leicester to grant Hugh Darker, a poor man, the right to "kill flesh in Lent," Mayor William Morton penned a lengthy letter of explanation. He first gave a variety of reasons why he had vowed to grant no such licenses, both because the Butchers' Company had requested it and the town's recorder advised it. But the mayor also said that if he saw fit to grant any licenses, Darker would definitely receive one, out of the town's "bounden duty" to the earl, "notwithstanding the said Darker and others that have aforetime been licensed never did any one of them good either to mend their estate or pay their debts, but have done much hurt to the Commonwealth."[47] Similarly, the townsmen rarely acceded to the earls' requests to allow country artisans to trade in Leicester's market.[48] The urge to gratify a patron was great, but it usually did not overcome the economic needs of the town.

The special link between patron and corporation encouraged each to take an interest in the economic life of the other, as well as the social and political life. While not a necessary part of the patronage relationship, economic relations nevertheless served to reinforce ties between patron and corporation where they existed. Corporate leaders looked warily upon excessive interference of the gentry and nobility in urban society, yet they also recognized the advantages that arose when people of that rank took a close interest in a town. When members of the elite formed a special attachment to a town, the citizens often enjoyed the benefits of schools, preachers, poor relief schemes, and hospitals that the landed elite had the money and the responsibility to promote. Corporations had to induce the elite to take a particular interest in their town, so they tried to integrate gentlemen into civic life in as many ways as possible, always stopping short of putting their own jurisdiction in jeopardy. Providing these sorts of benefits allowed patrons to fulfill their duties as Christian gentlemen and to show their honor and prestige and wealth to their peers. They also could improve their own positions by taking advantage of the offices and economic opportunities open to them as patrons of urban communities. Such patronage—social and religious and economic—was all a part of the same phenomenon of elite behavior and values in the early modern period, and should not be separated from the political and administrative patronage that more often receives attention from historians.

II

The paternalism of good lordship displayed in the support of social programs, religious institutions, and even local economies, offered advantages to both borough corporations and their elite benefactors. It allowed for social display and filled social needs. It also gave patrons a material stake in the locality. This was not without its dangers for local leaders, who had to protect their own authority even as they accepted the intervention of powerful men. The risk made corporators act cautiously, but it did not prevent them from cultivating patronage. Indeed, townsmen invited patrons to participate directly in civic institutions, making them members of borough corporations. Confounding the idea of "insiders" and "outsiders," townsmen asked peers and gentlemen to become part of their society. By offering local office to patrons, civic leaders worked to link themselves and their communities to the broader networks of authority that governed England. Corporators did this on their own terms; they did not relinquish their own authority to patrons. They fully understood the benefits, as well as the pitfalls, of integrating influential nobles and gentlemen into the business of a town. Corporations could not presume to exist independently of the networks of authority that ruled the realm. Civic leaders had the political intelligence and savvy to make use of these structures without giving up their self-determination. Not every corporation chose to include patrons in this way, and some probably regretted having done so when patrons made unwanted demands. Nevertheless, corporations all across England made peers and gentlemen part of their fellowship and aimed at wringing the benefits from this connection while keeping these great men at arm's length.

Corporations encouraged the direct interaction of patrons in borough government by appointing them to corporate office: high steward, recorder, mayor, alderman, justice of the peace. Examples have been found of peers or gentlemen filling each of these offices in this period, but the high stewardship was by far the most common. As noted in Chapter 1, the stewardship seems to have been created and developed by boroughs specifically to provide an office of honor for civic patrons. It existed to facilitate patronage. The role these officers played in the daily life of a town varied. Ideally townsmen expected their high steward to take an interest in local affairs, but not to attend corporate meetings or to visit the town with any regularity. In fact, most courtier high stewards never set foot in the towns in which they held office. Their main function was to watch out for the town's interests with the center.

While most corporations expected their high stewards to remain aloof from the day-to-day business of the locality, this did not always happen. Particularly in instances where the high steward had strong local connections, a corporation could expect him to participate in local events. We have seen the earl of Banbury's regular concourse with the town of Reading, and he participated occasionally in the business of Wallingford and Oxford as well.[49] In Oxford, he more than once adjured the corporation to maintain traditions that would uphold the city's honor: "it is dishonourable to the city to put away the giving of court dishes according to ancient custom, which is a badge of honor to the mayor of Oxford, in remembrance that he is butler by Charter to the King at the coronation feast."[50] Robert, earl of Salisbury, held many high stewardships and he rarely intervened in local events unless asked. His family's long connection with Hertford, however, prompted him to take action when he thought the corporators went astray. In 1610, the corporation of Hertford decided to pull down the old market cross, which had become "decayed" and "insufficient." Salisbury, high steward since 1605 and a substantial landowner in the area, felt that he should have been consulted in the matter. His ire grew when he heard that the corporation accused his own estate officers of bargaining for the lead from the old cross. The townsmen, fearing Salisbury's wrath, wrote immediately to explain themselves. While begging the earl's pardon, they named the particular officers who had bargained for the lead and described their own authority to take down the cross.[51] Corporators preferred for a high steward to remain at a remove from the daily events of a borough, but they prepared themselves for such involvement as a possible outcome of electing this officer.

In contrast to the high stewardship, the duties of a recorder required that officer to attend corporate meetings regularly. The recorder served as the chief legal officer of a borough, making legal expertise a necessity for holders of the office. Recorders frequently held the position of justice of peace in their borough, giving them power over the daily lives of townspeople. Nevertheless, some boroughs chose peers or gentlemen without legal training as recorders, essentially conflating the offices of recorder and high steward. Noble recorders usually appointed deputies who carried out the duties of the office, while the peer served more as a link to the center.[52] A few cases are more ambiguous. The city of Worcester chose Sir Thomas Coventry as counsel for the city while he was an up-and-coming lawyer in 1616. When the city's recorder left office in 1624, they gave the place to Coventry, and he served as a working recorder. By 1626, Coventry had risen to the office of lord keeper of the Great Seal, and soon thereafter became Lord Coventry. Initially, the new baron maintained a fair degree of interaction with the city, but as the burdens of his office increased, he seldom took direct action in the city's business. He retained the office of recorder, but in practice he operated like most high stewards, providing patronage from a distance.[53] Some noble recorders did attend corporate meetings and borough courts on occasion. William earl of Bath, recorder of Barnstaple, sat at the town sessions as JP in right of his place as recorder, even though he appointed a deputy to carry out most of his duties in that office.[54]

Noble recorders and high stewards could take direct action in corporate life and sometimes did. It seems, however, that neither townsmen nor honorary officers expected that it would be a common occurrence. Civic leaders jealously guarded their privileges and liberties, which over-eager participation by a noble officer might threaten. A delicate balance existed between opening the corporation to patronage and exposing it to unwanted inroads on civic authority. The solution to maintaining equilibrium lay not in excluding the landed elite entirely from corporate life, but rather in engaging them in ways that benefited the corporation. Sometimes, this meant including them as officers of the corporation, beyond positions of honor such as the high stewardship. Several boroughs, including Chester, Liverpool, Portsmouth, Abingdon, Evesham, Coventry, and Leeds, elected members of the landed elite, local peers and gentry, to sit as members of borough government, as mayors or aldermen.[55] Other towns selected peers and gentlemen as freemen of the borough, with the concomitant privileges of civic membership. It has been suggested that this simply indicated the inferior and weak position that towns held vis-à-vis the landed elite, that towns "gave in" to outside pressures in putting gentlemen into the corporation.[56] But this overlooks two important facts:

Townsmen did have control over the membership of the corporation, and participation by the landed elite did not automatically jeopardize the liberties of a town.

Examples of this sort of integration can be spotted across the country and in towns of varying sizes. Many corporations manifested their willingness to connect by offering the freedom of the borough to nobles and gentlemen they wished to oblige. Strictly speaking, the freedom provided exclusive rights to trade, work, and participate in the government of a borough. Townsmen prized it highly and attempted to uphold its exclusivity. According to the rules of most towns, a man could gain the freedom by serving an apprenticeship to a master of the town, by paying a fine to enter the borough liberties, or simply by being the son of a freeman. Freedom then allowed the burgess to ply his trade freely in the town, to participate in the local markets and fairs without fine. It also obligated him to be resident in the town and to serve in civic government if called upon by the magistrates to do so.[57]

Many boroughs gave their privileges to men of rank to whom they wished to show special favor. Coventry offered the civic freedom to the sons of two important friends of the town, Lord Harrington and Sir Edward Coke, in 1610 and 1614, respectively.[58] Dover's Assembly granted the freedom to Sir Henry Mainwaring, lieutenant of Dover Castle, without fee, "out of the assurance that Assembly conceived of his favor and endeavor to perform all good offices he may for this incorporation."[59] These examples could be multiplied.[60] Although technically these men had the same right to trade in the local market and serve in corporate office as any townsman, most in fact had no desire to do so. Rather, many towns developed a category of honorary freedom that they conferred on gentlemen who wanted the honor and respect that went along with the position, but not the responsibilities or the residency requirement. In Salisbury, the practice must have been accepted, as the corporation made orders in 1625 that if any gentleman residing in the city became a member of civic government, he need not carry out all the "formalities"—walking in scarlet robes, sitting in all assemblies and meetings—of the office. "He shall not be enforced to keep his place, as others who have been merchants and tradesmen have used to do, but shall resort to the company of gentlemen."[61] Some corporations had their right to choose honorary freemen written into their charters. Evesham's charter gave them the authority to make free persons "dwelling in or out of the borough" as "shall seem to be the most useful for the public advantage of the same borough." The charter of Hertford included a similar clause.[62] Honorary freedom was usually granted "gratis," or at no fee, as a way to honor men who had been helpful to the community or might be helpful in the future.

For a few towns, granting honorary freedom to prominent gentlemen seems to have been a regular practice. The city of Portsmouth, an important port and military base, had a constant stream of noblemen and gentlemen passing through on business or stationed at the naval defenses there. As a gesture of goodwill, the corporation conferred freedom upon large numbers of these men, as the mayor said of one of them, "in consideration of the great good will borne towards the town of Portsmouth by [him], and his friendly care to the furtherance and advancement thereof."[63] Between 1585 and 1640, the corporation granted the freedom of Portsmouth to 30 noblemen, including Henry earl of Southampton, Henry Lord Windsor, Charles Lord Howard (the Lord Admiral), Robert earl of Salisbury and George duke of Buckingham. In the same period, they made burgesses of at least 50 gentlemen, many of them associated with the port or the navy, such as the secretary of the lord admiral and the treasurer of the royal navy. The town also gave the freedom to two bishops, a cathedral dean, and three chaplains to important noblemen.[64] In a consistent pattern throughout the entire period, the civic leaders of Portsmouth used honorary freedoms as a way to encourage noblemen and gentlemen to take an interest in the port, quite unabashedly offering this privilege for an expectation of future favor.

While for Portsmouth honorary freedoms formed part of normal practice, other towns appear to have used them at moments of stress to gain particular ends. In the late 1610's, Liverpool made a variety of local dignitaries—including Sir Richard Molyneux and Sir Hugh Beeston—free burgesses of the town. This proved useful in the town's drive to obtain a charter in 1617–18, as the corporation rated all of the honorary burgesses, as well as the actual citizens, for a tax to pay for the charter.[65] It is unclear whether Liverpool created these honorary freemen simply in order to rate them, but the townsmen may well have made the grants in order to encourage elite interest in their charter project. Likewise, Boston's corporation made a sweeping grant of honorary freedoms to local notables in the mid-1630's, during the town's heavy involvement with drainage and sewer projects. In one day, 24 August 1634, the town Assembly admitted to the freedom of the borough three noblemen and twenty-five gentlemen. That this was an unusual move is marked by the fact that the admissions were made "gratis without fine . . . notwithstanding any order of the borough to the contrary." The gentlemen all swore the freemen's oath, while the noblemen "engaged upon their honors to observe the freemen's oath"—it might have been seen as beneath their dignity actually to have sworn it.[66] The corporation of Boston may have wanted some specific return from these peers and gentlemen, but certainly the townsmen wished to cultivate their general goodwill as the process of the fen drainage commenced. Several of the men to whom Boston awarded the freedom served as sewer commissioners, including the earl of Lindsey and the earl of Devon, who headed the commission. A few months later, Boston also granted the freedom to the king's master of the robes, the high sheriff of Lincoln, a member of the Privy Council, and four other gentlemen.[67] The award of the freedom served not as a quid pro quo, office for service transaction, but rather as a concrete reminder to potential patrons of the needs and advantages of the locality.

The freedom might also be used as a more direct form of reward, offering citizenship as an honor for having performed special services for the corporation. All parliamentary boroughs conferred the freedom on those men who were to represent the borough in the House of Commons. Local bylaws invariably required MPs to be freemen of the borough, but since many who stood for borough seats were nonresident gentlemen, they had to be made free burgesses before they could become burgesses to Parliament. This rather contradicted the spirit of the bylaws, but it allowed towns to choose those men as MPs who might do a town the most good, resident or not.[68] Freedom might also be awarded for services performed for a town as a sign of thankfulness and respect. In April 1623, the corporation of Shrewsbury admitted Sir William Herbert, Sir Percy Herbert, and Sir Basil Brooke burgesses of the town without fees or fines, in consideration of "their love and goodwill to this corporation, expressed in the cause lately depending before the Privy Council between this town and the town of Oswestry concerning the freedom of the market for Welsh cottons."[69] Similarly, Peter Langstone, gent., was admitted free of Oxford for his "courtesies to the city" in the matter of the amercements estreated out of the Exchequer Court against the city.[70] Honorary citizenship served as a symbol of civic respect and of the bond between town and honoree.

The most potent symbolic linkage occurred when corporations also included patrons in their ruling hierarchy as mayors, aldermen, or JPs. When Charles I incorporated the borough of Leeds in 1626, the new corporators chose Sir John Savile, the town's patron and procurer of the charter, as their first alderman. The Cheshire borough of Macclesfield also at various times in the sixteenth and seventeenth centuries chose gentlemen, some with authority beyond simply that of a local figure, as mayors of the town. Sir Edward Fitton, lord president of Munster, served as mayor in

1599–1600, 1600–1601, and 1602–3; Sir Urian Legh in 1607–8, 1615–16, and 1623–24; and Sir Edward Fitton (created baronet in 1617) in 1614–15 and 1637–38.[71] This practice can also be discerned elsewhere, as in Portsmouth, Abingdon, Newcastle-under-Lyme, and Evesham.[72] Even Coventry, a corporation that has been described as having little to do with the county elite, selected Lord Berkeley as an alderman in 1611.[73] As a general rule, smaller towns that had more need for particular aid from patrons and less ability to fend off unwanted advances were more likely to make them part of civic government. Upon becoming a member of a corporation, a peer or gentleman became part of that brotherhood in a real as well as a symbolic way. His membership in the community obliged him to take a special interest in the welfare of the borough, both in the locality and especially with the center. In return, patrons received the honor and deference that went with their position, as well as the possibility of gaining influence over other corporate offices and favors for their own clients.

Instances of the phenomenon can be found all over the country, but aristocratic office-holding seems to have had a clear regional bias, occurring most frequently in the northwest. The best example of this practice hails from that region and pertains to a specific noble family: the house of Stanley in Lancashire and Cheshire. While it may be improvident to generalize their experiences to the rest of England, an investigation of their activities in borough government provides important clues into the workings of urban patronage. The experience of these northwest towns with their noble patrons represents one end of the spectrum of this phenomenon. The Stanleys wielded broad power in the northwest of England, far outstripping all other families in the area in the sixteenth and seventeenth centuries. With two main seats at Knowsley and Lathom only a short distance from Liverpool, the town could not help but fall within the Stanleys' sphere of influence. The earls of Derby held no manorial rights in the town, but did own land and a house there, clearly seeing Liverpool as part of their "turf."[74] The Liverpudlians, for their part, seemed to view the earls very much as their good lords. When Henry, the fourth earl, succeeded to the earldom, the town held banquets "four sundry times" for "our good lord the earl of Derby." The earls gave gifts to the town, including venison for the town council and a donation to build a new pillory for the detention of criminals. Civic leaders accepted all the earls' gifts with thanks and acknowledgments of obligation.[75] Their behavior reflected the continuity of lordship from these great magnates who had dominated the area for generations, but it also recognized the earls' current prominent position as representatives of royal government. Members of the Stanley family consistently held the lord lieutenancy for Lancashire and Cheshire, making them the key connection between the Court and the northwest. At almost every level—local, regional, and national—the earls of Derby were the most powerful figures in the area.

In the face of this expansive authority, Liverpool and its leaders would appear to be subject to fairly easy exploitation. A more complex picture emerges on closer inspection. Town and lords received reciprocal benefits. The leaders of the borough's government seemed to have been on good terms with the Stanleys. The earls of Derby held a legitimate place as players in local affairs. In fact, the townsmen of Liverpool at times used members of the Stanley family to suit their own purposes. Five times between 1568 and 1625, the burgesses of Liverpool elected an earl of Derby or one of his sons to the highest borough office: Sir Thomas Stanley (second son of earl Edward), 1568–69; Henry Lord Strange (heir apparent to the earl), 1569–70; Ferdinando Lord Strange, 1585–86; William, sixth earl of Derby, 1603; James Lord Strange, 1625.[76] These selections indicate the deference and esteem with which the townsmen regarded their powerful neighbors, but they do not demonstrate simple obedience. On at least some of these occasions, the townsmen chose Stanleys as mayors in order to reap quite specific benefits. Until 1626, Liverpool remained a prescriptive borough with no royal charter of incorporation. When James I came to the throne in 1603, civic leaders hoped to obtain a corporate charter. Apparently with this in mind, they chose the greatest local magnate, the earl of Derby, as their chief officer when applying for incorporation. On one hand the mayoralty put the earl of Derby under some obligation to assist in procuring the charter; on the other it would reassure the crown that the plan had the approval of the most powerful royal officer in the region. As mayor of Liverpool in 1604, William earl of Derby helped to obtain a new charter for the borough of Liverpool. Unfortunately for the town, a technicality—the date had been written "anno 4 Jac." rather than "anno 2 Jac."—caused the document's abrogation. Although the townsmen appealed to the earl of Salisbury to have the mistake amended, the attempt failed.[77] In 1625, with the succession of King Charles, the town council of Liverpool again tried this plan and elected the heir to the earldom of Derby to the mayoral chair. With Lord Strange's help, in 1626 Liverpool achieved the status of an incorporated borough. By electing them mayors, the townsmen not only did honor to the members of the house of Stanley, but also obtained much-needed assistance in securing the town's liberties.[78]

Small towns like Liverpool and Preston might be expected to be more vulnerable to Stanley "influence," but even the ancient corporation and regional capital of Chester invited the Stanleys into civic government. The city fathers chose Ferdinando Lord Strange as alderman in 1586, William earl of Derby in 1610, and James earl of Derby in 1642.[79] It is not entirely clear where the impetus for these nominations came from, but there seems to have been approval from both sides. For earl William's selection, Alderman Hugh Glaseor and Recorder Thomas Gamull apparently wrote to the corporation proposing the nomination and expressing the earl's approbation of the idea. The corporation as a whole supported the plan and took Glaseor and Gamull's suggestion. According to an Assembly order of 2 March 1610, the Assembly "especially out of their mere love and affection did with a free and general voice elect and choose William earl of Derby, knight of the most noble Order of the Garter and Chamberlain of the County Palatine of Chester to be one of the Aldermen of this City."[80]

This statement acknowledged the many levels at which the leaders of Chester thought the earl deserving of the aldermanship. They emphasized that they made their choice freely, without external pressure, and that they had a personal, affective, attachment to the earl. They also paid tribute to his social rank, at the very top of the honor hierarchy—a noble lord and a member of the Order of the Garter. Having a person of such status in the city's government could only enhance the honor and dignity of the corporation and its individual members. Finally, they acknowledged his role as an instrument of central government in his capacity as Chamberlain of the Palatine Exchequer. This royal appointment gave the earl specific authority in the region on behalf of the crown. The Palatine Court at times conflicted with the jurisdiction of the city's courts and conflicts occasionally brewed between Palatine and city officials. For instance, a lengthy and bitter dispute arose between Peter Proby, an officer of the Chester Exchequer and a client of Sir Francis Walsingham and the earl of Derby, and the corporation over the reversion to a civic office. Ultimately, the corporation rejected Proby's claim to the office, but offered him an annuity, mostly to gratify "their Lordships" Walsingham and Derby.[81] Corporators had constantly to balance the need to maintain civic privileges with the need to remain connected to the wider networks of authority in the realm. While having a lower Palatine official in civic government was problematic, having the Palatine chamberlain on the city council clearly was not. It can, in fact, be viewed as a conciliatory move, intended to keep conflicts from arising. The aldermen apparently felt little fear that the earl would use his position to dominate the city. They believed that his honor and authority would be assets to Chester. By including Derby in their city's government, the leaders of Chester showed due deference to the earl, but they also placed an obligation on him to act in the interests of his fellow corporators and the city at large.

While members of the Stanley family did occasionally attend meetings of the corporation, they viewed their offices as essentially honorific and not active. Their presence on the civic Assembly is recorded only on occasions when matters of special importance or divisiveness arose in the city.[82] The city of Chester did, however, choose other gentle aldermen and mayors who actively served as members of the corporation. Possibly as a result of their long-established dealings with the Stanley family, the corporation showed little hesitation in integrating landed gentlemen into city government. Sir Peter Warburton, a lawyer and judge, and Sir Thomas Savage, a prominent local gentleman, both sat on the civic Assembly as aldermen. Both played active roles in the corporation, but Savage proved particularly useful to the city when, as Viscount Savage, he held a prominent place at Court. Among many other things, he determined a lengthy dispute over the collection of tolls between the corporation and Sir Randle Crewe.[83] Three gentlemen also served as mayor during the reigns of James I and Charles I: Sir John Savage in 1607, Sir Randle Mainwaring in 1618 and 1625, and Sir Thomas Smythe in 1622. All of these men also held seats on the aldermanic bench. Smythe and Savage, although not for the most part resident in the city, did own or rent property there and appeared at the Assembly with some regularity. Savage was in town frequently enough that he had a deal with the bell-ringers of St. Peter's church to ring for him whenever he came into the Pentice Court, for which they received a "gratuity."[84] For Chester, having noblemen and gentlemen on the civic Assembly was the rule, not the exception, in this period.

It may be that Chester, as an important provincial capital and county unto itself, had enough confidence in its economic and political autonomy to prevent undue influence of its gentle members and therefore saw the benefits of such a policy as greater than the dangers.[85] For their part, the earls of Derby and other prominent members of the elite established strong, active relations with Chester and other towns in the northwest. They took particular interest in these localities and willingly became members of them. This regional bias may stem in part from the different way the borderlands of the north interacted with the emergent Tudor state than did the "core" of England in the south. As Steven Ellis has shown, the marches of the north and west maintained a seigneurial, magnate-oriented structure even as the Tudors solidified their rule in London. By the late sixteenth and early seventeenth centuries, the north had been more thoroughly integrated into the state, but a residual respect for and obedience toward the great magnates of the region still seemed to have operated in that part of the nation.[86] At least in the northwest, townsmen did not seem to fear that elite participation in corporate life would jeopardize the authority of the civic leadership.

Chester's affiliations, while unusual in their extent, nevertheless make clear the dangers of trying to distinguish "insiders" from "outsiders" in corporate boroughs. That boundary, more permeable membrane than rigid wall, could be manipulated to suit the corporation's needs. While civic leaders strenuously defended their borough's liberties and their own privileges against the depredations of others, they saw the advantages of integrating men whose principal interests lay outside the town into corporate governance. Borough corporations seem increasingly to have believed in the efficacy of this strategy, just as they increasingly included high stewards into their constitutions. This courting of elite favor may not have been as popular with the urban rank and file as with the more oligarchical corporations, but it helped reinforce civic government. For the rulers of early modern England—whether corporators, county JPs, or the king—order and stability were the greatest goods. Including members of the elite in corporations helped forge that stability while keeping urban government linked more fully to the governance of the realm.

III

Direct participation of a peer or prominent gentleman in the offices of a borough signaled a clear intent on the part of the townsmen to cultivate patronage. Having an officer of such social prominence in the corporation redounded to the honor of the corporators and established a special relationship with someone who had the power to work for the town's good. Direct participation was not, however, the only way that boroughs sought to attract the goodwill of the elite. The more indirect tie of nominations to civic office also formed an important link in urban patronage relationships. One of the necessary features of patronage was the availability of offices to use as rewards for participation. In the highest levels of government, the crown held a large assortment of offices both in central bureaucracy and in the county hierarchy, as in the lord lieutenancy, which the monarch distributed to favored members of the elite who then undertook the business of governing.[87] Similarly, parliamentary patrons used their power over certain seats to reward their own clients and relatives. But patronage networks intruded much more deeply into the polity of England.

At the most local level, boroughs had a variety of elective and appointive offices that could be distributed in ways that expanded the town's connections. By cautiously disseminating the nominations to civic offices, corporations strove to strengthen the obligation of patrons, who could in turn oblige their own clients. Such nominations were not handed out willy-nilly, and unsolicited ones were regularly rejected. Corporations carefully considered the distribution of nominations to patrons for the advantages that they might bring.

Offices from the great to the obscure offered points of linkage between patrons and corporations. The office of recorder, a corporation's chief legal officer, stood at the top of this hierarchy. Because of its prestige, it was a prime candidate for patrons' nominations. Court figures and local magnates, as well as gentlemen writing on their own behalves, solicited corporations for this place. The corporation of Cambridge chose as recorder in 1624 a nominee of Viscount Mandeville and the duke of Buckingham, while Great Yarmouth selected a Mr. Gwynne as recorder at the request of the earl of Northampton in 1611.[88] Because this officer had such a direct impact on and important role in civic government, corporations considered such requests warily and did not always honor patrons' desires. Leicester accepted a nomination from the earl of Huntingdon in 1603, but rejected one a year later when the original nominee died. The corporators were so concerned to keep the goodwill of their patron that they sent a deputation of five aldermen to visit the earl at Donnington Park to explain their actions.[89] Doncaster's leaders went through much heartache trying to convince their high steward, the earl of Shrewsbury, that he did not have a right to choose the town's recorder.[90] Even King James once failed in his bid to select the recorder of Chester.[91] Corporations accepted nominations with great caution. Men thought to be unfit or unacceptable would not gain the place, no matter how great the patron.

A similar calculus went into the choice of nominees for lesser offices. Positions like town clerk, serjeant-at-mace, or swordbearer were appointive offices within a corporation's purview. Although not necessarily high-status positions in and of themselves, they added to the honor of the corporation as a whole. The serjeants and the swordbearer bore the civic regalia, the symbols of the dignity of the town, while the town clerk kept charge of the borough's records, including the charters that gave a corporation existence and a history. Patrons regularly asked for these offices to gratify their own clients and suitors. Towns with long-standing connections to particular families almost expected such nominations. The earl of Derby procured for his servant the place of serjeant-at-mace of the city of

Chester, while Lord Keeper Egerton's servant became clerk of the pentice there in 1599. Apparently not all citizens approved of the latter choice, however, as one year later a townsman was brought to the court for saying that Ellis Williams, the new clerk of the pentice, "was an ass" and had obtained his office "by a great lord's favor."[92] In 1619, Lord Zouche, lord warden of the Cinque Ports, nominated a client as town clerk for Rye corporation. The lord warden had no legal right to the place, but relied on the town's goodwill toward him. "Your kind entertainment of this my request I shall take as a testimony of your love to me." The jurats of Rye took the hint and chose the warden's nominee.[93] The earl of Huntingdon on various occasions recommended servants or clients of his for offices in Leicester, including serjeant-at-mace, bailiff, and steward of the court. Francis earl of Bedford, high steward of Totnes, nominated the town clerk of that borough in 1634.[94] Even those cities that typically appointed townsmen to corporate offices sometimes accepted the nominations of patrons or important gentlemen. The provincial capital of Exeter rarely accepted nominations from outside the aldermanic body, but city fathers proved receptive to the advances of several gentlemen and the bishop of Exeter in their nominations for the position of swordbearer.[95] Coventry chose Mr. John Verney as steward at the request of Lord Brooke and Sir Edward Conwey, while Great Yarmouth agreed to give a reversion to the office of haven master to Robert Goodale at the request of Lord Arundel and the earl of Northampton.[96] Virtually no town operated entirely independently of elite patronage. Corporations created obligations in patrons, which they hoped to presume upon when need arose.

Corporations also handed out the freedom of the borough to gratify patrons, but again, they did so with calculated caution. Towns granted the freedom to urban patrons' individual clients, servants, or suitors who wished to have access to the privileges of the town. The practice seems to have occurred throughout England. Cases have been found in Reading, Leicester, Chester, Liverpool, Coventry, and Dover, and surely occurred elsewhere as well.[97] Whereas most gentlemen offered the freedom had no real intention to participate actively in the economy of a borough, many of these servants and suitors wanted the freedom specifically for the right to ply a trade in the town, with all its concomitant advantages. Sir Philip Stanhope asked that William Hopkin, draper of Derby, be made free of the town of Nottingham in the company of mercers, drapers, and grocers, which was "done only to satisfy Sir Philip's request, which he taketh thankfully at the town's hands." The corporation of Ipswich granted the freedom to the son-in-law of Justice Clenche in 1594, "out of thankfulness to Mr. Justice Clenche." The judge, in addition to aiding the port with legal troubles, had also recently loaned the corporation £200 to purchase land.[98] The earl of Essex asked the corporation of Oxford to make Robert Booke, glover, free of the city, while the bishop of Chester asked that his servant, William Knight, be made free of Chester.[99] Such requests put corporations in the difficult position of wanting to gratify the men who asked the favor while still first and foremost protecting the economic interests of the borough. Corporations often limited such grants, noting in their official records that a particular freedom to a "stranger" was not to be seen as a precedent for future dealings.[100] The frequency of these grants also varied greatly from town to town. In Chester, it occurred regularly; in Exeter only rarely. Whether common or unusual, such freedoms could have an impact on a borough's economy, and civic leaders acted cautiously in granting them. Corporations wished to appease patrons, but only insofar as it did not jeopardize the locality.

Chester's use of the freedom illustrates how carefully corporations proceeded in making such grants. In the sixteenth and seventeenth centuries, it became customary for great patrons like the earls of Derby or the chamberlains of the Palatine Court to nominate clients and relatives to the freedom of the city.[101] The city fathers generally deferred to their patrons in these matters as a mark of respect, but they made distinctions in their responses to various requests. Some the corporators rejected altogether, while others they fully accepted without fee or fine. Most fell somewhere in between, being accepted but having to pay fees of varying amounts. On the one extreme, in 1585 the Assembly rejected a request from the earl of Leicester, then chamberlain of the Exchequer of Chester, to make Mr. John Edwards free. "The convenience and inconvenience thereof was duly considered of, and albeit the whole corporation was most desirous to accomplish his Honor's such request . . . the said John Edwards is no fit person to be received into the franchises of the city." It was feared that Edwards, a wealthy merchant, was so rich that he would overthrow the whole trade of their poor city.[102] The corporation's plea of poverty rings somewhat hollow here, as it was the wealthiest port in the region and not likely to be overthrown by one man. There must have been something particularly obnoxious about Edwards that made the corporation respond so vehemently, but the sources are unfortunately vague. Although the city's leaders felt a strong obligation to gratify the earl, they would not jeopardize the city's trade or integrity in doing so. At the other extreme, when Thomas Vawes, brick maker and "servant in livery" to the earl of Derby, brought in a letter from his master underwriting his request for the civic freedom, the Assembly of Chester, "for the love that the city beareth to his Lordship," made Vawes free apparently without an entry fee.[103]

A fine line separated acceptable from unacceptable requests. During the course of the first half of the seventeenth century, the earls of Derby recommended at least six servants or clients as freemen of the city. The Assembly granted all of these requests, but only after careful discussion and voting on whether to grant the freedom at all and how much to charge if granted. Henry Smith, gentleman usher to the earl, received the freedom gratis, but most had to pay. Assembly Files show the sort of debate that occurred over these requests. Marked at the bottom of the petition of William Houghton, servant of the earl of Derby, is the following vote: to be "free as an apprentice," 15 votes; to be "free paying £5," 9 votes; "not free," 18 votes; "free paying £10," 1 vote; "free paying £6 13s. 4d.," 2 votes. The Assembly granted the petition, but what fee they assessed Houghton is unclear. Another Derby servant gained his freedom "gratis, not hurting any trade, at the earl of Derby's request."[104] Although the Assembly Books, the official record of the city, give the impression that these freedoms received the full and free consent of the corporation, it is clear that the requests went through a process of negotiation and not everyone favored granting them.

The granting of freedoms, whether honorary or otherwise, had consequences on a town's economy and government, both good and bad. The goodwill of the elite provided a useful tool for urban governors, but extensive action by a patron in controlling local affairs would be unwelcome. It is also the case that the governing body of a borough might well view the practice differently than did the regular citizens of a town. Average townsmen felt more keenly the competition from extra freemen and might resent the fact that they paid for their privileges while others received them gratis. Urban governors, typically well-established businessmen, had less to fear economically and more desire to identify with the landed elite. In Chester in 1619, all of the companies of the city petitioned the Assembly against the enfranchising of strangers by means of "private letters of powerful friends." Local tradesmen believed that the growing practice discouraged the "natural" citizens and apprentices in their trades. The Assembly responded by rejecting the application for freedom before them that day, which apparently appeased the commons.[105] But they never took steps to check the practice in the future and it continued throughout the period. The social and political good that honorary freedoms could do outweighed the possible economic consequences in the minds of the city's leadership, although not necessarily the rank and file.

Chester's corporation exceeded many others in the amount of inter-action it had with various members of the elite and the level of receptive-ness with which it approached those relations. Not all corporations had the security or deemed it necessary to accept patrons as participants in their day-to-day activities. Nevertheless, Chester illustrates an interesting paradox in the relations between urban communities and their aristocratic patrons. On the one hand, corporations worked forcefully to maintain in-tegrity and privileges. Civic leaders attempted to avoid actions that might endanger chartered rights and distrusted the landed elite as a force that potentially threatened those rights. On the other hand, town governors understood the great advantages that association with the landed elite could bring to a borough. They saw the integration of potential patrons or brokers into civic life as an effective strategy for cultivating favor. Wheth-er by making a powerful peer an alderman or by offering borough free-dom to one of his dependents, a corporation created an obligation for re-turn, an obligation that lay at the heart of patronage.

IV

Patrons participated in the life of corporate boroughs in a wide variety of ways, from the nominations they made to borough offices to serving in offices of the corporation themselves to providing desirable services and institutions to a town. These formed the most common sorts of interaction between towns and patrons, all of which kept members of the elite inte-grated into and interested in the activities and needs of the locality. But another sort of interaction cannot be left out of a discussion of urban pa-tronage. Electoral influence and parliamentary patronage played a signifi-cant part in relations between boroughs and the landed elite.[106] Historians have in the past placed undue weight on parliamentary patronage, ana-lyzing it to the almost complete disregard of all other aspects of patronage. It is the most visible form of interaction, producing correspondence from both patrons and boroughs at known intervals. However, this focus on parliamentary patronage has made it seem a thing apart, a different spe-cies from the normal routines of business. In fact, parliamentary patron-age existed as one aspect of the larger nexus of patronage relations in early modern England, springing from assumptions about deference and lord-ship, social goals and political tactics, tradition and order. It could also become factionalized and politicized, depending on local circumstances. It is not the intention here to provide a comprehensive treatment of parlia-mentary elections and patronage—whole books have already been written on that subject. A few key themes deserve attention in order to fit electoral patronage into the larger framework of urban-elite relations: the logic of electoral choice, the demands and expectations of patrons, and the ties between electoral patronage and other types of connection.[107]

Parliamentary patronage has often been seen in black-and-white terms. Corporations by nature wished always to return two of their own residents to represent them at Westminster, while peers and gentlemen persistently coerced townsmen to accept "foreign" nominees. According to this line of argument, those towns that were able to preserve "unswerving independence" were "among the elite" and "meritorious." Those that accepted the nominees of others "fell from grace."[108] Sir John Neale discussed borough patronage in terms of a hierarchy of independence. Those that returned two residents as members held the noble position at the top of the order as completely independent, while those that returned two "foreigners" sank to the depths at the bottom of the list. Those returning gentlemen from the county were somewhat better, but still fell short of the goal of independence.[109] This argument, ignoring all other aspects of patronage, presumes that the relationship between towns and members of the elite could not be anything but antagonistic. Townsmen, against their wills, had to accept unwanted foreign nominees forced on them by the invasive practices of gentlemen and peers. Enfolded in this discussion is another assumption that in the main, patrons only valued their relations with towns insofar as they provided opportunities for parliamentary patronage. Boroughs wanted to be independent; lords and gentlemen wanted the political power of parliamentary seats. This inherent conflict of interest led inevitably to hard-fought electoral contests and discontent between towns and patrons.

While this analysis has elements of truth to it, it simplifies a complex set of relations and views them through an anachronistic lens. We would do well to remember that Parliament, while extremely important, was not the be-all and end-all for obtaining favor. In Elizabeth's reign, at least, borough corporations were not particularly successful at achieving their ends through Parliament. David Dean has shown that although some towns used Parliament to solve local problems, they relied more heavily on personal appeals to privy councilors, lord lieutenants, high stewards, and other leading figures to gain effective resolutions. Robert Tittler, in his work on Elizabethan parliaments, has shown the limited effectiveness of Parliament as a tool for corporations to accomplish their business. "During the entire sixteenth century only eight to ten per cent of English towns gained action for themselves alone through parliamentary legislation. . . .

By the same token, only a very small number of urban centres (including York and Exeter, two of the largest) seem to have thought in terms of legislative programmes."[110] Surely the fact that boroughs without the parliamentary franchise achieved marginally greater legislative success than did those with the franchise says something about the way this particular institution served early modern towns. It suggests that urban electorates were less concerned to have local men as MPs than modern historians of them are. Townsmen, while aware of the importance of Parliament, also knew that there were other ways than Parliament to get their business done.

Even when doing business in Parliament, townsmen looked beyond their own fellows in making electoral decisions. In his study of parliamentary choice, Mark Kishlansky argues that because elections in the late sixteenth and early seventeenth centuries revolved around personal honor and not around partisan politics in the modern sense, we must rethink our assumptions about these events. Kishlansky believes that we should see them as "selections," composed through consensus, and not as oppositional elections. In the specific case of borough selections, he shows that choosing a patron's nominee was not considered to be a "fall from grace," but rather a practical response to the circumstances that existed at the time. "Patronage was an effective means of settling the problems of parliamentary selection that allowed a corporation to cement social and political ties while avoiding contests."[111] In a society where social relations were organic, parliamentary patronage formed another means of connecting people rather than driving them apart.

This interpretation has much to recommend it, and it can be taken further. Parliamentary patronage of boroughs only makes sense when seen as a part of a larger social matrix in which patronage of all sorts forms a crucial connective tissue. As the present work seeks to show, borough corporations achieved much of their business through nonparliamentary means, making other aspects of patronage critically important. Furthermore, parliamentary patronage is not a separate item from a noble family's patronage of a hospital or a high steward's patronage of a borough's charter. They formed parts of the same whole. Boroughs did not invariably believe they were being prevailed upon by outside forces, nor did lords believe they could impose upon towns at will without any return on their part. Parliamentary patrons promised to do good for the towns that chose their nominees, and they might expect that townsmen would take advantage of those promises.[112] While it is not the case that boroughs and patrons always agreed about the decisions made in parliamentary selections, nevertheless the choices make sense when put into the context of local events and patterns.

For the corporators of early modern boroughs, choosing one of their own did not stand as the inevitable goal of parliamentary selection. Rather, doing what they deemed best for themselves and the borough as a whole determined their patterns of choice. In some cases, this meant choosing two of their own; in others, choosing the nominee of a patron or a member of the local gentry. The town council of Nottingham stated this view succinctly prior to the Parliament of 1628.

> This Company are all agreed that if a parliament happens shortly to be called (as the rumor already is) that then two gentlemen of the country shall be chosen for easing the town's charges; and the same strangers are thought fitting by all the Company except two, to be Sir Charles Cavendish [son of the earl of Devon] and Master Henry Pierrepont, eldest son to the Lord Viscount Newarke, in hope that the town, yielding to their request touching their elections hereafter to this Parliament ensuing (if any be) may gain the friendship and favor of those two noble families, and have their assistance to the town when any occasion shall be offered.[113]

Selecting nonresidents who could actually provide benefits to the borough made better political sense than selecting resident townsmen would have. The townsmen showed little regret for any lost "independence," but rather had assessed the situation thoroughly and realized they would be well served by men like Cavendish and Pierrepont, both in and out of Parliament.

Townsmen made these choices upon considerable reflection and in some cases showed themselves to be quite politically aware. Great Yarmouth's parliamentary election of April 1625 demonstrates the care the citizens took in this important business. The borough had received letters "from divers knights and on their behalfs," asking to be chosen burgesses for Parliament. They proceeded to the election as follows:

> And it was agreed and ordered upon good causes and considerations, that notwithstanding any former ordinance to the contrary, yet it should be lawful for this house to be at liberty to make their own choice of Burgesses for this parliament, either out of this town or within this town at their pleasures. And it was also agreed that the choice of Burgesses should be made out of town, and so that which of the knights had or should have most voices should be the first Burgess. And every one of this House present being so at liberty and to give the first voice to which of the said knights being four they thought best. It happened that Sir John Corbett, baronet, had the most

voices. And so he was with assent of the most elected the first burgess of the parliament for this borough.

With the first burgess chosen, they proceeded to the second place:

At this Assembly also it was agreed that the other three knights and three of the Aldermen of this Town selected from the rest should stand for the second voice. And that which soever of the three knights or three Aldermen should have the most voices he should be the second Burgess of the Parliament for this Borough. Whereupon every man's voice passing accordingly, it happened that Edward Owner, one of the three Aldermen selected had the most voices. And therefore by the consent of this house was elected the second burgess of the Parliament for this Borough.

This selection was not the end of the matter, however. One member of the corporation was believed to have spoken improper words concerning one of the unsuccessful candidates, Sir John Suckling, comptroller of the king's household, and a privy councilor. The townsman in question, wishing to exonerate himself, "entreated this House that the words which he had spoken, for the avoiding of misinterpretation, might be recorded in this Assembly, which was condescended unto, and thereupon recorded to be these, (videlicet) that Sir John Suckling, being one of the Officers of His Majesty's household, it would be a question whether Sir John should incline rather to the King than to the subject, as the case might be."[114] This man, at least, made distinctions between Sir John Corbett, a local gentlemen who would work on the town's behalf, and Sir John Suckling, whose interests were more questionable.

Each locality made its own calculations. Townsmen weighed the knowledge of local circumstances that a fellow resident would have against the connections and clout a nonresident nominee could bring to bear on local business. The townsmen of Dover had these things in mind when they chose Edward Nicholas, secretary to the lord warden of the Cinque Ports, as MP in 1628. Nicholas, though a nonresident, had the trust and respect of the jurats of Dover because of his connection to the lord warden and the many favors he had done for the port. Specifically, Dover corporation suffered from an ongoing dispute with the port's water-bailiff, who repeatedly invaded the jurats' jurisdiction. Nicholas acted as mediator in the conflict, arranging a composition between the town and the water-bailiff. The jurats of Dover wrote to Nicholas in March 1628, apprising him of his selection as their MP. They assured him that the election was "most free and general," both in respect of the lord warden's letter on his behalf and for their "many engagements" to Nicholas for his numerous benefits to the town. At the same time they begged what favor they could from him concerning their suit against the water-bailiff, "wherein we are already much indebted to you."[115] The fate of the jurats' suit rested with Nicholas, and the townsmen happily gratified both the lord warden and the gentleman himself as a way to achieve their ends.

Some corporations chose to go against past precedents in order to choose nonresidents for Parliament. Ludlow civic leaders, in the elections of 1621, overturned a previous order requiring that only members of the corporation's ruling body could be chosen. The old rule, "for great and urgent occasions touching the good and commonwealth of this corporation is for this time only made void." The electors then proceeded to choose Spencer, Lord Compton as a free burgess and then burgess for Parliament.[116] The townsmen clearly hoped to gain advantages from choosing this prominent member of the Council of the Marches of Wales as their burgess. The corporation of Cambridge, devoid of connections to the center at the calling of the 1626 parliamentary session, used the parliamentary selection as a way to remedy their trouble. The town's high steward, Viscount St. Albans, had been impeached by Parliament in 1621 and had essentially retreated from the Court by mid-decade. Cambridge did not regularly choose outside nominees, but when the new lord keeper, Lord Coventry, wrote to the corporation in January 1626 asking them to choose his secretary Mr. Thompson, the townsmen listened. Coventry explained his nomination by saying, "I am yet a stranger unto you, but haply hereafter I may be able to do you a pleasure valuable to my present request." He also said that Thompson would serve without payment from the corporation. The townsmen duly chose Thompson as their burgess for Parliament, and four months later, when St. Albans died, the corporators chose Lord Coventry to replace him as high steward.[117] Local business often required powerful connections, and granting patrons' nominations provided one means of achieving this.

For many towns, maintaining the general goodwill of a patron, rather than achieving a specific bit of local business, made accepting electoral patronage a positive choice. Boroughs of all types and sizes felt the pull to gratify important patrons. Even the great city of York chose to select a nominee of the archbishop of York, Toby Matthew.[118] The townsmen of Cambridge understood the need to gratify a patron as a sign of respect, even if it meant changing their original plans for selection. In 1614, they received notice from their high steward, Lord Ellesmere, that he hoped to have the nomination of one of the burgess places for the town. The corporation had already made electoral plans, but decided to rethink them. The mayor, John Wickstede, wrote to Ellesmere:

> Upon intelligence received by Mr. French that your lordship hath inclination to have one of the Burgesses of Cambridge for the next Parliament to be supplied by your honor's nomination, I thought it my bounden duty to know your lordship's pleasure therein that such a course may be taken as it may be effected. Albeit at the writing hereof the Queen's Majesty's Attorney, being at Cambridge one of the counsel and fee of the town, desireth one of the places for himself, and we had our purpose to elect our Recorder and one burgess resident in the town. Howbeit in weightiest affairs the town hath received your long and most honorable patronage, so in this or anything else upon your lordship's liking and direction known, I hope the town shall be ready to esteem your honor's desire as a commandment to be observed.[119]

In this case, the best decision for the good of the town was to consider Ellesmere's nominee as a sign and a reinforcement of the connections that existed between them.

Boroughs that had long-standing relations with a particular noble or gentle family or a provincial office (such as the Cinque Ports or the duchy of Lancaster) often used parliamentary seats as one more means of creating obligation on the part of their patrons. Just like other aspects of patronage—gifts, hospitality, honorary freedom of the borough, membership in the corporation—parliamentary nominations required reciprocation. Corporations expected the burgesses they selected to work for the good of the town, a fact patrons acknowledged in their request letters. The friendship of a successful patron extended well beyond the business of any particular Parliament, and townsmen understood this when accepting nominees on a regular basis. Most of the Cinque Ports chose one if not two of the warden's nominees for successive parliaments. While the lord wardens frequently placed their nominees, it is also the case that some of the ports were more obstreperous than others in granting places, and some lord wardens had more success in their attempts than others. The duke of Buckingham, for instance, suffered serious setbacks as an electoral patron.[120] The corporation of Leicester usually gave one of its nominations to the earls of Huntingdon, while the chancellor of the duchy of Lancaster usually received the other.[121] Thus the townsmen could appease two different patrons at once. Liverpool customarily gave at least one of its nominations to the earls of Derby. When the chancellors of the duchy of Lancaster also attempted to gain the privilege of nomination in Liverpool, the townsmen used their connections to the earl of Derby to ward off this encroachment on traditional electoral patterns.[122] The earl of Banbury invariably received the nomination for one seat at Reading, while the earls of Rutland named one or both burgesses in East Retford through most of the period and one burgess in Lincoln in the sixteenth century.[123] In all of these cases parliamentary nominations formed just one more sign of mutual obligation between patron and client town. Parliamentary patronage did not exist by itself, but was one strand in a web of interrelations.

Such examples could be multiplied many times. Given the nature of interaction between localities, patrons, and the crown in this period, nonresident MPs could, in some circumstances, serve the purposes of a borough better than residents could. At bottom, the welfare of the town—or at least of the corporation—determined patterns of choice.[124] This is not to argue, however, that an outside nominee always made a good or a popular choice. Some towns almost never accepted the nominees of patrons, instead choosing members of their corporation and taking on the expense of paying for their time in Parliament. Chester, despite its relationship with the earls of Derby and other patrons, always returned two of its own, and these were almost always freemen of long standing.[125] A large and prosperous city in this period, it jealously guarded its privileges and could well afford the expenses of MPs; it provided many other means of gratifying its patrons as well. Exeter also typically made its own choices, as did Norwich and Bristol. Some towns occasionally accepted their patron's nominees. Barnstaple selected nominees from the earl of Bath in 1597, 1601, 1604, and 1626, but not in 1614, 1620, 1624, or 1625.[126] In the selection at Ipswich in 1604, the townsmen asked their high steward, Lord Treasurer Dorset, to sort out the various candidates ahead of the election date. The corporation had already given their word to Sir Michael Stanhope, but they agreed to accept Dorset's candidate instead, if Dorset could get Stanhope to defer to the new candidate, Sir Francis Bacon. Ipswich voters accepted two nominees from their high steward in 1604 and one in 1614, but chose townsmen throughout the 1620's.[127] Other towns split the difference, so to speak, by choosing one resident townsman or their recorder for one seat and allowing a patron to nominate the burgess for the second. The townsmen of St. Albans, having been asked by the earl of Salisbury for nominations to both seats, struck a deal with their patron whereby he received one nomination and they kept the other.[128]

Local circumstances largely determined the success that parliamentary patrons would have in corporate boroughs. Even in places that sometimes selected the nominees of patrons, a local crisis could cause a change in strategy. In a 1609 election to replace a deceased MP of Ludlow, the corporation rejected the nomination of Sir Francis Eure by the lord president of the Marches and Sir John Leveson by the earl of Salisbury. The civic body, wishing to amend "divers imperfections concerning the state of this corporation," chose one of their own, Bailiff Richard Fisher, for the seat.[129] The citizens of Salisbury, in January 1626, had very specific reasons for refusing to accept nominations from either their high steward, the earl of Pembroke, or from Attorney General Sir Robert Heath. As the aldermen explained it to Heath, the town could not accept the nominees of either patron because they were "taxed with paupers" and needed to procure an Act of Parliament to solve their problem, "which it were impossible to accomplish by strangers." The aldermen hoped that Heath would make "good construction" of their decision, for even though they "could not in this one particular give you satisfaction, yet we and our whole city will ever contribute to your worthy memory."[130] Even a very powerful patron like the earl of Pembroke could not force a corporate borough into submission. The concerns and beliefs of the citizens could play a part, although this is more difficult to prove decisively. The men of Great Yarmouth politely but firmly rejected a nominee from the bishop of Norwich in 1620. Samuel Harsnett, their bishop for only a year, had already butted heads with the reform-minded corporators of Yarmouth, refusing to approve a Cambridge-educated divine the townsmen had chosen for town preacher. While it is possible that the town's electoral choice bore no relation to the bishop's refusal, circumstances seem to suggest that the two were connected.[131] Townsmen certainly took the potential consequences of a patron's ill will into consideration when making their choices, but they did what was right for their town in the particular circumstances.

Local conflicts played a role as well. The civic elite who attempted to control elections, and in some cases changed borough constitutions to create a narrower franchise,[132] could not always manipulate elections to their satisfaction. Franchise disputes in a borough could lead to fractious elections, where the corporators wished to appease a patron while the larger body of voters took a different tack. In the election of 1624, the aldermen of Leicester explained to the earl of Huntingdon that while they supported the earl's nominee, the more numerous common council would not conform to their superiors' wishes and chose a townsman instead.[133] The 1640 elections saw more than one instance where the will of the voters at large led to the rejection of a patron's nominee. The corporate leaders of Great Yarmouth wrote to their high steward, the earl of Dorset, in spring of 1640 to inform him that his nominee had not been chosen. At Dorset's request, they had put Sir John Suckling into nomination "in a fair way" with the others who stood for the place, but the recorder and an alderman were chosen by the majority instead. They wrote similarly to the earl of Northumberland, lord admiral, who had also put forward a nominee.[134] Similarly, the jurats of Sandwich warned the earl of Northumberland that while they wished to gratify him by choosing his nominee, Edward Nicholas, they could not guarantee that the freemen, "who have votes in the election as well as we," could be convinced to vote for him.[135] In some cases, this may have provided a convenient out for corporators who really did not want to choose a patron's nominee; they could claim that they had no ability to sway the "common sort." Outside nominees themselves might take advantage of friction over voting rights. Derek Hirst identifies various instances of gentlemen using this tactic to obtain votes from the general populace of a town.[136] Because of the shifting sands of local circumstances, parliamentary patronage was never a sure thing.

This uncertainty requires an assessment of the other side of parliamentary patronage, the patron's expectations and response. Urban patrons, while they clearly felt some assurance that they would receive parliamentary nominations, regularly found their demands unfulfilled. Yet this did not necessarily mean the end of the relationship. Parliamentary selections in the Elizabethan and early Stuart periods revolved around matters of honor and prestige.[137] Serving as an MP, even for an insignificant town like East Looe or Eye or Chard, brought with it an increase in dignity. The winner, or his patron, had the clout to convince the electors to choose him, and the acclamation of one's fellows went a long way in matters of honor in this period. Urban patrons wished to have their nominees chosen not only to gratify their relatives and other clients, but to make manifest their own prestige. Successful pursuit of parliamentary nominations reconfirmed a magnate's status as a powerful and honorable man, just as did other signs like gifts, hospitality, and deference. But while parliamentary patronage had these beneficial effects from the point of view of the patron, successful enjoyment of it was not a guaranteed part of urban patronage. The office of high steward, which has so frequently been associated with electoral patronage, did not always convey such patronage. Peers agreed to serve as high stewards of towns that had no parliamentary representation at all. Doncaster, Macclesfield, Tewkesbury, and Hertford had high stewards long before they had the right to return MPs.[138] Peers also willingly served as high stewards of towns that historically never accepted parliamentary nominees, such as Exeter, Salisbury, and Hereford. The patrons in question might make advances, but they had no assurance of succeeding. Nevertheless, failure did not lead to rejection of the relationship on the part of the patron. The earl of Pembroke, as noted above, contin-

ued as high steward of Salisbury throughout the period that the corporation rejected his electoral advances. Indeed, he was instrumental in helping the corporation obtain a new charter a few years later.[139] The voters in
Leicester failed to select the earl of Huntingdon's nominee in 1601 and instead actually chose a mortal enemy (they said, through a trick on the enemy's part). This enraged the earl and severely strained the relationship
between him and the town. Yet the connection endured, and earl George
continued to aid Leicester, although more warily than before.[140]

Because it reflected upon their honor, patrons disliked being turned
down in their nominations. At the same time, they seemed to acknowledge
nominations as a gift from the borough rather than as an absolute right.
The earl of Pembroke admitted this when he wrote to the earl of Salisbury
concerning the voters at Old Sarum, "the nominating of [MPs] depending
only on their [the voters'] choice and swayed by their affection."[141] Lord
Zouche, lord president of the Council of Wales, recommended a relative
to the corporation of Shrewsbury in the 1604 parliamentary election as a
"friendly motion . . . without prejudicing your due election." When he
heard of some opposition to the nomination, Zouche told the townsmen
that he would rather lose his suit than have their election placed in jeopardy. He would rather "willingly put up any disgrace offered to me and
those I love than to see any of you discouraged by the insolent disposition
of any. . . . I am resolved to keep within the bounds befitting my place and
trust imposed upon me." Regardless of the outcome, he promised to
"stand betwixt you and any hazard any such malignant spirit can work
you."[142] Zouche was certainly unusual in his willingness to defer in this
way, but he apparently saw peace and order as the greater good. Part of
the responsibility of the urban patron was to protect local interests, and
this might mean accepting some setbacks on the parliamentary front while
still maintaining ties with the locality.

Patrons knew that their influence on parliamentary choice was not
guaranteed. Their ability to affect the borough selection process became
even more tenuous in the elections called in 1640. While these elections
did not depart entirely from previous patterns of choice, they did differ in
the level of tension and strong opinion concerning candidates that determined the outcome in many parliamentary boroughs. Some towns, like
Leicester, that generally accepted the nominees of patrons moved away
from that practice and chose men more in tune with local concerns.[143] The
citizens of Great Yarmouth selected townsmen rather than gentry nominees in 1640, as did voters in King's Lynn.[144] The 1640 elections do not,
however, show a simple and universal rejection of patronage across the

board. Outside nominees remained acceptable if they suited local interests. The small borough of Grantham chose gentlemen Henry Pelham,
esq., and Sir Edward Bashe in spring 1640, and Pelham and Thomas Hussey, esq., son of Sir Edward Hussey, bart., in the autumn. The critical concern in these elections seemed to have been that the gentlemen would pay
their own expenses at Parliament. In Ipswich, voters chose a neighboring
gentleman, John Gurdon, esq., of Great Wenham, over Edmund Daye, a
townsman, in the March election. That this was not universally approved
of, however, is apparent from the tone in which the election was recorded
in the Great Court Book: "John Gurdon . . . being neither an inhabitant
nor a freeman of the said town of Ipswich and Edmund Daye of Ipswich
. . . one of the Burgesses of the Town in the last parliament [and] being an
inhabitant of the said town of Ipswich." Also unusually, a vote was recorded; Gurdon received 105 votes and Daye received 95.[145] In general,
borough voters seemed more interested in returning two of their own to
Parliament in 1640 than in previous years. The anxieties that gripped the
realm made themselves felt in the parliamentary elections and in some
cases broke—or at least bent—long-standing ties of patronage.

Despite the difficulties of 1640, parliamentary patronage, for those
who participated in it, meant something significantly more complex than
boroughs giving in to domineering lords. Townsmen made positive
choices for patrons' nominees and patrons continued to serve boroughs
despite electoral failures. Patronage went well beyond parliamentary
nominations, involving a whole range of interactions, both at the local
level and at the center. As an element of this larger connection, parliamentary patronage cannot be seen in black-and-white terms, but rather occupied a gray area that different localities negotiated in different ways. As
historian William Hunt has said, "The whole question of patronage and
influence has often been treated much too simplistically, as if the only two
alternatives open to a borough in its relations with a local magnate were
defiance or servility. Like the force of gravitation, influence in seventeenth-century politics admitted of subtle gradations."[146] These "subtle
gradations" appear throughout the workings of urban patronage, providing a flexible medium for political and social exchange.

Urban patronage, in all of its aspects, brought members of the landed
elite into contact with borough communities. A patron's active interest in
borough life could benefit the welfare of a town immensely, providing
needed social, religious, and educational institutions, as well as the necessary ties to the crown. To achieve and maintain this interest, civic governors made patrons part of the corporate body, hoping to link them to the

borough by common membership. The offices of high steward and re-corder, mayor and alderman, were all given to members of the elite in some towns. The conferral of honorary freedom on present and potential friends of the locality also served this integrative purpose. The benefits towns offered to patrons—from nominations for civic offices to nomina-tions for parliamentary places—all helped to maintain the interest of pa-trons and encourage them to provide reciprocal benefits. The trick, of course, was for these great men to provide the sort of benefits that corpo-rations desired—economic and social investments that augmented the lo-cality and connections to and influence with those in power. Townsmen did not want their patrons to become too active in the daily round of civic business. This problem could lead to friction between patron and corpora-tion, and civic leaders regularly had to make difficult decisions between pleasing patrons and protecting their own power. But as this chapter has shown, it is a mistake to characterize relations between borough corpora-tions and landed gentry as inherently antagonistic or alienated. Bringing prominent men into the corporation could be a better strategy than keep-ing them out. Both corporations and their patrons gained something. The reciprocity of the connection served as the foundation for its success, and this success needs to be measured according to the values of the time: benefit, prestige, favor, and order.

THREE

Peacekeeping and Patrons

Finding Solutions for Civic Discord

The desire for order and stability drove early modern Englishmen. The active cultivation of connection by corporate governors underscores this point. Involving powerful men in the life of a provincial borough conveyed an air of increased legitimacy to urban leaders. Although historians have argued whether urban oligarchy grew or declined in the seventeenth century, it is certainly the case that small groups of men held the powers of magistracy in England's towns.[1] By linking themselves to nobles and gentlemen, borough governors reinforced and reaffirmed their own authority in the locality. At no time was this more important than in times of disturbance and discord in the corporation. Urban populations seemed inherently unstable. Only a strong, solid, and unified local government could keep a lid on potential turmoil. Central government had every bit as much of a stake in seeing civic leaders maintain a firm grasp on their communities as did the urban oligarchs themselves. The threat of disagreement within the corporate body signaled danger. Discord at the top of urban society might open up opportunities for instability further down the social hierarchy.[2] Finding ways to preserve and maintain civic peace preoccupied town leaders, pushing them to look outside the locality for creative resolutions to periods of division. Using everything from law courts to local composition to the mediation of civic patrons, corporators strove to regain order and agreement as quickly as possible. Both conflict and its resolution went beyond mere local business, often having impacts that extended well past the boundaries of a borough. Christopher Friedrichs, describing conflicts in early modern cities in general, aptly states that "some disputes developed along factional lines that reflected networks of influence or patronage. Often these networks extended far beyond the city itself. . . . [W]hen urban routine was disrupted by conflict, the interests of regional nobles or national rulers were often deeply affected."[3] Patrons and patronage could thus play a critical role in bringing together feuding factions or reinforcing the authority of corporate leaders. Calling on civic patrons to mediate conflict helped to maintain local stability, allowed patrons to fulfill their role as protectors of the commonwealth and defenders of civic interest, and complied with the crown's need to reinforce stable order in the realm. Looking at relations between corporations and their elite patrons during times of civic conflict reveals much about how urban patronage worked and the assumptions that underlay the connection.

I

On 4 September 1619, the city of Chester celebrated unity. After months of friction, rival factions came together under the beneficent eyes of two of the city's friends, Sir Thomas Savage and Sir Peter Warburton. The mayor of Chester, Sir Randle Mainwaring, and his followers had been sparring with Recorder Edward Whitby and his supporters for most of the spring and summer. Division prevailed in the city, to the chagrin of the city fathers themselves and the disapproval of the Privy Council. In an attempt to settle the conflict and avoid direct council intervention, the corporation of Chester invited the city's patrons to mediate the dispute. William earl of Derby, Sir Thomas Savage, and Sir Peter Warburton, desiring not just absence of conflict, but true harmony in the city, capped their mediation with a symbolic act of reconciliation. They "made Mr. Mayor and Mr. Recorder friends" by inviting them to share a meal in the presence of the three patrons, the aldermen of the city, and a collection of other knights and gentlemen. This ceremonial feast exhibited to the whole community that discord had ended and that friendship and unity reigned. The assistance of powerful friends and a public show of love before the whole community created a sense of peace in the corporation. Order returned to Chester.[4]

For early modern Englishmen, "order" served as a watchword. As King James made clear in his *Trew Law of Free Monarchies*, God had determined a precise pattern, hierarchical in nature, to regulate society.[5] Those who exercised governance in England, both urban leaders and landed gentlemen, worked to reinforce this stable order in their local communities, and thus the commonwealth at large. The increasing economic instability of the late sixteenth and early seventeenth centuries gave rise to fears of social instability, which local elites worked hard to quell. While enforcing order on those of lower status by demonstrations of authority, governing elites also hoped to promote harmonious relations among the populace through their own good behavior. Their orderly concourse served as a model. Conflict, meanwhile, received strong censure as a poor example to others. Nowhere was this prescription for peace more important than in borough corporations. The law considered a corporate body of many members as a legal individual, making conflict contradictory and intolerable. For corporations, the metaphoric Body Politic served as much more than a figure of speech—it represented reality. Discord diseased the body. It also endangered the community by setting a negative example to the urban population, which, it was commonly assumed, might rise if not properly governed.[6] Corporation members therefore attempted to preserve order and unity, although not always permanently or completely, both among the borough inhabitants and among themselves.

Central government also both expected and encouraged borough corporations to act promptly in resolving internal strife. The Privy Council actively promoted the composition of differences within localities, to avoid central intervention. They explicitly requested the corporation of Chichester in 1626 to "lay aside all dissensions and live in peaceable and quiet manner" in order to benefit the city and advance the king's service. Similarly, the lords of the council commanded Chester's Assembly to find agreement among themselves, presuming the corporators would rather have their problems "ordered in love than censured by the Board."[7] Failure on the part of local authorities might mean sending in commissioners or calling the mayor and aldermen to London to answer for their behavior. Traveling to London to appear before the board, often for weeks on end, required large amounts of time and money; it was also a terrifying experience. In extreme cases, a disrupted corporation might be threatened with quo warranto proceedings, questioning the validity of the corporate charter.[8] At worst, a corporation could lose all of its privileges and franchises, and civic leaders could lose their control of local government.

This fear certainly gave corporators reason to take the Privy Council's advice and to accommodate internal disputes as quickly as possible. Although from the reign of Elizabeth the Privy Council added the resolution of municipal disputes to its duties, such matters made up only a small portion of business before the board. Those disputes the board did get involved in do not seem to follow a particular pattern over time, although it appears that questions of local franchise and religious conflicts came increasingly before the council in the 1620's and 1630's.[9] This may suggest that corporations found it more difficult to find resolution at their own initiative as Charles's government became more "determined to pursue

unpopular policies and singularly deaf to local complaints."[10] Regardless
of the reasons behind the apparent change, no corporation wanted to put
itself in a position of having to answer to the Privy Council. Attention
from the council could only mean a serious problem in local order, and
corporators were just as concerned to maintain order as were the lords in
council. Avoiding council regulation was not an attempt at exclusion from
the broader governing structures of the state. Rather, civic leaders, seeing
themselves as part of those structures, took the initiative to promote their
own good governance, finding means both inside and outside borough
walls to protect their interests.

The language of consensual decision-making provided corporations
with one important method of conveying a sense of order and harmony.
Corporators expected to make unified and unanimous decisions, reaching
agreement through discussion and compromise. Consensus was not simply an attitude of mind, it was also a method of procedure; townsmen did
not invariably agree, but they carried out their business in such a way as to
avoid conflict as much as possible.[11] Unusually thorny or divisive questions might end in a voice vote, but records of these appear infrequently.
Agreement proved the norm, or at least it was the goal to which corporations aspired and the face that they presented to the public. Even the way
they kept their official records assumed unanimity. Official court books
and assembly minutes almost invariably emphasized agreement, even
when corporation meetings demonstrably fell short of harmony. In Exeter, for instance, the town clerk apparently sometimes filled out pages in
the books as blanks for future meetings. These blanks listed the names of
all the aldermen who should be at corporate assemblies, followed by the
words "who wholly agree." Clearly, obstinate dissent was not supposed
to occur in Exeter's corporation, at least not in the official records.[12] In an
entry in Chester's corporation assembly book for May of 1619, the town
clerk simply noted that there were "some matters in question" about the
removal of a civic officer, but that the Assembly deferred a decision until
the man himself could be present. An eyewitness to the meeting, however,
gave a vivid—and less dignified—account of aldermen yelling at each
other, peremptory speeches, violent humors, a demand that two council
members be ejected from the meeting and their refusal to leave, and general disorder and ill-temper. One wonders how many other disputes are
disguised in borough records by the language of consensus.[13] Corporations strove to give the appearance of harmony, even in the face of evident
cacophony. Their written records stood as a testimony of how they believed things should be and how the corporate body should act in the fu-

ture, rather than as a precise account of reality. Corporations needed to confirm their well-being as governing bodies, not just to their citizens or the central government or the local gentry, but possibly to themselves as well.[14]

Despite a strong desire to maintain the ideal of unity, townsmen consistently faced the reality of division. They attempted to minimize conflicts and resolve them as quickly as possible, using means both within the borough and without. When the corporators of Coventry found themselves mired in conflict in 1615, they entered the following order into their official record:

> Whereas no government can long prosper where unity and concord is not preserved, the maintenance whereof causeth small governments to grow great, and the want thereof hath been the ruin of the greatest and most flourishing commonwealths in all ages, for the better preservation whereof (it being the mother of the common good of this City) do hereby testify by word and witness under our hands that we are in true brotherly love and Christian friendship one with another. And for the suppressing of contention & discord that may by any means arise between Brethren of this House, whereby the Peace and unity of the same may be broken, the business of the City hindered, or discord the Mother of confusion hatched up to implacable irreconciliation: It is therefore now ordered, that everyone that shall be hereafter chosen and sworn to be of the Council of the City, & a brother of this House, shall likewise testify & witness under his hand writing to this present Order, that he likewise is in true brotherly love and Christian friendship with every brother of this House.[15]

The men of Coventry attempted to enforce this Christian friendship by censuring or suspending those who abused civic government "with insulting or provoking terms" or "bad speeches." They hoped this oath of brotherhood would bring the "unity and concord" they desired. While intramural harmonizing of discord was common, it did not preclude the resort to other types of dispute resolution. Townsmen, although localists, clearly recognized their need to remain connected to the wider society and the central government. Town governors used all of the institutions and persons available to them to preserve order and to carry out the business of the borough. Corporations, as part of the larger body of governance in the English state, relied on this interdependence to reinforce their own authority and solve local problems. Mediation, whether by elite patrons or others, played an important part in finding solutions.

In resolving their disputes, borough corporations had many options, as well as many models for behavior. The settlement of differences—everything from the personal or business discontents of individuals to matters that struck at the very heart of civic governance—occurred regularly. The leaders of civic society could look to the daily business of the urban community to find examples of dispute resolution, from going to the law to seeking composition and mediation. The courts saw heavy use in this period, whether the central courts in London or the local mayor's court. We know that litigants resorted to borough courts frequently, for instance to settle failed credit arrangements.[16] Indeed, citizens risked disfranchisement if they took certain types of local matters outside the borough courts.[17] Disputes over moral behavior—defamation of character, quarreling—ended up before ecclesiastical courts or Quarter Sessions for resolution. The central courts at Westminster saw an all-time high in litigation in 1640.[18] There are even a number of cases where a disgruntled corporator, having been removed from the corporation for misbehavior, obtained a writ of restitution out of King's Bench to get his position back.[19] The courts—local, regional, and central—were familiar terrain for many townsmen.

While litigation, and the desire for victory over one's opponents, formed one model for dispute resolution, mediation and the desire to moderate conflict formed an even more prevalent one. Litigation itself sometimes served simply as a first step on a path to more friendly resolutions. In at least some of the cases where a corporator went to King's Bench to obtain a writ of restitution, the person in question was restored not because of his writ, but because he "submitted" to the corporation, apologizing and agreeing to behave properly in the future.[20] An historian of urban credit and debt in King's Lynn stresses the rarity of vexatious litigation in that town. Most complaints "were largely successful attempts to resolve disputes and maintain the bonds of credit."[21] Similarly, a study of defamation cases in the ecclesiastical courts of York shows that although many complaints came into court, few actually went through to a final decision. Many plaintiffs, after initiating a suit in court, withdrew their complaints and settled out of court through the mediation or arbitration of third parties. Avoiding the trouble and expense of law and a sense of friendship and love in the community motivated many to drop court proceedings.[22] Townsmen in particular disliked the adversarial nature of the law, especially common law, in their commercial business. Commercial opinion stressed fair-dealing and honesty; going to law, for instance to collect debts, was frowned upon.[23] Even in the midst of a great deal of litigiousness, finding solutions that preserved peace and friendship seemed attractive.

It is not surprising, then, that borough corporations faced with internal divisions saw a range of options for resolution, yet often chose those options that best protected their peace and allayed conflict. Legal action, both divisive and expensive, represented a breakdown of harmony, a failure to resolve matters in a more friendly fashion. Corporations, even more so than individuals, could not well afford the consequences of legal conflict. As did so many individuals, corporations regularly turned to third parties, often men not resident in the community, to resolve conflict and return civic government to order.

One way to avoid a suit at law but still to procure a more or less legal decision was to appeal to Assize judges for arbitration. In Lincoln, Assize judges Sir Peter Warburton and Sir Thomas Foster "heard and ended" a controversy over the office of town clerk. In the Western Circuit Assize, the judges mediated a dispute between the mayor of Lyme Regis and the overseers of the poor, while the civic governors of Ipswich agreed in 1603 that if further problems arose concerning the town clerkship, they were "content to refer the same to the order of Sir Edward Coke," a judge and a friend of the corporation. Similarly, the corporation of Chester appealed to the Assize judges to settle the city's conflict over the collection of tolls.[24] Judges made attractive mediators because of the qualities they brought to the process: they had legal expertise, were considered to be objective observers, and had the backing of the crown behind them. It does not seem that corporations followed a clear pattern in the types of problems they brought before judges as opposed to other mediators. Simple logistics may have played a role. If the Assize judges were in town, they heard the dispute. The corporate practice of giving gifts and banquets to judges in some way reciprocated the services judges offered.[25] In the air of mutual good feeling that such hospitality engendered, town leaders hoped and expected that Assize judges would assist them when the need arose.

While Assize judges were useful, they were not always available. Other authority figures also served this purpose. Conflict resolution appears to have been one of the expected duties of an urban patron. His services might be used in a wide variety of ways, depending on his level of interaction with the town and the seriousness of the differences involved. Religious conflict, trade disputes, disagreements over lands and leases, and disputed or disrupted municipal elections all came under the mediating influence of patrons of various towns during the period. Most important, patrons served to patch together those corporations riven with internal strife. Considered a member of a corporation, a patron had a strong interest in keeping peace in the borough. His presumed knowledge of the people and the problems of a particular community suited him well to play a mediating role. He demonstrated his natural place in the social hierarchy by preserving order and exercising his authority in the borough. This integration did not create perfect harmony or alleviate all discord, but it did provide a way for patrons and client boroughs to work together for the good of the locality.

Borough patrons settled disputes for corporations all across England in the early Stuart period and in towns of all sizes. Boroughs as small as East Retford, Nottinghamshire, and as large as Chester called on the assistance of local patrons. The Assembly of Boston agreed unanimously that "the difference about repairing and amending of the sluice and piles in the haven is absolutely referred to the determination and ordering of the right honorable the earl of Lincoln," high steward of the city at the time. The earl of Huntingdon mediated property disputes in Leicester, as did the earl of Shrewsbury in Derby. In Chester, the earl of Derby served as mediator in several disputes, including a disagreement between two aldermen over the building of new city waterworks.[26] Civic patrons sorted out disputes between corporations and their appointed officials—clerks, stewards, schoolmasters—in many localities as well.[27] The earl of Bath served as mediator when the civic authorities found themselves at odds with the town preacher, Mr. Trynder. After having been thrown in jail for carousing in an alehouse late at night, Trynder retaliated through the pulpit: "Sunday following, he [Trynder] preached two hours, being a cold day he wearied all his audience." Bath issued a decision aimed at establishing peace in the community. He warned the preacher that disorderly behavior would not be tolerated, but he also urged the townsmen to have more respect for their minister.[28] When participants could not find a solution to local problems, whatever their nature, established local patronage links could be called upon to reach one. A patron made a convenient referee.

The high stewardship in particular offered a platform for the mediation of local disputes. Townsmen brought all kinds of concerns before their high stewards, even resorting to that officer to complain against the depredations of the corporation itself. The earl of Rutland, high steward of East Retford, received letters both from a group of townsmen and from the town's bailiffs when a bitter feud broke out in 1593 over the custody of the charter and other treasured documents of the borough. Each group blamed the other for the trouble, and each clearly assumed that Rutland would resolve the matter in its favor. Similarly, a merchant in King's Lynn, on behalf of his fellow townsmen, appealed to the high steward, Lord Keeper Egerton, in an attempt to foil the actions of one of the town's aldermen. Alderman Thomas Baker, with the aid of his brother, supposedly was "maliciously and without any just cause" persecuting and plotting against some inhabitants, "to their continual vexation and great charges." The alderman and his followers justified their actions by claiming "the great favor they have of your honor and other great personages to bring their devices and malicious practices to pass."[29] The sparring parties in both towns expected to find resolution at the hands of their noble high stewards. They may have sought victory rather than compromise, but they nevertheless agreed that a high steward was an appropriate arbiter who could be expected to provide an orderly resolution.

High stewards provided townsmen with a mediator who was at once inside and outside the corporation. Their main interests lay well outside the town, but as an officer of the corporation, a high steward could be expected to reinforce the authority of the body to which he belonged. Lord Chancellor Ellesmere, high steward of Cambridge, acknowledged this dual role when he wrote to the corporation in 1610 to settle a conflict between a borough officer and the mayor and aldermen of the town. Henry Wulf, the city's bailiff, was setting "an evil example to others" by refusing to make certain payments required of him in that place. The corporation had written to Ellesmere complaining of the misbehavior, and the lord chancellor agreed to rectify the problem. He did this because "both in my love to the Town and in regard of the place I hold, I cannot but take the more particular notice as a thing more peculiarly belonging unto me, to see both the peace and good government of the town preserved and the disturbers thereof duly punished." But as a member of their corporation, he desired more "the reformation of offenses than the punishment of offenders" and hoped to cause Wulf to change his ways through admonition and not condign punishment.[30] Ellesmere identified himself with the corporation in his treatment of the incident, but also brought to bear his authority as an important crown officer. Townsmen saw him as an authority at once internal and external to the borough, not simply as an "outsider" forcing his will on the community. Corporations purposefully called on this dual interest in order to attain their goals.

Patrons, representing both local and central authority, performed a beneficial service for corporations confronted with conflict. Sometimes informal mediation restored peace to a town, but at times a more formal resolution was needed. Borough corporations also requested patrons to make rules for the civic body to follow. Chester's corporators asked Sir Thomas Savage and Justice Warburton to set out the official fees pertaining to the office of clerk of the pentice. Viscount Wallingford, as high steward of Oxford, devised official orders concerning the precedence of aldermen, at the corporation's request. In Reading, Wallingford (by then the earl of Banbury) set the table of fees to be collected by stewards of the borough court in 1627.[31] Thomas Lord Ellesmere and Thomas Lord Coventry, both lord chancellors of England, also served as Cambridge's high stewards during the early seventeenth century. During their respective tenures, both men helped to mediate disputes within the town government by drawing up official orders for the corporation.[32] Corporations depended at times on patrons to set policy, not just to serve as honorary figureheads.

These examples indicate the variety of strategies that a corporation might use to maintain the health of the body politic. Different types of disputes called for different remedies, and those remedies were not exclusively homegrown. Patronage could form an important part of local solutions. Urban communities had their own institutions for self-government, which they protected and cherished. Simultaneously, they existed as part of a larger commonwealth and its governing structures. Preserving local unity promoted national stability. Peacemaking in the town did not stop at the borough's borders, but extended to the personnel and institutions of the government at large.

II

Peacemaking seems to have been an accepted duty for urban patrons. Corporations relied on patrons to settle a wide range of troubles in the borough, but major disputes—ones that divided the corporate body itself—constituted their most serious business. Disorder and discord threatened the reputation, authority, and in the worst case the very existence of corporate government. Civic leaders needed prompt, decisive resolutions, preferably ones that firmly reinforced the ruling oligarchy and squelched any hint of popular sentiment. By asking a patron to help solve local problems, corporators gained both the prospect of peace and closer connections to a prominent member of the elite. A patron, as part of the ruling orders of England, had a stake in preserving the peace in the localities to which he was tied. Both corporations and patrons saw the reinforcement of their authority and the preservation of reputation as key. The best-documented examples of patron involvement in the resolution of corporate conflict show that patrons played an important role in sustaining the authority of civic government and impressing standards of order on townsmen as a whole.

A complex mixture of motives inclined civic authorities to reach out for help in solving their problems. The corporation of Barnstaple had several things in mind when calling on their recorder, the earl of Bath, to settle a dispute: concern for public order, desire to uphold the honor of the corporation, and the practical considerations of keeping urban government in proper working condition. In 1599, Pentecost Dodderidge, scion of one of Barnstaple's most prominent families, and three confederates refused to pay their rates in the borough, claiming they were not burgesses. The aldermen felt fully justified in rating them because, by rights, these men should have entered into the freedom of the borough to carry on their trades. Dodderidge's refusal to become a freeman is particularly difficult to understand given his family's position in the town. He himself went on in later life to serve as mayor and as MP for the borough. When the four "recusants" refused to pay, the town receiver distrained their goods.[33] In retaliation, Dodderidge procured a writ and had the receiver arrested. Events having reached this unpleasant impasse, the mayor and his brethren asked the earl of Bath to adjudicate the dispute.[34]

Bath had held the office of recorder since the late 1580's, usually assigning a deputy to carry out his duties. On this occasion, however, as in other matters of particular importance, the earl came to Barnstaple in person, sitting in the Guildhall with the Company of the corporation. The deputy recorder first recounted Dodderidge's alleged abuses. Dodderidge then gave his statement, claiming that he and his fellows were over-rated, not that they should not pay at all. The earl of Bath reprimanded him for his rash behavior, stating that Dodderidge should have first appealed to him as recorder before launching into disobedience. Bath apparently saw it as his rightful duty to take action in matters of this sort. Dodderidge attempted to appease the earl, replying that "he would have done it but that a hundred of the inferior sort would have attended him and thereby given him a deal of trouble." This appeal to Bath's sense of propriety backfired, however, as the deputy recorder jumped on Dodderidge's words and alleged that he "went to raise a tumult and insurrection in the town." The earl shared this opinion, committing Dodderidge to prison and binding him over to appear before the Privy Council for his disobedience.[35]

For the earl of Bath, this was the only correct outcome in the case: incitement of the populace and rejection of corporate authority could not be tolerated in a well-ordered society. The mayor and aldermen held legitimate authority from the crown in Barnstaple, and the earl—although he did not always see eye-to-eye with them—had to support their authority. Men like Dodderidge, who threatened to stir up the popular element, had to be stopped in order to maintain political and social structures. Because of the issues at stake, the earl of Bath took the matter personally. He clearly believed that the matter touched on his own dignity and status, as well as falling within his sphere of authority as recorder. Bath's decision ultimately found confirmation at the board, as the Privy Council ordered Dodderidge not only to pay his assessed rates, but also to submit to being made a burgess for a £10 entry fine, "as others do."[36] With the fear of popular discontent quelled, the corporation forced Dodderidge to take up his rightful place of responsibility in the borough. Reliance on a noble patron helped the corporation to reinforce its authority without compromising it. The earl of Bath's honor and authority received confirmation as well, both in the locality and in London. By turning over the determination to Bath, the corporation procured a lasting settlement, officially sanctioned but friendly to the corporation and its needs.

Matters tending toward civic unrest concerned corporators deeply. Nonconformity to the economic or administrative rules of the borough brought a swift response, as in the case of Barnstaple. Religious nonconformity proved to be even more problematic. Townsmen often disagreed among themselves about the proper outward forms of religious practice. When religious questions caused division, it could be convenient to look to a patron—particularly one with congenial beliefs—to find solutions. When strife over the choice of civic preacher arose in Dover in the spring of 1622, the jurats turned to the lord warden of the Cinque Ports, Edward Lord Zouche, for a remedy. Zouche, a reform-minded peer, had the trust of the corporation as well as a personal interest in the outcome of the matter. A group of inhabitants attempted to have Mr. Henry Chantler made the new civic lecturer for the town, a position to which the lord warden held certain rights of appointment. According to John Reading, the conformist minister of the parish of St. Mary in Dover, Chantler had gained the post by a conspiracy organized by "our holy brethren," implying that they held puritan opinions. Chantler's supporters obtained his license "by Mr. Hibbens mediation," Hibbens being lord warden Zouche's servant. Zouche himself apparently had no hand in the matter, although his reforming religious beliefs were well known. Hibbens may have used the lord warden's name without his knowledge. Mr. Reading and the mayor and some of the jurats of Dover deemed this a move to dishonor the minister and to decrease both his "auditory" and his income, while fueling the fires of the factious, the "adversaries of our peace." Reading insisted that the puritan group merely intended to increase their own power and not to advance the word of God. He had offered to fill the place of lecturer himself for free, but "they refused me and found them such a lecturer as pleased them." Reading had been opposed by this group of factious men before, and he pleaded with the lord warden to support him and to have Chantler's license revoked. "I do therefore humbly beseech your good lordship that as you have been pleased not only to place me, but patronize me among this people, so also still to keep me in the sanctuary of that power, out of which I am subject to the injuries of those that love me not, because they love neither the government nor the ministers of our Church."[37]

While the majority of the details of this story come from the account of John Reading himself and reflect his bias, even his slanted account points to the fact that groups with varying religious sensibilities had developed in Dover. It appears that the mayor and some of the jurats supported Reading's brand of religion, or at least supported his position as sanctioned by the lord warden. But the other group, the "holy brethren," had enough influence to be able to obtain the appointment of an irregular lecturer without the knowledge of the lord warden. This faction, active in the previous year, posed ongoing difficulties for the town, according to Sir James Hussey, the commissary of the archbishop in the area. Zouche, as lord warden, had a duty to maintain the peace of his town and to enforce religious propriety. He also had an obligation as a patron to his client Reading. Zouche did come to Reading's aid, quelling the "holy" faction by having Chantler removed as town lecturer.[38] Although his actions may not have eradicated completely the problem of religious division in Dover, Zouche did serve to remove the immediate trouble, reestablishing peace in the port and reaffirming the rightful authority of both the beneficed clergy and the majority of the civic leadership.[39]

Reaffirmation of corporate authority formed the core of what civic leaders hoped elite patrons would do. Discord, whether religious or otherwise, threatened the integrity of urban government. Corporators preferred to knit themselves together by their own agreement, but some gulfs of opinion simply could not be bridged through discussion within the civic Assembly. Business rivalries and competition for place and honor in the borough could factionalize corporations in short order. Recourse to patrons whose principal business lay outside the town offered feuding townsmen a more "indifferent" means of working out serious problems. These powerful men saw local issues from a different angle than did the heavily invested townsmen, and they had the effective force of social and political power behind them to bring divided sides together.

The contentious situation of Chester in 1619, noted above, provides a prime example of the effectiveness of inviting patrons to knit the torn fabric of civic government. The willingness of Chester's leaders to call out for help from two neighboring gentlemen and a regional magnate might seem odd. The city prided itself on its ancient self-government and its liberty from county institutions. But Chester also had a long tradition of connection with Cheshire's elite families.[40] Indeed, the three men principally involved in these events had long histories of involvement with the city: all owned or leased property there, and all held office in the corporation.[41] At the same time, all three stood outside the hurly-burly of day-to-day civic politics, associated as they were with the wider scope of royal office and authority. The earl of Derby was lord lieutenant of Cheshire and chamberlain of the Palatine Court of Chester; Sir Peter Warburton, a judge of Common Pleas; and Sir Thomas Savage (later Viscount Savage), a deputy lieutenant and JP of Cheshire. This combination of interests and qualities gave Chester's corporators confidence in their friends' abilities to settle civic strife.

Chester stood in particular need of help in maintaining local concord. The city had an unfortunate reputation for factiousness in the seventeenth century. Bouts of infighting among groups in the corporation broke out with alarming regularity. Rival groups changed personnel over time, but during the early seventeenth century they consistently revolved around two families: the Mainwarings, an old Chester family; and the Whitbys. Relative newcomers to the city, the Whitbys arrived around 1602 and immediately entered into local politics and administration. Robert Whitby, who served in the Exchequer Court of Chester, became clerk of the pentice of the city (essentially town clerk) in 1602. In 1606, he requested that his son Thomas join him as co-clerk. Robert then resigned the clerkship to his son in order to run for mayor, an office he gained in 1612. That same year, Thomas was chosen sheriff of the city, while the younger son, Edward, became recorder in 1613. This agglomeration of power in 1612–13 led to a period of protracted feuding within the corporation, as some aldermen tried to contain the Whitby juggernaut.[42] The Whitbys simultaneously accumulated their own set of backers. Never hard and fast, these groups shifted with the issues involved.[43] The kernel of the factions remained, however, providing preexisting camps of interest whenever new points of conflict arose.

Tensions reached fever pitch in 1618, when the anti-Whitby faction set out to damage their rivals. Upon the examination of witnesses in Portmoot Court in June of that year, corporators determined that Thomas and Robert Whitby had committed various offenses in the office of clerk of the pentice. The Assembly voted to remove them from office and to prevent their readmission. Very conveniently, the corporation just then received a letter from the king, recommending one Robert Brerewood as clerk. Brerewood sported sterling credentials as a man with long Chester roots, the son of a sheriff and grandson of a mayor. His main advantage, however, lay in his close connection, as son-in-law, to Sir Randle Mainwaring, foe of the Whitbys and soon-to-be mayor of Chester. According to one (admittedly hostile) source, Brerewood procured the king's recommendation "by great friends" in London, presumably through Sir Randle's connections.[44] In order to dampen factional passions, the corporation decided to call in Sir Peter Warburton and Sir Thomas Savage to settle the divisive issue of the fees the clerk could legitimately take.[45]

The settlement solved one problem, but failed to dissolve the tensions that dominated city government. Within a year, the Whitby family suffered another blow when mayor Mainwaring's backers accused Recorder Edward Whitby of official corruption. The charges had the flavor of vendetta about them: the Assembly in fact voted to remove Whitby from office while he was absent in London, pursuing civic business. Disorder marred the proceedings so much that corporators feared they had broken their own rules. The mayor called a second meeting for 1 June 1619, which again resulted in confusion. Men from both sides uttered "sharp interlocutions," while Robert and Thomas Whitby were threatened with exclusion from the House. The division, sharp and deep, could not be healed within the Assembly. Eager for order, the corporators finally agreed on two things. First, they deferred the hearing of the case against Edward Whitby until such time as he could be there in person to speak for himself. Second, they invited the earl of Derby, Sir Thomas Savage, and Sir Peter Warburton to hear the cause.[46]

When Edward Whitby returned to Chester in August, he defended himself before a full Assembly, including Judge Warburton and Sir Thomas Savage.[47] Although opponents objected "many matters" against Whitby, none of them stuck. Sir Peter and Sir Thomas cleared him of any misdemeanor and reaffirmed him in his office. While this may not have pleased Sir Randle Mainwaring, it provided a firm resolution backed by the civic Assembly and representatives of the king's government. To complete their settlement, the city's patrons offered a ceremonial symbol of Chester's peace and good order. On 4 September, they made the factions share a meal. Warburton and Savage brought the mayor and the recorder back into amity, and Sir Thomas Savage "bestowed a fat buck on either of them upon condition that the one should sup the other at their own houses, with the Aldermen and other friends on both sides." This they did, the "right honorable William earl of Derby being with them, and many other worshipful knights and gent."[48] The feast, symbolizing the restoration of friendship and brotherly love to the corporation, was every bit as important as the actual hearing. By intervening at the corporation's invitation, Savage, Warburton, and Derby used their status as both accepted members of the community and powerful figures in the regional and national elite to bring order back to the locality. They existed simultaneously as insiders and outsiders. Chester's corporators relied on that combination when they called out for help.

III

An examination of one corporation's struggle to deal with internal division shows that this very ambiguity of definitions, the multiplicity of interests on the part of townsmen, could allow patrons to restore order. The corporation of Oxford manipulated this ambiguity successfully when faced with strife. In a reversal of usual meaning of "insiders" and "outsiders," the corporators of Oxford identified with a noble patron to the exclusion of one of their own members. A disputed election of a town councilman in 1611 escalated into a vituperative attack by Alderman Thomas Harris against his fellow corporators and eventually against Lord Knollys, the city's high steward. Rather than defend their fellow's behavior, the town governors of Oxford disfranchised him and bound themselves more closely to their noble patron. Harris then appealed to Lord Chancellor Ellesmere for restoration to the aldermanic bench, producing a set of depositions recording the dispute. A story emerges of the contest over the honor and privileges of the corporation and of the high steward.[49]

"By the general consent of this house and of all the commons of this city in the guildhall assembled," the citizens of Oxford chose William Lord Knollys as their high steward on 11 January 1611. He succeeded to the office upon the resignation of Lord Chancellor Ellesmere, who became chancellor of Oxford University. Strife between town and gown over jurisdiction and precedence formed a basic structure of life in Oxford, making it virtually impossible for an officer of the university to serve as an officer of the corporation.[50] To protect the city's interests, and to obtain a powerful advocate to counterbalance the university, the corporation chose a new high steward from the same social rank as Lord Ellesmere. Lord Knollys hailed from a family with long roots in the region and a long history of government service. He served as lord lieutenant of Oxfordshire and as privy councilor to three monarchs—Elizabeth, James I, and Charles I. In an elaborate show, the mayor, six aldermen, the town clerk, the chief bailiff, and the recorder all went to London to present the patent of office and a gift to Lord Knollys.[51] While Knollys accepted the place with "hearty thanks," he also showed his annoyance at the corporation for their failure to choose him earlier, "in respect that his honorable father [Sir Francis Knollys] was in the same place, and he himself being of this Shire or County and of the Chiefest Rank of the same." Nevertheless, he agreed that he would "by all good means as well by himself as his friends protect and defend the same city." He then took an oath to maintain the liberties of the city of Oxford.[52] The corporators knew they must treat their high steward particularly well if they wished to enjoy his favor. With troubles afoot regarding the university and within the corporation itself, the townsmen needed the protection and support of this powerful peer.

The city that Lord Knollys took into his stewardship was not a city at peace. Against a backdrop of continuing conflict with the university, the corporation experienced turmoil stemming from the behavior of Thomas Harris. In 1609, during his mayoralty, Harris had offended the vice chancellor of the university, which "extremely provoked both him and the university against the city." Mayor Harris's erratic behavior compounded not only the town-gown conflict, but internal division as well. According to his fellow aldermen, he failed to defend the town's officers against the university or to write a letter asking for assistance from the then high steward, Lord Ellesmere. Harris claimed that he did this only out of respect for the lord chancellor, as the letter was going to be carried to London by a common carrier, a "sheepskin dresser"—a singularly unconvincing explanation.[53] After his mayoralty, Harris continued his disruptive behavior, holding subsidy assessments in his own hands (and, by inference, embezzling them) and disparaging his fellow corporation members when they disagreed with him. He seems to have been something of a loose cannon. His actions caused intense feelings in the corporation, eventually leading to the disputed civic election of 1611.[54] In that election, the question arose as to whether a bailiff could be chosen for the position of assistant in the corporation. This seemingly minor point had major ramifications: corporations that acted contrary to the precise specifications of their charters might have those charters revoked for noncompliance. The corporators could not come to a resolution. As an act of respect to Lord Knollys, their new high steward, they referred the matter to him for an official settlement.[55]

Knollys took great pains in his ruling. He carefully studied the city's charters and precedents, drawing up a long document explaining his resolution. Wishing "all peace, concord, and good agreements" to the people of Oxford, he stated that a bailiff could not be an assistant; to do so would be contrary to their chartered privileges.[56] While the council of the corporation accepted the determination, Thomas Harris did not. Harris encouraged the unsuccessful candidate for assistant not to accept Lord Knollys's decision, thus creating further disruption in the city. Most corporators viewed his behavior as "an opposition if not rebellion against the whole body of the city," impeaching the peace and injuring civic authority. It also had the effect of discouraging the high steward from ever trying to compose a dispute again, if "the party against whom it is or his adherents shall thus despitefully kick against it and despis[e] both him and it."[57]

Harris's insults moved beyond a simple disregard for authority, however, and launched into an attack on Lord Knollys's personal abilities and honor. Harris, in "very fleering and scornful manner," declared that Lord Knollys could not even read the city's charters, much less make an objective decision about them. He also refused to give any title of respect or honor to Knollys, but rather declared the peer an oathbreaker who had ignored the customs and liberties of the city.[58] Why Harris was so incredibly hostile remains obscure, but throughout his career in the corporation he had episodes of disruptive and erratic behavior. Nor does it seem that he acted on behalf of a "party" that opposed Lord Knollys. No evidence appears in the Council Acts to suggest that Harris had a following in his attitude toward Knollys or his fellow corporators. That does not preclude the possibility, given the nature of the source, but all available evidence suggests that the great majority of the corporation condemned Harris's behavior.[59] Whatever his reasons, by making these statements Harris brought shame upon the whole corporation and jeopardized not only the settlement of the civic issues, but the negotiations between the city and the university that Knollys was then undertaking.

The affront, not surprisingly, incensed Lord Knollys, who wondered that "in that city and amongst those citizens which should most respect him, and in the heart of that county wherein he dwelt and whereof he was lieutenant, he should be so highly disgraced and dishonored." He came to the city in July 1611, where the mayor and aldermen greeted him in their finest scarlet robes, presented him with gifts and a banquet, and showed him as much honor as possible. They wished to convey that the corporation as a whole revered him.[60] Knollys later appeared before the whole Assembly and charged Harris with his abuse. Harris refused to humble himself or show any desire for pardon, which further irked the high steward.

Lord Knollys declared that his honor could not stand sharing membership in the corporation with one as malicious and odious as Harris. He demanded that the council remove Harris from the corporation, or else he would remove himself from the high stewardship. The corporators now had a choice. They could support their fellow townsman or preserve their connection with Lord Knollys. They made their decision quickly: the next day they officially removed Harris from his aldermanship and from the corporation, "in respect of his great abuses done in words towards our most honorable Steward, the Lord Knollys, besides his very ill behavior, misusage, misdemeanor, and carriage of himself in the time of his late mayoralty towards this city and divers citizens thereof."[61] It was far more important to maintain the goodwill and support of the high steward at this juncture than to defend a fellow corporator, especially one as troublesome as Thomas Harris. The corporators identified their interests with those of Lord Knollys, and worked to preserve his favor as a way of preserving the liberties and peace of the city over time.

The matter did not stop there, however. Harris soon appealed to Lord Ellesmere, as lord chancellor, for readmission to the aldermanic bench.[62] The intense desire of the majority of the Oxford city council to exclude this man from their midst and the real need of the city to retain good relations with its high steward are apparent in the city's final statement to Ellesmere. Reinstating Harris would not only bring the dishonor of factionalism to the city and alienate Lord Knollys, but would also keep Oxford from establishing patronage ties with noblemen in the future.

> These things thus being, we appeal to the judgment of grave and honorable wisdom whether due respect to the honor of the king's Council and our own honorable Steward, as also a meet care to avoid that disgrace like to have fallen upon the City by being (as never yet it was) abandoned in displeasure by the Lord Steward thereof, if this man had not been ejected, were not sufficient motives and causes so to do; nay, whether we had not cause to think that if the city had been cast off for the abuse to the honorable Patron thereof not righted yet would have been for long time unreceived into Patronage by any other person of nobleness or honor.[63]

The corporation's arguments proved convincing: Thomas Harris remained excluded from the Oxford city council.

In this final statement, the men of Oxford clearly acknowledged their need for connection beyond the city walls. They willingly identified corporate interests with those of their high steward, to whom they owed honor and deference. Knollys had worked assiduously on the city's behalf, to solve both the internal dispute and the conflict with the university. He went on to compose a settlement with the university later that year, much to the delight and relief of the townsmen.[64] Harris's dishonor to Lord Knollys put the city's future in jeopardy, as it threatened to cut Oxford off from all potential patronage. After five years out of office, and with Lord Knollys's explicit consent and Harris's explicit promise to behave, this argumentative alderman finally regained his place on the corporation in 1616. In April, Harris, having apologized to Lord Knollys, asked the high steward to request the corporation to reinstate him. "His Lordship in his letter declared his free forgetting and forgiving the said Mr. Harris any error or injury by him heretofore offered towards his Lordship, but yet left a free will and power unto this house to accept and restore him again so as some submission and promise of future conformity by the said Harris were made." The city council, taking into consideration Lord Knollys's magnanimous example, agreed to forgive Harris his past sins and "lovingly received and restored" him into the corporation.[65] This was as it should be. Corporations like Oxford preferred the idea of harmonizing everyone within the body. Only in extreme cases—such as Harris's attack on corporate integrity—did they wish to exclude someone. A borough with a reputation for fractiousness and disrespect for authority found little favor with the ruling elite. Alienation of patronage meant that a town would not have a sympathetic mediator for dispute resolution or a protector of borough interests in the county or at Court. Treating a patron appropriately in matters of internal interest to the borough had long-term ramifications for a corporation's ability to succeed in the patronage-oriented political world of early-Stuart England.

IV

Maintaining the goodwill of a patron could prove critical both to a corporation's domestic felicity and to its ability to remain connected with the wider governing structures of the realm. Civic disputes were not simply parochial problems, but had a broader impact, as well. The crown had an important stake in the maintenance of urban order, using the Privy Council and regional magnates to fashion stability. But from a corporation's point of view, keeping all patrons happy while holding a firm grip on civic privileges could prove challenging. A patron's interest did not necessarily conform to a corporation's interest. Those incidents in which a patron worked against the desires and needs of a client corporation provide insight into both the ideals and the realities of patronage relations.

While flexible enough to accommodate a wide range of behaviors, these connections were not entirely within the control of a corporation. Disagreements in towns could spill over into or be influenced by regional politics and personal relations between important men of the area. The town of Evesham, for instance, had regular interaction with a number of neighboring gentry families, and it seems that in-fighting in the corporation in 1608 and 1609 stemmed from corporators' alliances with feuding gentlemen.[66] Civic disputes offered a platform upon which a variety of dramas might be played out, not all of which related directly to the town.

Doncaster's corporators found themselves confronted with such a dilemma as they attempted to run the gauntlet between a powerful patron and their own corporate privileges. A contested election in Doncaster brought the corporation in contact with the Privy Council, the Council of the North, judges of Assize, the lord chamberlain of the queen's household, and the most powerful local magnate, the earl of Shrewsbury. In 1589, a group of Doncaster's citizens, including some members of the corporation, called into question the manner in which the corporation conducted mayoral elections. Citing privileges granted by Henry VII in the "Grand Charter," the citizenry claimed a broader franchise than the aldermanic bench allowed. This resulted in electoral confusion and a double election: the commonalty chose as mayor Francis Copley, gent., while corporators chose their fellow Thomas Harryson. Copley, who was not an alderman, was ineligible for the mayoralty by the rules then used. Not surprisingly, "some tumult and disorder" ensued, which brought Doncaster to the Privy Council's attention. The board commissioned members of the Council of the North and Justices Clenche and Walmesley to investigate.[67] Not just these more distant officers of the queen, but also the town's "especial good lord" became involved. Members of both factions apparently hoped to gain the support of George earl of Shrewsbury, Doncaster's high steward. Shrewsbury asked that the Grand Charter be brought before him for his perusal, to which the mayor and aldermen assented. They asked, however, that "his lordship do not debate of any matter concerning the said charter before Francis Copley, gent., Francis Mapplis alderman, Henry Bingley, Mr. West, and their adherents." The corporators also agreed to have the charter perused by Justices Clenche and Walmesley if the earl could not make a satisfactory determination.[68] The mayor and his cohorts likely thought the matter closed.

They thought wrong. Shrewsbury's entry into the proceedings, rather than calming the storm, whipped up the winds of faction instead. His behavior illustrates the varying consequences of personal connection to a

great peer: sometimes a patron had more than an objective interest in a locality. No "indifferent" arbiter, Shrewsbury pressed his own privileges in
civic government by virtue of his high stewardship. He used the divisions
in the town to promote his right to appoint the town's recorder, siding
with Francis Copley and his faction against the mayor and his brother,
who was then recorder.[69] The earl in fact brought Recorder William Ferne
before the Privy Council for his "disordered and seditious proceedings
against his Lordship" in his "rash and unadvised acceptance of the office."[70] Ferne vacated his position under pressure. From the corporation's
point of view, this disastrous turn of events required a move away from
the earl. They wrote a long, respectful letter to him, expressing their hope
that he would "stand our good lord to our poor corporation as you always
have done," but they held firm on their claim over the recordership.[71] His
partial behavior alarmed the townsmen, causing them to doubt the earl's
ability or willingness to serve their best interests. Even the Privy Council
seemed to believe that Shrewsbury was too involved in the matter to be a
fit mediator of the disputed mayoral election. The board turned the matter
over to the Council of the North, the lord president of which, the earl of
Huntingdon, pledged "to do what is necessary for the quiet of the
town."[72]

The "quiet of the town" received a stroke of good fortune in autumn of
1590. Shrewsbury died.[73] The corporation proceeded immediately to look
elsewhere for patronage. They found it in the person of Henry Carey,
Lord Hunsdon. Hunsdon, an important Court figure as chamberlain of
Queen Elizabeth's household, also owned property near Doncaster. Corporators appealed to his friendship and proximity when asking for his
help to uphold their authority and condemn the "riotous and unlawful"
behavior of Doncaster's commons. Hunsdon accepted his new role as patron, personally presenting the corporation's petition before the Privy
Council, advocating the town leaders' position, and writing directly to the
earl of Huntingdon to see that the peace of the town be kept and "tumultuous and dangerous assemblies" be restrained and punished.[74] He also attended the meeting of the council that finally laid down the orders for
good government in Doncaster, which reinforced the authority of the
close corporation to elect the mayor of the town.[75]

In recognition for the great favor that Lord Hunsdon had shown them,
the corporators chose him their new high steward in March 1591. The
new earl of Shrewsbury, Gilbert Talbot, took this amiss. His ancestors had
been associated with Doncaster for generations, and he seemed to believe
he had a hereditary right to the place. It came as a great affront to his

honor to be overlooked in this way. The earl tried to obstruct the workings of the court of record in the town and to discover what he could about the lord chamberlain's intentions.[76] Although certainly Lord Hunsdon must have known the consequences of his actions vis-à-vis the new earl of Shrewsbury, he did not intentionally strike against the honor of his fellow peer. Maintaining order in the locality and defending the queen's peace largely motivated his actions. In a letter to the mayor dated 3 July 1592, the lord chamberlain declared that he had accepted the position, "which I have kept in my hands all this while, till matters might grow to reasonable pass of quietness amongst yourselves, which now I hope they are." Although he enjoyed the office and the modicum of local prestige that it brought, he nevertheless regretted the alienation of his fellow peer. Hunsdon wrote to the corporation requesting that they allow him to yield the office to Shrewsbury, who "has an honorable disposition towards you and the good estate of your corporation and whose ancestors have of long time held that place of office amongst you."[77] Hunsdon saw his primary task as that of restoring peace to the town that had honored him with the high stewardship. Once he accomplished that goal and the corporation no longer needed his immediate assistance, he magnanimously wished to give up his place to the new earl of Shrewsbury.[78]

The story did not end there, however. The corporation, while not pleased, accepted the lord chamberlain's request.[79] Surprisingly, the resistance came from the earl of Shrewsbury. By the autumn of 1592, he apparently refused to take up the position offered him by Hunsdon. Although couched in terms of doubting the legality of having both a recorder and a high steward in the corporation simultaneously, the earl's real reasons had more personal roots. It would have reflected poorly on his honor to come back to the town that slighted him, at the behest of the peer who had replaced him.[80] In what appears rather as a fit of pique, Shrewsbury sent back Lord Hunsdon's patent of office to him, renouncing the close relationship that his ancestors had previously maintained with the town. Hunsdon took back the patent and wrote to the corporation that "I am your steward still and do mean, God willing, so to continue." He agreed not to press the high steward's right to appoint the recorder, "for I would be loath you should do anything to your prejudice or hindrance to your charter and liberties which for my part I will maintain to the uttermost, and so I doubt not my lord of Shrewsbury would have done if he had kept it." Hunsdon concluded with this thought. "One thing I would heartily wish amongst you which is, to agree together, not for any small matter to contend one against the other, for that will decay all your wealths—

nothing so sure. And if you hold this rule you will all prosper the better and your town will flourish to all your comforts and commodities."[81] Peace equaled prosperity.

The evidence from Doncaster shows the complex web of relations that existed between corporate boroughs and their patrons. The earls of Shrewsbury, claiming privileges beyond what the corporation considered acceptable, damaged their reliability as friends to the town. Townsmen felt fully justified in looking elsewhere for aid. Lord Hunsdon provided the perfect alternative. He had both local and central connections, and he dealt impartially with the corporation, working to settle divisions without claiming extra privileges for himself. If Shrewsbury represented the old style of patron, looking back to ideas of medieval lordship, Lord Hunsdon represented a newer style of patron, directly linked to the crown and more concerned about general order in the realm than about personal interests in the locality. The flexibility of patronage as a tool for resolving conflict comes through clearly in this episode: if one strategy, or one patron, did not work, try another. Doncaster's experience also shows that civic conflict did not simply have a local impact, but might resonate at many levels, from county magnates to the Privy Council. Corporate interests did not stop with the boundaries of the town, so involvement with those men who could mediate those interests at multiple levels were invaluable to a corporation's peace and prosperity.

Doncaster's fraught relationship with the earls of Shrewsbury also gives vivid testimony to the fact that patronage relations were not without risk to borough corporations. Corporators dealt warily with the men who provided them with needed influence and access, but who also had the ability to use that influence in problematic ways. A fine line divided welcome intervention from unwelcome interference. The personality of a patron certainly had something to do with whether that line was crossed. If a patron had a personal stake in the outcome of civic discord, that, too, could affect the balance. Many great men stood as patrons to countless individual clients as well as corporate clients. When individual clients became the source of corporate discord, the circumstances were ripe for wrangling. The multiplicity of levels at which urban patrons functioned could itself make mediation of local problems more difficult.

The corporators of Reading found this out the hard way in 1623. After months of building tensions, the corporation of Reading came to (figurative) blows with their understeward. Edward Clerke, they claimed, charged exorbitant and unprecedented fees for his services in office. Clerke, on the contrary, asserted that townsmen detained his "ancient fees," and he demanded a higher salary to remunerate him fairly. Fed up, the corporators voted to remove Clerke and to replace him with Mr. John Saunders, counsel for the town and onetime burgess for Parliament.[82] The corporation, by its charter, had the right to remove officers for misbehavior, but Clerke proclaimed his innocence and defended himself with the aid of a powerful advocate. Viscount Wallingford,[83] the town's high steward and patron, was also the patron of Edward Clerke. The corporation had chosen Clerke as their understeward in 1605 at the explicit request of Wallingford (then Lord Knollys).[84] Wallingford thus had a commitment to both his corporate client, Reading, and his individual client, Edward Clerke. In this case, the individual won. Wallingford became an active player on Clerke's behalf. He came to believe that the townsmen not only intentionally slighted their understeward, but their high steward as well.

Throughout the spring of 1623, the dispute gathered steam. In the course of a few weeks, Wallingford wrote three letters to the corporation concerning the matter. At least one of these pressed the aldermen to restore Mr. Clerke. The townsmen proclaimed their wish to satisfy their good lord, but declared it "not in their power to do" as he wanted.[85] Wallingford remained unsatisfied. In an unusual move, he brought this bit of local business directly to the attention the Privy Council, of which he was a member. In mid-March, the board issued a close warrant for the mayor and three fellows to appear in London for their "undue carriage of some business and of your contemptuous behavior towards our very good lord the Lord Viscount Wallingford, High Steward of your town."[86] Wallingford's interest in the suit transformed it from a local squabble over legal fees into a drama concerning the preservation of hierarchy and the boundaries of obedience to a noble patron.

Wallingford tenaciously pursued the business both in London and in Reading. He engaged the Privy Council to peruse the town's charter and resolve the legal question of the understeward's fees. The board hoped to squelch the "factious disposition" of the townsmen.[87] They chastised the corporators especially for disrespect to Lord Wallingford, threatening to take further action against them "if they do not carry themselves with the respect to his lordship which the quality of his person and place doth require and the good offices he hath done to the said town have well deserved."[88] On the local level, the viscount used his physical presence to influence the townsmen's decisions. On 3 May he came to Reading and sat with the town council, called the Company, "desiring to compose the differences betwixt the Company and Mr. Clerke concerning his putting out of his stewardship." No resolution emerged. The clerk recorded somewhat cryptically that "some affirmed that they conceived he was justly put out and some made answer 'if,' etc. and some said they were absent at the time, etc." But on 7 May, in Wallingford's absence, the corporation voted once again, this time reaffirming their original expulsion of Mr. Clerke.[89] This last step resulted in disaster for several key members of Reading's corporation. Not only was the civic body in a disordered state, but the high steward and the entire Privy Council had adamantly turned against them. The lords called the mayor and his three fellows to London once again, where the townsmen's justifications were found "unjust," "frivolous," and "against all order, law and justice." Mayor Anthony Knight and his compatriots ended up in Marshalsea at the board's pleasure.[90] Because of Wallingford's partisanship of Clerke over the corporation, a difference that started in the Reading Town Hall led ultimately to a London prison.

While this episode caused serious distress to the borough, it was an anomaly rather than the norm for relations between Wallingford and Reading. The four prisoners eventually obtained release when they apologized for their "misbehaviour . . . to the Board and miscarriage toward Viscount Wallingford and unadvisedness in the manner of their proceeding with Mr. Clerke." Their behavior was not universally accepted at home, either. One-third of the corporators polled refused to agree that the four be reimbursed from the civic treasury for their troubles.[91] Not everyone supported wrangling with the high steward. Afterward, the corporation continued to choose his nephews for Parliament, give him gifts when he came to town, and depend on his assistance for their business. They were loath to lose him when he wished to resign as high steward in 1630. But as this series of events shows, even a close and generally effective patronage relationship could go awry at times of stress. Patrons had some expectation that their word would be obeyed; they naturally assumed the superior position to a town, based both on the hierarchical notions of society and on the rules of patronage. When the townsmen refused to rest with the settlement Wallingford made for them, he saw it as a great affront to his dignity as a peer and his position as high steward of the borough. The fact that the dispute in question involved a client of his made it doubly troublesome. The supposed disrespect to Mr. Clerke reflected back as a disrespect to Wallingford himself. A patron's authority and connections were what made him useful to a corporation, but these were also the qualities that had the potential to cause civic leaders serious problems. Peace might ultimately prevail, though not necessarily on the corporation's terms.

V

Connection to the powerful could have its dangers. No corporation had complete assurance that a patron would always act in civic interests. Yet such connections could be the saving grace of a corporation in need. Townsmen made a calculated gamble by cultivating ties with powerful peers, but the potential advantages outweighed the risks. The sorts of aid and protection a patron could provide were not available to corporators in any other way. Their position—situated between center and locality—allowed them to function both as civic member and representative of crown authority. A town in turmoil, threatened with Privy Council regulation, could use a patron to solve its internal dilemmas and to fend off formal sanctions from the crown. The fact that many high stewards were privy councilors is certainly not accidental. It served local needs to have such powerful men advocating for the community, and it served royal needs by helping to maintain peace in the commonwealth.

Cambridge corporators more than once avoided the full brunt of Privy Council investigation by appealing immediately to their high steward to provide guidelines for the restoration of order. Lord Keeper Coventry, named high steward in 1626, received such an appeal in 1629, when the corporation asked him to devise orders "for the better government and quiet of the town." A controversy over the proper form for mayoral elections and mayoral qualifications exercised the town council. The lord keeper, responsible to both the larger commonwealth and the local community, laid out rules for maintaining order in the town government by following a strict *cursus honorum* in mayoral elections. The mayor, along with representatives from the aldermen and the lower body of the town council, the Four-and-Twenty, signed the orders and accepted them as bylaws of the corporation.[92]

This settled the immediate problem but failed to root out dissension completely. By July 1632, local elections again came under dispute, and Lord Coventry chastised the corporation, insisting that they follow the orders he wrote for them in 1629.[93] In the summer of 1633, he found it necessary to write them once again, after a disputed election and "riot" over the government of the House of Correction. He urged them to follow his 1629 orders and warned that "these refractory courses are very much to be misliked . . . and fitter for severe punishment than any further admonition or advice." But as an officer and friend of the town, he agreed to show lenience: "out of my good wishes to your Town & the peaceable government thereof & the deserving members of the same, I have thought fit again to advise you to desist from cherishing these and all other disturbances stirred up within yourselves." Coventry desired reform, not punishment, and he used his special relationship to the town to try to achieve this. He would not tolerate further disorder, however. He expected their compliance, "otherwise I shall much repent my pains herein as in other things."[94] Not wishing to lose the favor of a powerful patron like Coventry, and threatened with further Privy Council intervention into the running of the town government, the leaders of Cambridge composed their differences using Coventry's orders as a guide. Although the depth of this composition is not clear, the corporators at least had no need to invite Coventry's further regulation.

Cambridge's story makes clear that corporations in early modern England could benefit from the attentions of powerful peers and governed with the help of seemingly extramural forces. The divisions between "insiders" and "outsiders" cannot be clearly drawn, for men like Coventry could exist simultaneously as both. Although a privy councilor, he was also a member of the corporation of Cambridge, and as such he was pledged to protect the interests of the locality. In his favor and good wishes toward the town of Cambridge, he preserved the corporation from condign punishment and further regulation by the full council. The townsmen accepted his regulations as orders of the corporation itself. Indeed, the corporators invited Coventry's action; the rules were not forced upon unwilling townsmen by the magisterial weight of the crown. Rather, Lord Coventry used his dual status as local governor and officer of state to bring order to a troubled borough.

Cambridge had the good fortune to solve its problems without formal Privy Council intervention. The townsmen called upon their informal, personal relations with Lord Coventry to stitch a serious tear in the corporate fabric. But for other towns, the magnitude of the issues involved—like serious religious or political disruption—almost automatically invited Privy Council regulation. The likelihood of board scrutiny of the matters increased during the 1630's, as King Charles stepped up his calls for order in the realm. In these cases, townsmen found it doubly important to have a strong advocate in their corner. If a patron could not completely stave off Privy Council investigation of a corporation, he might still be able to influence the council to be sympathetic to a town's plight and lenient in any punishments ordered.

The town of Great Yarmouth, riven by faction and faced with formal Privy Council regulation, succeeded in moderating its effects by acquiring a sympathetic patron who was also on the board. By 1629, two factions had developed within the corporation, roughly dividing along religious lines. One tended toward puritanism while the other favored the anti-Calvinist views of bishop of Norwich Samuel Harsnett, recently translated to the see of York, and of William Laud, then bishop of London. This second group, although numerically smaller, had strong connections at Court. The faction's leader, Alderman Benjamin Cooper, managed to prevail upon Attorney General Heath, among others, to help him achieve a change in the borough constitution that would assist him and his anti-puritan friends. He secretly moved to obtain a new charter, one calling for a single mayor, rather than the traditional two bailiffs; that sole mayor (not surprisingly) was to be Alderman Cooper himself. The new charter would also have halved the number of aldermen and common councilmen, naming Cooper's supporters to those positions. The rest of the corporation, led by Alderman William Buttolphe, abhorred this change and strongly desired to retain the old constitution.[95] Knowing they were in for a difficult ride, the corporation agreed to fill the then-vacant office of high steward with someone who could protect them effectively. In November 1629, they chose Edward Sackville, earl of Dorset—privy councilor, chamberlain of the queen's household, and proven friend to the town—for the job.[96]

Cooper's scheme to alter the charter came to a head in 1630. Alderman Buttolphe, leader of the group wishing to preserve the old charter, managed to halt the plot by postponing the passage of the new charter through Chancery. He petitioned the earl of Dorset, the lord keeper, and the king, who referred the matter to Dorset and four other members of the Privy Council.[97] Dorset wrote to the corporation that autumn, informing them of Cooper's machinations in London: "I am now by your last certificate confirmed in my former opinion that you never desired any innovation or change of government. I thought it my part to know your desires, that so I might truly inform his Majesty (as I shall not fail to do) and that you may therefore continue the possession of your ancient rights and privileges." He asked Buttolphe and his group to "arm me in your just defense" by sending him information with which to argue against the changes.[98] Because the pro-alteration faction had friends at Court, the "conservative" group vitally needed the solid support of Dorset to defend the customary liberties of Great Yarmouth.[99]

While Dorset took a firm stand in defense of the traditional constitution of the town, his chief goals remained the restoring of peace in the borough and assuring the town's religious regularity. He did not condone puritan excesses, but rather demanded the townsmen's conformity. When informed of religious irregularities in the town, he admonished the corporation. "I should want in my care for you if I should not let you know that his Majesty is not only informed but incensed against you for conniving at and tolerating a company of Brownists amongst you. I pray you, remember there was no seam in our Saviour's garment; root out that pestiferous sect forth your town; they are as dangerous to the soul as the plague to the body."[100] He also refused to allow the two parties continually to try to throw members of the opposing faction off the corporation, calling for peace and harmony instead.

> It is said that factions reigns [*sic*] amongst you, the which division much damnifies the peace and quiet under which all societies best subsist and prosper. I am not apt to credit rumor, yet persons of eminent quality have possessed me, as I cannot but believe there is some ground of it. Let me prevail so far with you, as to entreat you all to incline your wills and endeavors to make up such differences as rent asunder that unity which ought to dwell amongst you.[101]

He advised them of the dangers of division:

> How much concord advanceth both private families and politique bodies I shall not need to represent unto you, only I must with grief call to mind how miserably your Town is distracted within itself and what way that opens unto the daily attempts of such as truly wish not the prosperity of it. His Majesty (whose care embraceth the whole and every part of his kingdom) heartily wisheth a better correspondence amongst you.[102]

Dorset wanted composition, not division.

Despite his disappointment with the behavior of the battling corporators, Dorset did protect the town from the full brunt of Privy Council punishment when the matter came up before the board. The corporation ran afoul of the Privy Council by ejecting alderman Cooper—"the main incendiary (as we upon more than probable grounds suppose) in all our molestations and combustions"—from their fellowship. Cooper in turn appealed to the Privy Council, which responded with a peremptory letter to restore him. Although the "misdemeanor" deserved a "severe proceeding against" those who had engineered the dismissal, the board rested "content to forebear the same," presumably because Dorset was handling the matter personally.[103] Rather than solving the problem by cutting out unwanted parts of the body, as the rival factions had tried to do to each other, Dorset and the rest of the board believed that order could only be achieved by bringing the two groups together again within the corporation.

The difference finally ended in peace in July 1631, when Alderman William Buttolphe, "out of his voluntary and free motion (that the command of the Lords might be complied with, and the charters preserved from violation) desired this house, that he might be suspended, and sequestered from his place of Alderman, that so a way might be made for the readmission of Mr. Cooper. Which motion upon some consideration was well-liked and accepted of by this House."[104] Buttolphe did not give up in defeat. Rather, he provided a creative solution to a thorny problem. The corporation obeyed the king's commands, as required, but did not lose the service of their fellow, Buttolphe. For although he was suspended from his aldermanic place, Buttolphe retained his seat in church and his precedence in all things except the Assembly. He continued to serve the corporation as their agent in London and in other business. The Assembly officially restored Cooper, but with the statement that they had put him out validly in the first place.[105] Buttolphe eventually returned to the corporation in April 1633, when the next seat on the aldermanic bench opened. According to the official record of Buttolphe's restoration on 12 April, not only Buttolphe but another alderman, Mr. Edward Owner, had volunteered to give up his aldermanic seat in order to preserve the charter and obey the lords in 1631.[106] The factions in the corporation, as well as the Privy Council as a whole and the earl of Dorset individually, very much wanted the return of order and unity to Great Yarmouth, and they were willing to go to some lengths to achieve it. Almost certainly, the members' divergent views did not disappear with this resolution, but the fact that they agreed to present a unified public appearance speaks volumes about their ideals of order. The earl of Dorset, high steward of the town, deserves credit for helping to achieve this peace, working as he did both in the locality and at Court to bring the two groups together into a unified whole rather than to remove one or the other from the corporation. Great Yarmouth maintained corporate integrity explicitly because the corporators looked beyond town walls for the resolution of this dispute.[107] Their relationship with the earl of Dorset made the corporation not dependent, but stronger.

Problems like those that arose in Yarmouth played themselves out not only in the town but at the center as well, once again reinforcing the connections between various levels of royal government. The corporation honored the earl of Dorset with the high stewardship at a point when they needed a protector at Court and a defender of local peace. The townsmen chose a peer already on the Privy Council who had shown favor to the town in the past and made him a member of their society. For his part, Dorset both upheld the rights of the corporation at the center and mediated peace in the locality, preserving corporate integrity there, as well. Great Yarmouth's difficulties reflected both local and national concerns, and their solution to reestablish order combined local and central actions carried out by a member of the corporation, the earl of Dorset, who was also a great officer of state.

Patrons like the earl of Dorset filled the role of arbitrator in urban disputes perfectly. They were men of high social status, imbued with all the personal authority that went along with it in early modern society. They also had the authority of the central government behind them. This was particularly important in the case of Great Yarmouth, which needed protection and assistance at Court as much as at home in Norfolk. But despite their lofty status, patrons were also considered as members of the community, fully entitled to participate in the life of the town and expected to watch out for its interests. When disruptions of the civic peace occurred, patrons were expected to step in and help to resolve them. Having connections to both the center and the locality, they had the weight of authority and the knowledge of local affairs to accomplish mediation. Their position in the commonwealth at large also dictated that they work to preserve peace and good government, both of which were threatened by civic unrest. At moments of breakdown, urban patrons were invaluable in reestablishing the order that held early modern English society together.

The ways that corporations interacted with their patrons during times of civic stress reflect many of the assumptions that underlay urban patronage. Shared notions of the consensual nature of social and political relations are apparent, as both civic leaders and their elite patrons wished to preserve order in the community. For the most part, patrons reinforced corporate authority, predicating concord on the firm emplacement of hierarchical structures in the borough. Such close contact with powerful men was not without its dangers, but townsmen regularly invited it anyway. They viewed this not as an interference from above, but as a local solution to a local problem. In many cases patrons held civic office—as high stewards, recorders, aldermen, or at least freemen—and thus could be considered by the inhabitants of the borough as members. This was an important point for the leaders of corporations, who vigorously protected their jurisdiction and privileges. Corporations desired to exert control within their boundaries, making the idea of central regulation, as from the Privy Council, very unappealing. But the boundary between intramural and extramural had no clear definition. Layers of governance interpenetrated each other, from the heart of the borough out to the surrounding county and beyond to London. Townsmen relied on informal, personal connections to patrons for settling matters of internal dispute as well as obtaining services in the locality and influence at the center. Both the landed elite and the governors of boroughs had an interest in maintaining proper order in the commonwealth, at large and locally. Both townsmen and their patrons would surely agree with the diarist of Chester in his concluding comment upon the successful restoration of peace in that city in 1619: "God grant that peace and love may long continue and flourish within this city amongst all sorts of true-hearted citizens."[108]

FOUR

Corporations and Competing Authorities

*Solving the Problem of
Overlapping Jurisdictions*

The desire for order permeated early modern ideas of government. A corporation's internal stability helped solidify the government of the realm as a whole. But urban leaders' obsession with order did not stop at borough boundaries. As one type of jurisdiction among many, corporations had to deal with a whole host of other authorities, all of which together formed the English state. The "patchwork quilt" quality of early modern government made misunderstanding and contention particularly likely. Nevertheless, historians generally agree that the Tudor and Stuart periods saw an increasingly organized and centralizing state.[1] How early modern government achieved this is a critical question for historians. Institutions of central government—law courts, the royal Court, the lieutenancy system, the shrievalty—strengthened royal rule. The real success of orderly government, however, lay not so much in the institutions themselves as the people who ran them. Integration and communication between different authorities occurred because the same men had a hand in them all. Persons, not institutions, held the early modern state together. The men who could make the jumbled bits of the English state function more effectively were of great value to the crown. They were also of great value to the leaders of provincial communities who put their services to work.

Corporations found themselves surrounded by many different authorities and liberties. Urban government fell within the geographical parameters of county government, even if corporate charters forbade ingress by county JPs. Towns existed within diocesan boundaries, and those cities that had cathedrals had daily concourse with a "foreign" jurisdiction within their midst. Corporations also dealt with a variety of what might be called regional administrative districts, many of them medieval holdovers. Although organs of the central government, liberties such as the Cinque Ports, the duchy of Lancaster, and the palatinate of Chester nevertheless maintained broad and somewhat eccentric powers. Added to these were the regional administrations established by the Tudors, like the Councils of the North and of the Marches of Wales. All levels of government—including corporations—formed parts of the early modern state, ultimately responsible to the crown.[2] This amalgam of authorities lacked consistency or uniformity.[3] Corporate boroughs had to develop ways to protect their interests within this confusion, preventing undue incursions while encouraging cooperation when profitable. Personal connections to powerful individuals often helped corporations achieve this delicate balancing act.

Even for seventeenth-century administrators, sorting out the multitude of jurisdictions that made up the state proved no easy task.[4] Boundaries, both literal and figurative, lacked distinction. Even though corporations had charters defining their rights and liberties, townsmen nevertheless found their privileges questioned and limited. Urban magistrates could and did bring such disputes to court, making sophisticated use of the legal system to protect themselves. But they also regularly sought other means of resolution, through arbitration or mediation outside the courts. Regardless of whether corporations went to the courts or avoided them, they relied on the personal interest of powerful men to bring them good results. Patrons could provide mediation out of court, or could speak on a town's behalf in London if a dispute did go to law. The social prominence of patrons made them able to enforce decisions on both parties. Their role transcended that of mere enforcers, as they also helped towns to cooperate with other authorities when it was useful to do so. In many cases, a leading figure of one of the other jurisdictions—a bishop, a chancellor or president of a prerogative council, or a county gentleman—could himself stand as a patron to a town. The flexibility of personal connections allowed for mediation of conflicts that arose as well as for constructive interaction between elements in the state.

Patronage provided no panacea. Deep conflict could and did arise between corporations and other authorities. But to see corporate government as always and inevitably in opposition to other elements creates an overly polarized view. Some historians have emphasized the constriction of urban authority as the Tudors and Stuarts expanded the responsibilities of county government and prerogative jurisdictions. Peter Clark has suggested that towns became "vulnerable to outside influence" when the "Crown engaged in an almost continuous campaign of interference in urban affairs" from the 1570's onward.[5] Conflict doubtless flourished. These troubles seem to have become even more severe in the 1630's, when the force of royal policy added new urgency to old disagreements. Corporations, however, formed part of royal government, just as did county benches and prerogative courts. Borough governors purposely marshaled the forces that could be interpreted as "outside influences" as a means to secure their own prosperity. Early modern government required a degree of integration, and patronage provided a matrix in which this could occur.

I

The problem of multiple jurisdictions within a single area affected most early modern towns. A multitude of units for regional administration—some holdovers from a much earlier period and some established or strengthened by the Tudors—overlay and sometimes vied for precedence with urban corporations. Officials in these regional administrative bodies towered above urban leaders in both social status and authority. Yet these men did not simply enforce their prerogative powers against those of corporations. Instead, they regularly provided patronage to them. The interests of the various layers of English government were far from identical, but neither were they necessarily oppositional. Patronage provided a way for these potentially competitive authorities to interact and even cooperate constructively. Corporations used patrons to protect their interests as well as to knit themselves more tightly into the fabric of the state.

Jurisdictional confusion stemmed in large part from the inconsistent way in which the English state, at all levels, emerged. The state as it existed in the late sixteenth century had coalesced under a dynasty of strong monarchs from a patchwork of pre-Conquest administrative units, feudal holdings, near-independent regions, and royal enclaves. While the crown presided over them all, many of them had institutional histories that long predated the Tudors. When these disparate authorities came under closer central direction in the sixteenth century, new methods of interaction had to be devised. This proved especially true as the crown introduced new forms of local and regional administration designed to bring all the areas within the boundaries of England and Wales under tighter central control. The change included the rapid proliferation of grants of formal royal incorporation to towns during the sixteenth and seventeenth centuries, giving boroughs specific rights of self-government and altering their relations with older regional units.[6] Dover had its own corporate charter, yet remained within the administrative unit of the Cinque Ports; Shrewsbury and Ludlow both answered to the Council of the Marches of Wales, the towns of the north to the Council of the North; Liverpool, Newcastle-under-Lyme, and Leicester, among others, still owed service to the duchy of Lancaster; and the great city of Chester could not ignore the authority of the Palatine Court of Chester.[7] Despite any possible "Tudor revolution in government," no fully rationalized organization of this hodge-podge administration really existed. Local leaders frequently had to work these problems out among themselves. Sorting out how these different layers would work together formed an important part of the transition in the English state in the sixteenth and seventeenth centuries. Patronage aided this process.

Some towns formed close connections with regional authorities. This held especially true for the Cinque Port towns that fell under the purview of the lord warden. The Cinque Ports actually consisted of seven main towns plus various smaller "limbs" that had for centuries held a special status in England. The ports initially received their privileges because of their strategic position as the first line of defense against invasion from the Continent. The lord warden originally served as a military leader who organized coastal defenses and had almost total control in this district. The Cinque Port towns supported a heavy charge of ships and men for national defense, but in return received many special privileges, such as freedom from general taxation and rates levied on the rest of the country. The lord warden wielded great power, and the enclave that he controlled developed separate courts and separate lines of authority from the rest of England.[8]

While the institution persisted, the relationship between the Cinque Ports and the state, as well as the powers of the lord warden, changed dramatically in the early modern period. The local leaders of ports like Dover had strengthened their positions vis-à-vis the wardenship by gaining charters of incorporation from the crown. This did not separate the city from Cinque Ports jurisdiction, but it did formalize Dover's status as a corporation in its own right.[9] The status of the lord warden also changed. No longer a military command per se, the wardenship became a prime office of royal patronage, which the monarch presented to highly favored courtiers. The earl of Northampton served as lord warden under King James, and the duke of Buckingham held the post under Charles.[10] Practically a sinecure, the wardenship involved few real duties but it encompassed a large network of lesser offices that could be distributed to the warden's own relatives and clients. Everyone from the lieutenant of Dover Castle—the lord warden's second-in-command—to the lowly toll-gatherers and water-bailiffs fell within the warden's patronage network. It was these lower officers that the jurats of the various ports had to deal with every day. Civic officials spent much of their time attempting to guard their corporate privileges against incursion by the many minions of the lord warden, while still enjoying the favor of the warden and his highest deputies.[11]

Although it might seem like a confusion of interests, townsmen appealed to the lord warden when they wanted redress for wrongs done by the warden's subordinates. He appointed the officers who impinged on the privileges of the corporators of the ports, but he also stood as the main protector of corporate privileges. For instance, in 1635, the jurats of Dover sent their town clerk to London to petition the lord warden, the earl of Suffolk, concerning a number of "particular grievances" against the water-bailiff and the lieutenant of Dover Castle—both appointees of the lord warden—as well as several admiralty officers who had allegedly infringed the city's chartered rights.[12] The lord warden had both manifest duties as the keeper of courts, sheriff, and lord lieutenant in the ports and "latent" responsibilities as a patron to those under his authority.[13] His role as patron also had dual aspects. He looked after the towns' interests and mediated between townsmen and the crown; but he simultaneously acted as a patron in the narrower sense, as one who provides offices for clients within his patronage network.[14] These two sets of interests did at times clash in the Cinque Ports jurisdiction, but the process usually maintained a sense of equilibrium.

One strategy for cooperation combined the lord warden's multiple types of patronage. Some townsmen of the Cinque Ports themselves became part of the lord warden's patronage network. Linda Levy Peck has shown that the earl of Northampton, lord warden from 1604 to 1614, appointed townsmen to various posts within the Cinque Ports jurisdiction. In general, this earl made no consistent effort to place courtiers in local offices, but rather chose county gentry and members of the oligarchies of the ports. "The dynamic relationship established by the dispensation of court patronage to local governors is best illustrated in two cases where Northampton took into his household young scions of the Cinque Ports oligarchs and later appointed them into positions in the region." William Byng, younger brother of George Byng, a mayor of Dover, entered Northampton's service in 1602 and received the governorship of Deal Castle in

1608. Thomas Godfrey of Lydd, son of one of the jurats of Lydd, attended the earl of Northampton as a gentleman in ordinary for several years, then married and left the earl's household to return to the Cinque Ports. He settled in Winchelsea, where he was made a jurat immediately, providing an important conduit to the lord warden. He sat as parliamentary burgess for Winchelsea in 1614.[15]

Northampton's successor in the post, Edward Lord Zouche, likewise employed local men in his business. William Ward, who served as mayor of Dover in 1618–19, acted as personal agent for Zouche in the ports during the late 1610's, forwarding intelligence reports and taking care of the lord warden's business in the locality, especially his ship the *Silver Falcon*.[16] In October 1619, Zouche authorized Ward "to use and exercise the place of Lieutenancy of Dover Castle and to do all things belonging thereunto as freely and fully as if you had a deputation thereof at large, wherein I desire you to have a care of my honor and his Majesty's service." Ward carried out the lieutenancy for about five months, after which Zouche gave a permanent appointment to Sir Henry Mainwaring. This honor ended badly for Ward, whom the lord warden accused of juggling the books. Zouche's last official communication to Ward was a scolding note ordering him to provide "a more honest account than you have yet given me, which if you will not perform, I will trouble you if you live, and yours when you are gone, for I will not be cozened by all your running."[17] Appointments like Ward's were rare, and they could be risky. But they provided a way for individual corporations to interact with the Cinque Ports as a regional administrative unit. The lord warden, using both his manifest powers of office and his informal authority as patron, served as the medium for this connection.

The Cinque Ports were unusual for their coherent structure and the strength of the larger entity relative to the individual towns within it. Other corporations worked out relationships with more diffuse regional authorities over the course of the late sixteenth and early seventeenth centuries, as many boroughs tried to increase their jurisdiction through corporate self-government. In Chester, relations between the Palatine courts and the corporation remained uneasy, as the Palatine Exchequer claimed rights within what the corporation considered its private jurisdiction.[18] Palatine institutions had survived the reforms of the 1530's and 1540's, coming under royal control (as the duchy of Lancaster and duchy of Cornwall had). The courts of Great Sessions and Exchequer still had authority in the county.[19] Conflicts, sometimes bitter, arose between the corporation and the Palatine Exchequer, but at the same time, the city often looked to the chancellor of this court for patronage.[20] The process of defining the relationship between authorities continued throughout the sixteenth and seventeenth centuries.

Although wishing to preserve its rights, the corporation of Chester also had an interest in protecting the regional court, both for its convenience as a venue (as opposed to the central courts in London) and for its economic benefits. It brought business to the city and provided posts for the sons of local leaders. Both Sir Thomas Egerton, later lord chancellor, and Sir Peter Warburton, a justice of Common Pleas, got their starts in the Palatine court. These connections served the city well in later years, as Sir Peter especially became an important patron of the city.[21] Chester was not unique in wishing to retain connections to regional prerogative courts. Those cities that fell under the jurisdiction of the Council of the Marches of Wales saw the benefits. Worcester's citizens used the council's courts and sought personal favors from the lord president.[22] The civic leaders of Ludlow, where the Council of the Marches usually sat, well understood the economic and other advantages of the council. When the lord president held court elsewhere, as at Bewdley, the bailiffs of Ludlow would travel to the lord president to put him in mind of their town.[23] As Alan Dyer has said of Worcester, "Far from objecting to the jurisdiction of the Council, the city found itself with a powerful and comprehensive arbiter in local disputes at a much more convenient distance than the capital, despite the complications presented by the presence of powerful local political figures among the Council's members."[24]

The corporators of York likewise valued the Council of the North, which met in the city, and they regularly relied on the patronage of the lord presidents.[25] According to David Palliser, the third earl of Huntingdon, lord president, "took a keen interest in York's prosperity" during Elizabeth's reign, and this close connection would continue between the city and some of the early Stuart lord presidents.[26] The two authorities also had periods of quite intense disagreement, as in 1613 when the city claimed that the council's courts exceeded their jurisdiction and infringed on the corporation's rights. Lord Sheffield, the lord president, apparently spearheaded the attempt to expand the council's powers at the expense of the city. For redress, the corporation appealed to their high steward, the earl of Northampton, who, they hoped, would restore civic privileges and make the lord president see reason.[27] Despite periods of discord, the citizens appreciated the advantages that the council brought them, and they warmly welcomed the lord presidents when they entered the city. Even for Lord Sheffield, the lord president who caused the city so much grief, the city showed real fondness. When he came into York on 9 August 1615, the corporators agreed to meet Lord Sheffield at the Walmgate bar to welcome him to the city, having been long at London, and in the time since his last coming to the city, he "had all his three sons drowned and a daughter deceased."[28] The citizens of York bitterly regretted the abolition of the council in 1641. The corporation agreed to petition the king and the Parliament to reestablish the council in September 1641 and did so again at the Restoration of Charles II.[29] Townsmen did not consider these jurisdictions as automatically and necessarily invasive of their rights, but saw the benefits they could bring.

Corporations had to deal with a whole host of other jurisdictional authorities, from prerogative courts like the Council of the North to royal enclaves such as forests and honors to military establishments such as existed at Portsmouth and Berwick. Although towns vied for favor and for power with all of these other layers of government, urban leaders seemed to have understood that cooperation ultimately achieved better ends than did conflict. It paid to join forces over common interests. Thus some corporations attempted to mediate potential difficulties by bringing non-townspeople into the corporate fold. The town of Wallingford protected its interests by choosing the steward of the honor and constable of the castle to be the high steward of the town as well. The town fell within the boundaries of this royal honor, and Wallingford Castle was a parcel of the honor. For much of the later sixteenth and early seventeenth centuries, the stewardship of the honor remained in the hands of the Knollys family, who had powerful Court connections as well as local authority.[30] Portsmouth granted freedoms and corporate offices to a wide array of peers and gentlemen who came to the city as part of the military base there. The earl of Sussex, one of the chief naval leaders during the war with Spain, came frequently to the city. To honor him, the corporation made him high steward. Several other gentlemen and peers became freemen of the city during his tenure as well. In 1593, the town awarded the freedom to Sir Charles Blount, the captain of the Town and Isle of Portsmouth (i.e., its military governor) and his son Charles. Blount, newly created Lord Mountjoy, was chosen as high steward in 1594 to replace the deceased earl of Sussex. The corporation gave the new high steward special consideration in a lease from the town, selected his nominees as burgesses to Parliament, and elected him as an alderman of the city.[31] Portsmouth, like many other towns, saw inclusion as a more useful strategy than expulsion.

One of the ways in which this inclusion was accomplished was by giving a relatively small number of men a multiplicity of duties and positions.

The same peer who was a privy councilor also served as a lord lieutenant, a JP, and possibly also an officer of a regional court, like the duchy of Lancaster or the Council of the North, as well as being a high steward or informal patron of a corporation. The sixth earl of Derby, considered the chief patron of the corporation of Chester and an alderman as well, served as lord lieutenant of Cheshire, the chamberlain of the Exchequer of Chester, and justice of the peace and *Custos Rotulorum* for Cheshire. The third earl of Huntingdon served as a privy councilor and lord president of the Council of the North for Queen Elizabeth, while holding the positions of justice and *Custos Rotulorum* of Leicestershire, lord lieutenant of Leicestershire, and steward of the honor of Leicester. At the same time, the corporators of Leicester revered him as their chief patron. Likewise, Sir William Knollys, earl of Banbury, held a multiplicity of offices both at Court and in the towns and counties of his home region in the Cotswolds.[32] In the absence of a professional bureaucracy, patronage, or more accurately patrons, played a key role in mediating between and integrating the patchwork of jurisdictions that made up the early modern state in England.

The city of Chester provides insight into the value of multiple office-holding and patronage. Cestrians relied on the earls of Derby as key patrons. At the same time, the earls usually served as chamberlains of the Palatine Exchequer, the corporation's main rival for jurisdiction in the area. Given the squabbles between the two authorities, this might seem like a conflict of interest. But in fact, all concerned found this a workable arrangement. Chester's corporators apparently believed that the best way to protect themselves against incursions by Palatine officials was to have the highest officer of the County Palatine as a good friend of the city. Thus the corporation consistently gave gifts and hospitality to the chamberlain and his officers as a sign of goodwill. The earls of Derby accepted this treatment as just another mark of the city's attachment to the Stanley family. But the earl of Leicester, who served as chamberlain of Chester from 1565 to 1588, was also courted as a patron, although he had no particular local ties beyond his holding the chief Palatine office. His strength lay mostly at Court. Both the local office and the central influence brought with them the power to affect the city of Chester considerably. The corporation wisely understood the value of having such a figure as a good friend and gratifying him as far as possible within the chartered rights of the city.[33]

Other corporations used the strategy of inclusion to deal with extra-corporate authorities. The town of Leicester lay within the jurisdiction of the duchy of Lancaster, to which the corporation owed its fee farm payments and other forms of service. Inhabitants of the city and county could use the duchy courts for certain types of cases, and the duchy itself could bring suits against the town or individuals within it in some circumstances. The auditor of the duchy annually checked the town accounts to ensure that the duchy received its due, and the town leaders in turn took care to satisfy the auditor, always providing food and drink for him at the corporation's charge.[34] More important, the corporation courted the favor of the chancellor of the duchy, who had power over the duchy courts and who also frequently had considerable influence with the crown. While the corporation did not pander to the chancellors, it did follow the rules of patronage in dealing with them. Townsmen routinely gave gifts and hospitality to the chancellors, accepted some requests for privileges in the town, and regularly agreed to select duchy nominees for parliamentary burgesses. The corporators seem to have received a fair return for their troubles, especially from Sir Humphrey May, who was chancellor from 1618 to 1629. May had a special, though roundabout, relationship with the town. His sister had married Sir William Heyrick, native son and faithful friend of Leicester.[35] The townsmen appealed to May for assistance on several occasions in the 1620's. He helped them convince the king to give the corporation the mastership of the Newarke Hospital and then to grant a royal stipend to the minister who performed the ecclesiastical functions at the hospital. May agreed to intercede on the town's behalf with the earl of Huntingdon on a militia matter in 1625. The corporation also called on him in 1628, when all of the town's ministers were called as a group to London to testify in a case concerning puritans in Leicester. Townsmen, concerned for their clergymen, hoped that May would do his best to expedite the matter and to give the Leicester ministers his favor in London.[36] Sir Humphrey had an especially strong link to Leicester's corporation, but the town cultivated the favor of all the duchy's chancellors in the period as another way to link the corporation into the network of interest and influence that moved the government of early modern England.

This strategy reaped benefits for some corporations, staving off problems and preserving stability. Not all were so lucky—some corporations remained overshadowed by other authorities or found themselves too open to the influence of others. Even cities like Chester and York that interacted regularly with officials of other jurisdictions experienced periods of conflict and expended time and money to maintain corporate privileges. It was a delicate balance. Enlisting the aid of potentially rival officials could maintain a sense of order, keep a town connected to important patronage networks, and ultimately protect the jurisdiction of the corporation. Civic governments took action against direct interference in matters that fell to the corporation by royal charter; intervention caused resentment among townsmen. At the same time, isolation was neither possible nor profitable. All elements within the state ultimately answered to the same crown and all swore to maintain the king's peace. Despite the tensions that existed in the relationship, it behooved corporations to link themselves to regional authorities through networks of patronage, as this bound them more closely with the crown.

II

The growing complexity of the English state made lines of connection all the more necessary. A major contributor to the complexity was the Reformation and the concomitant creation of the Church of England as part of royal government. While many of the structures of the old church remained, the power dynamic between ecclesiastical and secular authorities changed dramatically. Medieval bishops had been great landed magnates and their cathedral churches were often the most powerful institutions in their region. For a number of cathedral cities, the bishop was their feudal lord, controlling the manor of the borough. Most of these—like Salisbury and Durham—developed some processes of self-government, but ultimate authority rested with the bishop.[37] The post-Reformation church paled in comparison. This dramatic transition and its aftermath can be seen very clearly in the cathedral cities.[38] Civic governments, once subordinate to episcopal power both legally and economically, now gained legitimacy as royally chartered incorporations. This changing relationship offered new opportunities for both contention and cooperation, giving testimony to the principle that patronage provided an effective means for mediating between competing authorities. Cathedral city corporations and their ecclesiastical counterparts used local interaction as well as appeals to central and regional authority to hammer out the boundaries of their respective jurisdictions.

Occasional conflict between citizens and cathedral denizens dates back to the medieval era. But the events of the sixteenth century exacerbated it, as many cathedral towns received charters of incorporation from Tudor and Stuart monarchs. This meant that two divergent authorities—equally part of royal government—existed in the locality. At the heart of most contention between civic and ecclesiastical powers lay the privilege of the cathedral close. A cathedral and its close might lie entirely within the bounds of a town, yet it was a liberty unto itself, over which civic authorities had no control. Hence, one portion of the city lived according to a different set of rules, with a different set of officers and courts, than did the other.[39] Regulations about markets and fairs, rates, and local responsibilities for fire and cleanliness might differ inside and outside the close. Civic governors saw these special privileges as a threat to their own chartered authority. Not only the clergy who served the cathedral, but also the lay people who lived within the close enjoyed these privileges. Civic leaders suspected that townsmen moved into the close purposely to avoid town rates or to avoid paying for the freedom of the borough in order to trade. Corporate authorities also argued that they could not properly keep the peace. The jurisdiction of civic courts did not penetrate into the cathedral precinct, and borough officers had no power there. While cathedral clergy presumably did not want to harbor criminals, they clung tightly to the privileges of the close as their authority diminished over time in other ways.[40]

Nearly all cathedral cities experienced some tensions between corporate and ecclesiastical jurisdiction. As urban magistrates' power waxed, cathedral personnel guarded their strongholds from encroachment by town authorities. Relations varied widely from city to city. In Hereford, the cathedral clergy obtained a clause in the corporate charter, maintaining the rights of the close.[41] The bishop of Lichfield granted the manor of Lichfield to the bailiffs and burgesses of that town in 1598, at the request of the earl of Essex, who made a special appeal to the queen for the favor. Worcester settled its relations with the cathedral early on in the sixteenth century, in 1516 granting the clergy all the privileges and immunities of regular citizens, "a considerable concession on the city's part."[42] Townsmen tried their luck with new bishops and new deans, hoping to press their own liberties forward, while some clerics pushed cathedral privileges more forcefully than others. No matter how clerical and lay officials worked out these agreements, the process required ongoing negotiation and rarely resulted in permanent peace.

Such negotiations often required assistance from above, and civic patrons were well placed to provide it. The men of Salisbury, for instance, relied heavily on patronage connections to free their city from their bishop's temporal lordship. Borough leaders argued that the ancient arrangement, in which the bishop had final authority in the city, ill-served the king's peace, since civic officers could not prosecute the laws as vigorously as they desired. Town governors quarreled with cathedral authorities from as early as 1225, but relations became particularly strained during the episcopacy of John Coldwell (1591–1596). Citizens accused him of using "sinister practices" to procure a commission to seize the subsidies of the city. Civic leaders finally managed to obtain a royal charter in 1612, when they had a more amenable bishop and the strong backing of friends at Court, particularly the earl of Pembroke.[43] This did not solve all of the potential issues of contention between town and clerics, but it went a long way toward defining rights and privileges.

Even those cities that had been incorporated for many decades still had to deal with the problem of multiple jurisdictions. The city of Exeter, a regional capital and an ancient city, had received royal charters for certain privileges as early as the reign of Henry II and received formal incorporation and status as a county in the reign of Henry VIII.[44] Exeter Cathedral sat at the heart of the city, the boundary of the close lying only yards away from the Town Hall. Despite having had most of the sixteenth century to work out the differences between the city and the cathedral, the two still squabbled regularly in the seventeenth century. The cathedral's dean and the city's mayor each thought the other guilty of deliberate acts of encroachment.[45] In the spring of 1600, the dean and chapter of Exeter lashed out at the city, accusing the corporation of exercising civic authority within the Bishop's Fee, of impaneling residents of the close on city juries, of carrying the city sword upright within the close and the cathedral, and—adding insult to injury—of erecting scaffolding onto buildings adjacent to the chapter college and thus shutting out all light to the prebends. The corporation, not surprisingly, declared itself innocent of all charges.[46] Such debates over authority and jurisdiction continued intermittently throughout the next decade.[47]

Conflict sputtered and flared until it reached white heat in 1615. This time, the corporation called on powerful friends to douse the flames. Corporators claimed that the dean harassed inhabitants of areas under civic control, calling them into his own courts and allowing his bailiff to enter the city proper to threaten citizens and impanel them for jury service in the bishop's leet court. They accused Bishop William Cotton of countenancing the bailiff's illegal actions, saying Cotton had attempted to extend the limits of the Bishop's Fee "in a more earnest and resolute manner" than had any previous bishop. According to the Assembly, the situation had "grown through the malice and instigation" of the bailiff, William Moore, but had been furthered by the dean and bishop. Under such antagonistic circumstances, the corporation had only two options—to take their suit against the cathedral to the law, or to appeal to a higher authority for arbitration. Exeter's civic leaders chose to petition the earl of Suffolk, their high steward, for redress. Although Suffolk's resolution is not recorded, soon thereafter Moore's questionable activities stopped and relations between close and city calmed.[48] Legal battles invariably involved large expense and trouble and did not necessarily end in victory. The alternative of a mediated decision, handed down by an influential man—with, it was hoped, affection for and loyalty to the borough of which he was an officer—seemed preferable. Having a powerful civic patron gave an advantage to towns at odds with their ecclesiastical neighbors.

Cathedral towns witnessed hotly contested battles between mayor and dean, leaders of civic government and church. Typically, these struggles revolved around issues of precedence and jurisdiction rather than theology. The symbolic power of the civic regalia lay at the heart of some of the most divisive disputes. Could the mayor's mace or city sword be borne upright in the cathedral?[49] The mayors of Chester certainly thought so and regularly brought this symbol of civic authority into the sacred environs. Ecclesiastical officials took this as an affront to the church, however. In 1605, a prebend, Mr. Sharpe, actually pulled down the sword while the city serjeant carried it before the mayor in the cathedral. The corporation looked to a higher authority to punish this brazen move. Chester's leaders wrote to the lord keeper, Sir Thomas Egerton, "so that his support might be obtained and further action be taken." They also informed Sir Peter Warburton, a judge in the Palatine administration and a consistent friend of Chester, to obtain his opinion of the matter.[50] These connections to important men reaped high dividends for the corporation. One Cestrian wrote that Lord Keeper Egerton, "a Cheshire man," ordered that the mayor might carry the sword before him anywhere in the cathedral, "without disturbance".[51] Egerton's pronouncement guaranteed the corporation's status throughout the city and the close, and in fact effectively reduced the authority of the cathedral clergy. Patronage paid off.

The lord keeper's pronouncement, so beneficial to the city, did not prevent the cathedral officials from trying to reimpose their authority.[52] The bishop, dean, and chapter continued to interfere in the already divisive internal politics of the corporation. In 1612, at one of the peaks of conflict concerning the Whitby family and its concentration of local power, both the bishop and the dean chose to step into the fray, not to calm it but to condemn the entire government of the city. Their actions took place in the context of a jurisdictional dispute between the cathedral and the corporation, in which the dean accused the corporation of oppressing the church and the poor of the city. He likened the aldermen to "railing Rabsach or destroying wicked Ishmael" who "had his hand against every man . . . like swelling toads railing at God's holy priests and trampling the poor under their feet like slaves and villains."[53] The dean also impugned the city's honor and accused the mayor and aldermen of misgovernment. He intimated that the mayor, Robert Whitby, used the office for his own private gain and attempted to increase his power at the expense of both the church and the poor people of Chester. Analyzing the proper relationship between civic government and ecclesiastical government in metaphorical terms, he said that the Sword (representing the mayor) and the Word (representing the church), "as the two eyes of the City, had been joined together; but if the Sword would not hear and be ruled by the Word, that it should be said of Chester as it would have been said of Greece if Athens had been destroyed, that she would become *Monocula*." He then went on to accuse the mayor of encroaching upon and restraining the liberties of the church, what "moieties and little pittances was left them." He joined this criticism with that of the corporation's love of faction and schism and their oppression of the poor.[54] The questions of good government, good stewardship, and the proper boundaries of civil and ecclesiastical jurisdiction were all bound together.

To resolve this ugly dispute, the corporation called upon their patron. The Assembly asked the earl of Derby, lord lieutenant of Cheshire, chamberlain of the Exchequer of Chester, and alderman of the city, to adjudicate the jurisdictional dispute and clear them of the charges of impropriety and misgovernment. They believed that the aspersions the dean cast upon their honor and good government amounted to slander and defamation.[55] Although townsmen chose the earl as arbiter, one who stood above the fray, nevertheless they clearly presumed that Derby would look favorably upon them. As a member of their governing body, he would want to defend the honor of Chester corporation as well as their magisterial rights in the city. While the corporation remained divided in opinion over the Whitby family and their accumulation of power in Chester, the corporators could unite around the defense of their integrity. A stain on the mayor's reputation sullied them all. The corporation as a body appealed to the earl of Derby in search of vindication.

Mayor Aldersay and 32 of his cohorts wrote to the earl of Derby, asking his favor "for redressing the several wrongs offered and done unto us by Mr. Dean of Chester as others as well by infringing our liberties and wrongfully entering upon our possessions as also for vilifying and condemning the government of the same city in several open sermons." According to the letter, "both the city and the country do take notice and much admire" the accusations against "a late governor of the city," presumably Whitby. Whitby not only served as a member of Chester corporation, but also held a post as an attorney in the Exchequer of Chester, of which the earl of Derby was chamberlain. This made Whitby a servant of the earl, and the corporation emphasized this fact in order to strengthen their position. They hoped that the earl, "as our chief patron on whom we only depend under his majesty," would want to defend the rights and the reputation of his favored city, as well as to guard his own reputation through defending that of his subordinate, Whitby. Asking the earl to call both the dean and Mr. Whitby before him to hear their cases, the corporators expected the earl to clear Whitby of the charges of villainy and oppression and censure the dean for having made the remarks.[56] It clearly fell within the earl of Derby's area of responsibility to restore the proper balance between corporate and ecclesiastical jurisdiction within the city's boundaries. The corporation benefited greatly from having an advocate of the earl's magnitude.

Men like Derby regularly participated in the negotiation of boundaries between secular authority and the church that went on in all cathedral cities. Prior to the 1630's, the crown had no overarching policy to define these relations, leaving corporations and cathedral clergy to sort it out in the locality. Both sides called in figures with national stature to gain victory. Lack of such connections resulted in weakness. For a cathedral city corporation, the absence of powerful connections at Court could lead to serious difficulties if ecclesiastical officials chose to press their privileges. This became especially true as the crown grew more amenable to supporting the ecclesiastical hierarchy vis-à-vis corporations. The city of Exeter experienced this problem firsthand in the early 1620's when the bishop of Exeter lobbied the crown to be made a justice of peace of the corporation. The city fathers opposed this move vigorously, but they found themselves seriously hampered by a lack of patronage at court. The episode shows how both sides tried to line up support in London to achieve their ends. For the corporation, having an episcopal JP crossed the boundary of their authority, and they worked to generate new patronage connections to aid them in their struggle.

In 1622 the corporation of Exeter faced a strong challenge to their jurisdiction in the person of Dr. Valentine Carey, newly consecrated bishop of Exeter.[57] Soon after arriving in his diocese, Bishop Carey began a campaign to have himself placed on the commissions of the city, both for justice of peace and of gaol delivery. Exeter had county status in its own right, and bishops did appear on county commissions throughout England. However, the corporation of Exeter saw the inclusion of a bishop as JP as a dangerous infringement of civic liberties. The practice of placing bishops on civic commissions was not new, but some towns seem to have taken much greater exception to it than others.[58] Corporators argued that the bishop commenced his suit not out of "evidence of utility," or "urgent necessity in regard of any insufficiency of government," but rather simply out of "some spice of contempt and disdain" for the corporation. Civic leaders immediately sent a man of business—William Prowse, brother of the then mayor—to London to plead for the permanent exclusion of the bishop of Exeter from the city's commission of peace.[59]

Prowse fought an uphill battle. At the heart of the problem stood the city's high steward, the earl of Suffolk. Suffolk had lost most of his influence at Court following his family's implication in the Overbury murder and his trial in 1618 for official corruption while lord treasurer. He rarely or never appeared at the Council Board and offered little help to the corporation in combating the forces of the bishop. Nevertheless, he refused to give up his office as high steward, leaving the city in a patronage crisis. The city's solicitor had to find aid wherever he could get it, heading off advances by the bishop and currying favor for the corporation when possible. In a series of letters over the course of the spring and summer of 1622, William Prowse detailed his activities to his brother and the rest of the corporation.

The letters show that Prowse undertook his commission vigorously. With an ear to the ground for information, he roamed Whitehall. The suit, he heard, was "set on foot" by the "earnest solicitation of the Lord Keeper." The lord keeper, Bishop John Williams of Lincoln, had ordered his subordinate, Mr. Benbow, to draw up the bishop of Exeter's commission and ready it to be sealed. Prowse, however, knew Benbow and elicited from him a promise to protract the process as long as possible in order to give the city's attorney time to counterpetition. With this assistance, Prowse began the first moves in his strategy. He enlisted his "cousin" Mr. Hakewill, a court official who clearly sided with the corporation in this cause, to make a close study of all the points of law and relevant precedents. Armed with documents, some inside information, and the aid of friends, Prowse began his long campaign of pleading before various courts and officials to make his case heard.[60]

Although the bishop had powerful supporters, Prowse found several courtiers sympathetic to the city. Lord Mandeville, lord president of the Privy Council, was a "well-affected friend to the city to my [Prowse's] especial knowledge, for the favoring of your suit." Lord Hobart, chief justice of Common Pleas, also supported the city's case on legal grounds. He feared the legal consequences of the change, "for that the precedent will not only be dangerous but it will occasion much heart-burnings and contention." Hobart "entreated a friend to entreat the Lord Keeper" to forebear sealing the new commission. Lord Keeper Williams felt no sympathy, however, vowing "with might and main, all his power to obtain" the bishop of Exeter's suit. Prowse reported that Williams responded to Hobart's legal finding with, "if the King may not do it by law, yet his Majesty's will is to have it, and therefore it shall be done."[61] Bishop Carey apparently made a convincing case to Williams that his inclusion in the city's commission would assist in the better governance of the inhabitants, punishment of malefactors, and relief of the poor of the city. The lord keeper directed the clerk of the crown once again to draw up the commission.

Matters looked dismal for Exeter corporation. But Prowse battled back, petitioning the lord president and the king. Prowse bemoaned the city's lack of a high steward during this crisis and strongly encouraged the corporation to choose an assistant high steward, "that may in time of need stand by you and back you."[62] The city had special need of strong friends, as Prowse discovered that not just the lord keeper, but King James himself favored the bishop's suit. James had apparently been told of the corporators' penchant for puritanism. It was the king's explicit pleasure that Bishop Carey be a JP of the city, "he being a worthy prelate" and the city being known for its unseemly and "forward carriage" toward its bishops in the past.[63] Prowse could only appeal to the attorney general to defend the city's rights. Exeter's charter limited the civic bench to eight members, all of them aldermen. Because the bishop's suit clearly had the strength of Court patronage behind it, the city governors had to combine their Court connections with a strong legal case if they hoped for success.

In the end, the corporation of Exeter prevented the bishop from becoming a JP.[64] They enlisted the aid of both Secretary Calvert and Lord Treasurer Cranfield, whose influence, combined with the corporation's strong legal position, served to defend the civic magistrates from sharing their bench with their ecclesiastical neighbor.[65] The men of Exeter sorely felt the lack of their high steward at this critical juncture, but were able to protect their interests by cultivating other influential figures at Court. Not all Court officials felt as strongly as did the corporation about distinguishing civil and ecclesiastical boundaries, since both Lord Keeper Williams and the king clearly desired to see Bishop Carey on Exeter's commission. But the townsmen were able to find enough support to preserve the limits of their authority. Matters of jurisdiction could be played out in London as well as in the locality, and having a protector in both places could be important to a corporation's liberties.

Cathedral cities did not see constant conflict between church and corporation. Civic records give clear evidence of gifts and hospitality and genuine cordiality between townsmen and ecclesiastical officials. Some towns even solicited their bishops as patrons in civic business.[66] But at the same time, both townsmen and clerics maintained a vigilant watch over their boundaries. The evolution of the early modern state left corporations and cathedrals as competing jurisdictions with no uniform policies for interaction. The church, having lost considerable worldly authority since the Reformation, strictly defended its privileges and attempted to exert temporal power where possible. Corporations, whose authority waxed from the time of the Reformation, worked vigorously to guarantee their newly chartered privileges and to extend their authority where possible. Corporate and ecclesiastical officials constantly negotiated the boundaries of their authority. Their negotiations took place not just in the locality, but frequently at Court through the medium of patronage.

III

Not every borough corporation had to deal with a regional authority or an ecclesiastical enclave, but they all had to deal with county government. Corporate towns gained a large measure of independence from county authority by strength of their charters, which gave townsmen their own courts, justices of peace, and governments. Some towns enjoyed the status of counties in and of themselves—Bristol, Exeter, Worcester, and Coventry, among others. Despite their extensive self-government, corporate governors had constantly to interact with the gentry who ran the county surrounding the borough. Before borough incorporation became common, county authorities had jurisdiction over town leet courts and appointment of borough officers. In many towns, the gentry continued to try to wield power, even after incorporation freed the borough of such intervention.[67] For instance, the corporation of Leicester paid attorney John Freeman 10s. for his counsel and to "move the Justices of Peace of the county of Leicester at the Castle [of Leicester] at a Privy Sessions that they should not infringe the liberties of the Borough."[68] Not only was it a matter of jurisdiction, but of honor as well. Gentlemen felt that their higher social position should give them rights and privileges in a town, while the borough leaders attempted to maintain their own dignity and that of the corporation by controlling their own privileges.

Some historians have emphasized the antagonism between towns and gentry, arguing that urban oligarchs strove to gain independence for their towns while actually losing out to county authority.[69] This antagonism was real and should not be dismissed. But putting these relations in stark, polarized terms tends to gloss over a more complex reality. Both conflict and cooperation characterized county-corporate interactions. As magistrates, both town and county officials had many common interests, chiefly preserving peace and good order in the provinces, but also more personal ones such as friendship and family connections. Some corporations were more apt than others to cultivate these connections, but for all towns it was advantageous to sustain good relations with the local gentry. They had the ability to provide connections to the center and to other authorities, serving a brokerage function for the townsmen. Central government also benefited from having town and county authorities coexist peacefully, and the crown did what it could to foster such connections, for the better government of the provinces.

That tensions existed between towns and counties is clear from the records of most boroughs. The county elite exercised authority in many towns until the mid-sixteenth century, and they were apt to continue to trespass upon the privileges of boroughs, regardless of any royal charter of incorporation. Frequent quarreling with gentleman-landowners induced many towns to obtain charters in the first place. Walsall, in Staffordshire, lobbied for and obtained incorporation as late as 1625, after a long, drawn out dispute over the leet court with the lord of the manor, Sir Richard Wilbraham.[70] A Warwick town clerk, writing in the 1640's, complained of the gentry's tendency to impinge on corporate privileges. Gentlemen, wrote Edward Rainsford, "will be satisfied with no reasonable respects except such croaching observance as standeth not with the honour of a corporation to perform . . . who make no other use of them but as they do of their stirrups to mount their horse, so to serve their times they will bestow a salute on them or some formal compliment when they have scorn in their hearts."[71] This was a particularly bitter view, voiced during a time of great strife, but it nevertheless shows that both jurisdiction and honor were at stake in relations between town and county.

Corporations looked to representatives of higher authority to preserve their rights against the encroachments of the gentry. In 1607, the mayor of Barnstaple and his fellows petitioned the Privy Council concerning Mr. Hugh Acland, a justice of peace in north Devon, for the "enormities, injuries, and ill demeanors daily committed by him against the state and government of this town, although he had always among them good entertainment." Mr. Acland was called before the judges of Assize, who reprimanded him for his behavior. Acland's brother Sir John Acland, a prominent member of the Devon bench, then requested that he have the hearing of the cause at difference; the judges objected to this seeming conflict of interest, unless the corporation consented. Surprisingly, the mayor and aldermen, "by the earnest request of Sir John Acland," agreed to give the hearing of the suit to Sir John, who promised that he and his brother would from thenceforth "bear good affection to the town and do anything for their good." Sir John's promise appeased the city fathers, and the cause proceeded no further.[72] Corporators in Worcester brought their suits to the president of the Council of the Marches of Wales to counter county officials who affronted borough privileges, as when the undersheriff of Worcestershire served a writ within city boundaries in 1580 or when county JPs arrested a freeman of the town for an offense committed inside the borough boundaries in 1594.[73] Corporations made use of these institutions of central and regional authority to preserve their privileges against encroachment by socially and politically powerful gentry.

While townsmen felt free to utilize the courts and the council, they often preferred to use less formal means, and called on the services of patrons to solve their difficulties with the county. The corporation of Chichester had a sometimes antagonistic relationship with the Sussex justices, who resented the town's independent jurisdiction. In preserving their rights, the townsmen relied heavily on the favor of the earl of Arundel, their high steward. In 1617 two county JPs, including Chichester's main adversary, Richard Higgins, managed to obtain places on the corporation's commission of peace, "without notice, love, or liking of their [civic] Bench." The earl of Arundel intervened and procured a new charter for the town in 1618, a charter that firmly denied the county gentry's power in corporate governance. The corporation actually succeeded in barring the county sessions from meeting within the corporate boundaries; from 1618 until 1621, when the charter was revised and reissued, the sessions had to be held in the cathedral close instead.[74] Chester, too, relied on patrons to mediate with gentlemen who imposed on the city's privileges. When Sir Randle Crewe claimed that he had the right to exact tolls from people who passed through the East Gate of the city (a gate for which he did, in fact, hold the lease), the citizens strongly objected. The city had "from time out of mind" been free of that toll, no matter whether the corporation or a private person held the lease. Crewe was a prominent gentleman with connections both in Cheshire and in London, and the corporation had to marshal all of its forces to win the suit. Fortunately, they had the support of Viscount Savage, great friend of the town and an official in the queen's Court, who obtained a mediated settlement between Crewe and the corporation. Savage used his influence at Court to fend off Crewe's exertions against the city in London, convincing Crewe to pursue mediation rather than legal action. Interestingly, Savage was a friend of Crewe's, as well, but he clearly weighed in on the side of the corporation. When the dispute finally came to an end, the corporation wrote to Savage, acknowledging his "extraordinary pains concerning the business."[75] Patrons like Arundel and Savage could be vitally important to corporations in trying to maintain their rights in the face of a powerful and intrusive gentry.

Although corporations fought tooth and nail to preserve chartered privileges, this does not mean townsmen remained in constant conflict with shire officials. Positive interaction between the county bench and the civic assembly could and did occur. Provincial magistrates, whether urban or rural, had a strong common interest in the maintenance of peace and order. Fearful of the prospect of popular unrest, the elite felt the need both to enforce strict rules of action for the population and to set a good example of order and decorum.[76] Town governors found it expedient to work with county gentry as a way to protect themselves from pressures from below. Maintaining ties to the gentry also connected corporate leaders into the larger network of personal relations that helped unite center and provinces. Corporations could protect their interests both at home and in London by seeking out good relations with the local landed elite. "Borough independence" would have been an untenable concept to early modern townsmen. They protected their chartered rights and privileges, to be sure, but beyond that they worked to integrate themselves into society at large. As Rosemary Horrox has noted for fifteenth-century towns, they never tried to exclude outside influence altogether, but to "keep its manifestations within limits acceptable to the town." Town and county were not separate worlds that had to be chosen between, but integrated elements of a single society. A common set of social values, as well as personal ties, linked corporate and landed elites, and the central government smiled upon their cooperation.[77]

Both the internal decisions of corporations and the orders of royal government encouraged this interaction. The corporators of Boston, when deciding to revise borough ordinances, turned to the county for affirmation. The aldermen sent the deputy recorder and the town clerk to endeavor to get the Lincolnshire JPs to subscribe the new rules and also to get the recorder, Lord Keeper Coventry, to "subscribe and confirm the same."[78] The mayor of Oxford was offered a seat among the Oxfordshire justices, through the patronage of the city's high steward the earl of Berkshire, while other corporations had county justices as members, at least on an honorary basis.[79] In a few cases, a citizen of a borough served as sheriff of the shire as well. Mayors also served with county JPs on commissions determining matters that affected a whole county.[80] In Somerset, the recorders of some boroughs received places on the county commission of peace. Thomas Barnes, the historian of that county community, suggests that the lord chancellor did this purposely "to help ease possible jurisdictional disputes and increase cooperation between county and borough Benches."[81] It is quite clear that the crown promoted this sort of interaction, as the commissions of peace and gaol delivery for numerous towns contained the names of gentlemen and nobleman—in some cases the borough's high steward as well.[82] Both the locality and the center saw the benefits of cooperation between town and county.

The important men of the county could be of great use to a town in its attempts to gain advantage. The corporation of Oxford stated this explicitly when they agreed that "Mr. Hugh Candish, being a gentleman of whom this House may haply receive some favor and kindness in his place or office either now or hereafter, shall be admitted and made free of this city; and for that his love is such unto this city, this House doth freely grant him a Bailiff's place."[83] These relations could be reciprocal, as favors gained by a town might also be advantageous to the surrounding country. The city of Lincoln obtained gentry backing to a scheme to benefit both city and county. In 1617 the corporation organized a project for repairing the Fossdyke, a channel that came in from the sea. Mayor Robert Morcroft solicited gentry support, as well as that of the earl of Rutland, high steward, who pledged £100 under certain conditions. The county gentlemen agreed to raise £300 for the project if the city would match it. The project, unfortunately, never came to fruition and the investors ended up squabbling over their lost money. Despite its failure, the Fossdyke project's origins showed that corporation and county could work together, especially when a person of status, such as the earl of Rutland, sanctioned the cooperative effort.[84] In 1607 the corporation of Leicester recruited the support of almost the entire county bench of Leicestershire in a dispute involving freedom from toll. One Randle Mainwaring, "by some sinister information," had managed to purchase the right to take concealed tolls in Leicester. Mainwaring's intrusion harmed both the shire and the town, giving the county JPs a common interest with the corporators in refuting Mainwaring's supposed grant. Nearly all of the most prominent gentlemen in the county signed a letter written to the lord treasurer on behalf of the town, asking that the toll be abolished, "in respect of the long continuance of this so ancient a privilege & being a thing very convenient (in our knowledge) for the general good and peace for the whole country."[85] The support of the gentry could be crucial to a corporation in matters of this sort.

Sometimes, however, the magistrates of town and county needed encouragement to cooperate. Local patrons were well placed to help them to work together for things of common interest, especially those that helped preserve public order. While local magistrates saw the advantages of common projects, they often got hung up in quibbling over the financial questions involved. Both sides wanted to protect their own purses as well as their privileges, and sometimes required a certain amount of compulsion to make compromises. When the mayor of Kingston-upon-Hull attempted in 1639 to get a contribution from the surrounding county to repair the ditches, roads, and bridges in the town's environs, county officials did not refuse outright, but they did ask the mayor to show some record of how their money was to be used and where previous contributions had gone. Eventually, the lord president of the Council of the North was asked to look into the matter and ensure the collection of the contribution.[86] In Leicester, bridge repair became a crucial issue when the king visited the town. In 1613 a poor man's cart fell off a decrepit bridge soon before the king was to arrive. Having the bridge collapse under some poor farmer was one thing, but to have it collapse under the king was something else entirely. The corporation appealed to the earl of Huntingdon to request the JPs to contribute county funds to the project. Because of the earl's mediation, town and county cooperated to make the bridge safe for the passage of King James.[87] Civic officials felt free to call upon higher authority, especially their patrons, to persuade the local JPs to cooperate on a project when the townsmen themselves did not have the clout to achieve it.

Public order as well as honor and reputation caused county and borough officials to work together on common projects. Maintaining the peace and suppressing disorder concerned shire JPs just as much as town magistrates, so projects that helped preserve public order made good candidates for cooperative efforts. County jails, for reasons of convenience and centrality, were usually situated in the county town or another local population center. When these buildings required repair or new construction, county and town governments sometimes combined to undertake the work. Not surprisingly, the JPs of Leicestershire chose Leicester for the site of a new House of Correction. Quarter Sessions and Assizes for the shire met there, so it offered the most logical location. Henry Lord Grey, on behalf of the JPs, requested the corporation to grant a piece of property for this use. Because the building in question was in some disrepair and would require extensive refurbishing, Grey asked that the corporation grant the lease on good terms, and that the corporation would render all possible assistance to the new keeper of the jail, Henry Cowper. "In which doing," Lord Grey stated, "myself and the rest of the country shall think themselves beholding unto you, And yourselves shall find some ease by the erection of so good a work." The townsmen saw the benefit of this cooperation, and assisted with the jail as requested, although ten years later they built another House of Correction for civic use.[88] Similar cooperation occurred during public health emergencies. The town and shire of Worcester apparently worked harmoniously to fend off the ravages of plague and famine on more than one occasion in the late sixteenth century.[89] During an outbreak of plague in Leicester in 1610, the corporation effectively solicited the earl of Huntingdon to appeal to the county JPs to help relieve the sick poor of the town. As a preventive measure during an outbreak in the town in 1614, the JPs and the corporation wrote a mutual letter to the lord chief justice to allow the removal of the county jail from Leicester for fear of the infection; the prisoners were the county's but the effects would fall upon the town that housed them if plague were to be spread.[90] It behooved the county JPs to assist corporate leaders in plague measures as it helped prevent the spread of the disease and suppress potential unrest among the poor and infected. But it sometimes took outside intervention to encourage the county officials to assist civic governors.

Despite evident tensions, town and county magistrates still shared many interests, both administrative and social. Town dwellers purposely sought out such connection and cooperation, for reasons of private interest as well as public safety and order. By encouraging ties to the gentry, townsmen could move their families into the higher social ranking of the landed elite. But they also protected their specifically urban interests by tapping into the network of patronage connections of which many of the gentry were a part. Town government could call on the links made by individual corporators with important local gentlemen in order to achieve civic business. Corporators often formed close relationships with county gentlemen, who became firm friends of the town. Members of the Carewe family and later Sir John Acland at Exeter, the Stanleys, Smiths, and Savages at Chester, the Withipolls at Ipswich, the Fanes at Maidstone, the Irbys at Boston, the Flemyngs and Sandyses at Winchester all formed long-lasting relationships with the respective boroughs and personal friendships with individual members of the corporations.[91] The scions of some of these houses were great peers who had the power and influence to act directly as patrons to the communities. Other families, while operating on a more local level, could still aid a town by serving as brokers, offering public services, and participating in the life of the community.

Examples of close relationships abound. At Chester, the Smith and the Savage families held prominent places in the county. Both forged close ties with the city and its governors. Savages and Smiths served as aldermen and mayors of the city as well as being JPs for the county. Sir Thomas Savage, bart., was both a friend of the town in general and a personal friend of certain members of the corporation. This closeness benefited the corporation, as Sir Thomas went on to become a prominent member of Queen Henrietta Maria's household and a friend of both King Charles and the duke of Buckingham. As Lord Savage he retained his friendships in Chester and continued to work for the good of the city, becoming one of its greatest patrons in the 1620's and 1630's. John Morrill suggests that gentry families like the Smiths and the Savages, who also held office in the corporation, may well have "helped to mediate in the jurisdictional and fiscal disputes which frequently simmered between city and county."[92] The corporators of Oxford made Mr. George Calfield of Kettleby a member of their society, regularly turning to him for counsel and support. He also served as MP for the borough in all of the last five parliaments of Queen Elizabeth's reign. Although he did not reside permanently in the city, he spent considerable time there and served as the city's legal advisor for seventeen years. The corporation granted him special consideration for his services in the form of corn, ground at the town's mill, for the provision of his household. Although never an alderman, Calfield received the honor of sitting among the corporators as if he were an alderman of high seniority.[93] Leicester, in addition to its relationship with the earl of Huntingdon, had an especially close friendship with Sir Edward Hastings, the younger brother of the third and fourth earls. He lived just outside the town at Leicester Abbey and showed consistent friendship to the town throughout his life.[94] Similarly, Sir Anthony Irby, a Lincolnshire gentleman and a master of Chancery under King James, had a close connection to the town of Boston. He served as recorder of the town for many years and was also elected a member of the corporation, an alderman. The town relied on his connections in London to benefit the town. Sir Anthony was held in high regard in Boston and treated the town generously in return.[95] While these gentlemen occasionally tried to throw their weight around in towns, such alliances benefited boroughs in the long run. Providing important brokerage services to their respective towns, they kept the locality in touch with those who had the power to affect the borough for good or ill. Corporations purposefully cultivated connections like these to strengthen their position in the state.

The desire of urban magistrates to associate themselves with the county gentry made sense for a variety of reasons. Maintaining good relations with local gentlemen helped to preserve order in the locality and led to cooperation on projects of mutual benefit to town and county. Magistrates quarreled about specific actions or policies, but they shared a desire for order in the locality. On another level, the county gentry had a social authority that gave them influence far beyond what an urban magistrate was likely to have. Gentlemen participated in the networks of patronage that extended to the Court and back out into the provinces, holding the potential to affect the distribution of goods, services, and influence that occurred at the highest levels of central government. While corporations wished to have a single prominent patron to act as the main connection between the borough and the Court, town leaders desired the goodwill of as many influential people as possible, people with their own contacts who could bring benefit to a borough.[96]

Undoubtedly, different towns had different levels of interaction with the gentry. Ann Hughes shows that while Warwick, the county town of Warwickshire, had regular concourse with local gentry and counted Lord Brooke as the town's patron, Coventry, as a county unto itself, "remained aloof from the general life of Warwickshire." Even Coventry, though, was not immune from the urge to connect. Sir John Harrington was made a freeman of the city in 1610, and Henry Lord Berkeley was chosen an alderman in 1611.[97] Gentry connections brought urban governors in contact with patronage networks both locally and at the center, providing increased possibilities for favor and benefits to come into the town. It should be remembered that many towns, of their own volition, returned members of the county gentry as burgesses for Parliament. A gentleman could sometimes achieve things at Westminster that a borough resident could not. Corporate cooperation with the gentry should not be overdrawn, but neither should it be assumed that corporations strove invariably for "independence." By maintaining direct links to the landed elite and making use of the mediating services of influential patrons, corporations could work to preserve their own privileges while remaining firmly fixed in the network of connection that linked all the parts of the early modern state, from the center to the localities and back.

IV

The connective power of patronage had its limits. Some conflicts ran deep enough that they could not be worked out through mediation or influence. But changing government policies also helped determine the boundaries of patronage. As central government increased the burden on local communities, it exacerbated old rivalries between competing jurisdictions and left little room for compromise or change. During the late sixteenth century and the first years of the seventeenth, corporations' conflicts with other authorities had much to do with civic privileges and honor and little to do with policy. Patrons could be particularly effective in sorting out such disputes by wielding their influence in the locality and with the center. The crown benefited from this by remaining informed of and involved in local business. Part of a patron's strength lay in the very fact that central government had no set-in-stone policies as to how urban governments should interact with others. These great men had broad discretion in hammering out solutions for regional problems. The advent of more determined policies on the part of Caroline government, most especially the universal imposition of Ship Money in the 1630's, forced corporations into a defensive posture. Townsmen, unhappy with paying these new exactions, wished to be free of them; this was something no patron could negotiate. The situation left corporations disgruntled with their neighbors, their patrons, and most likely with central government as well. Ann Hughes aptly states that "there was not necessarily any conflict between local and national interests: it depended on what the government was calling on local governors to do."[98] King Charles's administrative activism, which strove to create a more orderly and stable government, made the problem of competing jurisdictions more rather than less acrimonious.[99]

Serious problems arose with the universal imposition of Ship Money beginning in 1635. Levied as a lump sum on each county, Ship Money required that local men, in particular the sheriff, decide the share of the burden for each part of the county. This method almost automatically gave rise to disputes, as individuals and towns struggled to have their portions reduced. In several towns, Ship Money brought out bitter rating disputes between county and town officials, who revived old jurisdictional squabbles in order to save their own pocketbooks. Privy Council records reveal a steady stream of rating disputes between town and county officials. In one year, from July 1635 through July 1636, the board dealt with disputes in King's Lynn, Cambridge, Norwich, Lincoln, Boston, Ipswich, Maidstone, Canterbury, Shrewsbury, Colchester, and Northampton.[100] In Coventry, townsmen felt that they had been rated unfairly and they also questioned whether the sheriff of the county had any right to rate them at all. In military levies, Coventry traditionally paid one-fifteenth of the county's total charges. For Ship Money, the sheriff of Warwickshire rated the city at the seemingly arbitrary sum of £500, nearly twice as much as it would owe under the traditional rating system. Coventry consented to pay £266, or one-fifteenth of the county's total, but the sheriff, Robert Morden, continued to demand his specified amount. The dispute ended up before Bishop Wright of the diocese of Coventry and Lichfield, who in the end found for the town. This appeased the civic leaders but not the sheriff or his fellow gentlemen, who had to make up the lost revenue elsewhere.[101] In Chichester, the corporation, faced with a rate of £150, tried to tax the cathedral close as part of the borough, thus lowering the cost to the citizens. The Privy Council disallowed this move, and the Ship Money sheriff Sir William Culpepper even decreased the separate rate that the cathedral close owed, a clear dig at the corporation.[102] These disputes raised the level of acrimony between town and county magistrates to unusually high levels and did not allow for much, if any, compromise.

Corporations continued to appeal to tried-and-true methods to get satisfaction. Solicitations of patronage continued. In the midst of a row with the sheriff of Norfolk over the town's Ship Money assessment early in 1635, the corporation of King's Lynn chose the earl of Arundel and Surrey as their high steward. They also invited Lord Maltravers, Arundel's son, to visit the town and enjoy their hospitality. This calculated strategy failed to have the desired effect, however. The Privy Council still required the town to submit their original assessment.[103] Dover appealed to the lord warden of the Cinque Ports Thomas earl of Suffolk to have the town's charge reduced, while York sent letters to their high steward Lord Keeper Coventry complaining about the rate. In neither case does the lobbying seem to have been particularly fruitful, although Lord Warden Suffolk pledged to give Dover what aid he could.[104] Problems usually reached resolution through direct Privy Council enforcement, rather than through more informal channels.

The well-documented case of the assessment of Ship Money in Chester shows how such rating disputes could develop into more principled resistance, which could not be sorted out through mediation. When Charles imposed the general rate in 1635, it resurrected a long-standing dispute between city and county over the jurisdiction of Gloverstone. Gloverstone, an enclave within the boundaries of the city, escaped corporate control in the city's charters. The corporation usually chose to enforce its will over the enclave, despite their lack of clear authority, while the county JPs also laid claim to its jurisdiction when it suited them. In 1635 both county and city wanted to claim Gloverstone in order to spread the levy out among a larger number of people. At the same time, Sir Thomas Aston, sheriff of Cheshire, tried to escape from being assessed in the city for his farm of the customs on French wines in the port of Chester. The city lobbied hard to preserve its rights over Gloverstone and to charge Aston in Chester. Corporators must have been very pleased when the Privy Council assigned the earl of Derby and the Assize judges of Cheshire as commissioners to hear the suit. Yet even such a friendly commission could not give the corporators their desired ends. The commissioners found that the county, not the city, had the right to collect in Gloverstone. But they gave Chester some satisfaction by requiring Sir Thomas Aston to pay his rate in the city. Two years later, the corporation's pursuit went on, as they attempted to lighten their burden.[105]

While these events may have been just one more manifestation of the jurisdictional disputes that occurred periodically in Chester, they seem to have held a greater significance. Peter Lake, who has studied the case thoroughly, argues that although the players couched their debate in these localist, jurisdictional terms, in fact both the gentry and the civic leaders expressed dislike of the rate itself rather than mere unhappiness with the manner of its collection. Each side could blame the other for obstructing the service, thus appearing at home to be a champion of local rights while appearing to the center to be working assiduously to collect the levy.[106] The Privy Council, while supposed to be an objective arbiter of the local dispute, in fact had a very strong interest in the outcome, since it could set a precedent for other counties. Thus those directly in charge of settling the dispute—the judges and the earl—had little room to maneuver, since in the end the full amount of the levy had to be collected. Enforcement, not mediation or favor, fundamentally motivated the commissioners. Whatever their decision, the arbitrators would be seen by the locality to be enforcing an unpopular tax, while the crown demanded vigorous action in the service. A patron could not really do anything to satisfy the desires of the people in the localities, since to do so would be to damage his ties with the center, which could in turn destroy much of his effectiveness as a patron.[107] What the people in the locality wanted was the absence of the levy, not simply a reduction of it.[108] No amount of influence or patronage would achieve this.

Almost universally, the collection of Ship Money exacerbated old conflicts and made "friendly" resolutions nearly impossible. Many cathedral
cities saw the resurgence of bitter debates between corporate and ecclesiastical authorities. Typically arising out of a corporation's attempt to collect Ship Money within cathedral precincts, these conflicts looked similar
to earlier jurisdictional disputes. But they took on added heat and a theo-
logical tone as King Charles's policies became more clear-cut. The king
staunchly supported an Arminian episcopate and tried to conform the
Church of England to his strongly ritualistic and liturgical preferences.[109]
He viewed most townsmen, magistrates and average citizens, as particular
problems, deeming urban areas the main stronghold of puritans and other
enemies to religion. In this he was partly correct. Most towns, even those
that would become royalist during the civil war, had generally reform-
minded populations.[110] As tensions arising between towns and the ecclesiastical hierarchy took on a more doctrinal cast, Charles made clear that
his sympathies lay with the church.

In Canterbury, Lichfield, Chichester, Winchester, York, and Chester,
and probably Exeter and Salisbury as well, old grievances resurfaced
when corporations attempted to increase their tax base by rating cathedral closes for Ship Money.[111] In every case, cathedral authorities pro-
tested loudly, arguing their exclusion from civic jurisdiction. Rather than
being negotiated in the locality, these disputes came directly to the attention of the Privy Council and often that of King Charles himself, who
regularly sat in council to hear these disputes.[112] The board defended the
privileges of the church, denying corporations the right to collect from
anyone residing within a cathedral's jurisdiction. In Canterbury, the cathedral clergy gained permission to assess themselves, while in Chichester,
the Privy Council instructed the dean and chapter to pay their rates directly to the sheriff on the rumor that the mayor was going to try to assess
them with the town.[113] Of these seven cathedral cities, only Salisbury received permission to rate the residents of the close.[114] The Ship Money disputes as a group ended unfavorably for corporate government.

Although the council decided the Ship Money disputes, the lords failed
to stamp out controversy. These disputes in effect became catalysts for
more conflict over the balance between cathedral and corporate authority. Cathedral clergy, seeing that the political winds of royal favor blew
quite definitely in their direction, used the opportunity to remind the
crown that the privileges of the church had been under assault for years
from corporate authorities. They opened up anew the old issues of gov-

ernance and jurisdiction and religious conformity, but this time the churchmen had the power of the king's council, and the king himself, staunchly on their side. In 1635 the corporation of Lichfield found that the rating dispute with the cathedral led directly to the city's charter being threatened by quo warranto.[115] The Ship Money conflict in Chichester gave rise to a Privy Council investigation of the corporation's intrusions into the privileges of the close, and the council heard similar suits against the corporations of Salisbury, York, Winchester, and Exeter, all between June 1636 and November 1637.[116] In every instance, the Privy Council made determinations that were favorable to the cathedrals in question and curtailed the extent of corporate privileges. And in four of the six cases noted above, King Charles himself personally sat in council and made the determinations that so favored the ecclesiastical establishment. With the crown actively interested in the outcome, corporations had little hope to achieve their ends through patronage.

The hardened positions of king, church, and corporation can be seen clearly in the city of York in the 1630's. Troubles began in 1633, when the archdeacon of the cathedral sat in a higher seat than the mayor in the minster, much to the city's chagrin. This affront to the civic dignity caused the corporators to vote to "forebear going to the Minster."[117] To resolve the dispute, the city appealed to their high steward, Lord Keeper Coventry. Coventry, along with the archbishop of York, engaged in ongoing attempts to compose the differences.[118] But even as these negotiations went on, the Ship Money assessment began. The seating dispute became tied to a rating dispute, as the corporation assessed the levy on lands that had formerly been attached to the cathedral.[119] At this point, the dispute left the hands of the high steward and went directly into the hands of King Charles. The cathedral clergy appealed for redress from the king, who sided resolutely with the church. He first ordered a revision of the city's charter, taking away corporate authority over the parishes in question.[120] When the corporators seemed less than submissive to the authority of the church, he issued a peremptory order requiring the mayor, aldermen, and their companies to attend divine service at the cathedral on all Sundays and holidays, and to take communion "at some solemn times every year." While in the cathedral, and in coming in and going out, they were to behave themselves "as beseemeth them in obedience to the Canons of the Church and the customs of those cathedrals." The mayor was not to use the ensigns of civic authority within the cathedral, in order to keep inviolable the rights and privileges of the church.[121] The order was enforced not only in York itself, but in all cathedral towns in Archbishop Neile's archdiocese.[122] In essence, the king claimed that the corporation was and always had been subordinate to the cathedral, and that the mayor stood subordinate to the bishop.

For corporate authorities, these actions held great significance. Old patterns of dealing with cathedral personnel were destroyed, and the king and Privy Council dictated what the new relationship was to be. Issues they believed decisively resolved long ago once again came into question. In Chester, Charles's new policy concerning civic insignia meant an absolute reversal of the decision made by Lord Keeper Egerton in 1606, which had explicitly given the corporation permission to carry the civic sword anywhere in the cathedral and its precincts. For Salisbury, where the corporation had gained exclusion from episcopal control by their 1612 charter, confirmed in 1630, the king (at the request of cathedral authorities) now determined that the bishop, dean, all the resident canons, and the chancellor of the diocese would be justices of the peace of the city.[123] Corporators in Norwich, Worcester, and Winchester were commanded to enter the royal orders concerning church attendance and civic insignia into the official records of the corporation, preventing future questions as to proper behavior.[124] Charles's unilateral pronouncements in favor of cathedrals over corporations left little or no room for mediation or negotiation. While the bond between patrons and local communities could be called on to solve a wide variety of problems, it was not strong enough to hold in the face of such divisive religious issues.

As the issue of Arminianism added a new and more discordant element to the jurisdictional battles that occurred between corporations and the ecclesiastical hierarchy, so the financial exactions of the 1630's did for relations between corporations, counties, and the crown. The crown enforced unpopular policy upon the provinces; the different elements within the localities, although they may well have been sympathetic to each other's views on the taxes, instead squabbled among themselves over how the service was to be done, since they were not prepared to take issue with the crown directly. Local patrons, who had previously been able to help mediate jurisdictional disputes and to get the parties to work together for their common good and the common peace, could not do the one thing that would satisfy local people: convince the king to discontinue his policies. The crown and the localities were forced into hardened positions that did not allow for compromise, thus making the job of the patron, who provided connection between the two, much more difficult. Once jurisdictional disputes took on principled stances, the network of patronage that had helped to link the various elements in the state together could not effectively do its job.

The changes in the administration and policy of English government had a clear impact on the leadership of the realm's many towns. Those who had ruled the towns in earlier centuries—the church, the great regional magnates, even the local gentry—were no longer welcome to participate in civic government the way they once had. Corporate leaders worked hard to maintain the privileges they had won through their incorporation by royal charter, which bound them to the crown and excluded many other layers of authority. These other authorities routinely challenged the privileges of the corporations, trying to recover the influence they had once enjoyed. The irony is that the men who threatened corporate authority were from the same group, and often were the same people, as those who could benefit towns substantially. The trick was to learn how to interact in new ways. To protect themselves, corporations used a variety of methods, including the law, arbitration, and simple compromise. In all of these methods, towns relied on the services of patrons to assist them in getting their due. Because the English state lacked a formal means of integration between its multifarious institutions and organizations, problems that arose found resolution on a case-by-case basis, relying heavily on the actions of the Privy Council or of powerful individuals. Most corporations maintained patronage ties to one or more prominent figures as a crucial aid to civic well-being.

Corporate leaders knew full well that they had to remain on constant guard to protect their privileges. They also knew that turning their backs on authorities outside borough walls could result in disaster. The idea of "borough independence" simply would not work, given the nature of government in the late sixteenth and early seventeenth centuries.[125] Townsmen needed the connections that members of the landed elite, even those actively involved in bodies that competed with corporate governance, could bring. Because to a great degree personal connection, and not the institutions of royal bureaucracy, held the English state together, corporations had no choice but to tap into this network in order to obtain benefits and uphold their privileges.[126] All of the institutions and groups that made up royal government competed with each other for favor and advantage. The crown knit this patchwork together, but the monarch relied on the most prominent men in the land to maintain order and peace and to extend royal bounty out into the provinces. Borough corporations, like any other element in the state, found areas of common interest where possible, and sought protection and defense when not. It seems that these areas of common interest became more difficult to find as the financial and religious strains of the 1630's mounted, making patronage less effective in fulfilling the needs of both center and localities. Networks of personal connection had many strengths and served a constructive purpose throughout the period, but they could not solve all the problems that troubled the realm.

Corporations and the Crown

Mediating the Interests of
Center and Locality

The business of government in early modern England required reciprocity. Both local leaders and central authorities had needs and responsibilities that could only be fulfilled through cooperation. They shared certain assumptions about their society: its hierarchical nature, the duty of inferiors to obey and superiors to govern responsibly, and the necessity of consensus and concord for a healthy commonwealth. This by no means precluded disagreements and disputes, but it did require that constant attempts at communication and interaction be made. Hence the leaders of borough corporations maintained an eternal pursuit of access to the halls of power. Corporations had to turn to the crown for the charters on which their existence depended, but they also needed more mundane things like better and safer harbors, new beacon lights, and other improvements that benefited the economic and social life of a town. They increasingly had to confront issues of taxation and military expenditure that epitomized the relations between center and locality. As the demands of government mounted upon local leaders, the desire for patronage to mediate with the center grew as well.

Civic leaders fully understood the crucial importance of communication and access to the crown for their own ability to govern. Only by letting local needs be known could they achieve much of their business. But it was not enough simply to send petitions; those petitions had to be heard to be effective. Some things could be accomplished at Westminster, and citizens expected their burgesses to Parliament to act in the locality's behalf in passing statutes beneficial to the town. As one scholar has said, however, "All localities saw parliament as only one means to an end, and a pretty poor means at that." Many grants derived directly from the monarch, the

Privy Council, or one of the high courts, Chancery or Exchequer.[1] Provincial towns, by definition peripheral, did not have natural access to the centers of decision-making in London. Rather they sought out channels of access, powerful people within and outside the bureaucracy, who might have influence and who would be willing to act on behalf of townsmen.

The crown likewise had expectations of urban government. Civic leaders carried out a critical function in maintaining stability in the provinces. They had day-to-day contact with a potentially volatile portion of the population, and the crown expected enforcement of order for the safety and well-being of the realm.[2] Towns served as centers for regional government and business, and they also contributed significantly to tax revenues and purveyance. In short, civic leaders supported the state (of which they were a part) financially, administratively, and socially. In communicating royal wishes to urban government, the crown used a variety of means. Some were direct, as in royal orders or commissions.[3] Others operated more obliquely, through the same network of connection that townsmen used to gain access to the center. Known patrons, particularly high stewards, could provide a conduit of information between crown and town.[4] Without formal institutions of royal authority, such as the system of *intendants* created by the French kings, English monarchs had to rely on the goodwill of their most important subjects to enforce policies throughout the realm.[5]

Mediating between local authorities and the powers at the center lay at the heart of urban patronage in the late sixteenth and early seventeenth centuries. Obtaining or renewing charters of incorporation, procuring favors from the crown, and negotiating the contentious issues of taxation and the militia all required corporate governors to gain access to royal favor. Townsmen did so by cultivating connections to those most likely to effect local business at the center. Through these connections, boroughs strove to achieve their economic and political goals, and the crown, in turn, maintained the link between the central and peripheral elements of the state. When these same connections were put to use to mediate the increasingly problematic matters of taxation and the militia in the 1620's and 1630's, they proved less able to bring the needs and desires of center and locality together. Yet as long as localities fulfilled their responsibilities and the center was seen to be responsive to local needs, the English state functioned—not perfectly, but adequately.

I

For the governors of early modern towns, the world could seem a dangerous and not very peaceful place. At every turn, some group of merchants or gentlemen or another town seemed to be plotting the harm of others, either in the locality or in London. Borough leaders, constantly on guard to protect local interests, formed a sometimes paranoid view of the world. The language that townsmen used about their precarious status reflects this paranoia. Thomas Chettell, mayor of Leicester, insisted that the town had "privy enemies" both at home and in London undermining his efforts to procure a charter for the town early in the seventeenth century. Similarly Giles Carpenter, a member of Exeter's corporation, wrote to fellow corporator Ignatius Jurdain of "a dangerous plot against the City." According to Carpenter, certain "undertakers, Londoners, and decayed courtiers" lobbied to get a commission to reedify the castle at Exeter and to establish a garrison there. The supposed undertakers aimed at gaining exclusive rights to fairs and other privileges, leaving city magistrats with no jurisdiction whatever in the castle area. The rumor proved false, but it frightened the city fathers enough that they took the opportunity to push for a renewal of their charter.[6]

These seemingly irrational fears of urban leaders rested on some truth. Thomas Milles, in his *Catalogue of Honour* (1610), stated, "If you seek for such as they [the Romans] called *patricii* or Senators (whom the Romans reverenced as men sent down from heaven) you shall find them nowhere but in the cities, exercising Usury and Merchandise (trades utterly forbidden the Romans) at whom (although within their own walls they be much regarded and esteemed) our *Noble Courtiers* were wont to scoff and jest." Townsmen were not always held in high esteem by the landed elite. The portmen of Ipswich felt this disparagement first hand in 1610, when they had to send a solicitor to call on all their friends at Court to clear the town "from the great imputation of faction and schism which some lewd persons had filled the ears of the Lord Treasurer withall." The townsmen's solicitor spent £5 in going to the lord treasurer, the high steward of Ipswich the earl of Suffolk, the archbishop of Canterbury, and "divers others of the Privy Council," to assure them of Ipswich's good reputation and conformist nature.[7] In order to protect themselves from sinister plots, privy enemies, and any number of other threats, civic leaders willingly turned to central government. They relied on established patronage and brokerage connections to link them to the powers in London who could provide satisfaction. Forging relationships with men in power allowed townsmen to bring the authority of the crown to bear on their opponents. Threats to corporate well-being led corporators not to retreat into a protective shell, but rather to look outward for solutions and protection.

Townsmen maintained constant vigilance for encroachments against their privileges. The centrality of trade and commerce to the life of towns meant that civic governors spent considerable time and energy promoting and securing the local economy. In doing so, townsmen regularly turned to higher authorities for assistance. A near-constant stream of letters complaining of the depredations of London merchants went out from provincial ports to their patrons. Totnes carried on a long feud with the London merchants who traded with the Continent and attempted to shut out merchants from other English ports. The mayor and his brethren wrote to three successive high stewards of the town (the earls of Salisbury, Northampton, and Pembroke) over more than a decade to complain of the Londoners and to reinforce their own rights. Merchants from Dartmouth, regional rival of Totnes, actually sided with Totnes on this issue of mutual interest and also wrote seeking assistance against London merchants.[8] When Turkish pirates menaced the shipping interests of Totnes in 1636, the corporation appealed directly to Archbishop Laud to help them raise funds to fight. Laud's—and the king's—particular interest in this issue was well known. After receiving a petition from Totnes, Laud granted a personal interview with the town's solicitor, during which the archbishop, "striking his hand upon his breast," declared that while he had breath in his body he would advance "so necessary and good a business."[9] Clearly, the men of Totnes knew in what quarter to appeal and elicited a vigorous response from a powerful Court figure.

Another target for the ire of civic leaders was not rival towns or marauding pirates, but the officers of royal government itself. Inferior officers of the crown, for instance of the customs or the admiralty or purveyance, regularly dealt with town officials and sometimes went too far in carrying out their duties. When no agreement could be reached directly between the corporation and the royal officer, patrons served one of their most important services in mediating between the multiple layers of government. They helped royal government work in the localities. Several port towns had chronic troubles with royal officers who remained permanently in their midst. The mayor and jurats of Dover battled frequently with the successive water-bailiffs assigned to their port, claiming that the bailiffs took excessive fees and exceeded their jurisdiction. On two separate occasions, relations came to such a pitch between town and water-bailiff that the lord warden had to step into the fray. The warden stood as the water-bailiff's superior in office, but his dual nature as patron gave the townsmen of Dover hope that he would support their interests over those of his officer. The corporation frequently appealed to the lord warden and the lieutenant of Dover Castle to moderate the activities of water-bailiffs.[10] Customs officials who overstepped their bounds met a similar response. The Bristol corporation petitioned their high steward, Lord Weston, to free them from the unfair exactions of customs officers in the city. Although Weston first supported the position of the customs men, he later thought better of it and revoked his warrant to them, freeing the Bristolians from the charge. He even ordered the customs officials to pay back the excess they had collected.[11]

The financial consequences of matters large and small often motivated corporations to call upon patrons for resolution. Civic leaders might apologize for troubling great men with small problems, but continued to do so anyway. In 1614 Exeter corporation wrote to "our especial good lord," the earl of Northampton, with some hesitancy, fearing that by appealing to him too often, they would be considered "clamorous or backwards from yielding (as some think) to small matters." Nevertheless, they asked him to stop the deputy aulnager of Exeter and Devon, Thomas Bridgeman, from demanding excessive fees on Devon kersies and harming the city's trade. Northampton, as lord privy seal as well as high steward of Exeter, had both the local connection and the central influence to require Bridgeman's conformity.[12] When the corporation of Leicester was amerced for purveyance at an excessively high rate on the king's 1614 progress by an officer with a dubious royal commission, the townsmen called upon the earl of Huntingdon and the chancellor of the duchy of Lancaster for relief. Seemingly minor privileges could cause major concern, as when the corporation of Boston appealed to the earl of Salisbury in 1605 about their right to keep a "whale fish" caught within the liberties of the borough. They reminded the earl that his father Lord Burghley had always been their "singular good lord" and that he had procured them the right to keep whale fish in the first place. Pointing out both his traditional ties to the town and his influential position at Court, the men of Boston entreated Salisbury to maintain their rights.[13] Corporations believed that giving in on even small privileges put them on a slippery slope to the loss of other rights. Patrons solved problems between different elements within the state without forcing the parties into expensive and time-consuming lawsuits.

Patronage also provided a means by which corporations obtained

grants and favors that would bring benefit to the locality, not simply protection from harm. Favorable leases, grants for monopoly of trade, rights
to use crown lands or buildings, and grants of staple status for trade all required crown approval. Civic leaders relied heavily on patrons and brokers to provide them with access to the Court. Their suits might ultimately
come before a particular arm of the central government, the court of
Chancery or of Exchequer, for example. Yet unless a town's petition requesting the favor had an advocate at Court, the likelihood of its success
decreased drastically. Successful petitioning required the attention of the
king and the people who actually made the decisions. King Charles acknowledged this when he commended Viscount Ayr as high steward to the
corporation of Doncaster: "in anything where your corporation or the
members thereof shall stand in need of our grace and favor, by his inter-
cession you shall find ready access, and a gracious answer from us."[14] Patronage provided access.

This reality encouraged corporations to identify potential patrons
whom they believed might be sympathetic to the cause at hand or the locality in general. Chester corporation decided to write to Viscount Cranborne to help obtain the impost of Gascony wines for the use of the city
because he had taken an interest in the city's business in the past: "your
former respects to this city by your special furtherance of the business of
the late attendance of Mr. Mayor upon you encourages us to become suitors for the continuance thereof."[15] When Great Yarmouth's fee farm lease
came due in 1632, the corporation worried mightily that the favorable
lease granted them 40 years previously would be redrawn. The fee farm of
£45 per annum had been granted to the queen consort, and the aldermen
feared that she would not remit them the 40 marks annually that Queen
Elizabeth had. The corporation wrote to the earl of Dorset, the town's
high steward but also the chamberlain of the queen's household, to ask
him to "mediate and be an honorable good friend therein as formerly,"
and solicit a remittance from King Charles and Queen Henrietta Maria.[16]
Dorset's useful multiplicity of offices made him the obvious person to ask
for this particular favor. His history of good lordship to the town, his
authority as a member of the Privy Council, and his specific connection to
Henrietta Maria inclined him to bring Yarmouth and the queen to a composition on this issue.

In gaining this sort of access, corporations often relied on gentlemen
serving in the capacity of brokers, men who could make introductions and
put townsmen in contact with the decision-makers at Court. Brokers
linked townsmen to particular officers of state who had power to confirm

or deny petitions, and usually threw their weight in on the side of the petitioners, helping to persuade the "petitionee" of the justness of the town's request. The men of Chester relied on a broker when seeking to obtain a grant to a royal property in 1579. The corporation wished to erect a new shambles, or meat market, in order to make space available to poorer butchers. The logical spot for it seemed to be the site of the decayed old shire hall, a crown property. Civic leaders hoped that the queen would grant the shire hall to them outright as a gift rather than charging them for it. They wrote directly to Lord Burghley, who made most decisions about the queen's lands, asking for the property and for permission to raze the building and erect a shambles. They also sent him half a dozen cheeses as a gesture of friendship and thanks. Unconvinced of the efficacy of cheese alone, however, they wrote to Sir Henry Cholmondley to gain his assistance. The townsmen prevailed upon Cholmondley, a local gentleman prominent in the city as well as being the surveyor of the queen's lands in Cheshire, to write at least two letters to Lord Burghley on behalf of the city. Although it took some time, the petition finally met with success in 1581.[17]

The town of Leicester's grant to become a staple town for wool early in 1618 likewise resulted from concerted lobbying of officials of central and regional courts by a gentleman serving as a broker. Townsmen sought the assistance of Sir William Heyrick, master of the king's jewels under King James, but also a native son of Leicester and the brother of one of the most wealthy and prominent aldermen. Sir William helped the corporation greatly on several occasions and served as MP as well. He agreed to accompany George Wadland, the town's attorney, to wait upon "Mr. Attorney" (presumably Attorney General Henry Yelverton, although possibly the attorney of the duchy) in London to try to procure the grant of the staple. Unfortunately, on their first attempt the two men could not speak with him, he being "so pained with toothache that his cheeks were swollen exceedingly and his mouth even drawn awry (as his man said)."[18] The persistent Sir William and Mr. Wadland eventually did solicit the favor from the attorney. After several months of lobbying, the men of Leicester received their grant of a wool staple in February 1618. The corporation sent a formal letter of thanks to Sir William for his "special love and care" of the town of Leicester.[19] When Sir William fell ill soon after this victory, Mr. Wadland proclaimed that "the whole town have need to pray for him. For if it should please God to take him, we shall all have a great loss of him, and hardly have such another friend left."[20] Heyrick filled the role of broker perfectly, introducing townsmen to the decision-makers in London and adding his own voice to the petition.

Sir William served in the capacity of broker to Leicester on many occasions, helping the corporation with both internal and external difficulties. The townsmen in return treated him with tremendous respect, including him in the activities of the town and choosing him as their MP. The Leicester records show the warmth and strength of the relationship that could grow between townsmen and gentlemen. As a native son, Sir William was inclined to assist the town of Leicester, but the corporators also continually reinforced their great need for his assistance and their personal esteem for him. This pattern of mutual obligation and almost ritual thanking can be seen in the town's attempt to obtain a charter for incorporating the Trinity Hospital in Leicester. When, in November 1613, the corporation found that an almsman in the hospital had petitioned the king for the incorporation, the civic leaders decided that they should investigate the matter and take it over themselves, hoping to place the mastership of the hospital in the hands of the civic corporation. They immediately wrote to Heyrick to inform him of the suit, to give him the full details, and to ask his "good direction" to bring it to pass. Within a few months, the mayor wrote again to Sir William, thanking him profusely for his great pains for the corporation. The case must have been moving slowly, however; by May the desired grant had not been obtained. Heyrick continued to work for it, and the corporation wrote him again to thank him for his pains in the business and to ask him to introduce Mr. Wadland, the town attorney, to "Mr. Chancellor [of the duchy of Lancaster], Sir Daniel Day, or any other Burgess, or others that may do him good in his suit for the incorporating of the Hospital." The corporation (including Heyrick's older brother Robert) continued to assure him of their duty to him, hoping to keep his love, "for we shall have none that will offer no such kindness as you do."[21]

During the summer, Sir William continued to work on the town's behalf, introducing solicitors from the town to important officials who had the hearing of the suit. As the matter seemed to be coming to a critical juncture, the townsmen expanded their field of patrons. They wrote to the earl of Huntingdon to inform him of what they had accomplished in the suit thus far, and obtained his support for it. They also got Sir George Hastings, the brother of the earl, to act as mediator to the attorney general for the town. All the while, they continued to solicit Sir William, asking him to be on the lookout for people who were likely to attempt to influence the king against Leicester's cause. This he obviously did, as two weeks later the townsmen wrote him again, thanking him for "your great pains, travail, and good endeavors to many persons and in several places on the behalf of our poor Town." They heartily desired the continuance of his favors, "for upon yourself we and our whole corporation are bound wholly to rely, without which we know not what might befall us." When the king and his entourage came to Leicester on progress a week later, the townsmen requested Sir William's presence there so that the case for the hospital might be made directly to King James. The suit, with Sir William's great assistance, finally resulted in a patent under the Great Seal in March 1615. The whole process took sixteen months. Leicester's corporators never forgot the services of Sir William Heyrick, which in many ways went above and beyond the call of duty for one of his status. This favorite son of Leicester continued to receive gifts, banquets, good wishes, and even celebratory poetry from his place of birth. The town persisted in seeking his aid even after he had effectively retired from active life in London to his newly purchased estate of Beaumanor in Leicestershire.[22]

This example of Leicester's dealings with Sir William Heyrick indicates the complexity of elements involved in obtaining patronage and putting it to work at Court. Clearly patronage had both social and material aspects, which seem to have been all part of a seamless garment to the participants. Patterns of language formed an important part of the transaction, as almost ritualized forms of asking for favor and returning thanks appear again and again in the records.[23] If clients did not request favors properly, patrons were less likely to grant them. Ungratefulness was the great sin of the client. Gift-giving, entertainment, and other shows of connection and fidelity also played a crucial role in the transaction.[24] Gifts implied obligation. Yet gifts, while a necessary part of patronage, were not considered a corrupt quid pro quo. Townspeople clearly had scruples about what constituted appropriate gift-giving. In December 1633, the Exeter Assembly agreed to send a gift of £20 in plate to Lord Keeper Coventry, "in respect of his great favor and regard to this city." A month later, the Assembly Book records that presentation of the gift "hath been forborne to be done hitherto in regard of a cause of the city's . . . is in the beginning of the next term to be heard before his Lordship." They agreed to bestow the plate "after that cause shall be heard."[25] Townsmen believed in the giving of gifts, but they distinguished between legitimate and illegitimate uses of material favors in patronage relations.

Nevertheless, relying on patronage meant spending money and time. Not only did corporations pay out relatively large sums for gifts and entertainments to present and potential patrons, but they also had to deal with the army of doorkeepers, serving-men, secretaries, and clerks who actually did the work for the great men who made the decisions. Townsmen soliciting a favor at Court had to be well aware of exactly who they must speak to and "gratify" in order to achieve their ends, a difficult task in the rather disorganized Tudor and Stuart Courts.[26] Townsmen also had to understand the internal politics of the Court, knowing when and where and to whom to bring a solicitation. When some Exeter men asked the burgesses to Parliament from the city to present a petition to the king on their behalf, the two MPs discouraged it, "knowing this to be no time fit for such complaints when corporations are noted out by great men in public speeches with disgrace."[27] Without a strong patron to work on behalf of the town at the highest levels, a knowledge of the ins and outs of the central government—who to meet, who to "gratify" for favor—and the funds to be able to make gifts to patrons and pay fees for underlings, success in petitioning for favor could be hard to achieve.

While according to late twentieth-century standards these connections might be viewed as corrupt, they proved highly serviceable to contemporaries.[28] Patronage relations allowed for the maintenance of social conventions, as deference, obligation, hospitality, and other aspects of "good lordship" continued, while also providing a way for provincial people to interact with the center and to navigate the complexities of early modern government. Corporators appreciated the vitality of these connections, taking the initiative to acquire and maintain elite interest. They well understood the workings of central institutions and made full use of the channels of patronage that existed. Not simply manipulated by a system that favored powerful insiders, townsmen exploited it to their advantage. By working with judges and lord lieutenants, and especially by making good use of the civic office of high stewardship, townsmen found ways to obtain needed services from the center. Corporations looked to the crown as the ultimate fountain of bounty. Through patronage connections townsmen could tap into that fountain's flow. Although not a flawless and smooth-running system, patronage was a crucial process that bound together the state in both its central and local aspects.

II

One of the best ways of tracking the workings of patronage in the interactions between corporations and the crown in a systematic fashion is by looking at the business of procuring charters of incorporation. Corporations and the crown took charters very seriously, which is a boon to the historian. The complicated process of changing the corporate constitution left a paper trail both in the locality and in central archives. A charter constituted the instrument of government in a borough, guaranteeing the town's political and economic privileges.[29] In it, the monarch gave existence to the fictive individual called the corporation. Its importance gave the charter an almost sacred quality in the minds of most citizens. Because new privileges could only be obtained from the crown, a corporation needed access at Court as well as convincing arguments to obtain them. In these circumstances, town leaders sought out patrons, old or new, who could provide the necessary connection. Charters provide important keys to understanding urban patronage in early modern England.

For both boroughs and the crown, the process of incorporation and the language of charters themselves made important statements about the relationship between center and locality. A charter meant that a borough's government owed direct responsibility to the monarch. Incorporation brought a measure of self-determination to urban communities and provided security in various forms. First, it protected the economic privileges of a borough, built up through custom over the years—freedom from tolls, the right to hold fairs and markets, and the like. A charter also transformed a group of civic leaders into a legal individual, a body that could own, buy, and sell land. This corporate person could also sue and be sued, just like an individual, and could be held accountable for its actions. Unlike a real person, though, a corporation enjoyed legal immortality, and its institutions and liberties existed in perpetuity. Only the monarch could end the life of a corporation, by calling in its charter. Charters also conferred political and administrative privileges, constituting a body of men to govern over the populace, allowing for local elections, giving them the right to make by-laws, and giving directions for the replacement of deceased members. In most cases this governing body was closed, with vacancies filled by co-optation rather than election.[30] While these charters gave corporations greater autonomy and self-governance, at the same time they integrated towns more fully into the English state. Typically, only a narrow group of men served in borough government, making them more easily regulated by the center. According to some urban historians, this trend toward oligarchy became stronger over the sixteenth and seventeenth centuries.[31] Both the crown and the local elite viewed this as the best way to control the potentially unruly urban populace, open elections being deemed conducive to instability.[32]

In addition to securing the commonwealth from the potential dangers of urban unrest, charters also protected urban government from incursions by other authorities. For instance, the inhabitants of corporate towns could not be forced to serve on county juries, while county JPs had no legal jurisdiction within corporate boundaries. Most charters included a clause establishing or maintaining borough courts, especially a court of record, and named certain members of the corporation (usually the mayor, recorder, and some senior aldermen, although occasionally other gentlemen as well) to be JPs for the borough. These measures effectively made towns responsible for themselves and established by law a corporation's right to exclude external jurisdictions. But in fact borough leaders did not isolate themselves from interaction with the rest of the political nation. Abingdon's charter named William Lord Knollys, Sir John Parry, and Sir David Williams as JPs. Wokingham's charter made the high steward a justice, along with the mayor and recorder. Evesham's 1605 charter named Sir Thomas Challenor, Sir David Fowles, Sir William Fleetwood, and Adam Newton, esq., as JPs in addition to various corporate officers.[33] The same charter that gave Tewkesbury's corporation control over the town's manor, adjuring county JPs not to "intermeddle" in intramural affairs, also established in law the corporation's right to select a high steward (an office used by custom in the town since the earl of Leicester procured Tewkesbury's incorporation in 1574) and gave the corporation the power to elect "strangers" as burgesses.[34] Such strangers were often not artisans and merchants but rather gentlemen who might do some favor for the town in the future. Other corporations, including Maidstone, also had this clause added to their charters in this period.[35] Charters, in fact, show a new level of interpenetration between provincial boroughs and the rest of early modern government.

This integration arose in response to the developing state in the Tudor and early Stuart periods. Formal incorporation by royal charter only came into its own in the sixteenth century. Before the fifteenth century, boroughs received charters from their manorial lords, giving them particular privileges and franchises, for instance to hold a fair. Gradually borough leaders set up courts, institutions of self-government, and methods of administration and enforcement that allowed them to carry on borough business without, or sometimes in spite of, the lord's active interest.[36] By the sixteenth century, and especially after 1540, town leaders increasingly turned to the central government for grants of incorporation, giving boroughs self-government and making the mayor or bailiff an officer of the crown rather than a servant of the lord. This "urban policy" went hand-in-hand with the Tudors' desire to make local authorities responsible to the crown alone. Attempts at incorporation sometimes failed, and the crown did not always follow a consistent policy toward towns, but increasing numbers of boroughs applied for charters in order to guarantee rights and liberties from the monarch.[37]

While such charters gave townsmen a degree of autonomy with respect to their former lords, to interpret this as independence and incipient democracy, as the nineteenth-century Whig historians might, would be mistaken.[38] The very act of procuring a charter required civic leaders to cultivate ties with the landed gentry and nobility. These ties were now ones of patronage rather than lordship. Corporations maneuvered to gain the trust and aid of the powerful men in the realm who could accomplish local business at Court.[39] Town leaders had to make sure both that no local lord was implacably set against the incorporation and that the town had at least one important ally at Court who favored it. The absence of the latter and the presence of the former could spell disaster for a borough aiming at incorporation. Towns like Doncaster and Leicester, and even the important city of Salisbury, lost bids to gain new privileges under exactly those circumstances.[40] Obtaining a charter did not remove boroughs from connection with the landed elite, but rather forced corporators to engage with them in new ways. Through these connections to patrons and brokers, corporators endeavored to navigate the labyrinthine halls of central government.

Charters usually required an extended round of petitioning and negotiation at Court, so civic magistrates had to be prepared both administratively and financially to meet the challenge. As a first step, borough leaders sent a petition to the monarch requesting a new charter (or confirmation of a previous one) and justifying their reasons for it.[41] But simply sending a petition to the crown could be like sending it out into a void. A petition needed advocates who would personally bring it to the attention of the decision-makers at Court. Corporations invariably sent one or more of their own members to act as solicitors of the business on the borough's behalf. Whom they chose varied from place to place, but often a town's recorder, the chief legal officer, undertook the job. In some corporations, particularly where the recorder did not reside in the town and had less detailed knowledge of the borough, an alderman or even the mayor would act as agent. The corporation of Liverpool, when attempting to procure a charter in 1617, sent the mayor, Edward More, to London for the purpose; Leicester did the same in 1605, sending Mayor Thomas Chettell. Sometimes towns also delegated local lawyers who were in London on business anyway. These men, experienced in working with the central courts, knew how to make the necessary connections and follow the appropriate forms. Exeter employed two aldermen to solicit a charter renewal in 1614, while sending an Exeter attorney to work on the city's behalf in 1622.[42] No matter who went to London to see the business through, they required knowledge of local circumstances, some understanding of the ins and outs of petitioning at Court (often learned on the job), and, importantly, persistence if they wanted to succeed.

Second, the townsmen had to raise money in order to pay for the solicitation and the charter itself. Procuring a charter could be extremely expensive, requiring fees and tips to clerks and scribes, gifts to patrons and their servants, and usually wages to reimburse the solicitor for his time and expenses while staying in London. Coventry spent £180 2s. 6d. to procure a charter in the 1630s; between 1631 and 1634, Ipswich spent over £250 defending the civic charter against a quo warranto and obtaining a new grant.[43] Corporations sometimes had to do some creative fundraising to be able to afford these large expenditures. Lincoln mortgaged several borough properties and took deductions from the mayor's annual allowance for a venison feast to raise the £250 required to obtain their charter in the late 1620's. To pay for its attempt at a charter in 1618, Liverpool levied a tax on its inhabitants and also on 73 nonresident freemen, including the earl of Derby, Sir Richard Molyneux, and other knights and gentlemen.[44] Liverpool's example shows that a corporation's solicitation of elite interest in the borough could pay off handsomely.

The third element necessary in making preparations was gaining the assistance of particular men in authority to back the borough's petition. These provided local leaders with the thing they needed most—access. Unless a petition came before the right people and moved through the system under someone's watchful eye, it would most likely fall through the cracks and fail. Corporators engaged in doing business at Court, writing back to their fellows at home, provide some insight into the hazards of their task. A "remembrance for myself" taken by Thomas Chettell of Leicester, sojourning in London to obtain a new charter for the town in 1605, indicates the complexity of his business. He lists about 30 things to do and people to see to accomplish his business, including:

+ remember my lady Arbella
+ remember my lady Fortescue
+ remember the King's hand to the book charge
+ remember the Privy Seal to pass charge
+ remember the Privy Signet to pass charge, of both of these 9s. 10d.
+ remember the Great Seal by God's grace to be done

+remember to acquaint my lord of Huntingdon to crave his honor's favor if
we have just cause
+remember to see Sir Thomas Hesketh, Attorney of the Court of Wards to
crave his favor if we have cause
+remember the two noblemen of Scotland, the Constable and the Treasurer
if we have need of them[45]

This is only a portion of Chettell's list, but it conveys the difficulties that
he faced in securing his ends in London. Chettell failed in his purpose that
year, and the town received a new grant only in 1609. By the time the
charter finally received its seal in April of that year, the chamberlains of
Leicester had paid out over £300 in the attempt. Much of the money went
simply for Chettell's living expenses, as he often had to stay in London for
long stretches to make sure that a petition moved forward through the
correct channels.[46] Solicitors for Coventry, Exeter, and Great Yarmouth
told similar tales.[47] Familiarity with the procedures at Court and diligence
in following the business could go a long way to achieving success.

But knowledge and persistence alone were not enough to gain access.
Personal connection opened doors. Borough solicitors needed the amplifi-
cation of great men in order to make their voices heard. Not only could a
patron offer townsmen access at Court, but his association with a request
for favor also reassured the crown of the legitimacy of the petition. In
launching a bid to renew their charter in 1614, the mayor and Assembly of
Exeter wrote to Lord Ellesmere, the lord chancellor who gave final
authorization for all charters, as well as to the earl of Northampton, the
city's high steward. To Ellesmere, they emphasized that a new charter
would lead to the good government of the city, and they pointed out his
favor to them in the past:

> May it please you to be informed (to further the good government of this his
> Majesty's city of Exeter and to reform some defects which are hindrances
> thereto) we are now determined to be humble suitors to his Highness [for a
> confirmation and expansion of the charter]. We humbly pray your honor, in
> regard of the great love you have still borne to the welfare and prosperity of
> this little city, to afford your countenance and ready help, for which we will
> remain truly and heartily thankful, and will account your lordship one of the
> strong pillars of our support.[48]

To their high steward, the men of Exeter took a similar but slightly different tack. While they stressed the need for a new charter in order to
strengthen and improve government, they also commended the city's solicitors directly to the earl of Northampton's attention:

Our often necessities do occasion us to be often times troublesome unto you, yet we shall never be willing to engage your Lordship in any business which shall either want reason or require too much pain. . . . [The business] we have commended to the care and diligence of Mr. John Prowse and Mr. Thomas Martyn, our two Burgesses, to whose labors (we humbly do entreat your honor) to vouchsafe favor and help. And as we [tear] covet to be protected by your love, so shall we still endeavor to perform our best services to your Lordship.[49]

Exeter's magistrates knew that their potential for success lay in the hands of men like Ellesmere and Northampton. They called on the patronage relations they had already established with these men to steer them through the hazardous waters of government bureaucracy.

As with urban patronage relations in general, the patrons that townsmen chose to aid them in their pursuit of charters varied with local circumstances. Those boroughs with long-term ties to a local magnate would likely solicit his services in these all-important negotiations, as occurred in Leicester in the late sixteenth century. A cathedral town with good relations with its bishop might call on him for assistance, while a coastal town would approach the lord admiral or another maritime official. For other towns, a regional choice made sense: West Country towns looked to the earls of Pembroke and Bedford for patronage, while some boroughs in the northwest relied on the earls of Derby. Cinque Ports boroughs needed the assistance of the lord warden to carry out successful charter negotiations. The high stewardship also had clear links to the process of chartering.[50]

Townsmen curried favor predominantly among the powerful, but they solicited the favor of anyone who might be able to provide inside information, hurry along some paperwork, or slip a petition to an important courtier. The city fathers of Exeter realized the truth of this in 1622. During a difficult period when their high steward had fallen from the king's grace, the city's attorney cultivated the friendship of Mr. Benbow, a clerk of the crown, which gave Exeter a useful access point at Court.[51] Clerks and doorkeepers, as well as privy councilors and high Court officers, all received the attentions of urban solicitors. But while local authorities tested all routes of access, they increasingly found it necessary to cultivate the favor of one powerful man, usually centered at Court, to act as patron for the locality. According to Linda Peck, the early Stuart Court saw a decrease in the channels of access to the crown as favored courtiers, most notably the duke of Buckingham, attempted to set themselves up as exclusive brokers of the king's bounty.[52] Urban leaders (with the possible exception of the lord mayor of London) ranked far down the scale of social importance in this hierarchical world, and hence found this trend even more difficult.[53] As suggested above in Chapter 1, towns began to single out the great officers of state, men with the most influence at Court, who seemed most able to help in these matters.

Evidence for the critical role of patronage in obtaining charters can often be found in the documents themselves. In some charters during this period, the wording explicitly declares a particular patron's role in the process. King James granted Evesham's 1605 charter "at the humble petition and request of our most dear and well-beloved first-born son, the Lord Prince Henry, being the first petition which he hath made to us in our kingdom of England." The charter also named the prince's governor, Sir Thomas Challenor, as first high steward. Dr. Lewis Baylie, the prince's chaplain, served as vicar of All Saints, Evesham, from 1600–1611. He seems to have used his influence with his master on behalf of the town.[54] Similarly, William Lord Knollys, along with Sir John Parry (chancellor of the duchy of Lancaster) and Sir David Williams (a judge of Common Pleas), solicited the king for Abingdon's charter in 1609. The role of all three as patrons of the charter is explicitly stated in the document. Northampton's charter of 1618 states that it was granted "at the instance of our beloved and faithful servant Sir Henry Yelverton, knight, the Attorney General and Recorder of the town," while Cambridge's 1605 charter was granted at the "humble petition" of Thomas Lord Ellesmere and Sir John Fortescue, the town's high steward and recorder. Sir John Savile, later created Baron Savile by Charles I, solicited Leeds's charter of incorporation in 1626 and was named first alderman of the borough in the charter as well. Salisbury's 1630 charter was granted "at the request" of Philip earl of Pembroke, and Derby's 1638 charter "at the instance and request" of Sir John Coke.[55] Not every charter of the period named the patron or patrons who solicited it, but those that do show both the importance of patrons to the process and the range of men who served in that role.

In the absence of sponsors' names in a charter, local records often reveal the sometimes ephemeral evidence of patronage. Letters written, gifts presented, and entertainments made to local magnates and courtiers provide hints at links between corporations and patrons. For many towns, the link had been formalized through the office of the high steward. Townsmen usually turned to that officer first when in pursuit of a charter. Although a high steward might provide a variety of other services, he functioned most importantly as a liaison between the center and the town at those times when the corporation needed access. The earl of Exeter performed this service for Stamford in procuring that town's charter in 1604.

When the port town of Great Yarmouth petitioned King James for its incorporation in 1608, it specifically requested that the petition be referred to the consideration of the earls of Nottingham, Suffolk, Northampton, and Salisbury. All were extremely powerful men, but Nottingham served both as lord admiral of England and as high steward of Yarmouth. The four earls recommended passage and the town received extended liberties, including special admiralty privileges and formal incorporation from the crown. Similarly, the earl of Pembroke, despite being troubled with "the stone," forwarded the city of Salisbury's petitions for a charter confirmation in 1631.[56] The Council of Oxford actually agreed that no charter of theirs should go through to the Great Seal until it had been read before the corporation and "further allowed of by the right honorable Lord Wallingford, our Steward."[57] For many towns, the high steward stood as the doorkeeper to the crown, through which they found access to the monarch.

Through the late sixteenth and early seventeenth centuries, the participation of high stewards in charter procurement became increasingly standard. Not only did towns use incumbent stewards to aid them in their pursuits, but sometimes awarded a newfound patron with the office of high steward as a response to the nobleman's aid to the town in obtaining a charter. Tewkesbury offered the high stewardship of the borough to Robert earl of Leicester in 1574, after he obtained for them their first charter of incorporation from Queen Elizabeth. The earl of Essex, lord lieutenant of Staffordshire, became high steward of Newcastle-under-Lyme when he procured that town's charter in 1590. Essex also obtained a charter of incorporation for Tamworth, whose new corporators chose him as their high steward as well. When Sir John Savage, longtime friend and patron of Macclesfield, helped the borough obtain incorporation in 1595, the charter named him as high steward, an office newly established by the document itself.[58] In fact, this pattern of making a patron high steward upon receipt of a charter became quite common, as crown and community acknowledged a patron's assistance by naming him as an office-holder in the charter. The appearance of this relatively new office in these vital documents provides a measure of its growing importance to corporations.[59]

Some corporations, however, had no high steward, while others found their stewards ineffective. In these circumstances, townsmen often tried to spread a wider net for patronage, looking for aid wherever they could find it. The city of Exeter had experienced difficulties with its high steward, Thomas earl of Suffolk, in the mid-1620's, which inclined the corporation against relying exclusively on that officer for patronage.[60] When needs arose, they appealed to various men with connections to the center. In attempting to renew their charter in 1627, the men of Exeter sent a £20 gift to Lord Keeper Coventry for his "many honorable favors." They also agreed to give a piece of plate worth 20 marks or £15 to the earl of Dorset to "secure his Honor's favor in the city's business" and to write to him expressing Exeter's "particular occasions." Dorset had no particular connection with Exeter, but he held an important position at Court and corporators obviously perceived him as friendly to the city.[61] The earl of Pembroke held the office of high steward at this time, and although there is no direct evidence of it, the city's attorneys almost certainly approached him for his favor. In any event, the city received a new charter from King Charles in 1627.[62]

Having the attention and support of powerful friends made the painstaking process of obtaining a charter work. It was particularly important when not all townsmen agreed to a charter's contents. Great Yarmouth's divisive charter problems have already been discussed. Coventry experienced difficulties, as well, when confronted in 1611 by a "domestic adversary" who thwarted the corporation's attempts to renew their charter. The enemy made "certain advertisements and informations (or rather scandals) . . . to Sir John Harrington and the Prince's Council," through whose mediation the corporators had hoped to obtain the charter. The civic attorney in London who discovered the scandal recommended that it was "high time to unbutton the bosom of the city to search if it were a Serpent that so hissed in your ears, who since put forth his foreprovided sting." To "avoid the venom," the attorney thought it best for himself and the other solicitors of the business to make a personal appearance before Lord Harrington, Sir John Harrington, and the Prince's Council to satisfy them concerning the corporation's behavior.[63] Only by maintaining the goodwill of these powerful men could the corporators expect to achieve a positive result.

Conflict over the makeup of the corporation itself could also make effective patronage a critical factor in procuring charters. This situation can be seen clearly in Totnes late in the reign of Elizabeth. Faction badly fractured the town in the 1590's and into the first years of the new century. A group of the more prominent men in the town, mostly merchants, strove to obtain a charter that concentrated power in their own hands while excluding some of those previously eligible to participate in civic government. Freemen threatened with exclusion fought against the trend, but did not have the leverage to maintain their position. In 1595–96, the "oligarchic" faction prevailed on their connections to the center and secretly obtained a new charter that closed and narrowed the corporation. The merchants relied heavily on the brokering services of Sir George Carey, the recorder of the borough and a client of the earl of Essex. In 1600, the burgesses succeeded in persuading the crown to question the validity of the 1596 charter and quo warranto proceedings began in King's Bench. The oligarchs' charter survived the scrutiny intact, however, and it remained the town's ruling charter throughout the early seventeenth century.[64] No direct evidence of the architect of the charter's survival remains, but circumstantial evidence points to Sir Robert Cecil, named high steward by the Totnes corporation while the quo warranto suit progressed.[65] The crown maintained a general pattern of supporting closed, narrow corporations in boroughs. The merchants of Totnes, well aware of this trend, had the support to secure their authority.[66] They also knew how to exploit connections to the most powerful men at Court, like Cecil, to gain their own ends.

Unhappiness with corporate privileges often came not from within the borough, but from outside it. While corporators found patrons at Court to solicit privileges from the crown, they often also had to rely on patrons to ward off the opposition of neighboring gentry or noblemen who claimed rights in the borough. Leicester ran into difficulties with the powerful Cavendish family when trying to renew the civic charter in 1629–30. Despite spending £144 4s. on the attempt, the townsmen could not garner the support to gain their ends.[67] Poole also struggled in obtaining a charter slightly before our period, in 1568, when the lord of the manor, Lord Mountjoy, opposed the process. The townsmen received the aid of Dr. Walter Haddon, a prominent divine and a client of Lord Burghley. Haddon spoke directly with Queen Elizabeth to ask her to agree to the incorporation. After "much argument" she finally did, but said she did so "only because they had long been suitors and to save my [Haddon's] reputation, as she termed it, for that I had given them hope." But even with the queen's permission, Haddon still faced the opposition of Lord Mountjoy, who "stirreth in this matter by indirect means." Haddon, acting as broker, used his personal connections to get beyond Mountjoy. He wrote to his own patron, Lord Burghley, who had the authority to make sure that the incorporation went through. Ultimately, with Burghley's backing, Dr. Haddon and the town of Poole procured Lord Mountjoy's approbation and the charter received the Great Seal. Haddon's troubles in the matter made him wary about getting involved in such a situation again, however. He wrote to Lord Burghley, "As I promised the Queen's Highness, so I will promise you, it shall be the last incorporation that ever I will deal withall except I be specially commanded."[68] The corporators of Poole succeeded in the end, but their bid almost failed because their opponent nearly matched the strength of their "friend." Only the aid of Lord Burghley brought the incorporation to fruition.

The antipathy of a powerful figure could lead to great difficulties for townsmen, who then had to find another person willing or able to overcome that opposition. The city of Salisbury, from the 1580's through the 1610's, carried out a more or less constant search for "friends" who might procure a charter of incorporation. Salisbury received its early charters from the bishops of Salisbury. By the sixteenth century, however, this arrangement had begun to chafe the civic leaders of this prosperous city. They made repeated attempts to gain greater self-government, agreeing in the Assembly that their city should be made a county, with all the jurisdictional privileges endowed by that status. Their desire became even more urgent in the summer of 1590, when the townsmen accused Bishop Coldwell of attempting to seize the subsidy collections and other "indirect dealings." The Assembly commissioned the mayor and others to go to London to complain about the bishop and to seek incorporation from the queen.[69] In November, townsmen chose Sir Francis Walsingham as high steward of the city; in December the Assembly moved to offer Sir John Popham, the queen's attorney general, an annuity of £3 6s. 8d. for his good favor.[70] Unfortunately for the city, these attempts fell short, as did others over the next twenty years.[71] Finally, in 1610–11, the civic leaders made another serious try at incorporation by the crown. First and foremost, they obtained the acquiescence of their bishop, William Cotton, who wrote to Lord Chancellor Ellesmere on their behalf. They also had the backing of the earl of Pembroke, their new high steward.[72] But the men of Salisbury would not allow any opportunity for patronage to go to waste, as they worked on gaining the friendship of dignitaries who passed through town.

The most interesting and well-documented case of this appears in the entertainment the city provided for the prince of Brunswick, nephew of James I's wife Queen Anne, when he visited the city in May 1610. The Assembly greeted him in full civic regalia, accompanying him to his lodgings at the Antelope Inn, while the church bells of the city pealed in his honor. They attended him to divine service at the cathedral and showed him the Council House at his request. He in turn asked the mayor and aldermen to dine with him at the Antelope, at which banquet the townsmen gave him a purse with "ten pounds in good gold, which he also gratefully received, letting us to know that he hoped to see us more oftener." At this juncture, the mayor acquainted the prince with their suit to the king for incorporation and new privileges, without which the city "will hereafter be utterly decayed and overthrown in all civil government." They concluded with a petition that the prince of Brunswick "would be so gracious unto us as to be our mediator unto his Majesty on that behalf." In response, the prince "did promise that he would be mindful of our request; and also do us what good he could with this, that we had obliged him thereunto by acceptance of our gift, and that he would move his Majesty for us effectually." For insurance, the townsmen also extracted a promise from Mr. Amsterdary, the prince's interpreter as well as a gentleman of the bedchamber, that he would "assuredly call upon the prince and put him in mind of our request." They then gave Mr. Amsterdary "20 shillings in gold, to bind him the better to remember his promise."[73] With aid from various quarters and also the favor of Bishop Cotton, the city of Salisbury received its formal incorporation from King James in 1612.[74]

For Salisbury, the attempt to obtain incorporation and the consequent solicitation of noble patronage energized the townsmen. City leaders had a solitary goal on which to focus and had to bring the bishop into harmony with the city in order for the plan to succeed. The members of the corporation knew exactly how to manipulate the system in their favor, especially regarding the prince of Brunswick. They entertained him with a lavish civic ceremony, demonstrating the honor and gravity of both the corporation and their cause. The townsmen also orchestrated a display of regard that, according to the rules of patronage, required some reciprocation. The prince himself admitted that by his acceptance of their gift, he counted himself obliged to do what favor he could for Salisbury. This was not the sort of ongoing relationship that some towns cultivated with their patrons, but it demonstrates nicely the way civic government could bring the honor of the corporation and the symbols of obligation to bear when courting a patron.

This example from Salisbury also suggests that the traditional symbolic aspects of lordship remained important in this very political context. In soliciting charters, corporations looked to obtain or confirm their core privileges—even their very existence—from the pinnacle of authority, the crown. They did so by gaining the backing of the men at the centers of power. Yet the interaction between those seeking aid and those in power was far from being coldly political. Such relationships, even those formed to gain this very specific end, required the symbolism and ceremony of patronage. Gift-giving and hospitality could play crucial roles in the process. The inhabitants of Tewkesbury presented the earl of Leicester with a silver cup worth £16, as well as an ox, when he assisted them in becoming incorporated in 1574.[75] The borough of Nottingham made a present to the earl of Shrewsbury of "a veal, a mutton, a lamb, a dozen of chickens, 2 dozen of rabbits, 2 dozen of pigeons, four capons, wine and sugar" in early 1605, which circumstantial evidence suggests was a gesture in response for the aid he gave the borough in gaining a new charter. The corporators also named him high steward in January 1606.[76] When seeking a new charter in the late 1620's, the wealthy men of Bristol made quite lavish gifts to the powerful men who helped them. The high steward, the earl of Pembroke, benefited most from this largesse, receiving large amounts of wine, a chest of dry "succades," half a hundred-weight of loaf sugar, a similar weight of oranges and lemons, two boxes of marmalade, two boxes of prunes, a jar of olives, four rundlets of sack, and two barrels of claret in 1627. Bristol further honored him by having his portrait painted for the city. Lord Chief Baron Hyde, the city's recorder, received a Persian carpet and a large gift of food and wine as well.[77] Although the importance of charters to civic government made the stakes particularly high, townsmen seem to have viewed the patronage relations involved in charter procurement not much differently than they did connections for other purposes. No matter what ends were sought, by either urban patron or corporate client, the relationship involved traditional, ceremonial elements as well as the more political or pragmatic.

While this combination of pragmatism and symbolism involved in patronage characterized the chartering process throughout the period under consideration, it did not remain stagnant. Over time, corporations tended to focus on pragmatic ends, seeking out patronage from those men most clearly linked to central government, sometimes to the disadvantage of traditional, more locally based patrons. The townsmen of Barnstaple, in the midst of a dispute with their recorder the earl of Bath, applied for a renewal of their charter. They were at loggerheads with their neighbor the earl because of the construction of the so-called "New Work," a series of houses and warehouses along the harbor to which Bath objected. Attempting to procure a large favor from the crown at a time of serious discord with a patron might seem foolish on the part of the corporators. But the men of Barnstaple had an ace in the hole. John Delbridge, one of the most prominent men in the town, was also a client of the earl of Salisbury, who on several occasions acted on behalf of the townsmen.[78] In addition, the town could rely on the counsel of John Dodderidge, the king's solicitor, a native son who remained attached to Barnstaple throughout his life.[79] With Salisbury and Dodderidge willing to speak on the town's behalf, the corporators evidently felt the support of the earl of Bath unnecessary for the passage of the charter. Indeed, the evidence strongly suggests that once the new charter obtained its seal, the townsmen planned to drop Bath as their recorder, an office he had held since the 1580's. On 24 January 1611, King James sternly warned the corporation that they must choose the earl once again. Bath's services to Barnstaple in the past had been both useful to the good government of the town and "an honor to you that a man of such rank should have [the office]." He ended by stating that "we do therefore require you, that you do elect him to be your Recorder . . . which we do not doubt shall be much for the quiet of the town. So if you shall neglect to do it, we shall think our favors lately done to you ill-bestowed."[80] Later in that same year, a slightly amended charter passed the Great Seal, explicitly including the office of recorder in the document and naming the earl of Bath as the holder of the office.[81] The men of Barnstaple thus observed the forms of behavior toward their traditional lord by giving him gifts and banquets and maintaining him in the honor of his civic office. But townsmen understood that those closest to the king held the real power, and it was to them that corporations increasingly appealed.

It also seems that the crown became increasingly interested in corporate charters, who was involved in them, and what they contained. Charters fairly commonly included names of prominent men as high stewards or recorders and often suggested the role of the patron in procuring the charter. Colchester's 1635 charter includes "our dearly beloved cousin and counselor Henry earl of Holland" as the "first and new High Steward."[82] Holland had been recorder before the stewardship became part of the borough constitution, so his link to the locality is clear. Nevertheless, the strong personal identification with the king seems new, or at least intensified, under King Charles. Charles also appeared willing to change a corporation's charter in order to gain his own ends. He asked the corporation of Doncaster to choose his cousin, Viscount Ayr, for the place of high steward of the borough. When the townsmen dragged their feet, Charles wrote to them more sternly, describing his dissatisfaction with their behavior. He declared that if they made scruple that their charter contained no high stewardship, he would take that as no answer, "because we are able both to supply that defect and dispense with any error formerly committed in that kind."[83] He would alter the charter for the circumstances. Caroline government also seems to have become more active in pursuing quo warranto proceedings that questioned the chartered rights of boroughs, especially after 1628–29.[84] Charles's more activist stance vis-à-vis the localities manifested itself clearly in the way charters were obtained and protected.

This is not to suggest that Charles was engaged in "creeping absolutism" or that the crown had a well-considered policy for reining in corporations and their charters. While certain instances of the crown purposely taking aim at a borough's charter can be identified, these cases are rare and often were accompanied by local initiative. The quo warranto brought against Great Yarmouth, for instance, was in part a sign of the king's anger against the townsmen's supposed religious irregularities and disturbed government. But the suit was triggered in the first place by Yarmouth alderman Benjamin Cooper, who wanted to gain greater authority in the corporation by being made mayor.[85] The crown seemed to be reacting, on a case-by-case basis, to the problems and pains produced in the growth of the English state. Similarly, the local men who increasingly involved themselves with the center and who used the good offices of patrons to do so were not engaged in incipient nationalism or following an ideologically charged pattern. Indeed, ideology seems to have had little to do with charter procurement. Borough leaders solicited aid from anyone who could help them attain their goals. Intensely practical, townsmen clearly came to see that the personnel and the structures of crown government offered them the best means of obtaining their local ends. They did not always have identical interests with either central government or their mediaries, and strife arose at times. Nevertheless, townsmen bound themselves more closely to the crown, even as royal government worked to bring the localities more firmly within its grasp.

While urban communities may have been moving away from some of the traditional forms of lordship, they clearly did not reject it outright, but found new ways to interact. The substance of charters as well as the process required to obtain one provide solid evidence of the workings of patronage in early modern government. Obtaining a charter required townsmen to work with members of the elite, both locally and at the center, displaying the high level of integration that existed between provincial governors and the crown. Every step of the process required townsmen to interact with people outside the confines of the borough. Attempts to obtain, confirm, or expand privileges reinforced corporate authority, but also bound boroughs more closely into the state.

III

In petitioning for charters and other favors, towns attempted to obtain goods and services from the crown. They formed relationships with those men who could make local voices heard in London. But much of the interaction between center and localities that occurred in early modern England consisted of the central government asking for goods and services from the provinces—purveyance, military service, taxation, and other financial exactions.[86] While local people accepted their duty to serve the crown in these ways, they did not always agree on the level of taxation or the type of service being required. For corporations, these issues held a further concern, that of their chartered liberties. Incorporated boroughs usually had their own militias and were to be taxed separately from the counties. Townsmen kept up a nearly perpetual battle to keep their rates as low as possible and to maintain the privileges of the borough. They did this by calling on the services of patrons, just as they did to obtain other sorts of grants.

The men responsible for enforcing military and monetary duties in the provinces received their appointments from the monarch. Lord lieutenants controlled military services, while the crown appointed commissioners to assess and collect particular levies, such as subsidies and loans.[87] These men with royal commissions were often the very same men who served more informally as patrons to local people for other concerns. Townsmen made use of them in their official capacities as well as in their unofficial capacities as patrons. The patterns of gift-giving and entertainment worked similarly, and the expectation of reciprocation existed as well. Corporations appealed to lord lieutenants and commissioners to convince the crown to reduce levies or to protect civic privileges. They also called on lord lieutenants like any other patron to help solve local problems that may have had nothing to do with military service. Because of who they were, these powerful men could not help but receive the attentions of local people on all sorts of issues. The one thing they most assuredly received was a near-constant stream of requests to protect local liberties and to reduce the exactions of the crown. However, the nature of these issues could bring the desires of the localities head to head with those of the crown, making mediation by patrons more difficult. Especially with the strongly enforced and increasingly unpopular levies ordered by King Charles in the 1620's and 1630's, corporations became less able to rely on patrons to procure them favors from the crown in matters of taxation and the militia.

The subject of the militia often touched a raw nerve for corporate towns.[88] On one hand, the civic trained band and soldiers added to a town's prestige, an outward symbol of their chartered status. Townsmen wanted to control these companies themselves and used the training days as shows of corporate honor. On the other hand, townsmen disliked paying for the militia and perpetually tried to get away with paying as little as they possibly could. This contradiction can be seen in towns that voluntarily formed a special military outfit, but then had to be prodded to keep it going and pay its officers. Great Yarmouth's corporation asked the Privy Council to grant them an artillery company and artillery yard in 1626; by 1635 the band had fallen apart and the lord lieutenant of Norfolk had to ask the citizens to reinstitute it. Crown directives for "perfecting" the militia often met with small enthusiasm in the corporate boroughs.[89] These two issues, control and cost, loomed large in the interactions between corporate leaders and lord lieutenants, as townsmen used the practices of patronage to gain their ends.

Townsmen took pride in their local militia regiments. Mustering allowed them to show their loyalty to the crown and to participate in a certain amount of pomp and circumstance (and, if the reports are correct, drinking and carousing) more frequently associated with the gentry than with urban dwellers. To increase the excitement of the spectacle of the training, the corporation of Leicester purchased 156 yards of scarlet and white ribbon, at a cost of £2 1s., to deck out its trained band in 1620.[90] Beyond ceremonial value, the local militia company also signaled a town's status as separate from the jurisdiction of the county. One of the rights usually conferred by charter to a borough was that of training and exercising the militia company within the town walls, led by men chosen by town authorities. The question of officers usually caused few problems. Most corporations accepted the men that the lord lieutenant chose for them, and lieutenants often selected townsmen to help train the regiment, although sometimes in commission with others. The city of Exeter, as a county of itself, had deputy lieutenants of its own, distinct from those of Devon. When one of their DLs died or left town, the aldermen wrote to the lord lieutenant suggesting a few names, usually of fellow townsmen or gentlemen with close ties to the city. While the lord lieutenant had the final say, the corporation largely dictated the choice.[91] In Chester, Lord Strange, lord lieutenant in 1587, gave the corporation the choice of either Mr. Edwards, an alderman of the city, or Mr. Thomas Stapleton, Strange's servant and not a freeman, to train the city's soldiers. While the choice of Edwards would have made a statement about the city's privileges, the townsmen appeared more concerned about remaining in Lord Strange's good graces for the future. Wanting to be "dutiful in all things" to Lord Strange, the Assembly agreed that "for the honorable good favor of the said L. and in respect of his Ho: goodness to this incorporation; and for performance of such good will promised by him the said Thomas Stapleton . . . viz.: to be solicited for all city's causes and to procure his Ho: to show himself favorable to the city," they would give Stapleton the charge of the soldiers and make him a freeman as well.[92] This example shows clearly how the roles of crown military officer and local patron could be intertwined in the same person and the same events.

Unfortunately, within a few years the aldermen came to regret their choice of Stapleton, whom they disliked not simply as a "foreigner," but also for his behavior, he "rather seeming to rule the whole incorporation than to obey the same or any government thereof." The Assembly asked the earl of Derby to give the charge of the soldiers to the mayor and sheriffs of the city.[93] Desire to retain control of the militia in corporate hands appears almost universal, not only over the men doing the training but also over the venue. Corporations frequently faced the situation of having deputy lieutenants demand that they muster the civic regiment with the rest of the county's units, outside the boundaries of the town. This "trenched largely," as early modern townsmen would say, on their corporate privileges, and lord lieutenants received repeated requests from corporations not to make a trained band muster away from its native town or under the scrutiny of county officers rather than borough officers. The leaders of Salisbury raised this issue with the earl of Hertford, lord lieutenant of Wiltshire, complaining that his deputies encroached on civic privileges concerning musters. The earl repeatedly upheld the town's privileges against the demands of county officials, saying that the military service "shall be so performed as the present ability of the city may afford; neither shall any other direction proceed [*sic*] from me be any way prejudicial to the town but will be still ready to give any furtherance to help for the advancement or benefit thereof."[94] Similarly, the portmen of Ipswich more than once appealed to the earl of Suffolk, lord lieutenant of Suffolk, to defend the town's rights against the demands of the county DLs. When the portmen begged him in 1625 to prevent the town soldiers from having to train at Languard, they at the same time presented him with his annual fee as high steward of the town, thus reminding him of his role as patron of Ipswich, not simply as lord lieutenant.[95]

When the lord lieutenant and the townsmen agreed on how to proceed about the militia, the lieutenant could act as both commander and patron, defending the town's interests and maintaining its chartered liberties. Matters could prove more difficult when the lord lieutenant himself enforced orders that prejudiced a town's rights over its militia. In these cases, corporations might solicit the patronage of another lord who would redress their grievances. The men of Dartmouth, unhappy that one of the deputy lieutenants repeatedly tried to force the town militia to muster outside the civic liberties, wrote to the earl of Northampton to complain. The earl of Bath held the lord lieutenancy of Devon, but he had defended the actions taken by Sir Edward Seymour, the DL in question. The townsmen asked Northampton both to write letters to the DLs in the county to force them to refrain from making the Dartmouth trained band muster outside the town, and to cause the earl of Bath to appoint a new DL, one who would support the town's liberties, in place of Seymour, lately deceased. Dartmouth's plea proved convincing. Within a month the Privy Council had written to the earl of Bath, recounting the townsmen's complaint. They ordered the lord lieutenant to respect the town's liberties, in light of Dartmouth's important position as a port town and its good service to the crown in the past. The Council also required Bath to appoint the mayor of Dartmouth as a deputy lieutenant for the town. Bath complied, without enthusiasm. He wrote to the Privy Council a year later that many of the "better sort" saw it as a grief that Dartmouth did not show its men at the general musters. To the earl it appeared a bad precedent for other towns, and "much to the destructing of the service."[96] Conflict with a lord lieutenant over musters could be difficult, but townsmen sometimes solved their problems by finding other patrons who would support their cause.

Other strategies, playing on ideas of mutual obligation, also proved successful. A corporation faced with a lord lieutenant unwilling to support civic privileges over musters might remind the lieutenant of all of his favors to the corporation in the past as a patron of the town. This worked particularly well when the locality had established a long-term relationship with a nobleman as a local patron, where the lieutenancy was just one of the roles that the lord played vis-à-vis the town. Leicester's relationship with the earls of Huntingdon fits into this pattern, and the townsmen used this strategy frequently, especially when the earl most actively attempted to reform and train the militia. In 1625, during a push to "perfect" the Leicestershire militia, the fifth earl ordered a mass training of all the county's militia units at Lutterworth, in the southern end of the shire. The corporation wrote to the earl asking him to let their unit muster at home, both because the expense would be too great and because it went against their privileges. Juggling semantics, the earl refused their request, stating that their corporate privilege extended only to musters, and this exercise was to be a "training" not a "muster."[97]

Undaunted, the men of Leicester undertook two simultaneous strategies. First, the corporation wrote directly to the earl, appealing to the long history of trust between Leicester and himself.

> We then presume so far upon your Lordship's accustomed favor to us and our poor town, that as your Honor will not in a plain case willingly do anything to infringe our liberties as your Lordship in your love to us and our town hath been pleased often to profess, so in a case doubtful your Honor will rather be a little too sparing to us, for the preservation of our liberties, than anyways too urgent to press us to that which may prove to be an infringing thereof.[98]

But as an insurance policy, they also wrote to another friend of the corporation, Sir Humphrey May, the chancellor of the duchy of Lancaster, to ask him to influence the earl of Huntingdon to change his mind about the venue of the muster. A month before, the corporation had selected Sir Humphrey as their burgess to Parliament, so they figured he might look favorably upon their suit. May did write a letter to the earl, which he gave to the corporation for their perusal before they delivered it to Huntingdon. Sir Humphrey's letter proved unnecessary. Before the townsmen had a chance to deliver it, the earl informed them that they had his permission to muster the town militia within Leicester's walls.[99]

The success of this strategy made the men of Leicester turn to it again the next time the militia came up as an important issue in Leicestershire. When the crown mobilized local militias in the late 1630's as England went to war with the Scots, the diligent lord lieutenant called for a general muster of the county's troops at Loughborough, a market town near his two seats of Ashby and Donnington. Again, the corporators of Leicester tried to exempt their troop from the general muster by claiming the defense of their charter rights and by appealing to Huntingdon's goodwill to the town in general. They first wrote to the earl's son Henry, who would actually supervise the muster, due to his father's frail health. They assured him that they would happily have the trained band viewed and impressed, but averred that it should be done in Leicester, "for the maintenance of the ancient liberties of our corporation which your noble father and others of your noble predecessors have of long endeavored to maintain." Addressing their next letter to the earl himself, they hoped for his "accustomed favor" toward their poor corporation. In addition to this direct appeal, the townsmen also wrote to Lord Newburgh, chancellor of the duchy, for his assistance in the matter. Newburgh took the cause of the town to heart, going to the earl personally and requesting that the corporation retain the right to exercise its trained band at home. He secured from the earl a promise to instruct the deputy lieutenants accordingly. Like Sir Humphrey May before him, Newburgh had reason to support the town's interests. Leicester had just chosen Newburgh's nominee, Simon Every, as a burgess to the Short Parliament for the town.[100] Clearly, patronage of various sorts—parliamentary as well as more general—could have an important effect on issues that at first glance seem purely in the realm of military administration.

Questions over militia rates brought out similar patterns of relations. Corporations demanded control over military issues in the borough, yet they sometimes dragged their feet on paying for the support of the soldiery. Towns did not always relish the expense involved in keeping the local troop in clothing, victuals, up-to-date arms, and appropriate officers. They spent considerable time attempting to have their rates reduced, both for the expenses of training and for the number of men impressed out of the town to fight in the monarch's wars. For instance, in 1618, the corporators of Coventry complained to the earl of Northampton, lord lieutenant of Warwickshire, that they were rated too high for militia munitions. Northampton responded by saying that if the DLs agreed to change the city's rate, the earl himself was "willing to condescend unto" the decision.[101] Towns like Leicester, which had a long-standing patronage relationship with a lord who was also the lord lieutenant, could more readily call on that patron to protect the town against exactions that he himself enforced. The earls of Huntingdon historically spared Leicester from some of the heaviest burdens. When Sir George Villiers, captain of the Leicester men at the camp at Tilbury in 1595, made off with £20 of the town's money that he was supposed to give to the soldiers, Henry, third earl of Huntingdon, took order that the money be restored to the corporation. After the third earl's death, his brother George, the fourth earl, tried to keep up the image of defender of the town, by lowering Leicester's militia exactions. In February 1600, the earl assessed Leicester six soldiers to be sent for the war with Spain. Each soldier was to be fully furnished and supplied with 40s. Believing this rate too high for their poor town to bear, the mayor and the five "ancientest" aldermen rode to see Earl George at Donnington Park to request a reduction. After consulting with the townsmen, the earl lowered the assessment to three men. In 1615, the corporators made a deal with the fifth earl over a troop levy. They agreed to pay the muster master £20, a sum higher than had ever been paid previously, and in return he freed them from providing more soldiers for that year.[102] Townsmen depended on good lordship and the earl's willingness and ability to manipulate the levies to protect them from what they considered unreasonable rates.

In general, however, Henry, the fifth earl, seems to have been less likely than his predecessors to accede to the townsmen's requests for relief, especially at crucial junctures like the mid-1620's and the late 1630's. The fifth earl saw the lieutenancy as a major component and symbol of his personal honor and familial authority. Anything that might work to the reduction of the military service he took as a poor reflection on him. He also came under pressure from the Privy Council to perform the service rigorously. When the townsmen asked him to lower the assessment of £50 for military provision in August 1626, they pleaded poverty caused by a recent bout of plague. The earl evidently allowed the town to postpone payment, but once the plague had subsided, he again required them to pay the full sum without further delay. At this, the corporation again wrote to the earl, arguing that the town's financial straits prevented them from paying, but still craving the continuance of his love for them. The earl balked. Not only did he force them to pay up, but he also demanded that they send their trained band to Market Harborough for training. By appearing neglectful of his orders, the townsmen, in his eyes, took direct aim at his personal honor. He wrote to them,

> As I would not go about to deprive you of that right the law gives you which is every man's birthright, so would I not lose anything that belongs unto that high office that I hold, being his Majesty's Lieutenant of the whole shire in which place the late King of blessed memory his Majesty's father and his Majesty that now is hath graced and trusted me with these 20 years, so it is likely I should be a Master of Arts in the execution of this office.[103]

For the fifth earl of Huntingdon, his honor was wrapped up in his role as lieutenant as well as his role as local patron. At a time when he felt his place in the hierarchy in question, from the town and from the county gentry and most importantly from the Court, he made defense of his honor the pinnacle of his existence, which made him less flexible as a patron to the town.

Leicester had an unusually intense relationship with its patron and lord lieutenant, but other corporations exhibited similar patterns. Chester's lord lieutenant, the earl of Derby, also had a long-standing patronage connection to the city. In 1621, the earl ordered that 100 men be levied out of Cheshire for possible service in Ireland. The deputy lieutenants, Sir George Boothe and Sir William Brereton, commanded the city of Chester to provide twenty of these men, as well as the regular trained band, to be viewed and mustered. The corporation objected. First, Chester historically had been free of such impositions, as a result of a grant given the city by Henry VIII. Second, they had already been at great expense in provisioning the soldiers for Ireland and were now, they claimed, in a very poor state. In soliciting the earl to free them from this service, they appealed to the long history of patronage between the city and the Stanley family. The mayor of Chester wrote that he and his fellows were:

> desirous to flee unto your Honor as one whom we have much cause to rely on for all honorable favors towards us, as our city hath for many years been much bound to your honorable ancestors, your grandfather, your father, and now most especially unto yourself, who have most honorably vouchsafed to be a member of our city, and the most honorable and chief pillar and countenance to the same, as also your said ancestors formerly have been.[104]

Again, townsmen tried to gain their ends by calling on the lord lieutenant not simply in his role as the military officer for the county, but as a protector and friend of the corporation and citizens.

For military issues, corporations had an obvious choice of whom to approach for relief. The lord lieutenant oversaw the entire service for the county, and it was to him that local authorities had to appeal to make changes in personnel, in training venues, or in assessments and levies. Militia trainings and their concomitant expenses continually raised problems in corporations, particularly during the crown's most active period in the 1620's and 1630's. This led to a continuing campaign for reduction of service and protection of corporate rights throughout the seventeenth century, a campaign often waged through channels of patronage. The same could be said for the financial demands of the central government upon boroughs, subsidies, privy seal loans, the Forced Loan, and Ship Money.[105] Taxation, then as always, found little popularity. Parliamentary subsidies, the most popular form of taxation, were not collected with complete ease, and subsidymen usually tried to obtain the lowest assessments possible.[106] Nonparliamentary taxation posed yet more difficulties. Even when the cause was a good one, Englishmen hesitated to spend more money than was absolutely necessary. While they believed firmly in fighting the Spanish and defeating the Catholic menace both on land and at sea, the practicalities of paying for it seemed less appealing.[107] Questions of finance and

taxation formed one of the bases of discord between the crown and the localities, and some historians have argued forcefully that the inability to
deal with the problems of crown finance helped lead to the breakdown of
the mid-seventeenth century.[108] Be that as it may, it was certainly true that
local taxpayers worked to keep their assessments as low as possible. Although they did not wish to disobey their sovereign, they also did not want
to pay at the levels set by the central government. In the face of increasingly heavy burdens, corporations struggled to come to terms with the
crown through the mediation of patrons.

One way to reduce levies was to have assessment commissioners considered to be friendly. English taxpayers were notoriously underassessed,
mostly because friends and neighbors often assessed each other. Citizens
of boroughs hoped to have members of the civic government as the commissioners, and failing that, friendly gentlemen. Central government,
rather than the locality, drew up the commissions, but local men did their
best to influence their composition. Ipswich petitioned the earl of Suffolk
in 1612 to be a means to the crown to allow the portmen to set the assessments for the privy seal loans of that year themselves. The town of Leicester, at least in the reign of Elizabeth and early in the reign of James, managed to get a significant proportion of the local subsidy commission to
consist of townsmen. In August 1590, the commission consisted of the
earl of Huntingdon and the mayor, recorder, and three aldermen, along
with two county gentlemen. In 1610, the commission consisted of Sir
Henry Hastings, Mr. Walter Hastings, Sir John Grey, and Sir William
Heyrick, three of whom were proven friends of the town, along with the
mayor, recorder, and four aldermen. As the years wore on, the townsmen
worked more actively to get friendly commissioners, writing to Sir William Heyrick for assistance in procuring the commissioners that they desired and presenting him with a list of names of possibilities. In 1624, the
corporation asked Sir Humphrey May, then the chancellor of the duchy of
Lancaster as well as their parliamentary burgess, to solicit the lord keeper
to appoint commissioners preferred by the town.[109] This would not prevent the townsmen from paying, but it might keep the rate of the assessments lower than if men hostile or indifferent to the town made the levy.

Even after commissioners prescribed the rates, townsmen continued to
work through patrons to attempt to have the levies reduced. In 1596, Dover's corporation, "by the mediation of the Right Honorable our Lord
Warden," managed to have their Ship Money assessment substantially
lowered.[110] Privy seal loans are another case in point. In response to the
1591 loans, the bailiffs of Derby wrote to the earl of Shrewsbury, the

town's high steward, asking for his aid in reducing their £240 assessment. The loans of 1611 seem to have been particularly irksome, the corporation of Exeter calling them "generally distasteful and unwelcome." Robert Heyrick, alderman of Leicester, wrote to his brother Sir William, "We hear that my good lord [Huntingdon] is gone to London about Privy Seals. I fear we shall hear of them too soon." Given this attitude, it is not surprising that corporations spent a good deal of time looking for ways to have the assessments reduced. The mayor of Exeter prevailed on the earl of Bath to delay the collection of privy seal loans in that city. The high cost of corn and the "multitudes of our poor and miserable people," made this the worst time to try to collect money from the populace. He hoped that Bath would allow the delay, in order to keep the people's "dutiful affection to their gracious sovereign."[111] The bailiffs of Great Yarmouth went personally to the earl of Northampton, high steward of the town, to see if he would help them get the privy seals recalled or at least abated.[112] Just as with any other type of favor that a town desired from the crown, corporations appealed to patrons who had influence with those who would be making the decisions.

As the seventeenth century wore on, however, the regular channels proved less successful at bridging the gap between central needs and local desires. Many of the fiscal exactions of the crown, especially during the reign of Charles I, were both unparliamentary and unpopular. If subsidymen dragged their feet on the exactions made by Queen Elizabeth and King James, they balked at the Forced Loan, knighthood fines, and Ship Money. Although in most cases townsmen paid their due, some refused to pay at all and corporations constantly attempted to have the levies reduced. When the commissioners for the Forced Loan for Oxford came to town in January 1627, the town council petitioned them to be excused from payment. The commissioners included the earl of Banbury, high steward of Oxford, and Lord Carleton. To sweeten their request, the townsmen presented the high steward with a pair of gloves of the value of 40s. "at least" and another pair to Lord Carleton. While the city often gave gloves to visiting dignitaries, the value of the gift to Banbury exceeded the norm. Given the magnitude of the request, however, even expensive gloves were unlikely to entice the two lords to grant this particular favor, and Oxford paid its required levy.[113]

The citizens of York also balked at these financial exactions. The corporators complained that not only had they been required to pay loans to the king in the amount of £400 (a reduction from the original assessment of £1800), but they also had to pay Ship Money, the five parliamentary subsidies, a rate for powder and match, and a loan of £1000 to the king of Sweden that King Charles had personally requested.[114] The corporation appealed to Lord Scrope, lord president of the North, emphasizing the city's poverty and Scrope's position.

> This city hath many times received comfort and help from your honorable and most noble predecessors, whose place you now possess, who have upon such like occasions afforded it their best help, And now we hope that it shall receive no less favor from your honor's noble disposition, for which gracious respect your Lopp. shall ever by this city be most worthily honored, And we the citizens thereof shall have just cause to pray for your Lop's health and happiness with much increase of honor.[115]

At the same time, they also took the opportunity to choose a new high steward in the person of Thomas Lord Coventry, lord keeper of the Great Seal, whom they petitioned multiple times for a reduction of their charges.[116] It is notable that despite the extremely political nature of this issue, the townsmen went about to solve it in the same way they would less highly charged matters.

One of the reasons for the successful collection of the Forced Loan, at least among towns, was that loan payments were sometimes used as trade-offs for other services or favors desired by boroughs. According to Richard Cust, in his definitive monograph on the Forced Loan, some corporations came to agreements with their patrons on the Privy Council to procure needed favors in return for full payment of the loan by the town. In 1626, several of the port towns of Suffolk and Norfolk desired to have naval escorts for their fishing fleets as they headed out to the North Sea fisheries, to defend them against marauding Dunkirkers. Many townsmen refused to pay the Benevolence because they felt impoverished by the pirates and neglected by the crown. But by dealing through the earl of Suffolk with the duke of Buckingham, lord admiral, the fishermen of the ports came to the understanding that a demonstration of loyalty by paying the loan promptly might well result in the desired favor. Indeed, most of the towns paid in full, and soon after this the petitions of several coastal towns requesting naval escorts came directly into the king's hands through the duke. Similar deals occurred elsewhere. Some ports, including Norwich, charged with Ship Money in 1626 lobbied to be freed from that exaction in return for full payment of the loan. This strategy proved successful in several cases.[117] By prevailing upon patrons for favor, townsmen could sometimes work out an advantageous arrangement even in the face of firm policies that divided local from central interests.

The Forced Loan, while widely unpopular, nevertheless proved successful monetarily for the crown, as the Privy Council worked so assiduously for its collection. Other assessments raised yet more questions among corporations. In 1630, the king attempted to collect distraints from all those who had failed to take up knighthood. These fines, long in abeyance, pleased few. When the earl of Huntingdon, head of the commission for collecting the distraint in Leicestershire, asked the townsmen of Leicester to compose for a lump sum rather than be assessed individually, the corporation tried to squirm out of it. They sent three of the most senior aldermen to speak personally with the earl, but he did not like what they had to say, it "neither answering [my] expectations nor the propositions made to you." He wrote to the full corporation, demanding that they rethink their rash answer, "hoping that as the second thoughts are the best, so consulting again the fruit of your counsels will produce this good effect." The members of the corporation managed to drag out their "second thoughts," delaying their answer until April 1631. Then the corporation agreed to the composition in general, but asked the earl of Huntingdon to reduce the amount of the town's composition from the £300 originally assessed. The townsmen claimed that they did not object to the composition, merely the level of the charge.[118]

Attempts to reduce the imposition of Ship Money used similar language. The town council of Boston agreed in 1635 to send a representative to London to attempt to obtain a reduction of their Ship Money assessment. The town clerk solicited the lord keeper and others, sending Lord Coventry, the town's recorder, a present worth nearly £20 for his favor.[119] Presumably, the corporators believed that Coventry would encourage the sheriff of Lincolnshire, who actually assessed the levy, to lower the city's charge. When Reading received the order for a levy of £260 in 1636, the corporation immediately agreed to petition for an abatement. They wrote a general letter to the lords of the Privy Council, but they also wrote individual letters of request to Archbishop Laud, a native of Reading, and to the earl of Holland, the town's high steward and a companion of King Charles.[120] It seems a rather forlorn hope that either of these two servants of the king would gratify Reading's taxpayers. Yet it is telling that the corporation chose to follow a traditional practice of appealing to patrons to gain relief.

Given the crown's financial needs, such appeals for patronage could meet with little success. The regular channels of patronage could only work well when the requests of clients did not run directly into strongly held policies on the part of the crown. This can be seen in the experience of

Leicester's corporation in dealing with the earl of Huntingdon in 1639. In the highly politicized atmosphere of that year, Huntingdon decided to increase the town's troop levy from 40 to 100 men. The corporators believed Leicester could not support that heavy a burden and agreed to petition the earl for a remission. This evidently met with no success, for in July the Common Hall held a vote as to whether they would yield their consent to this addition of 60 extra men to their levy; it was agreed "by the most voices" not to accept the enhanced levy. Appeals to Huntingdon's good lordship were abandoned, at least on this issue.[121] When the interests of local authorities and those of the crown diverged, patrons could not always smooth over the dissonance. In fact, they were more likely to feel the need to reinforce central policy than to look favorably on the desires of the locality; after all, they usually had received much of their authority directly from the crown. Corporations attempted to work through these same channels of patronage for the contentious issue of state finance as well as for less controversial matters. But as the demands of the state became less amenable to compromise, patrons proved less able to mediate effectively between the needs of the king and the desires of the localities.

For most corporations, the acquisition of a patron or patrons became a necessity of life. Those who sought to obtain bounty from the monarch had to discover and exploit channels of connection to those who had the ear of the king. These links, though informal and personal rather than institutional and bureaucratic, helped bind the English state together. Localities could not and did not exist in isolation, as the English state extended from London into the provinces. Urban governors, in order to secure their privileges and to achieve economic and political ends, tapped into this network of connection, seeking out patrons to mediate for them in obtaining bounty from the crown. They made particularly good use of the relatively new office of high steward, which in a concrete way bound a town to a particular lord or patron, who assumed an obligation to reciprocate by offering to bring local petitions to the attention of the crown. In some cases, they themselves were the representatives of the crown who made decisions on the monarch's behalf.

This form of "lordship" was based on chosen obligation to a person with apparent ability to do good for the town. The connection did not rest significantly on ideological affinities, but rather on a combination of traditional social exchange—deference, honor, hospitality—and more pragmatic considerations of influence and office. Townsmen tapped into the network of patronage to obtain many sorts of favors, from charters to leases to fairer customs officers to lower militia rates. The crown, as well, appreciated the benefits of patronage. Having little bureaucratic connection to the provinces, early modern monarchs relied on more personal ties to communicate with local communities and enforce policy throughout the realm. These connections required flexibility, and hence became less effective in the increasingly stiff structures of Caroline government. Nevertheless, both corporations and the crown continued to work through established lines of patronage and clientage in trying to maintain their respective interests. Using these networks of exchange, corporations maintained a level of self-determination while remaining integrated with the rest of the political nation.

SIX

Urban Patronage at Work

A Case Study of Leicester and the Earls of Huntingdon

In November 1612, the corporation of Leicester sought a new recorder. Sir Augustine Nicholls, after occupying that office for seven years, had risen to the judiciary in the court of Common Pleas, requiring him to relinquish his position in Leicester. Within two days of Nicholls's resignation, the earl of Huntingdon wrote to the corporation recommending a nominee. As Leicester's most important patron, Huntingdon used the opportunity to look after the interests of the town as well as his own. He wrote to the corporation, saying:

> Out of the love and affection which I bear unto you I cannot but in this offer you my advice whom I conceive would be fit to succeed so worthy a person, and herein I am carried and supported by no particular reason or respect but with the eyes of my little judgment do I look upon one herein who I hold and I hope you will in your judgments conceive fit for it, for out of long experience I have had of him he is very religious, honest, and learned in the laws.

He recommended to them Mr. Francis Harvey of Northampton, a man indeed well known to the town. Harvey also happened to be one of the earl of Huntingdon's men of business and a relative (possibly a brother) of the steward of the earl's household. Huntingdon signed off his missive with "if you shall satisfy this my desire I shall have cause to redouble the bond of my affection towards you and study your good as much as if I were a member of your Body." Despite—or maybe because of—Harvey's close connections to a great local magnate, the aldermen accepted the nomination and unanimously chose Harvey as recorder. They acknowledged themselves "much bounden to your Honor in commending so worthy a man." They also returned "many thanks for your Honor's love and good affection, which your Lordship doth bear towards us and our poor corporation, with much desire of the continuance of the same."[1] Patron and town found harmony.

This vignette shows the smooth working of urban patronage, with noble lord and corporation working together to reach mutually beneficial goals. Of course, the relationship did not always work so neatly. Periods of constructive cooperation laced with moments of strife characterized urban patronage during the early modern era. A delicate balance existed between parties: patrons had to be gratified, yet corporations had to maintain their integrity. Relations shifted and changed. Harmony rarely lasted long. Yet contention could exist without destroying the connection. Townsmen juggled between concern for ancient loyalties and deference, and the political realities of the day. Most dangerous to the relationship was a patron's inability to bring benefits to the local community through connection to the crown. Patrons who maintained close links to the crown flourished and gained more clients, while those who no longer could provide connections and access might find themselves unable to retain their clients' loyalties. The events in Leicester took place in a context of an ongoing and intense relationship between the town governors and the successive earls of Huntingdon. Only by viewing individual events within the larger picture of relations between the town and the earls can they be fully understood.

A systematic investigation of how Leicester dealt with the earls of Huntingdon over a long span of time helps illuminate the complex nature of urban patronage in early modern England. Relations between corporations and patrons were dynamic, not static. Analyzing long-term patterns of exchange that existed between patron, client, and the crown, and how each party responded to changing events over time provides a vital sense of the ebbs and flows of these relations. Patronage was not a formal institution or system, but rather a process whereby different layers of government and society interacted with each other, from the king on down to the lowliest town or village officer.[2] Although no one corporate borough can be said to be representative of any others, it nevertheless can serve to mark out the boundaries of urban patronage in this period. These relationships, after all, took place in particular historical circumstances and across changing events. Neither Leicester nor the earls of Huntingdon may be "typical," but their story brings together the many complexities, successes, and difficulties of urban patronage and the trials of early modern government.

I

Leicester, the county town and sole parliamentary borough of Leicestershire, enjoyed a long history in which the inhabitants took great pride. The borough had, in the medieval period, been governed by the earls of Leicester and later the dukes of Lancaster. The Honour of Leicester became part of the duchy of Lancaster, and even in the seventeenth century stewards appointed by the duchy still presided over the court of the Honour. But borough institutions also evolved as the burgesses busied themselves in their town, gradually distancing themselves from seigneurial control and acquiring for themselves more authority in the overlapping jurisdictions of town and Honour. The tradesmen who populated the town, many of them involved in the cloth or leather trades, kept a tight rein on civic governance in the sixteenth and seventeenth centuries. An annually elected mayor, twenty-four aldermen, and forty-eight assistants constituted the corporation, according to the charter of Queen Elizabeth that granted formal incorporation to Leicester. These prominent men made a close-knit group, as two and three generations of men named Wyggeston and Heyrick and Abney took their places as mayors and aldermen. Concerned to maintain order, to manifest their own authority and status, and to preserve the honor of the ancient borough, the close corporation took a vital interest in the town's life.[3]

Yet Leicester faced difficulties that the corporation alone could not solve. The town experienced a growing poverty problem and a perceived general economic decline exacerbated by recurrent bouts of plague. The corporators worked hard to counter the effects of these troubles, in part by trying to broaden their own jurisdiction. At various times during the period, the corporation attempted to gain new royal charters that would extend civic boundaries and privileges, giving the mayor and his brethren tighter control over Leicester's polity and economy. But the town needed to have friends in positions of power in order to overcome its difficulties and to preserve its rights and privileges.[4]

Throughout the early modern period, the earls of Huntingdon fulfilled just this function for the town of Leicester. The Hastings family, which had its medieval roots in the Midlands, had first found royal favor in the reign of Edward IV, when that monarch created Sir William Hastings Baron Hastings in 1461. Although this first lord Hastings lost his title and head by the command of Richard III, the family was soon restored in the blood, and by 1529 the lords Hastings had advanced to the dignity of earls of Huntingdon. They dominated the political and administrative life of the county, consistently holding the offices of lord lieutenant of Leicestershire, justice of the peace, and *Custos Rotulorum*.[5] Along with these marks of royal favor, the earls of Huntingdon also owned large tracts of land in Leicestershire. Their wealth dwindled over the course of the late sixteenth and seventeenth centuries, as the family faced increasing financial difficulties, but the earls maintained their status as the premier men in the county to the end of the seventeenth century. As local magnates, embodiments of social status and privilege, the earls stood closely bound to the county and the town of Leicester. Holding offices in both the borough and the shire, they wielded the authority of the central government in the locality. The office of the steward of the Honour of Leicester had been granted to William Lord Hastings in 1461 and remained in the Hastings family. It gave the steward powers in the borough court, although in reality the earls left the operation of the court almost entirely to the civic magistrates.[6] The earls of Huntingdon also represented the central government in the town as lord lieutenants, exercising the militia and overseeing local governance for the crown.

Although this relationship existed on an official level, the earls were not distant symbols of central authority but rather neighboring magnates who had a personal relationship with the townsmen of Leicester. From the middle of the sixteenth century, the earls maintained a residence in town, giving them a base of operations when they came to Leicester for the Sessions or Assizes or musters. Because of this propinquity, lord and town maintained direct contact in both official matters and more intimate ones. In 1549 Francis, the second earl, reckoning the men of Leicester to be his "very friends," required them to send several able men to fight with him over the seas. This they soon did, and he thanked them for their "friendly and hearty good will." He regretted that he could not be with them at Christmastime, "whereof I would have been glad," but he sent his servant to them with a gift of "two does to make merry with at your pleasures."[7] This gift expressed the affective as well as the official tie between them.

Such gift-giving played an important part in the dealings between town and lord. Leicester, like most early modern towns, always reserved some of its revenues for expenditure on wine, sugar, and sundries to be given to various "friends" of the town. The earls of Huntingdon, as Leicester's major patrons, received several gallons of wine and pounds of sugar nearly every year as a New Year's gift, as well as more casual gifts throughout the course of the year. Although the corporation gave presents to other local and visiting dignitaries, the earls always received the largest.

In return, the earls of Huntingdon sent venison or sturgeon or some other lordly gift to the corporation. Symbols of a deeper bond of respect and affection, gifts both acknowledged and created a sense of mutual obligation between parties.[8]

Henry, third earl of Huntingdon, combined both the official and more affective aspects of his position of patron, so that the people of Leicester considered him the epitome of the "good lord." As a trusted servant of Queen Elizabeth, he served as a privy councilor, lord president of the Council of the North, and lord lieutenant of Leicestershire and Rutland. Despite these heavy official responsibilities, the third earl always remained involved in local issues, an involvement that went far deeper than simply carrying out the military training for the county and town. He took a personal interest in the well-being, especially the spiritual well-being, of the people of Leicester. Although some members of his family remained Roman Catholic, the earl himself believed strongly in reformed religion.[9] His puritanism struck a responsive chord in the town's inhabitants. Under his authority, the first civic preacher came to Leicester, in a position established according to his orders. He involved himself in the operation of the grammar school and assisted the town in setting up a scheme of work to relieve the poor. He also donated £6 annually to the corporation in order to buy coals for poor townsmen.[10] Although he never held any official title in the corporation, such as high steward, the third earl did hold the duchy office of the steward of the Honour of Leicester, an office he later relinquished to his brother Sir Edward Hastings.[11] He wielded his real power in the town by dint of his local prominence and central connections.

When the earl visited Leicester, the corporators appealed to him to resolve their differences, both internal and external. In April 1590, the mayor and burgesses presented him with a petition that addressed the following subjects: their overly high (in their opinion) charge of soldiers; a mischief-making salt-peter man; inhabitants who procured gentlemen's livery in order to avoid local rates; the freemen of the Bishop's Fee being charged in both the town and the county; and the civic preacher.[12] Huntingdon, as lord lieutenant, had the direct authority to moderate the town's militia charge, but his responsibility for the other matters is debatable. The corporation nevertheless clearly viewed him as a protector of their interests and a person who made decisions that would stick.

The third earl performed another crucial task for the borough of Leicester in mediating with the surrounding gentry and with the officers of the duchy of Lancaster. When the plague hit Leicester hard in 1593–94,

Huntingdon personally commanded the JPs of the county to take a special collection for the relief of the poor afflicted in the town. He settled a dispute between the town and Dr. Chippingdale over the use of the Castle Mills, and he also aided the town in purchasing a tract of land just outside the town wall from Sir Francis Hastings, his younger brother. In 1585 the earl intervened on the town's behalf in a suit before the duchy when a question arose over one of the borough's leases.[13] The people of Leicester held Henry earl of Huntingdon in the deepest respect because of his power in central and local government and his willingness to take an interest in his native county. This made him the perfect arbiter of provincial disputes.

While the third earl provided many local services to Leicester, he also aided the townsmen faithfully in their dealings with the queen's government. Earl Henry played a key role in procuring a royal charter of incorporation for the borough in February 1589.[14] Huntingdon also served as the chief militia and subsidy commissioner for the county and the town. He had a large part in the assessment process, and the townsmen often appealed to him in order to moderate their rates. When the corporation received an order to provide horses for military purposes, the town leaders asked the earl to write to the earls of Warwick and Leicester, who had issued the order, to free the town of the charge. The earl complied, and the town clerk rode to London with his letters to give to the two other peers. Huntingdon also acted as the main enforcer of crown policy in Leicestershire, conveying the needs and wishes of the queen and Privy Council directly to the borough.[15] The townsmen saw these activities not as unwelcome interference of an external authority, but as a useful and desirable sign of friendship and aid from a powerful patron. Huntingdon, in return, received reinforcement of his authority and prestige, both from the town and from the crown.

While the townsmen had a deep commitment to their lord, they did not abjectly obey him. The members of the corporation deferred to his rank and authority, but they did not invariably take his advice or fulfill his expectations. In particular, the close corporation—which alone had the franchise in parliamentary elections—failed to select some of the nominees that Earl Henry proposed as burgesses to Parliament. In 1593 the townsmen rejected his nominee as well as that of the chancellor of the duchy, returning two townsmen instead. Despite his great stature, he was never an omnipotent figure as the town's patron. Local leaders had their own integrity and interests to maintain, and this meant doing what they believed best for themselves and the town. This lack of conformity to his wishes irked the earl, yet he remained a staunch patron of the town even after his electoral disappointments. He continued to aid the town until his death, and his memory as the town's good lord lingered well into the seventeenth century.[16]

The third earl's bond of honor and respect with the town can be graphically seen in a portrait of him commissioned and given to the corporation of Leicester by Sir William Heyrick in 1623. The earl, gray and grave, wears his ermine robes and his chain of the Order of the Garter, showing the power of his title and lineage. He also bears the white staff of the president of the Council of the North, the office he served in from 1570 until his death in late 1595. A text appears in the corner, recounting the many good deeds he did for the town as their lord and patron. All of these layers of honor and authority—identification with central government authority, seigneurial relations carried over from the past, the local authority and prestige of the Hastings family, as well as affection for the man himself—made the third earl the town's ideal good lord. He, more successfully than his heirs, achieved a close and generally harmonious relationship with the townsmen of Leicester.[17]

His successors found it difficult to live up to the third earl's lofty reputation. Having died childless, the third earl was succeeded by his brother George. Sir George Hastings had lived principally in Leicestershire and had fewer connections with central government than did his elder brother. He also faced continual financial struggles. Although Earl Henry had been a popular and hard-working lord, his income perpetually failed to match his expenses. Earl George inherited a seriously debt-burdened estate, and he spent much of his time trying to ward off creditors and keep hold of the family's lands.[18] He also felt the burden of his brother's sterling reputation, a reputation he could never emulate. With heavy financial burdens and fewer ties to the center, Earl George sat less securely in the position of Leicestershire's chief magnate.

Yet Leicester's townspeople viewed the fourth earl of Huntingdon as their patron, just as they had his predecessors. He received gifts of wine and sugar from the corporation on a regular basis, and the mayor communicated frequently with him on matters of public order and military service. The corporators of Leicester appealed to Earl George for assistance with problems at all levels, internal borough matters, disputes with county or duchy officials, and mediation with the crown. When the townsmen wanted to ensure that Sir John Grey—who had threatened revenge on the corporation the previous year—was not put on their subsidy commission for 1600, the townsmen decided to write to the earl of Huntingdon to procure his letter to the lord keeper, supporting the town's request.[19] Earl George also involved himself in specifically civic concerns, such as elections for mayor and other town officers. When the earl nominated Mr. Stanford to be recorder in 1603, the mayor wrote that they had elected the man, and thanked the earl for having named someone so "well approved." He hoped "for the continuance of your Honor's love and affection toward our corporation, assuring your Lordship that our duties & loyal affections towards the honor of your Lordship's house shall not be wanting, when just occasion shall be [illegible] to make testimony thereof."[20]

Such tranquillity did not always characterize relations between the townsmen and Earl George, however. Corporators routinely chose to ignore the earl's advice, and the earl at times crossed the corporation's purposes as well. When the recorder, Mr. Stanford, died only a few months after the corporation elected him at the earl's recommendation, Earl George wrote again to nominate a replacement. This time the corporation was not so amenable. The corporators had no knowledge or experience of Mr. Cheyney, so they considered him unfit for the office.[21] The townsmen also twice failed to elect Earl George's nominees as burgesses to Parliament. The most notable case of this occurred in 1601, when an enemy of the earl, Sir George Belgrave, offered himself as burgess of Leicester. The earl warned the mayor to see that Sir George not be elected, and the mayor gave assurances of the corporation's love and respect for their lord. But on the day of the election, Belgrave presented himself before the electors in Huntingdon's livery, claiming that he was now Earl George's man and that the earl had made him his nominee. The corporation chose to take Sir George at his word and elected him, only to learn that the story of the reconciliation had been concocted by Belgrave. The mayor made apologies to Earl George, who seemed to accept that the townsmen had been duped by Belgrave's evil practices. But the earl also claimed that they had a "false brother" among them who facilitated the deception.[22] Clearly, not all members of the corporation held strong loyalties to the earl, and this 1601 incident introduced a note of strain and distrust between lord and locality. Until his death, the corporation continued to address him as "our very good lord" and he signed himself "your very loving friend." But the fourth earl's lament that "I have found you stand off and on with me in that I have delivered unto you" accurately reflected the uncertainties in their relationship.[23]

II

When the fourth earl died in December 1604, he thus left his heir a mixed legacy. On one hand was the happy memory of the third earl, who continued to be seen as the ideal patron of the borough. The townsmen remembered old Earl Henry's goodness to the town, his steadfastness in religion, and his authority on both local and national levels. The third earl's successors believed they saw in his earldom a perfect obedience to all his commands and a true rendering of affection by his people to their lord. On the other hand was the memory of the fourth earl, who, for all his good deeds for the town and his continued desire to stand the town's good lord, had never received the same affection from the townsmen as had his brother. The fifth earl, another Henry, came to the dignity with a strong desire to re-create the authority of his great-uncle and namesake.[24]

Earl George's son Francis died in 1595, so the title descended to George's grandson Henry in 1604.[25] At eighteen years of age, Earl Henry had all the exuberance of a young man and a firm belief in his own importance. Raised in the household of his great-uncle the third earl, young Henry held soundly reformed, though not stridently puritan, beliefs. He had married at fifteen, his grandfather having arranged an alliance with Elizabeth Stanley, co-heiress of Ferdinando, fifth earl of Derby. This marriage strengthened both his pocketbook and his family connections. While the power that rested in his lineage held great weight, he was himself an untried young man, not yet of age. This fact told against him in the faction-ridden arena of Leicestershire politics. The Grey family of Bradgate, rivals of the Hastings's for many years, tried to strip the young earl of his local offices. The Greys lost their political power in the sixteenth century with the ill-fated attempt to make Lady Jane Grey queen in Mary Tudor's stead. In the early seventeenth century, the family was trying to recoup local and national authority, at the expense of the new earl of Huntingdon.[26] Under age when he inherited the title, Earl Henry could not assume the offices of lord lieutenant or *Custos Rotulorum* that his predecessors had held. Henry Lord Grey used this opportunity to try to gain these offices for himself by energetically lobbying Sir Robert Cecil, Viscount Cranborne. In the event, Cranborne supported the claims of young Huntingdon, holding the offices in abeyance until the earl came of age.[27] Although successful in maintaining his offices, Earl Henry struggled to preserve a somewhat shaky inheritance, still burdened by debt. Unsure of his ability to "bear the port" of a great lord, and insecure in his place in county politics, he used his position as local authority in Leicester, and a strict attention to his personal honor and prestige, to undergird his position as a great peer of the realm.[28]

Huntingdon's personality and activities had a direct bearing on the townsmen of Leicester. They looked to him as their chief patron, offering him honor and deference of many kinds. As such, the corporation had to work out ways to deal with their particularly sensitive lord while maintaining civic integrity. Leicester encountered the fifth earl's sensitivities head on very soon after he succeeded to the title, when the corporation attempted to gain a new charter.[29] During this era of economic and social stress, the close corporation of Leicester consistently attempted to consolidate its authority over the town and its people. With the help of the third and fourth earls, the townsmen had procured a royal charter of incorporation in 1589, followed by a confirmation and extension of privileges in 1599. The corporation realized, however, that the new charter left the question of the town's jurisdiction over the Bishop's Fee and the Newark (two of the extramural rural areas adjoining the town) in doubt. It also failed to make clear the powers of the corporation over the borough court and the court of the Honour of Leicester.[30] In 1604 the corporation agreed to obtain a new charter expressing their full privileges as they defined them. To do this, they had to cooperate with the new earl of Huntingdon.

The fifth earl's predecessors had been key in securing the town's privileges, but the young peer took issue with the terms of the new instrument. In its wording, the proposed charter touched on Lord Huntingdon's rights as the steward of the Honour of Leicester. While previous earls of Huntingdon had held the office of steward of the Honour, none of them had particularly concerned themselves with the court's functioning. The fifth earl now chose to make this hitherto unremarkable office a symbol of his prestige. He saw the town's attempt to procure this charter as a plot to divest him both of his economic and judicial rights in the court and of his personal honor as steward.[31] His county offices had just been threatened by Lord Grey, which made the earl especially sensitive about his other privileges. While the corporators hoped the earl would stand their good lord in procuring the charter, as the third earl had done in 1589, instead they found him set against them. In the ensuing months and years, the corporation struggled to come to an understanding with the new earl of Huntingdon, one that balanced corporate privilege with the dignity of the earl and the wishes of the crown.

When the earl learned the details of the new charter from his kinsman Sir Henry Harrington, he took action. Early in 1605 he wrote a lengthy letter to the attorney of the duchy, Sir John Brograve, complaining of the wrongs that would be done him under the new charter. He argued that the town's proposal denigrated the authority and prestige of the crown as well as himself personally. He complained that the mayor desired rights over the stewardship of the Honour, with the castle and court appurtenant. This, however, "cannot be granted away from the Duchy without the disherison of the King and the great diminishing of the jurisdiction of the Dukedom." It would also establish a bad precedent, disabling the duchy from enforcing its rights over the corporation ever again.[32] The earl phrased his objections to reinforce the idea that the town intended to infringe the king's rights and create disorder in the region. But the earl made the issue one of personal honor as well as public order. Part of his own standing in the area stemmed from the royal offices he and his family held. It damaged his honor to have even a fraction of his privileges infringed. Allowing a mere mayor to perform the duties that members of his own family had done would undermine the prestige of his ancestry. Under the new charter, the townsmen would "execute those offices in their own right which heretofore hath been executed by men of greatest birth and ability under the Dukedom (many of my own ancestors having enjoyed the same for many years)."[33] For the earl of Huntingdon, Leicester's proposed charter was not a plan for rationalized local jurisdiction, but rather a direct attack on his own honor and lineage and on the authority of the crown.

The corporation saw things differently. They argued that the stewardship of the Honour and that of the town were separate entities, and that the mayor had always had rights over the latter. None of the earls had been steward of the town except the third earl, and his patent of stewardship had ultimately been demised to the corporation. The townsmen also denied that royal authority would be diminished. By expressly requiring the mayor to take his oath at the castle, something previously done only by custom, the new charter would, in fact, bind the mayor and corporation more closely to the crown.[34] Corporators simply wished to maintain their own privileges and distance the borough from the old manorial ties that still bound it, not refute the authority of the duchy. Leicester had no interest in cutting itself off from the crown or from the earl of Huntingdon. The town leaders did, however, desire to find a new way to relate to their powerful patron.

The earl's obstructionism thwarted the corporation's aims. Apparently on Huntingdon's objection, Lord Chancellor Ellesmere (who had married Huntingdon's mother-in-law, the dowager countess of Derby) slowed the passage of the charter through Chancery, to the chagrin of the corporation. Thomas Chettell, mayor of Leicester and chief solicitor for the town in this business, made dire statements to the aldermen, complaining that "great men oppress themselves against Leicester about the Stewardship" and that "Leicester hath more privy enemies than ever I did expect." Chettell refused to give up, vowing to speak with everyone necessary in order to have the charter passed. "Great men shall not put me out of conceit of good so long as they be but subjects as I am." With those rather daring sentiments and his persistence, Chettell and the town's attorneys nearly brought the business to fruition. But despite these efforts and an outlay of over £380 on "many fees, rewards, and giftures," the charter was stayed at the Great Seal and never came into effect.[35]

This failure soured relations between town and earl. In 1606 the earl threatened lawsuits against the corporation, which responded by sending more men to London to help in the business rather than by acquiescing to his demands. Resentment had risen to such heights by the end of 1606 that for the first time in many years the corporation failed to send the earl of Huntingdon a remembrance for the New Year.[36] To deny such a gift was a bold and unequivocal statement: in this cause, at any rate, the earl had not taken the interests of Leicester to heart. Reciprocity faltered. The townsmen well knew what might be the outcome of such a symbolic gesture. The town's recorder, Augustine Nicholls, warned the corporation about their action. "I am sorry," he said, "you did not bestow a New Year's gift upon the earl of Huntingdon. I do assure myself it would have been very well taken. And I hope if no offense be given of the town's part the cause will this term receive an end one way or other; it is meet the town seek my Lord and not he them."[37] Nicholls knew that if the earl did take offense, it would bode ill for the town.

Understanding the danger of the earl's enmity, the townsmen embarked upon a plan that developed into one of the more poignant episodes between locality and lord. Having expressed their displeasure by withholding one gift, the members of the corporation sought to win back the earl's "friendship" through the bestowal of another, more valuable than the first. With the earl away in London in February 1607, the townsmen attempted to ingratiate themselves through his wife, the young countess Elizabeth. They sent a delegation to her at Ashby de la Zouche to present her with a "fair gelding," worth £30, as a sort of peace offering. But to accept the gift would mean accepting the obligations that went with it, and this Earl Henry refused to do. He warned his wife to receive nothing from the corporation. When the delegation appeared at Ashby, the countess sympathized with their actions, but obeyed her husband's command. She told them that she refused not out of "proud disposition," but because she had not "desired it and knew no means how to requite it." Mr. Hunter, leader of the delegation, begged her to accept the gift and "to be a means to procure an end of their suit without the law." The countess assured them that the earl did not wish to overthrow those who had behaved themselves "unfittingly," but that if they would submit properly, he would be "willing to embrace the love of those that formerly had erred." While refusing the horse, she promised to speak to her husband on their behalf.[38]

Although repulsed by the countess, the townsmen remained encouraged. They felt sure that she would eventually accept the gelding, and made repeated attempts to present it to her. In late March Mr. Hunter wrote to one of the earl's gentlemen, Mr. Chatwyn, inquiring whether the countess would now take the horse and "procure my Lord his love towards us who love him in our hearts as I myself do think." Chatwyn informed him that the countess, while remaining their good friend, would still not accept the gift. At about the same time, the mayor of Leicester wrote to Mr. Walter Hastings, the earl's uncle, to discover his lordship's pleasure, "because they desire his love and would by no means have him their adversary." As late as May, the corporation agreed to pay 40s. to the man stabling the gelding spurned by the countess, hoping she would still take it.[39] Having once alienated their lord, the townsmen struggled to win back his favor.

After a period of uneasy relations between town and earl, complicated by a spate of enclosure riots in the Leicester area, the parties began to hammer out a compromise in the autumn of 1607.[40] Under the agreement, the earl would allow the town's charter to pass in exchange for the nomination of the officers of the borough court in turns with the corporation. At the first turn, the earl would nominate the steward of the court, and once that officer died or left office, the corporation would have its turn. Bailiffs, too, were to be chosen by alternate turns.[41] Neither town nor lord would be permanently excluded from the nomination. This compromise shows the interdependent nature of relations between town and patron. The corporation needed a charter and wanted all of the advantages of increased jurisdiction that came with it. They could not gain their ends by excluding the authority of the duchy and the earl, so they agreed to give

Huntingdon a recognized role. The earl needed this compromise, as well. It reinforced his status in the community, proving to the crown and to the townsmen his necessity to both of them. Each party compromised on its position. The town accepted the nomination of court officials in turn, and the earl agreed that his patent would be limited in descent to the heirs male of his body only, not his heirs general. This guaranteed to the town that only the direct line of the fifth earl's family would be connected to the town in the future, as so many of his ancestors had been connected in the past. This arrangement allowed the connection to be retained and the honor of both the corporation and the earl to be confirmed.[42]

Once again, Leicester returned to a more steady course of relations with the earl. Although not all corporators liked this compromise, they all wished to have a quick resolution in order to obtain the charter. In 1608, the earl, "by the earnest persuasions of Mr. Hastings and Mr. Recorder," consented to the compromise. After several months of negotiation and waiting, the corporation finally received the charter from the lord chancellor on 17 April 1609.[43] At the same time, they made a separate agreement with the earl of Huntingdon to grant him the nomination of the steward and bailiff by turns with the corporation. Under this agreement, the corporation would issue a patent under the corporate seal to the earl, a book of nominees would pass between them upon the alternation of turns, and bond would be taken from both sides as a sign of good faith. It seemed that all of the troubles and ill-feelings had ended.

But the townsmen dallied in completing the bargain. In early June 1609, the earl wrote to the corporation in an aggrieved tone, asking for the speedy delivery of his patent. They made excuses, and the patent remained unwritten in August.[44] On the eleventh of that month, Huntingdon wrote to the corporation in high dudgeon, accusing them of bad faith and of breaking the tenuous but real affective bond between them. The letter is worth quoting at length:

> I have long expected to have heard from you that the . . . agreement might have been sealed, but now your own ends are served your performances are answerable unto men of your condition. And though upon your reconciliation and mine I buried all your unrespective courses towards me, yet seeing you run your former I shall hold you in my thoughts and value you at no higher a rate than I had cause to heretofore. The world may see that out of fear and not out of love you respected me. For my part I had rather have been linked unto you by your affections. It is now made evident unto me that though you carried honey in your mouths, yet there was but gall in your hearts. And seeing it is so I shall try by course of law how to be righted of

the indignities it seemeth you would put upon me. Let me be carried on no further with delays but receive your speedy answer (which is all I covet). . . . And so if you do deserve it I rest,

Your loving friend, HH[45]

Lord Huntingdon's remarkable missive gives a clear account of his understanding of the patronage relationship by decrying the men of Leicester's failure to live up to that standard. The earl saw things in very traditional terms, in which lord and people are bound by ties of love and respect. They owed him deference because of the power of his status and honor, which he manifested in his goodness to them. In Huntingdon's eyes, the personal bond of lord to people ought to be founded on affection, not on fear of retribution. All disagreements should be settled through compromise and consensus. To go to law is to admit that the traditional relationship, which should produce harmony, has failed. Insecure in his own status, the fifth earl of Huntingdon emphasized a traditional view of lordship and took the town's intransigence as a slight to his personal honor.

The corporation generally agreed with the earl in their conception of patronage relations. They believed in the power of gifts, in the importance of traditional ties, and in the need to retain respect and honor for the earl. But the town fathers also believed in the integrity of the borough and of their own authority, which they had a pragmatic interest in maintaining. They would not deny that the earl of Huntingdon had authority, but their own economic and jurisdictional concerns made them unsympathetic to Earl Henry's need to make an outward show of power. The corporators saw that their own authority over the town could only be guaranteed by royal charter, granting them specific privileges from the central government. They looked to the earl of Huntingdon for aid, friendship, and advice, but they continued to uphold their own status and to work for what they considered the best interests of the corporation.

This episode exemplifies the complex nature of patronage relations in Leicester and in early modern towns in general. It shows the necessity of patronage relationships for towns in this period, especially in crucial situations such as charter procurement. Although the earl of Huntingdon caused the townsmen of Leicester difficulties, he was still their major channel of communication with the crown, from which they hoped to receive their new charter. The corporation for the most part tried to cooperate with the earl as the best way to accomplish their goal. The crown, as represented by the lord chancellor, confirmed that the process should be negotiated through the patron: as long as Huntingdon objected, Ellesmere held up the process. When the earl finally gave his consent, Ellesmere granted the patent.[46] Nevertheless, it is also clear that this was not simply a case of a noble lord forcing the town leaders to obey his will. The townsmen had a certain amount of leverage and negotiating latitude. There was a point at which they would go no further, in order to preserve corporate dignity and privilege. The earl did not like this, but he ultimately accepted it.

Leicester's experience also points to the trend away from the older practices of lordship. The earl of Huntingdon at times tried to wield final authority over the town of Leicester, summoning up an ideal of lordship that had not existed for many decades, if it ever had. Townsmen rejected such domination. They happily preserved some of the outward forms, such as gift-giving and hospitality, but they would not let their corporation fall completely under Huntingdon's sway. In addition, the situation in Leicester demonstrates the great importance of local circumstance in urban patronage relations. The ongoing strife between the houses of Hastings and Grey, as well as Huntingdon's own financial problems, created a local framework that placed a premium on honor and influence. The earl of Huntingdon clung tenaciously to every privilege, fearing a diminution of his own authority in the eyes of the country and the potential expansion of Lord Grey's. Thus Leicester's behavior toward Huntingdon and the corporation's actions in general had greater resonance in local politics than it might otherwise have had. The local context must be carefully analyzed in any urban patronage relationship, as it had a clear effect on the closeness and direction of the relationship.

III

The period from 1605 to 1609 proved the defining one for the relationship between Leicester and the fifth earl of Huntingdon. Ever after, the earl remained wary of the corporation's treatment of him, and the corporators knew that they could not push the earl too far before he balked. Nevertheless, the town remained an important part of the earl's patronage network, both as a source of his personal prestige and potential office and favor for his own clients. He developed a reputation among local gentry and the crown as a man of great influence in Leicester. Preserving his connections there enhanced his position in the eyes of both center and locality.[47] Huntingdon continued to view Leicester as "his" town, despite his occasional clashes with the corporation. The corporators, for their part, knew the earl to be a crucial link to the central and provincial governments, and they would by no means cut themselves off totally from the earl's patronage. While the relationship had its highs and lows, the connection between the two remained close throughout the next several decades.

The strength of this bond lay in the complex mix of ritual, ceremonial exchanges and the more concrete elements of office and favor. The events of 1606–7 aside, the corporation never failed to send the earl and his lady a New Year's gift of wine and sugar. The corporation gave gifts to several people every year, some of them other members of the Hastings family, as well as to Lord Grey, the Hastings's chief rival. But the earl of Huntingdon always received the most valuable present. Even in those years when the town found itself in financial straits, the corporation made this symbolic statement.[48] In addition to these annual gifts, the earl also received many informal tokens of regard from the corporation throughout the course of the year. The aldermen invited him to dine with them when he was in Leicester on official business and gave him small presents whenever he came to town. The townsmen sent more substantial gifts to the earl on those occasions when the king or part of the royal entourage came to call on him at Donnington or Ashby. When the king came to Leicester on progress in 1616, the corporation paid £6 for "a hogshead of claret wine given to the right honorable the earl of Huntingdon at the King's being at Leicester, his honor then being at great charge in making provision to entertain the noblemen which came with his Majesty." A royal visit offered a great financial opportunity to the town's merchants and traders, so the corporation happily assisted the earl, who helped attract the king's entourage to the town. Again in 1617, when James passed through Ashby on his way back from Scotland, the town sent the earl "a yoke of fat oxen" to assist in feeding the entourage.[49] For his part, the earl reciprocated by sending the occasional buck to the corporation, "to make merry withall."[50] Such exchanges repeatedly affirmed and reinforced the ties between patron and clients.

Beyond giving gifts, the corporation honored the earl in other ways. The bells of St. Martin's church pealed for the earl and his family when they came to town. The churchwardens' accounts show payments not only to bell ringers, but to workmen for fixing the earl's seat and for "sweeping the church walls against the earl of Huntingdon's coming thither."[51] These marks of deference and celebration made clear the townsmen's respect for the earl. Townsmen welcomed not just Huntingdon's physical presence, but also his advice and consent. On many occasions every year, representatives of the corporation rode to the earl at Donnington or Ashby to consult on town business. They made some trips to seek specific favors from the earl or to inform him of a particular event in civic government. On other occasions, corporators simply sought his advice before taking action on an issue. When the schoolmaster Mr. Ferne died in 1618, the corporation sent Roger Hawfield, the town clerk, to meet with Huntingdon. The corporators acknowledged that Dr. Clarke, master of the Newark Hospital, had the right to appoint a new schoolmaster, but given the importance of the matter, the corporation wanted the earl's advice. They also asked him to send his letter to Clarke so that the minister would make a wise decision.[52] Whether for things over which he had specific power or not, the corporation still sought out the earl of Huntingdon's opinions on a regular basis.

Demonstrations of regard and mutual obligation provided a vital base for patron-client relations, but the exchange of more tangible benefits also played a role. Like the social rituals of gift and deference, these more practical exchanges involved reciprocity. Throughout the first half of the seventeenth century, the earl of Huntingdon and the town of Leicester exchanged the tangible benefits of office and favor and kept the lines of patronage open. Huntingdon asked for and received licenses to "kill flesh in Lent," alms places in Leicester hospitals, and freedom of the borough for his servants.[53] Similarly, the corporation asked for a number of favors from the earl.[54] But while the relationship persisted, not every attempt at gaining office or favor was successful. The corporation accepted many, but not all, of the earl's nominees to office; similarly, the earl usually, but not invariably, gratified the townsmen's requests for favor. Huntingdon made several attempts to convince the corporation to choose one of his clients, Thomas Clarke, for the position of town serjeant. He even went so far as to procure another, better position for the man who already held the office, so that he would create a vacancy for Clarke to fill.[55] The townsmen refused every time, claiming that "the said Clarke was thought not to be a fit person for that office." Clarke served as the deputy "amnor" [almoner?] for the counties of Leicester and Rutland, and the corporators thought him an inappropriate choice "by reason of his said office of Amnorship, which oftentimes would call him away when we might have most occasion for his service."[56] Not averse to the earl's nominees simply on principle, the corporators nevertheless guarded their own interests by refusing to select nominees they thought might harm the town. There was no simple case of the corporation striving to be independent or the earl completely dominating the townsmen. The relationship, rich and complex, depended both on immediate circumstances and on the longer-term dynamics between town and patron.

A similar pattern can be seen in the nominations for parliamentary burgesses in Leicester. In 1610 the town needed to replace Sir William Skipwith, a burgess since 1604, who died in early May. The earl of Huntingdon informed the corporators of Skipwith's death and asked them to "make choice of my cousin Mr. Henry Rich." Rich "is one who is very nobly born and that will well supply the place, and whose friends and allies are such as he may be able to do you favors." Huntingdon assured himself that his good friends at Leicester would gratify him in this as in so many other things. His friends in Leicester complied. There seems to have been little or no objection to or discussion concerning Rich's selection, the only point at issue being whether he could receive the oath of office by proxy in London.[57] The corporators clearly believed that while Rich was a stranger to Leicester, his election would benefit the town at Westminster.

When King James called a new parliament in 1614, local circumstances created a more complex situation than in the 1610 by-election. Multiple candidates coveted the parliamentary seats at a time when the corporation particularly needed patronage. The corporation was deep in negotiations at London to obtain a patent for the mastership of the Newark Hospital. Several of the men interested in the parliamentary seats had pledged their aid in the hospital suit. The earl of Huntingdon once more nominated his kinsman, now Sir Henry Rich, for one place. He also asked for the second place for one he declined to name, although it was, in fact, his brother Sir George Hastings. The chancellor of the duchy of Lancaster, Sir Thomas Parry, recommended a candidate, Mr. Henry Felton, grandson of Lord Grey. This made things awkward for the corporators, who now had to navigate between the two greatest families in county politics.[58] Meanwhile, Sir William Heyrick, the Leicester native who frequently aided the townsmen in their business in London, asked the corporation to "nominate me for one, [and] I will vow unto you to give as honest an I and an Ø [*sic*] for the good of the town and all corporations as any man you shall make choice of whatsoever." For the second place he recommended their recorder Mr. Francis Harvey.[59] The corporation depended on Huntingdon, Parry, Heyrick, and Harvey to advance the suit for the hospital. No choice seemed good.

As the day for selection approached, the corporators thought carefully about how their choice might affect their suit. They got some relief from the fact that Recorder Harvey declined to stand and the earl of Huntingdon chose to have his brother Sir George stand for knight of the shire. He was still "very importunate" for Sir Henry Rich, however. According to one alderman, Mr. Morton, "we may in no wise say my Lord [Huntingdon] nay, for he will . . . speak concerning the hospital to the Chancellor, to the King, nay if there be cause, my Lord will move the Parliament House." Robert Heyrick, Sir William's brother and a prominent alderman, noted that "the voices go in our Hall, that if the chancellor [Parry] be said nay for Mr. Henry Felton, then our old Hospital is quite gone; so that, you see, many heads, many brains." Corporators clearly feared the consequences to the town and the future of the hospital if they contradicted their patrons' wishes. Alderman Heyrick hoped his colleagues would write to the earl to "see if he will be content to release us of Sir Henry Rich, which by no means we would have if we could get his Honor's consent." In the end, however, the need for patronage prevailed, as the corporators agreed to take one of the earl of Huntingdon's nominees and one of Chancellor Parry's, a well-established compromise in Leicester's parliamentary history. Fortunately for the corporation, Mr. Felton declined to stand, saving the townsmen from having to choose a relative of Huntingdon's nemesis. Parry instead named Sir Francis Leigh, related by marriage to the lord keeper.[60] Corporators duly selected the two knights on 2 April 1614.[61] While they disappointed Sir William Heyrick, the bulk of the corporators made what they thought was the best choice given their position vis-à-vis the old hospital.[62]

The earl of Huntingdon lived up to his word concerning the hospital and other favors for the town as well.[63] The townsmen continually negotiated the boundaries between cooperation with the earl and their own demands and choices. As the 1620's progressed, however, tensions arose that had as much to do with national policy as with the local relations between the town and the earl.[64] Questions about the militia, especially, made the corporation feel the need to appeal to their patron for succor, but the earl, as lord lieutenant and chief military officer for the king in Leicester, had to carry out royal policy. This change strained relations between town and earl. At the heart of the matter lay the right to exercise the civic militia company within the town walls and the rate that the town had to pay both in men and in money. Not simply a question of having to make greater financial sacrifices during a period of economic downturn, the militia issue touched on corporate privilege and pride. It also involved the honor and authority of the earl of Huntingdon, who took his military duties seriously and used the militia as a way to enhance his own prestige. He, like all lord lieutenants, felt pressure from the crown to perform well and to "perfect" the militia in the crown's campaign to rationalize and invigorate local government.[65] Thus both local circumstances and national matters impinged on the way Leicester and Lord Huntingdon interacted in the 1620's.

For the most part, the town and the earl found ways to compromise that did not cripple the other's position. The corporators called on the earl's past good lordship to the town when they requested their service to be reduced or changed, and Huntingdon respected that. A personal plea from the mayor provided an effective strategy. The earl did in fact lower the town's levy on at least one occasion, and changed his mind about requiring the town militia to train outside Leicester with the county troops. His need to show his authority and the pressure he was under to improve the county militia grew stronger, however, causing him to demand that the corporation send its troops to the countywide muster early in 1627.[66] When his grandfather George had dealt with similar problems in the reign of Elizabeth, there had been room to maneuver. The fourth earl on several occasions lowered the town's troop allotment or moderated their service in some way.[67] But circumstances had changed by the 1620's. In the war years late in the decade, the rules that the fifth earl had to enforce grew more rigorous and less flexible.

The increasing difficulties of the 1620's impacted the town's selections for Parliament as well as military matters. Pinched between the desires of the earl of Huntingdon and the chancellor of the duchy, the corporation found itself with too many nominees, just as in 1614. The compromise of taking one nominee from each of the two patrons, thus pleasing them both, helped resolve this difficulty. In 1621 the town selected Sir Richard Morison, Huntingdon's candidate, and Sir William Heyrick, the nominee of duchy chancellor Sir Humphrey May, Heyrick's brother-in-law. The process of choice was actually more complicated than the result might indicate, however. Several other candidates came forward, one from the recorder and one from the countess of Devonshire, who had recently taken up residence in the Bishop's Fee just outside the town. The corporation politely dismissed the claims of the countess and Recorder Harvey, leaving only the nominees of the two patrons to stand for the final selection. The corporators may not have been particularly enthusiastic about Morison. They had expressed their desire to choose a freeman, which Morison definitely was not.[68] They could only have been delighted, however, with Sir William Heyrick, their great friend and a prime mover in their suit to obtain the hospital. These two men, both with court connections and one with very strong local connections as well, stood the town in good stead at Parliament.

The 1624 election again saw the corporation attempting to balance the wishes of several patrons. The chancellor of the duchy, Sir Humphrey May, requested one place for himself. The corporation happily consented. May also had taken the extra precaution of getting the earl of Huntingdon's letter of endorsement, so that voters had a double reason to select him. They received the nomination "with joy and thankfulness" from both Huntingdon and May. Meanwhile, Huntingdon had tried to get his brother Sir George Hastings selected as knight of the shire. Failing that, he recommended Sir George to the corporation, "presuming upon your wonted affection to me which upon all occasions I have had good testimony of that you would add this to the heap of your former respect." The corporation had a strong desire to select one of its own, however, and chose William Ive, a senior alderman and one of the wealthiest men in town. They were able to make their excuses to the earl by claiming that they had taken his one nominee, as custom dictated, and this nominee was Sir Humphrey May.[69] Whether this satisfied the earl is unlikely, but despite the outcome, Huntingdon did not give up nominating men to the corporation, nor did the townsmen turn their backs on the earl as their good lord. In October 1624, the corporators invited the earl to join them for the election feast and to administer the oath to the new mayor. In December, three aldermen, the recorder, and one of the chamberlains rode to Ashby to visit the earl "to confer with him about the businesses and affairs of the town so soon as with convenience they may."[70] The corporation reserved the right to protect its own interests and choose for its local officers those men who would best serve its needs, yet the connection between town and lord remained.[71]

A continental war and the succession of a new king brought forth a new set of issues that affected the way the center and the localities related. The crown pressed military service and rates strictly, and King Charles and his council devised nonparliamentary ways to finance royal expenditures. How these matters unfolded in Leicestershire had an important effect on the earl of Huntingdon's patronage of Leicester, altering his ability to serve as an effective mediator between central and local government.[72] On the one hand, he enforced the militia regulations almost too strongly, thus antagonizing the county. On the other hand, he chose not to pay the Forced Loan, destabilizing his position vis-à-vis the king. These things combined to complicate and hinder the earl's role as a patron. It also left the borough of Leicester in a weakened position: the corporators could not be sure that their wishes would be properly communicated to the center through the earl, but no clear alternatives existed, either.

Huntingdon's troubles began in 1624 and 1625. In 1624 the earl enthusiastically worked to perfect the Leicestershire militia, as required by the crown. Because of the financial straits of his family, the earl seems to have used the militia as a way to enhance his prestige without spending his own money. He rated the county to pay for all sorts of trappings—including knapsacks and a marquee—for the militia, all sanctioned by the Privy Council but considered unnecessary luxuries by Leicestershire taxpayers. They also grumbled about the high charge for paying the militia officers and for supplying arms and powder, although in fact the rate differed little from other years.[73] The earl did no more than enforce rules made by the crown, but he applied them more thoroughly and possibly more arbitrarily than did other lord lieutenants.

Huntingdon's failure to pay the Forced Loan provided a second source of his trouble. He never interfered with its collection in Leicestershire nor spoke openly against it, but he tried to excuse himself from it by pleading his extreme poverty.[74] While his claim of financial difficulty rang true, the earl nevertheless found the wherewithal to buy luxuries for himself and his wife during this period. He took a lengthy and expensive journey to Bath at the same time that he claimed poverty to the king.[75] He had also felt solvent enough, just a few years previously, to give a large donation to the king of Bohemia for the defense of the Protestant cause. He strongly supported this cause, and in fact exhorted others to contribute freely, as well.[76] Whatever his reasons, Huntingdon did not pay the loan, undermining his position with King Charles. This state of affairs may have made him enforce his military office even more strongly, hoping that the king would perceive his loyalty and forwardness in that service.

Unfortunately for Huntingdon, his plan backfired. Leicestershire's notorious factional politics put a dangerous spin on Huntingdon's activities. The Grey family and their supporters made political hay by accusing the earl of what amounted to official corruption. Various gentlemen of the county complained to the Privy Council about their lord lieutenant, claiming that he levied exorbitant rates and that he kept the county's money in his own pockets for personal gain. The council put enough credence in these accusations to call for all of the earl's accounts for the Leicestershire militia and for the testimony of the collectors and the receiver. The earl himself was called before the full council to state his case, a deep humiliation for him. He also feared that people at home would be unable to distinguish whether he was being accused of failing to pay the Forced Loan or of abusing his privileges as lord lieutenant and bilking the county.[77] Either way, it damaged his reputation and put him out of favor with both his countrymen and the crown.

How did all of this affect the town of Leicester in its relations with the earl? The tension between the two is apparent, although no direct and consistent correlation exists between the earl's problems and the town's actions. As we have seen, the corporators pleaded with the earl to allow the civic troop to muster within the town liberties in order to uphold their chartered privileges. He had the power to make this decision, and they could use their long relationship to his family as leverage in making their case. But they also took the precaution of getting the chancellor of the duchy, Sir Humphrey May, to write a letter to the earl on their behalf. In 1626, when the earl charged the town £50 for militia rates, the corporation agreed to send only £25, citing their recent visitation by the plague and the "deadness of trading" and "scarcity of money" in the town. Sixty-nine people refused to pay their assessments toward the £50, including some from the civic elite. The corporation as a body disapproved of such rank refusal, but they did appeal strongly to the earl to reduce the levy.[78] Of course, whatever the townsmen may have wanted, the earl could not simply grant their wish, given his personal circumstances and his orders from the crown. Had he allowed the Leicestershire militia to be laxly exercised or underfunded, it would have been another large black mark on his already mottled record. Huntingdon, bruised by royal demands, local desires, and personal circumstance, found accommodation nearly impossible to achieve.

The earl of Huntingdon's untenable position soon came to have a direct impact on the corporation. For several generations, the Hastings family had held the office of keeper of the forest of Leicester from the crown. The forest lay just outside the borough of Leicester, and the inhabitants of the town had common rights there. In 1626 King Charles decided that he wished to "disafforest" the forest so that it could be rented out for arable fields.[79] This meant that the earl would lose the office of keeper, along with the prestige and the privilege of hunting that went with it, while the borough would lose its customary rights. Under other circumstances, a nobleman with such long-standing traditional privileges might have been able to convince the king not to proceed. But Huntingdon had very little influence with the crown while he remained out of favor over the Forced Loan and the charges of corruption in the militia rating. Thus the town's close connection to the earl, often useful in the past, now worsened Leicester's position with the crown.

This crisis forced the townsmen to scramble to find support for their opposition to the disafforestation. While the earl could not pull strings for them at Court, he did help them in planning their strategy. On the earl's recommendation, they had the recorder frame a petition to the king to stop the disafforestation because of the damage it would do to Leicester. They asked for the earl's continued support and solicited his advice as to whether they should get the county JPs to petition the king as well.[80] In order to obtain effective communication with the crown, however, the townsmen had to turn to others. On 4 November 1626, they wrote to Sir Humphrey May, chancellor of the duchy and MP for the town, asking for his assistance in preventing the disafforestation. They also sent an alderman, Richard Inge, to speak to Sir Humphrey directly. May asserted his willingness to help the town in any way he could, but as a member of the Privy Council and one of the commissioners in the matter, he could not advise them in the business. Nevertheless, he said that "the town of Leicester should ever find him their faithful friend." Inge spoke to the attorney of the duchy as well, obtaining his goodwill for the town. Next, he "moved my Lord of Devonshire that he would be pleased to deal with such of the commissioners that conveniently he might, which he promised to do." Devonshire and his mother, the dowager countess, had acquired property nearby and become actors in the life of the town. The corporators took advantage of this relationship as much as they possibly could, in the absence of effective patronage from the earl of Huntingdon.[81]

Along with these more informal channels of connection and interest, the townsmen also made use of the formal action of petitioning. They made a petition to the earl of Huntingdon as lord lieutenant of Leicestershire to use his influence to stop the disafforestation, but given the circumstances, this may well have been simply a formality.[82] More to the point, the corporation petitioned King Charles, begging him not to take the proposed action, out of kindness to his poor subjects in Leicester. To get their petition to the king's notice, the corporators sent a second petition to the duke of Buckingham, hoping to gain the support of the royal favorite. In framing their appeal, the townsmen played up the damage that the disafforestation would do to their poor town and also to the county. They emphasized the duke's connection to the locality, for Buckingham had been born in Leicestershire, son of Sir George Villiers of Brokesby, knight of the shire and onetime sheriff. Buckingham had little to do with his home county once he left it, but the townsmen willingly exploited any connection they could.

> We your humble petitioners being by oath and duty bound to provide for the safety and good of this incorporation and to prevent the hurt thereof to our powers, and having ever found your gracious favor and honorable disposition towards the weal of this poor town, are bold to become petitioners, that your Grace would be pleased to mediate unto his Majesty or others by his Highness authorized for these affairs for the preventing of the great and inevitable losses that disafforesting will produce, both to this town and the whole county, which if it please your Grace to do you shall not only do a work of great mercy and piety to this town of Leicester and your native country in general, but to thousands of poor souls in particular, bordering upon the same, whose prayers will never cease to be poured forth to God for your Grace's long and happy continuing in this life and afterward eternal blessedness in the Kingdom of Heaven.[83]

Such pitiful and effusive petitions were common currency in this period, and the men of Leicester knew how to pull out all the stops to make the strongest possible impact on the recipient.

Unfortunately, their petitions failed. At one point, the corporators had even thought about using a monetary reward to achieve their ends: they agreed to "make known privately to the earl of Huntingdon and the earl of Stamford that if means can be made to his Majesty that the Forest may contain as formerly it hath been, that this corporation will give five hundred pounds towards the raising of money for his majesty's satisfaction in that behalf."[84] This too availed them nothing. The forest met its end in 1627, provoking resistance from some of the local poor, who were tried at the summer Assizes of 1628 for casting down the ditches and forcibly resisting the clearance. Leicester lost the forest, but in the end the crown granted the town 40 acres for the use of the poor and 20 acres specifically in lieu of the common lands lost in the disafforestation.[85] The earl lost the income, privileges, and prestige that went with the keepership of the forest and spent the ensuing several years seeking compensation for his losses, the honorific ones just as much as the monetary ones.[86]

These events changed the relationship between the town and the earl. The corporation could no longer depend on Huntingdon for patronage with the Court, since his connections there remained tenuous. He managed to retain his local offices of lord lieutenant, *Custos Rotulorum*, and justice of the peace, but just barely.[87] Although the townsmen put less reliance on him in accomplishing their business, they still considered him their patron, asking favors of him and providing him with honor and favor in return. In the parliamentary election of 1628, the corporation as usual appeased its two most important patrons, selecting Sir Humphrey May at his own request and Sir John Stanhope at the earl of Huntingdon's request. There seems to have been little or no discussion about the earl's nominee. The corporators did the earl this favor, since he had made a choice so congenial to them. Stanhope, though a Derbyshire gentleman, had connections in Leicestershire, as well.[88] Huntingdon also continued to sit on commissions for affairs in the county, such as the one for the collection of knighthood fines in 1630. Although the townsmen asked him to reduce the sum, the earl had little option but to carry out the commission vigorously.[89] The corporation thus had a very mixed relationship with the earl. While he made unpleasant demands of the town, the townsmen still wanted to remain in his good graces. He continued to wield authority over things such as militia rates or composition fines. He felt pressed himself, since the demands he made of the town were being enforced upon him by the king, into whose good graces he hoped to restore himself. A complex mixture of central and local considerations determined the relationship between Leicester and the earl.

The earl of Huntingdon's troubles over the Forced Loan, the militia, and the forest of Leicester seemed to have a strong psychological effect on him. The 1630's saw him retreat increasingly from public life. He disliked London and the Court, at times sending his wife to do his business for him. Ensconced in his congenial country estates, he warned his sons not to enjoy the high life at Court too much. He wrote to his second son Henry,

> I should be sorry that you should like a Court life too well, for it is but *splendida miseria*, and Sir Walter Mildmay, a great courtier and Councilor of State in Queen Elizabeth's time, in a little book of his hath this saying, "Know the Court but spend not thy time there." And I can say in my own experience that have tasted the waters that have issued from honest delights that no life for the good of the soul, of the body, and of the estate are answerable to a country life.[90]

Such sentiments convey his alienation. He also spent a large amount of his time and energy pursuing lawsuits against two Leicestershire gentlemen, Sir William Fawnt and Sir Henry Shirley, both of whom had insulted his honor and questioned his governance in the late 1620's.[91] The earl's preoccupation with his own business left the borough of Leicester adrift.

No longer so closely tied to Huntingdon, the corporators found themselves butting heads with other peers in the area. The countess of Devonshire, who had purchased Bishop's Fee, a property just outside the town wall, caused the corporation serious problems. When they attempted to renew their charter between 1629 and 1632, they met with stiff resistance. While the corporation wished to increase jurisdiction over the suburbs, the countess wanted to retain control for herself. The townsmen first petitioned the king for a new charter in July 1629, at which time Charles ordered Sir Robert Heath, attorney general, to peruse it and give his recommendation. Heath responded that some of the new branches of the charter had no precedent and required further study. The corporation continued to strive for passage of the improved patent, but without a powerful advocate to speak on their behalf, the countess of Devon easily outmatched them.[92]

Continuing prior practice, the townsmen turned to the earl of Huntingdon for relief. They sent the town clerk to the earl to "acquaint him with the late proceedings of the countess of Devon against the corporation concerning the Bishop's Fee, and to entreat the continuance of his Honor's favor and furtherance to us in that business." They based some of their arguments on the earl's opinion that the Bishop's Fee lay within the borough of Leicester.[93] The earl's apparent sympathy with their cause availed them nothing, however, as he did not or could not turn his wishes into actions in London. The countess of Devon, on the other hand, used connections at Court to exhibit her suit before the Privy Council. In the end, the board ruled that the borough of Leicester had never legally exercised jurisdiction over the Bishop's Fee, and that they would not in the future ever be allowed to do so.[94] Thus the charter came to nothing, the corporation lost its de facto authority over the suburbs, and the countess showed herself as a force to be reckoned with in the town's business.

The "vacuum of patronage" in Leicester also led Henry Grey, earl of Stamford, to increase his dealings with the town. Although the Grey family lived at Bradgate, just outside of the borough of Leicester, the family historically had much less influence on the town than the geographically more distant earls of Huntingdon. After decades in the political wilderness, the family saw its fortunes flourish in the early seventeenth century. Sir Henry Grey became Lord Grey of Groby in 1603 and advanced to the earldom of Stamford in 1628.[95] As the Grey family's stock with the crown rose, they attempted to exert more influence over their neighboring town. Their efforts offer a clear example of the reciprocal nature of patronage relations. Lord Grey needed to cultivate local connections to prove his usefulness to the crown. In turn, local people saw his star rise at the center and wished to connect themselves to him to improve their own positions. The two things constantly reinforced each other, just as the reverse happened when the earl of Huntingdon fell out with the crown. The effects of this shift in relative prominence of the two lords is apparent in the town records for the 1630's. As an attempt to win the corporation's goodwill, the earl of Stamford invited the mayor and aldermen to join him in the "fishing of Groby Pool" in the summer of 1633. The townsmen happily accepted, later sending him their thanks and a gift of twenty gallons of wine and a sugar loaf. When the king and queen came northward on progress in 1634, the royal party stopped in Leicester and at Bradgate. The corporation sent a hogshead of claret to the earl of Stamford at Bradgate for use in the monarchs' visit, as they had done for the earl of Huntingdon in the past.[96] These small but significant signs indicate that the earl of Stamford gradually gained influence in Leicester, as he purposely cultivated the interest of the corporation.

As with the earl of Huntingdon, the corporation did not unthinkingly concede to the earl of Stamford's authority. In 1635, Stamford obtained a patent granting him sole control over the brewing of beer and ale in Leicester. In return for this monopoly, Stamford promised to designate £20 per annum from the profits to be given to the poor of Leicester. While this arrangement might provide a steady income to the corporation for the use of the poor, the brewers of Leicester and the borough corporation that regulated all the trade in the town believed it would be "very prejudicial" to their privileges. The Common Hall decided to challenge the earl's patent with a petition to the Privy Council.[97] The corporation also made a direct appeal to the earl of Stamford himself. Although they would readily pleasure him in "any design which may appear to be to or for the public good," they could not "conceive but that the business intended is like rather to turn to the great prejudice of our town in many respects, than to any public good." They then astutely appealed to Stamford to be their patron in preserving the welfare of the town: "wherefore we become humble suitors and petitioners to your Honor that you will vouchsafe the continuance of your honorable favor and respect to us and this poor corporation, and be a means to prevent the proceedings in any thing that may turn so much to the prejudice of the corporation as we conceive your Honor's propositions will."[98] In this way, the corporators attempted to transform Stamford from a great lord demanding an unpopular favor to a patron of Leicester who worked to preserve the town's best interest.

The corporation's plea fell on receptive ears at Court, if not at Bradgate. The Privy Council apparently supported the corporation's arguments against Stamford, preventing him from enforcing his plan on the town. He later asked the corporators if they wished to purchase the patent of monopoly from him, a proposition they firmly declined. They sent one of their members to Bradgate to thank him for making the offer, but told him they thought it "neither good nor fit for the corporation to accept the same."[99] Stamford's influence in the corporation rose, but he could not expect the men of Leicester to obey him all of the time.

The 1630's posed new challenges for Leicester corporation, as for all local government. While trying to negotiate the changing local circumstances of the leading families of the shire, the corporators also had to contend with the increased demands of the crown. Militia rates and Ship Money exercised the townsmen, who once again sought relief through the good lordship of the earl of Huntingdon. Chamberlain's accounts show the corporation's concern about the levies, as they sent two men to the earl at Donnington "about the Ship Money." The records do not indicate whether they hoped to persuade the earl to help them lower the rate, but the corporators clearly felt it important to consult with him. The townsmen paid the full amount of £200 in the first assessment, apparently without much difficulty, but the task became more difficult with each succeeding year. In 1636–37 the corporation had to make up £6 11s. 6d., while the following year they made up £28 in defaults.[100] Beyond the passing mention in the chamberlain's accounts, the Leicester archive contains no other commentary on the townsmen's attitude regarding the levy, nor are there any petitions to Huntingdon, Stamford, or the chancellor of the duchy complaining of the town's assessment. While silence cannot be taken for hard evidence, it may be that the townsmen realized that on this issue, their local patrons could not grant the favor, since the king himself so ardently promoted the policy.

Regardless of their views on Ship Money, the townsmen of Leicester clearly disliked the burden being placed on them for men and money in the late 1630's. By 1639–40, the corporation seemed almost in a tug-of-war with the earl of Huntingdon who, as lord lieutenant of Leicestershire, enforced many of these policies on the county and the town. In June 1639, the corporators were of two minds as to whether they should accede to another request for a military levy. The earl had apparently written to the mayor, asking that he supply a list of the names of the members of the corporation and others of worth in the town to be used for assessment purposes. A meeting of the Four-and-Twenty agreed to send two of their members to the earl of Huntingdon, but disagreement arose over what to tell him. The town clerk first wrote down that they were going "to certify his Lordship of the 24 & 48 & the gents & attorneys & other inhabitants of the Borough of Leicester that are able to bear any charge toward [tear]." This whole sentence was lined through, however, and below it was written, "to entreat his Lop. that Mr. Mayor may be spared from giving any list of the 24 & 48 . . . according to a letter received from the said Lord." Ten days later, the full Common Hall agreed that "a list of the 24 & 48 and the rest of the great and men of ability within the corporation shall be s[ent] unto my Lord of Huntingdon in satisfaction of a letter sent from his [Honor] to Mr. Mayor for that purpose."[101] Ambivalence about how to proceed with the earl arose among the members of the corporation as they tried to reconcile his role as their good lord and as enforcer of unpopular policy.

This ambivalence can be seen in the way that the corporation dealt with Huntingdon as he levied both troops and money from the townsmen for use in the war in Scotland. In the spring of 1640, the earl ordered the corporation to send the trained band to Loughborough for a muster. Just as in the 1620's, the townsmen objected to this on the grounds that it infringed on their corporate privileges and they asked the earl and his deputy lieutenants to withdraw their demand. The corporation wrote to the new chancellor of the duchy of Lancaster, Lord Newburgh, asking him to intercede with the earl of Huntingdon on the town's behalf. This Newburgh did, making a personal appeal to the earl to let the town trained band muster at home, "whereby the liberties and privileges of your corporation may be preserved."[102] Recorder Thomas Chapman, commenting on Lord Newburgh's action, said that the corporation had great reason to thank him for it, for the earl of Huntingdon would never have changed his order without Newburgh's personal request.

> Though my Lord of Huntingdon gave an indifferent answer to your letter, yet delaying to write unto you, we thought fit to write another letter in your names to Mr. Chancellor of the Duchy & to deliver that also & to move him about the business, for fear my Lord of Huntingdon might in the interim while he delayed us should complain to the Council of you, & get a messenger sent down for you, while we waited upon him for his letter. . . . Though my Lord of Huntingdon at his [Lord Newburgh's] request hath spared you, yet I believe if he had not moved him therein, he would one way or other have done you a displeasure, or at least have endeavored it.[103]

While Chapman's suspicions cannot be proved, his language shows his belief that the earl did not have the best interests of the town in mind.

Huntingdon had no intention of modifying his demands to suit the corporation. Whatever had been his feelings about the Forced Loan, the earl in 1639–40 staunchly supported the king and his prosecution of the war. In November 1640, the earl commanded the corporation to collect £50 in the town for their arrears in militia payments. Instead of proceeding immediately, the Common Hall met to confer, concluding that they could not possibly make the collection. They had already been at great charge that year in sending their pressed soldiers to Loughborough and billeting them there, along "with our other expenses for his Majesty's service in the North." This amounted to £150, "which as yet we know not how to raise by way of tax by reason of the small trading we have had of late in our poor Corporation." They had also been visited by pestilence, which had not only cost them £150 outright, but had decreased trade and traffic in the town. They humbly requested that the earl would spare Leicester from the payment of the £50, "we not knowing well how at this time to collect the same."[104] Although the corporation went through the formalities of making a humble request of the earl for favor, the letter leaves the impression that the corporators could not and would not assess this tax.

The tensions that arose between town and lord in 1639 and 1640 came into sharp relief in the elections for the Short and Long Parliaments. The earl of Huntingdon's desires still carried weight with the townsmen, even in these highly charged elections. But other figures entered the field as electoral patrons, and the corporators themselves had strong feelings about their choices. Henry Hastings, second son of the earl, who was himself standing for knight of the shire, went to Leicester in early spring of 1640 to report to his father on the disposition of the corporation. He said that Lord Newburgh had written to the town on behalf of Mr. Simon Every, receiver of the duchy, for the first place, and that the townsmen were well affected toward him, although some believed that only a townsman should be chosen. The rest were solicited for Sir John Bale and Sir Thomas Hartopp, knights resident in the shire, who Henry Hastings said would remove themselves from the running if the earl disapproved. Hastings also put in a kind word on behalf of the civic magistrates:

> I must needs do the Mayor and the chief of the Aldermen this right as to let you know how forward and willing they are to observe you in what choice soever they shall make and that they likewise express their respects to you both in their words and affectionate kindnesses to me, which I desire your Lordship to take notice of as from me, and to write them thanks in general terms for the report I have made to you of them; by this you will oblige them to [give] me their best assistances by procuring what voices they can (to make me Knight of the Shire) and there is many in that town.[105]

Obviously, the mayor's and aldermen's behavior pleased Hastings, and he happily exploited it as much as he could for his own benefit.

The earl of Huntingdon took his son's advice, and penned a thank-you letter to the corporation for their willingness to give their voices to Henry as knight of the shire. In addition, the earl asked them to give his son a burgess place if Henry failed to be chosen for the county. Lord Newburgh had already recommended Mr. Simon Every for one seat, and the earl seconded the nomination, vouching for Every as his neighbor. The earl of Devonshire, Charles Cavendish, also made a bid for parliamentary patronage in Leicester. He put forward the name of Mr. Thomas Coke, son of Secretary Sir John Coke, presuming that "at this time" the townsmen would "have a greater eye to the sufficiency of those you choose than to the friendships they make." Lord Newburgh, in his recommendation of Mr. Every, acknowledged that he had "no power or interest" with the corporation to force them to choose his nominee, but left them to a "free election."[106] The peers angling for seats seemed just as aware as the townsmen themselves that something different was going on in 1640 than in any previous election.

In the end, the corporation gratified all their patrons, although not entirely intentionally. The townsmen chose as their burgesses Mr. Simon Every, appeasing Lord Newburgh and the earl of Huntingdon. For the second place they chose Mr. Roger Smith, esq., a thorough-going Puritan. Smith's election clearly signaled that the corporation of Leicester felt strongly about reformed religion and probably voted in part along religious/ideological lines. Smith, however, had such a precise conscience that he could not swear the oath of office for the place of burgess. He politely declined the seat. This being the case, the townsmen turned to the other man that had been recommended to them, electing Mr. Thomas Coke to serve in the place instead.[107] Although no informal comments about the election exist in the archive, the results suggest that the townsmen of Leicester, at least, were not in a strictly antipatron, anti-Court mood during the course of this election. They saw it as in the best interests of the town and themselves to gratify their neighboring peers in this way, as long as the nominees proposed were acceptable men. The Leicester corporators may well have been expressing an opinion about public policy in choosing Roger Smith, but once he left the field they made use of the obligations that their acceptance of their various patrons' nominees would create.

The abrupt dismissal of Parliament in the spring and the announcement of a new election for the fall of 1640 gave Leicester's patrons another opportunity to recommend nominees. The election writs followed hard on the heels of the king's commission to Huntingdon to raise troops to fight the Scottish rebels.[108] Despite the anxiety of the times and the position they played in Leicester politics, none of the Hastings family seems to have used the opportunity to nominate a burgess to the corporation. Into this apparent void stepped the earl of Stamford, the earl of Huntingdon's bitter rival for authority in the county and a vigorous promoter of puritanism and of parliamentary right. For the first time in the seventeenth century, the Greys wrote formally to the corporation of Leicester, asking for a parliamentary place. The earl of Stamford wrote on 9 October 1640, recommending to the townsmen his eldest son, Thomas Lord Grey, "in respect of my neighborhood to your town." Stamford promised that his son would carry out the office diligently, since he wished to be burgess of Leicester more than of any other place. He would also bring benefit to the town: "if you gratify his desire and my request, you shall tie both him and me to do you any courtesies shall lie in our way, either for your corporation in general or any of you in particular." While Stamford made a strong plea, his was not the first. Lord Newburgh and the earl of Devonshire also wrote to the corporation, Devonshire on behalf of Mr. Thomas Coke and Newburgh on behalf of Mr. Simon Every, as in the spring election. But Every was a Court appointee, while Lord Grey was a local dignitary with sympathetic religious beliefs. The third candidate, Thomas Coke, provoked fewer objections than Every, although he was the son of a Court official. As in the April election when they first selected Roger Smith, esq., the townsmen chose someone whose religion they could trust, who would be sure to uphold the reformed tradition in the church. On election day, 23 October 1640, the assembled corporators chose Thomas Grey and Thomas Coke of Gray's Inn as burgesses for Leicester.[109]

The corporation's choice of Grey made clear the townsmen's preferences. But the earl of Huntingdon's apparent lack of intervention in this crucial election seems perplexing. It could be that he saw the handwriting on the wall and forbore to make a nomination in order to avoid sure public rejection. The county went to his rivals Henry Lord Grey of Ruthven and Sir Arthur Hesilrige, both firm puritans, and the mood of both county and borough was anti-Court. Huntingdon, though far from being a courtier, did vigorously support the king and his policies in 1639–40. He wrote to his fellow peer, the earl of Arundel, in 1639, declaring his firm attachment to King Charles.

> I think a man may say "O Mores, O Tempora" that any of his Majesty's Nobility of this kingdom should refuse to serve the King his Majesty, going

[to York] in his own person, but sure they must be of the new stamp that should make scruple of it. It is an offense of so transcendent a nature as I think a greater cannot be committed unto his Majesty, God bless his person and make him victorious in all his designs against his enemies.[110]

Huntingdon set himself in direct opposition to the Grey family, who disagreed with the actions of the crown in this period.[111] Set on top of the longstanding rivalry for prominence in the county between the two families, this ideological difference gave the electors of Leicestershire a clear choice in autumn of 1640. The majority of the political elite in both the borough and the county had greater affinity with the parliamentary/puritan stance of the earl of Stamford than with that of the Hastings family, and hence the earl of Huntingdon lost his influence as a parliamentary patron. The potential good he could do for them was far outweighed by the importance of having a voice in parliament that reflected the beliefs and desires of the voters of Leicester.

Patronage, as it developed in the reigns of Elizabeth and James, could not function in the face of the divisive politics of the 1640's. No longer did lineage, wealth, prestige, and connections provide the sole basis for authority, but rather more political issues, particularly religion and views on the role of parliament, played a much greater part than they had previously.[112] A patron's greatest asset was the ability to mediate between parties, based on social authority and dignity. When the parties held increasingly hardened positions, this mediating power shriveled. Thus the earl of Huntingdon's decline as a patron derived not simply from his personal decrepitude and his retreat from governmental activity, but because political realities made his style of patronage—based on prestige and not "interest"—untenable.

IV

The earl of Huntingdon's power as a patron received its death-blow in the turmoil of 1640. The townsmen continued to send him gifts and occasionally to consult him, but as a mark of respect rather than of clientage. As king and Parliament went to war, the earls of Huntingdon lost their political clout in a largely parliamentarian county. The fifth earl died frail and disillusioned in 1643.[113] His heir Ferdinando succeeded him, while his second son Henry became an important Royalist general in the Midlands. Ferdinando withdrew almost entirely from public life, and took no interest in interacting with the corporation. When the corporators asked him to administer the mayor's oath in 1644, he claimed that the right had ended with his father. He may well not have wished to give the oath to a Parliamentarian mayor, but even after the town fell to a Royalist siege in 1645, earl Ferdinando declined to perform the service.[114] Parliament sequestered Ferdinando's estates after the war, and he eventually had to beg a parliamentary act to break the entail on his estates in order to pay his taxes and fines. Meanwhile, Lord Grey became prominent as the leading Parliamentary general in the area, and became lord lieutenant of Leicestershire after the war. The corporation interacted regularly with him, but he was more military governor than patron.[115] The old style of patron, who thrived on honor and tradition rather than ideological stance, seems to have died with the old earl of Huntingdon. The war reduced Huntingdon's authority, like Ashby Castle, to rubble.

Yet ties to the house of Hastings never fully died out. With the Restoration in 1660, the townsmen turned immediately to the head of the Hastings clan, Henry Lord Loughborough (earl Henry's second son), to reestablish the relationship that had essentially been in hiatus since the early 1640's. The earl of Huntingdon, Theophilus, was a child of ten years, his father Ferdinando having died a broken man in 1654. Henry Hastings, Lord Loughborough, had suffered as a delinquent under the Parliamentary regime, but with the restitution of royal government, he was very much in King Charles II's good graces and well placed for Court favor. The corporation recognized this and immediately called on him to reestablish the links between their town and his family, emphasizing the favor his ancestors had always borne toward the corporation. Not only did they turn to him for parliamentary patronage, but for favor from the king as well. The townsmen wished to present the king with a gift of £300 in September 1660, and they asked Lord Loughborough if he would attend the king with them so that the gift would be accepted. This he did, much to the pleasure of the corporation, who showed sincere gratitude to the peer. They expressed the "great duties which we do much owe to your Honor and your noble family for this and all former favors received by us and our predecessors, much rejoicing that we have so noble a friend of that noble family that can and will befriend us." The corporation also asked him to reinstate the practice of administering the mayor's oath at Leicester Castle, a practice that had been discontinued by his brother during the troubles. Loughborough happily complied, working to reforge the links between the town and his family and to establish himself as patron of Leicester, a position in which the townsmen seemed pleased and ready to accept him.[116] The question whether that relationship was the same as the one that had existed before the war does not fall within the limits of this study.[117] Clearly, though, the corporation of Leicester found something in that earlier relationship important enough to make them wish to reconstruct it once circumstances permitted. Patronage was not something merely forced onto the town by power- or prestige-hungry peers, but was rather a relationship entered into willingly, with open eyes and with expectations of benefit in return.

Leicester's long history with the earls of Huntingdon shows graphically the many complexities in relations between towns, patrons, and the crown in this period. While the patron-client relationship lasted over a long span of time, it shifted and varied as local and national circumstances changed. It must also be said that Leicester's experience with its patrons is unusual for its intensity. The combination of propinquity, long roots in the locality, and a history of close ties with the central government made the house of Hastings a particularly potent force in Leicester. Leicester's example shows one end of the spectrum of urban patronage in this period.

Nevertheless, the pattern of relations between the corporation of Leicester and the earls of Huntingdon exemplifies many of the larger issues at work in urban patronage more generally. Of first importance is the fact that towns needed patrons. Patrons helped make government work. Without the vital connection of men like Huntingdon, interaction between the central and local manifestations of the monarch's government would have been extremely difficult. Such formal bureaucracy as existed was not designed to make these connections, while the institutions that could serve the purpose—for instance Parliament and the Assizes—met only intermittently. Thus it fell to prominent, usually noble, men to bridge this gap. The earls of Huntingdon, in particular the third earl, achieved this successfully for the town of Leicester. The fifth earl's loss of favor with King Charles made the process more difficult, but the townsmen still tried to work through the earl. Even at moments of contention between patron and client—as during the charter controversy in 1607—the corporation of Leicester never entirely forsook the earl of Huntingdon as their patron. The corporators well knew that the earl was still their best link to the crown and the most powerful man in the county. Patrons offered crucial support for the well-being of their boroughs, as they linked towns to the national government. Losing an established patron could cause serious problems.

Leicester's relations with the Hastings family also show clearly the local context of patronage. The earls of Huntingdon took an active part in civic life, economically, socially, and governmentally. The outward forms of exchange, such as gifts and hospitality as well as office and parliamentary seats, formed an important part of the relationship between town and lord. Leicester offers a complex counterbalance to oversimplified explanations of such interaction—either that boroughs were striving for independence or that great lords forced towns into submission. The townsmen of Leicester on many occasions actively welcomed the earl of Huntingdon's participation in borough life. They frequently solicited his advice and mediation. They regularly accepted his nominees for office and favor, whether for a place in the hospital, a position in borough government, or a seat in parliament. None of these are the actions of a corporation trying to exclude all external forces from its jurisdiction.

At the same time, neither did the townsmen allow their patron to dominate borough life and government. The corporators kept a strict hold on their own dignity and privileges, defending corporate rights when dealing with noble patrons. While the corporation would accept the earl of Huntingdon's nominees when these nominees could do good for the town, the aldermen rejected those who posed danger to civic liberties. Strangers, nonresidents, and men with other offices typically failed to find preferment in Leicester corporation, despite the earl's nomination. A delicate balance existed between welcome participation and interference. The corporators of Leicester constantly renegotiated this balance with their patrons. Leicester, like most towns, drew the line where the benefits of gratifying a patron no longer outweighed the potential consequences to a borough's privileges.

Leicester's experiences with urban patronage show how important this relationship was in the life of the town and of it major patrons. The earls of Huntingdon provided the corporation with a channel to the crown as well as with assistance in local government and in sorting out local differences. The earl received the deference of the townsmen, a means of expanding his personal clientage network, and reinforcement from the crown as the premier authority in the locality. The fifth earl's decreasing clout, both in the county and with the center, jeopardized his position as patron and highlights the movement away from reliance on local magnates and toward stronger connections to the Court. Leicester's case may not be a model for others, as its main patron was something of a dying breed and the relations between town and lord were particularly intense. Its example does, however, set out the boundaries and range of interactions that made up urban patronage and shows how both local and national circumstances altered those connections over time.

Conclusion

The fifth earl of Huntingdon knew his duty. Service to the king through government of the locality constituted his most important work. His status, wealth, family legacy, and noble title placed him at the head of Leicestershire society and his royal offices of *Custos Rotulorum*, justice of peace, and lord lieutenant gave him authority to act. He valued (and indeed fought to maintain) his position in the eyes of his king and of his neighbors. His role as patron to the borough of Leicester offered him one way to make manifest his position. He made the most of it, browbeating the townsmen at times, but also truly acting as their good lord, providing favors and supporting the town's causes. The corporators of Leicester had a complicated and occasionally tense relationship with the earl, yet on the whole he served their purposes well. Theirs was not a relationship of simple resistance or servility on the part of the town and domination on the part of the earl. Townsmen both feared the earl and loved him. But his days as a player were numbered. Huntingdon's style of patronage was becoming increasingly obsolete. Power resided at Court, and the earl's absence from the centers of power hindered his ability to act effectively. Not simply who you were, but what you could do, made a patron powerful.

The relationship between the corporation of Leicester and the fifth earl of Huntingdon illustrates both the significance of patronage to urban government and the changing circumstances in which patronage took place. Towns needed patrons. This was a fact of corporate life. Except for London, all towns were peripheral, at least in the geographical sense. Civic leaders worked hard to craft lines of communication to the crown. Those corporate boroughs that could attach themselves to a great peer or powerful gentleman strengthened their position not only with the monarch but in the eyes of other provincial authorities as well. In this status-conscious society, an earl's word meant more than an alderman's. Townsmen knew the realities of their world and made the most of the situation. A borough corporation protected its rights and privileges by maintaining connections to a variety of powerful nonresidents who could provide access and protection.

In cultivating the connections by which they gained advantage, corporations used the most traditional of methods, emphasizing honor, ritual, and custom. Most of the interaction that took place between patron and client took the form of ceremonial language and actions. Patrons and clients exchanged gifts, shared hospitality, and acknowledged each other's honor. Deference on the part of the townsmen and respect on the part of the patron were vital methods of exchange, just as important as the more tangible benefits of office and parliamentary seats. The willingness of corporations that often teetered on the brink of insolvency to engage in gift-giving and hospitality to favored friends and neighbors suggests the significance they attached to it. Patronage was not a matter of quaint custom. It was central to the business of governing. Patrons provided a wide variety of services for civic leaders, everything from maintaining order within the governing body to promoting the corporation's business at Whitehall. Patronage could sort out differences between rival jurisdictions or provide a link to the crown in moments of necessity. Procuring charters, negotiating tax levels or militia rates, and obtaining new markets all occurred through the mediation and goodwill of patrons. A vital tool for drawing together center and locality, patronage served the needs of town and crown while also appealing to the desire for status and honor of the men who provided the service.

Those who served as patrons clearly saw the benefits of it. They received both tangible and intangible returns from these connections: honor and deference, office and privilege. More clients meant more honor. A following in the provinces offered an important display of the respect in which a patron was held. Those that felt they were losing their grip on power and reputation clung determinedly to their roles as urban patrons as a way to affirm their status in the eyes of both the locality and the crown. The family and friends of the young earl of Rutland in 1590 laid elaborate plans to persuade the corporation of East Retford to choose the earl as the town's high steward, even though he was a minor. A family confidant urged the dowager countess of Rutland to invite civic leaders "to your own table with some kind courtesies" in order to ensure that the young earl would not lose even this "little office" from his patrimony.[1] Having patronage links to a town helped prove to the crown that one had authority in the locality, and esteem in the eyes of the crown was one of the paramount achievements for people in this period. The crown gained from the situation as well. Having some of the most prominent men in the land attached to specific communities in a clearly defined relationship gave royal government a means of communication to and enforcement in that community. In the absence of a formal bureaucracy, patronage helped the crown govern better.

Throughout this process of exchange between crown, patron, and civic government, the initiative of town leaders comes through clearly. Corporations were full participants in patronage, not simply pawns acted upon by their betters. A narrow focus on parliamentary patronage has often painted a picture of patrons forcing lowly townsmen to accept their parliamentary nominees without question. A broader look at urban patronage as a whole suggests something different. Townsmen saw parliamentary selections as one among several types of interaction between themselves and the great men of their society. Gratifying a patron at a parliamentary election could play a part in a larger strategy of enlisting aid for the business of the borough, in parliament or elsewhere. Deeply pragmatic, corporators saw the value, as well as the dangers, of inviting members of the landed elite to participate in local affairs. They learned to play the patronage game well. In choosing patrons and making connections, they made careful calculations, weighing the potential benefits of particular men. Understanding where the power lay, civic leaders in general moved away from local magnates, identifying prominent courtiers as the best targets for effective assistance. With these connections, civic leaders worked to advance their own best interests during increasingly difficult times, while also reinforcing their own authority.

This movement away from local magnates toward peers with more clout at Court is a distinctive feature of this period. As government became more complex, and as the crown placed greater burdens (both administrative and fiscal) on local elites, those men had to find ways to respond to and connect with the center. Civic leaders perceived the significance, and even necessity, of patronage to the success of urban government, turning to those they believed most capable of delivering the goods. The development and formalization of the office of high steward provides evidence of the increased urgency with which corporations pursued the goodwill and practical assistance of their social betters. It also suggests the support for this office among those in power, who allowed it to become an increasingly standard part of borough constitutions. Only by making connections did civic leaders expect to be able to accomplish their business, and the crown, in turn, relied on these connections to regulate local government.

The crown's regulation of local government, however, had a clear effect on the ability of patronage to work effectively. Patrons required some latitude if they were to mediate between center and locality. As royal government's expectations of local authorities became increasingly rigid, negotiation became more difficult. Particularly in matters that concerned taxation and religion, corporations found their traditional sources of patronage unable to achieve local ends. This is especially apparent in the events surrounding the Forced Loan, where some negotiation did occur, and the collection of Ship Money, where few towns escaped with a reduced level of the exaction. As has been seen, debates over Ship Money actually propelled some corporations into further difficulties with the crown, as townsmen became tarnished with reputations for faction and irregularity in religion. The result was a scramble for assistance from the men most close to the king. Peers like the earl of Dorset, the earl of Strafford, and even Archbishop Laud become the targets for corporations seeking patronage in the 1630's. Ironically, of course, these very men were probably the least likely to carry out local wishes, if local wishes entailed reducing militia charges or absolving a borough from financial contributions. The mediation of patronage was simply not going to moderate the requirements that the crown placed upon local government. Civic leaders clung to the hope that patrons could bring about change, as evidenced by the attempts of such boroughs as Leicester to recall and bring to bear their patrons' historic goodwill toward the town on the vexing problems of the day. Urban patronage could still work in the 1630's, and sometimes it still did. New relationships formed and old connections strengthened. But the network of patronage came under increasing strain as patrons became less able to mediate between center and locality, less able to gratify both local clients and the king's will.

The patterns of patronage, although altered by the events of the 1620's and 1630's, held their own throughout the period. But they would not survive the turmoil of midcentury intact. People on the peripheries tried to manipulate traditional patronage relations to gain their own interests, but such personal connections could not well mediate between strongly held, principled positions. While patronage was able to encompass some conflict, it failed when the parties made entirely incompatible demands. Relationships built principally upon honor and traditional social ideals of authority rather than firm political or religious beliefs did not flourish when beliefs became more central to political discourse. The disruption of older connections is apparent in the parliamentary elections of 1640. Parliamentary patronage, never a sure thing in any election, became even more tenuous in those for the Short and Long Parliaments. In many—although by no means all—boroughs across the realm, voters chose members of Parliament based on ideas rather than on the nomination of a patron. Urban patrons of long standing, such as the earl of Huntingdon in Leicester, simply lost out in the changed political scene of the 1640's.

It is outside the scope of the present work to explain the changes after 1640, but a brief look beyond our terminal date is in order. If patronage were a completely effective means of making connections among different parts of the English state, one might question how the civil war could have happened at all. Of course, patronage did not work in every instance, nor was it the only mode of interaction between center and locality. As the highly charged political situation descended into war in the 1640's, patronage as it had been practiced in the previous 60 years became a casualty. Corporations chose to find other means to accomplish their business as traditional patrons appeared less able, and quite possibly less willing, to do favors for civic governments. Urban patrons of long standing withdrew themselves from that role when they no longer had the ability to command the loyalty of their local clients or influence decisions at the centers of power. The structures of authority were contested in ways they had not been before; it was no longer clear just where the lines of authority ran, and having the ear of the king did not mean what it once did. Having the ear of the Parliament could be far more important. The fact that Parliament was in regular session throughout the 1640's, and that it became the most important venue for business, significantly altered the way government worked. The two decades from the calling of the Long Parliament to the Restoration also saw the development of more organized and professionalized bureaucracies within English government.[2] Patrons, who had always worked in the interstices of government, may have had less latitude to operate, less room to make a personal impact. Ideology and institutions made government by personal connection not obsolete, but certainly less significant.

It seems as though the war itself also diminished the desire of local leaders for compromise and consensus. Partisanship flourished in the tumultuous atmosphere of civil war even while the rhetoric of unity and uniformity continued to be heard.[3] Excising wholesale those who disagreed with the political views of the day became the norm at all levels of government by midcentury. The impact of this on corporations was direct: with the Restoration, parliamentary statute required the surgical removal of dissent.[4] Paul Halliday has shown how the politics of division arose in the decades of war and republicanism and also how these divisions—once thought evil and destructive—came to be accepted into the normal course of civic government and English society as a whole.[5] Urban patrons of the later seventeenth century tended to be more politicized, favoring one local faction over another (usually the "well-affected" over the "malignants") or trying to enforce policy on behalf of the crown. Theophilus, the seventh earl of Huntingdon, resurrecting the role of urban patron that his predecessors had played in Leicester, played his most notable part in the turmoil of the early 1680's. In an attempt to recraft the corporation more to the king's liking, Huntingdon worked assiduously behind the scenes to persuade the corporators to surrender the civic charter to the king and accept a new one with a more circumscribed constitution.[6] The earl succeeded, and those who disagreed were excised from the corporation. But Huntingdon's influence with the corporation later faded to black when he followed the lead of King James II into the political wilderness. Theophilus's world of partisanship and contest was a far cry from the world of his grandfather Henry.

It is the world of Henry earl of Huntingdon and the corporators of Leicester that this book has attempted to illuminate. For these people, participation in the work of the state was a given. Civic governors could not function in isolation or alienation from the crown, since many of the issues most crucial to urban life and government were affected by royal action. Nor could corporations maintain a strict policy of exclusion toward members of the landed elite. Townsmen relied too heavily on them to provide a means of communication to the center and influence with other authorities in the provinces. Many corporate towns interacted regularly with members of the elite. These relationships, dynamic and flexible, could run the gamut from happy and harmonious to bitter and oppressive. They varied widely in scale and intensity. Yet their significance in helping to get the work of government done is attested to by the frequency with which borough corporations sought them out. Local leaders discovered routes to power and worked out the most effective ways to ply them. This initiative on the part of civic leaders suggests that we rethink the larger problem of relations between center and locality in this period. Society was not fragmentary, with different parts unable to comprehend or communicate with each other. Late Elizabethan and early Stuart government was more than a simple matter of central authority being imposed onto the localities, where center and locality were automatically and inherently at odds. Governance was dynamic and interactive, and the impetus to forge these mutual relationships came as much from the localities as from the crown. Patronage provided a medium for this exchange. All of the elements within the English state were interdependent, from the central to the peripheral. Without such connection, the business of governance could not have been accomplished at all.

APPENDIX

Borough High Stewardships, 1580-1640

Abingdon

Henry Lord Norris	1574	P. Hasler, *The Commons 1558–1603*, vol. I (London, 1981), p. 114
William Knollys, earl of Banbury	1610–1630	Bromley Challenor, ed., *Selections from the Municipal Chronicles of the Borough of Abingdon* (Abingdon, 1898), p. 56
Henry Rich, earl of Holland	1630–1640+	Ibid.

Andover

Robert Dudley, earl of Leicester	1574–1588	Hasler, vol. I, pp. 167–68
Robert Devereux, earl of Essex	1597–1601	Ibid.

Banbury

William lord Knollys (earl of Banbury)	by 1608–1632	J. Gibson and E. Brinkworth, eds., *Banbury Corporation Records, Tudor and Stuart*, Banbury Historical Society, vol. 15 (1977), p. 99 Alfred Beesley, *The History of Banbury* (London, 1841), p. 266
William Fiennes, Viscount Saye and Sele	1632–1640+	Ibid., p. 282

Barnstaple

William Bourchier, earl of Bath (Recorder)	by 1596–1623	The Diary of Philip Wyot, in *Sketches of the Literary History of Barnstaple*, ed. J. R. Chanter (Barnstaple, 1866), p. 103

Edward Sackville, earl of Dorset	1637–1643	NDRO, B1/612

Boston

Henry Clinton, earl of Lincoln	–1616	John Bailey, ed., *Transcription of the Minutes of the Corporation of Boston*, vol. 2 (Boston, 1981), pp. 185–86
Thomas Clinton, earl of Lincoln	1616–1619	Ibid.
Thomas Lord Coventry (Chief Recorder)	1634	Ibid., p. 678
Robert Bertie, earl of Lindsey (High Steward)	1634	Ibid., p. 684

Bristol

Robert Dudley, earl of Leicester	–1588	John Latimer, *Annals of Bristol* (Bristol, 1900), p. 8
William Cecil, Lord Burghley	1588–1597	Ibid.
Robert Devereux, earl of Essex	1597–1601	Ibid.
Thomas Sackville, Lord Buckhurst (earl of Dorset)	1601–1608	Ibid.
Robert Cecil, earl of Salisbury	1608–1612	Ibid.
William Herbert, earl of Pembroke	1613–1630	Ibid., p. 114
Richard Weston, earl of Portland	1630–1635	Ibid.
Philip Herbert, earl of Pembroke	1635–1640	Ibid., p. 135

Bury St. Edmunds

Thomas Howard, earl of Suffolk	by 1645	HMC *Fourteenth Report*, Pt. 8, Bury St. Edmunds Mss., p. 142

Cambridge

Roger North, Lord North	1572–	F. A. Keynes, *By-Ways of Cambridge History* (Cambridge,1947), pp. 38–44
Thomas Egerton, Lord Ellesmere	1600	Ibid.

Francis Bacon, Viscount   1617   Ibid.
St. Albans

Thomas Coventry,   1629   Ibid.
Lord Coventry

John Finch, Lord   1640   Ibid.
Finch

Canterbury

Thomas Egerton, Lord   1606   PRO, C181/2, fol. 16
Ellesmere

Chichester

Thomas Howard, earl   1618–1640+   VCH Sussex, vol. 3, p. 99
of Arundel

Chipping Wycombe

Lord Windsor   1605   Neale, p. 145

Colchester

Sir Francis Walsingham   1579–1589   Hasler, vol. 1, p. 159
(Recorder)

Sir Thomas Heneage   1589–1595   Ibid.
(Recorder)

Robert Cecil, earl of   1595–1612   PRO, C181/2, f. 112; Hasler, vol. 1,
Salisbury (Recorder)   p. 159

Henry Rich, earl of   1635–1640   *The Charters and Letters Patent
Holland   Granted to the Borough of Colches-
                                        ter* (Colchester, 1904), p. 92

Congleton

Sir Thomas Savage,   1625–   PRO, C233/3, fol. 53
bart., and Sir John
Savage

Coventry

John Harrington, Lord   1611–1614   Benjamin Poole, *Coventry: Its His-
Harrington   tory and Antiquities* (London and
                                        Coventry, 1870), p. 369

Sir Edward Coke   1614–1630+   Cov.CRO, BA/H/C/17/1, fols. 201v,
(Recorder)   306v

Thomas Coventry,   1633–1640   T. W. Whitley, *The Parliamentary
Lord Coventry   Representation of Coventry* (Coven-
                                        try, 1894), p. 78

Earl of Northampton   1640   Poole, *Coventry*, p. 369

Dartmouth

Robert Cecil, earl of Salisbury	by 1603	DRO, MS DD61670
Henry Howard, earl of Northampton	1613	MS DD61838
Thomas Howard, earl of Suffolk	1614	MS DD61879A
Henry Montagu, Viscount Mandeville	1626–1636+	MSS DD61874, DD62637

Derby

Gilbert Talbot, earl of Shrewsbury	by 1603–1616	Lambeth Palace Lib., MS 3203, fol. 115
Edward Talbot, earl of Shrewsbury	1616–1617	Robert Sampson, *History and Antiquities of Derby* (Derby, 1826), pp. 93–94
William Herbert, earl of Pembroke	1617–	Ibid.

Doncaster

George Talbot, earl of Shrewsbury	–1590	*A Calendar to the Records of the Borough of Doncaster*, vol. 4 (Doncaster, 1902), pp. 62–63
Henry Carey, Lord Hunsdon	1590–1596	Ibid., p. 64
Sir Robert Cecil (earl of Salisbury)	1596–1612	Ibid., p. 125; John Tomlinson, *Doncaster from the Roman Occupation to the Present Time* (Doncaster, 1887), p. 54n
William Crichton, Viscount Ayr	1630	Ibid., p. 114n

Dorchester

James Stuart, duke of Richmond	1641	David Underdown, *Fire from Heaven* (New Haven and London, 1992), p. 187

East Retford

Roger Manners, earl of Rutland	1592–1612	HMC Rutland, vol. 4, p. 303; GEC, vol. 11, p. 259
Sir Gilbert Clifton, bart.	by 1640	M. F. Keeler, *The Long Parliament, 1640–41: A Biographical Study of Its Members* (Philadelphia, 1954), p. 59

Evesham

Sir Thomas Challenor	1605–1615	*Evesham Borough Records of the Seventeenth Century*, ed. Stephen K. Roberts, Worcestershire Historical Society, vol. 14 (1994), pp. xiii, 19
Lewis Bailey, Bishop of Bangor	1615–1625	Ibid., p. 19
Edward Conwey, Lord Conwey	1625–1630	Ibid., p. 25
Thomas Coventry, Lord Coventry	1630–1640	Ibid., p. 31
Thomas Coventry, Lord Coventry	1640+	Ibid., p. 41

Exeter

William Cecil, Lord Burghley	by 1592	DRO, ECA Accounts, 33–34 Eliz.
Sir Robert Cecil (earl of Salisbury)	1599–	ECA Act Book 5, fol. 438
Thomas Sackville, earl of Dorset	1608–	ECA Act Book 6, fol. 320
Henry Howard, earl of Northampton	1612–1614	ECA Act Book 7, fol. 49
Thomas Howard, earl of Suffolk	1615–1625	Ibid., fol. 176
William Herbert, earl of Pembroke	1625–1630	Ibid., fol. 624
Richard lord Weston (earl of Portland)	1630–1635	Ibid., fol. 754
Philip Herbert, earl of Pembroke	1635–1640+	ECA Act Book 8, fol. 38

Gloucester

Sir Edward Coke	1615–	Samuel Rudder, *History and Antiquities of Gloucester* (Cirencester, 1781), p. 117

Gravesend

James Stewart, duke of Lenox and his heirs	1635–	PRO, C233/4, fol. 97

Great Yarmouth

Robert Dudley, earl of Leicester	1572–1588	NRO, Y/C18/6, fol. xlvi

William Cecil, Lord Burghley	1588–	Ibid.
Robert Devereux, earl of Essex	1597–1601	Ibid.
Charles Howard, earl of Nottingham	1601–	NRO, Y/C19/5, fol. 22
Henry Howard, earl of Northampton	1613	NRO, Y/C18/6, fol. 196
James Ley, Lord Ley (earl of Marlborough)	1625–1629	NRO, Y/C19/6, fol. 8v
Edward Sackville, earl of Dorset	1629–1640+	Ibid., fol. 141v

Grimsby

Sir George Heneage	–1638	HMC *14th Report*, App. 8, Great Grimsby MSS, p. 282
Robert Bertie, earl of Lindsey	1638–	Ibid.

Guildford

Charles Howard, earl of Nottingham	1585–1624	Vivienne Hodges, "The Electoral Influence of the Aristocracy, 1604–1641" (Ph.D. diss., Columbia University, 1977), p. 443

Hereford

William Herbert, earl of Pembroke (Chief Steward)	1617–1630	Richard Johnson, *The Ancient Customs of the City of Hereford* (London, 1882), p. 229

Hertford

Robert Cecil, earl of Salisbury	1605–1612	N. Salmon, *The History of Hertfordshire* (London, 1728), pp. 36–37
William Cecil, earl of Salisbury	1612–1640	Ibid.

Hull

Sir Francis Walsingham	1583–1590	Hasler, vol. I, p. 288
Sir Thomas Heneage	1590–1595	Ibid.
Sir Robert Cecil (earl of Salisbury)	1595–1612	Ibid.
Thomas Egerton, Lord Ellesmere	1612–1617	GEC, vol. 3, p. 476; L. M. Stanewell, *Calendar of the Ancient Deeds [Kingston upon Hull]* (Hull, 1951), p. 327

George Abbott, arch-bishop of Canterbury	1617–1633	VCH Yorkshire, East Riding, vol. 1, pp. 101–2; Stanewell, *Calendar*, p. 329
Thomas Coventry, Lord Coventry	1633–1640	Ibid.
Thomas Wentworth, earl of Strafford	1640–1641	Keeler, *Long Parliament*, p. 74n

Ipswich

Sir Francis Walsingham	1581–	SRO/I, C6/1/2, fol. 35
Henry Carey, Lord Hunsdon	1590–1596	GEC, vol. 6, p. 628; SRO/I, C9/2 (2), fol. 58v
Robert Devereux, earl of Essex	1596–1601	SRO/I, C5/14/1, fols. 192, 232
Thomas Sackville, Lord Buckhurst	1601–1608	Ibid., fol. 232v
Robert Cecil, earl of Salisbury (elected but declined)	1608	SRO/I, C6/3, fol. 227v
Thomas Howard, earl of Suffolk	1608–1627	SRO/I, C5/14/1, fol. 264v
Theophilus Howard, earl of Suffolk	1627–1639+	Ibid., p. 336

King's Lynn

Robert Dudley, earl of Leicester	1572–1588	Henry Hillen, *History of the Borough of King's Lynn* (Norwich, 1907; repr. Wakefield, 1978), p. 292
Thomas Egerton, Lord Ellesmere	1598–1617	*Stiffkey Papers*, Camden Society Third series, vol. 26, pp. 16–17
Thomas Howard, earl of Arundel	1635	King's Lynn Town Hall, KL/C7/9, fol. 404v

Leominster

| Sir Thomas Coningsby | –1625 | Hodges, "Electoral Influence," p. 445 |
| Fitzwilliam Coningsby | 1625–1640+ | Ibid. |

Lincoln

| Robert Bertie, earl of Lindsey | by 1638 | GEC, vol. 8, p. 17 |

Macclesfield

| Sir John Savage | 1595–1597 | J. P. Earwaker, *East Cheshire*, vol. 2, p. 416 |

Sir John Savage, bart.	1598?–1615	Ibid., p. 467
Thomas Savage, Viscount Savage	1616–1635	Ibid.
Thomas Savage, Earl Rivers	1636+	Ibid.

Maldon

Robert Dudley, earl of Leicester	1565–1588	Hasler, vol. I, pp. 160–61
Robert Devereux, earl of Essex	–1601	Ibid.
Sir Thomas Mildmay	1604	Hodges, "Electoral Influence," p. 446
Sir Julius Caesar	1614–1636	Ibid.
Sir Henry Mildmay	1636–1640+	Keeler, *Long Parliament*, p. 46.

Nottingham

| Edward Manners, earl of Rutland | by 1582 | W. H. Stevenson, ed., *Records of the Borough of Nottingham*, vol. 4 (London, 1890), p. 200 |
| Gilbert Talbot, earl of Shrewsbury | 1606–1616 | Ibid., p. 278 |

Oxford

Sir Francis Knollys	to 1592	H. E. Salter, ed., *Oxford Council Acts, 1583–1626* (Oxford, 1928), p. 68
Henry Carey, Lord Hunsdon	1592–1596	Ibid., p. 102
Robert Devereux, earl of Essex	1596–1601	Ibid.
Thomas Egerton, Lord Ellesmere	1601–1611	Ibid., p. 139
William Knollys, Lord Knollys (earl of Banbury)	1611–1632	Ibid., p. 205
Thomas Howard, earl of Berkshire	1632–1649	M. G. Hobson and H. E. Salter, *Oxford Council Acts 1626–1665* (Oxford, 1933), pp. 39, 164

Plymouth

| Sir Robert Cecil (earl of Salisbury) | by 1597–1612 | R. N. Worth, ed., *Calendar of the Plymouth Municipal Records* (Plymouth, 1893), p. 139 |

Thomas Howard, earl of Suffolk	1613–1626	Ibid., p. 148
Francis Russell, earl of Bedford	1627–1631	Ibid., p. 155

Portsmouth

Henry Radcliffe, earl of Sussex	1590–1594	Robert East, ed., *Extracts from the Records of the Borough of Portsmouth* (Portsmouth, 1891), p. 137
Charles Blount, Lord Mountjoy	1594-	Ibid., p. 143

Reading

Robert Dudley, earl of Leicester	to 1588	Hasler, vol. I, p. 116
Sir Henry Neville	1588–1593	Ibid.
Robert Devereux, earl of Essex	1593–1601	Ibid.
William Knollys, Lord Knollys (earl of Banbury)	1601–1632	HMC, Eleventh Report, App. 7 (Reading Mss), p. 184; J. M. Guilding, *Diary of the Corporation of Reading*, vol. 2, pp. 8, 10, 11
Henry Rich, earl of Holland	1632–1640	Guilding, vol. 2, p. 115

Rochester

Charles Howard, earl of Nottingham	1624	Hodges, "Electoral Influence," p. 450
George Villiers, duke of Buckingham	1624–1628	Ibid.
Philip Herbert, earl of Montgomery (earl of Pembroke)	1628–1640	Ibid.

St. Albans

William Cecil, Lord Burghley	–1598	HALS, Off Acc 1162/312, fol. 69
Robert Devereux, earl of Essex	1598–1601	Ibid., fols. 69, 80
Thomas Egerton, Lord Ellesmere	1601–1616	Ibid., fols. 80, 103
Francis Bacon, Viscount St. Albans	1616–1626	Ibid., fol. 103

Thomas Coventry, Lord Coventry	1632-	PRO, C233/4, fol. 39v; A. E. Gibbs, ed., *The Corporation Records of St. Albans* (St. Albans, 1890), p. 6

Salisbury

Sir Francis Walsingham	1590–1591	Robert Benson and Henry Hatcher, *Old and New Sarum or Salisbury* (London, 1843), p. 296
Sir Christopher Hatton	1591	Ibid.
Sir Thomas Heneage	1591–1595	Ibid.
Sir John Puckering	1595–1610?	Ibid., p. 305
William Herbert, earl of Pembroke	1610–1630	Ibid., p. 364
Philip Herbert, earl of Pembroke	1630–1640	Ibid., p. 377

Stafford

Henry Howard, earl of Northampton	1602–1614	John Bradley, ed., *The Royal Charters and Letters Patent Granted to the Burgesses of Stafford* (Stafford, 1897), p. 150
Robert Devereux, earl of Essex	1614-	Ann Kettle, ed., "Matthew Cradocke's Book of Remembrance 1614–15," in *Collections for a History of Staffordshire*, Staffordshire Records Society, Fourth Series, vol. 16 (1994), p. 86

Stamford

Thomas Cecil, earl of Exeter (Recorder)	1604+	John Drakard, *The History of Stamford* (Stamford, 1822), p. 102
William Cecil, earl of Exeter	1627–1640	Ibid., p. 106

Tamworth

Robert Devereux, earl of Essex	1588–1601	Charles Palmer, *History of the Town and Castle of Tamworth* (Tamworth, 1845), p. 112
Sir Humphrey Ferrers	1601	Ibid., p. 114
Sir John Egerton	1602	Ibid.
Sir Humphrey Ferrers	after 1603	Ibid.

Tewkesbury

Robert Dudley, earl of Leicester	1574	James Bennett, *History of Tewkesbury* (Tewkesbury, 1830), p. 43

Totnes

Sir Robert Cecil (earl of Salisbury)	by 1600–1612	DRO, MS 1579A/7/122; John Roberts, "Parliamentary Representation of Devon and Dorset 1559–1601," (MA thesis, University of London, 1958), p. 233
Henry Howard, earl of Northampton	1612–1614	DRO, MS 1579A/5/25
William Herbert, earl of Pembroke	1616?–1630	DRO, MS 1579A/5/27
Francis Russell, earl of Bedford	1630–1641	DRO, MS 1579A/5/30

Wallingford

Robert Dudley, earl of Leicester	1569–1588	Hasler, vol. I, p. 117
Henry Lord Norris	1588–	Ibid.
Sir John Fortescue	1601–	Ibid.
William Knollys, Viscount Wallingford	1621–1632	John Hedges, *The History of Wallingford* (London, 1881), p. 106
Thomas Howard, earl of Berkshire	1632–1640	Ibid., p. 121

Westminster

Robert Cecil, earl of Salisbury	–1612	Hodges, "Electoral Influence," p. 453
George Villiers, duke of Buckingham	1618–1628	Ibid.
Philip Herbert, earl of Montgomery and Pembroke	1628–1640	Ibid.

Winchester

Sir Francis Walsingham	1581–1592	HRO, Winchester records, W/B1/1, fol. 221
Thomas Sackville, Lord Buckhurst	1592–1593	Ibid., fol. 269
Sir Thomas Heneage	1593–1596	Ibid., fol. 272
Charles Blount, Lord Mountjoy	1596–1606	Ibid., fol. 286v
Thomas Sackville, earl of Dorset	1606–1608	Ibid., fol. 312

Robert Cecil, earl of Salisbury	1608–1612	W/B1/3, fol. 157
Henry Howard, earl of Northampton	1614	Ibid., fol. 178v
Henry Wriothesley, earl of Southampton	1618–1626	W/B1/4, fol. 6v
George Villiers, duke of Buckingham	1626–1628	Ibid., fol. 51
Thomas Wriothesley, earl of Southampton	1629–1640	Ibid., fol. 60v

Windsor

Charles Howard, earl of Nottingham	1592–1624	Hodges, "Electoral Influence," p. 453
George Villiers, duke of Buckingham	1624–1628	Ibid.
Henry Rich, earl of Holland	1628–1640	Ibid.

Woodstock

Sir Henry Lee	–1611	Marjorie Maslen, ed., *Woodstock Chamberlain's Accounts, 1609–50*, Oxfordshire Record Society, vol. 58 (1993), p. xviii
Sir Thomas Spencer	1612–1622	Ibid., p. 26
Philip Herbert, earl of Montgomery	1622–1640+	Ibid., p. 89

York

Sir John Fortescue	–1607	YCA, B.33, fol. 119
Robert Cecil, earl of Salisbury	1608–1612	Ibid.
Henry Howard, earl of Northampton	1612–1614	Ibid., fol. 297v
Thomas Howard, earl of Suffolk	1614–1626	B.34, fol. 272v
Thomas Coventry, Lord Coventry	1626–1640	B.35, fol. 25v, B.36, fol. 36v
Thomas Wentworth, earl of Strafford	1640–1641	B.36, fols. 36v, 39v

REFERENCE MATTER

Abbreviations

Add.	Additional Manuscripts, British Library
APC	Acts of the Privy Council
BL	British Library, London
Bodl. Lib.	Bodleian Library, Oxford
CRO	Cheshire Record Office, Chester
Ches.CRO	Chester City Record Office, Chester
Cov.CRO	Coventry City Record Office, Coventry
CSPD	Calendar of State Papers, Domestic
DNB	Dictionary of National Biography
DRO	Devon Record Office, Exeter
ECA	Exeter City Archives, in DRO
G.E.C.	G.E. Cockayne, *The Complete Peerage*
HALS	Hertfordshire Archives and Local Studies, Hertford
Harl.	Harleian Manuscripts, British Library
HMC	Historical Manuscripts Commission
HRO	Hampshire Record Office, Winchester
HWRO	Hereford and Worcester Record Office, Worcester (St. Helen's branch)
Hunt. Lib.	Henry E. Huntington Library, San Marino, California
KAO	Kent Archives Office, Maidstone
Lam. Pal.	Lambeth Palace Library, London
LRO	Leicestershire Record Office, Leicester
LA	Lincolnshire Archives, Lincoln
NRO	Norfolk Record Office, Norwich
NDRO	North Devon Record Office, Barnstaple
PRO	Public Record Office, London
SRRC	Shropshire Records and Research Centre, Shrewsbury
SRO/B	Suffolk Record Office, Bury St. Edmunds
SRO/I	Suffolk Record Office, Ipswich
VCH	Victoria County History
YCA	York City Archives, York

Notes

INTRODUCTION

1. NRO, Y/C18/6, fol. 255.

2. See below, Chap. 3.

3. Keith Wrightson, *English Society 1580–1680* (New Brunswick, NJ, 1982), pp. 66, 149, 184, 222; Susan Amussen, *An Ordered Society: Gender and Class in Early Modern England* (New York, 1988), pp. 2, 134–35. See also many of the essays in A. Fletcher and J. Stevenson, eds., *Order and Disorder in Early Modern England* (Cambridge, 1985), particularly the editors' introduction.

4. For an older, but still compelling, discussion of this process, see G. R. Elton, *The Tudor Revolution in Government* (Cambridge, 1953) and *England under the Tudors* (London, 1955). More recent work includes David Loades, *Tudor Government: Structures of Authority in the Sixteenth Century* (Oxford, 1997), and Steven Ellis, *Tudor Frontiers and Noble Power: The Making of the British State* (Oxford, 1995), which stresses differences in Tudor control over the borderlands.

5. The social scientific literature on patronage is vast. Much of the current discussion is based on Eric Wolf, "Kinship, Friendship, and Patron-Client Relations in Complex Societies," in Michael Barton, ed., *The Social Anthropology of Complex Societies* (London, 1969), especially pp. 16–17. Wolf provides one of the clearest accounts available. Other works covering this subject are S. N. Eisenstadt and Louis Roniger, "Patron-Client Relations as a Model of Structuring Social Exchange," *Comparative Studies in Society and History* 22, no. 1 (January, 1980): 42–77, and "The Study of Patron-Client Relations and Recent Developments in Sociological Theory," in S. N. Eisenstadt and Rene Lemarchand, eds., *Political Clientism, Patronage and Development* (London, 1981), pp. 271–329.

6. Wolf, "Kinship, Friendship, and Patron-Client Relations," p. 17.

7. Ibid., p. 18.

8. Sharon Kettering, *Patrons, Brokers, and Clients in Seventeenth-Century France* (New York, 1986), p. 4.

9. Lawrence Stone suggests this equation in *The Crisis of the Aristocracy* (Oxford, 1965; reprint 1979), especially in chapter 5, entitled "Power."

10. Victor Morgan, "Some Types of Patronage, Mainly in Sixteenth and Seventeenth Century England," in *Klientelsysteme in Europa der Frühen Neuzeit*, ed.

Antoni Mączak (Munich, 1988), p. 102. Morgan uses this terminology as a reference to Max Weber's concept of "patrimonial bureaucracy."

11. Ibid., p. 104.

12. Many historians have discussed patronage from the center's perspective. John Neale, in *Queen Elizabeth* (Oxford, 1958), interpreted most of Elizabethan politics in terms of factions that were held together through networks of patronage. Wallace MacCaffrey's "Place and Patronage in Elizabethan Politics," in S. T. Bindoff, J. Hurstfield, and C. Williams, eds., *Elizabethan Government and Society* (London, 1961), pp. 95–126, makes the extension out from the Court and into the localities, showing how Elizabeth doled out patronage to the peerage and gentry in order to govern the realm. Linda L. Peck, *Court Patronage and Corruption in Early Stuart England* (New York, 1990), focuses on the uses of patronage by the early Stuart Court and argues that a movement from neutral "patronage" to negative "corruption" occurred in this period and contributed to the breakdown of government.

13. MacCaffrey, "Place and Patronage," p. 98.

14. Clive Holmes, "The County Community in Stuart Historiography," *Journal of British Studies* 19 (1980): 54–73; Ann Hughes, *Politics, Society, and Civil War in Warwickshire, 1620–1660* (Cambridge, 1987).

15. For a more systematic treatment of this transition, see Robert Tittler, "The End of the Middle Ages in the English Country Town," *Sixteenth Century Journal* 18 (Winter 1987): 471–87.

16. Robert Tittler has shown that although an increase in borough incorporations can be spotted from the late fifteenth century, the most intense period of incorporation occurred between 1540 and 1558. There were 13 borough incorporations between 1485 and 1540, but 44 in the 18 years between 1540 and 1558. (Robert Tittler, "The Incorporation of Boroughs, 1540–1558," *History* 62 [1972]: 24.)

17. For the general argument, see Martin Weinbaum, *British Borough Charters, 1307–1660* (Cambridge, 1943). For specific town histories, see for example J. Reilly, *History of Manchester* (Manchester, 1861); J. A. Picton, *Memorials of Liverpool* (Liverpool, 1875); Joseph Gribble, *Memorials of Barnstaple* (Barnstaple, 1830); or W. R. James, *The Charters and Other Documents Relating to the King's Town and Parish of Maidstone* (London, 1825).

18. John Neale, *The Elizabethan House of Commons* (London, 1949), pp. 164, 165–66, 168–69.

19. Peter Clark and Paul Slack, *English Towns in Transition 1500–1700* (Oxford, 1976), p. 13.

20. Alan Dyer, *The City of Worcester in the Sixteenth Century* (Leicester, 1973); W. G. Hoskins, *Industry, Trade, and People in Exeter* (Exeter, 1968), *Provincial England* (London, 1968), esp. chaps. 4 and 5. Even the principal collection of urban history articles from the 1970's (Peter Clark and Paul Slack, eds., *Crisis and Order in English Towns 1500–1700* [London, 1972]) consists predominantly of economic studies. Of eight substantive articles, one is on civic cer-

emony, one is on politics, and six are on economic topics—guilds, demography, urban decline, poverty, etc.

21. Wallace MacCaffrey, *Exeter, 1560–1640* (Cambridge, MA, 1958).

22. Allan Everitt, *The Community of Kent and the Great Rebellion* (London, 1966).

23. Holmes, "County Community"; Hughes, *Warwickshire*; Richard Cust, *The Forced Loan and English Politics, 1626–28* (Oxford, 1987); Peter Lake, "The Collection of Ship Money in Cheshire during the 1630s: A Case Study of Relations between Central and Local Government," *Northern History* 17 (1981): 44–71. See also Thomas Cogswell, *Home Divisions: Aristocracy, the State, and Provincial Conflict* (Manchester, 1998).

24. D. H. Sacks, "The Corporate Town and the English State: Bristol's 'Little Businesses' 1625–1641," *Past and Present*, no. 110 (1986): 105. See also his monograph, *The Widening Gate: Bristol and the Atlantic Economy, 1450–1700* (Berkeley and Los Angeles, 1991).

25. Richard Cust, "Anti-Puritanism and Urban Politics: Charles I and Great Yarmouth," *Historical Journal* 35 (1992): 1–26. See also Robert Tittler, *The Reformation and the Towns in England: Politics and Political Culture, c. 1540–1640* (Oxford, 1998).

26. Rosemary Horrox, "Urban Patronage and Patrons in the Fifteenth Century," in Ralph Griffiths, ed., *Patronage, the Crown, and the Provinces in Later Medieval England* (Atlantic Highlands, NJ, 1981), p. 147.

27. Michael Braddick, "State Formation and Social Change in Early Modern England: A Problem Stated and Approaches Suggested," *Social History* 16 (1991): 2–3.

28. G. R. Elton, "Tudor Government: The Points of Contact. I, The Parliament," *Transactions of the Royal Historical Society*, 5th ser., 24 (1974): 183–200; "II, The Council," ibid., 5th ser., 25 (1975): 195–212; "III, The Court," ibid., 5th ser., 26 (1976): 211–28.

29. See, for instance, T. G. Barnes, *Somerset, 1625–1640: A County's Government during the "Personal Rule"* (Oxford, 1961); Anthony Fletcher, *Reform in the Provinces: The Government of Stuart England* (New Haven and London, 1986), *A County Community in Peace and War: Sussex, 1600–1660* (London, 1975); Holmes, "County Community"; and Hughes, *Warwickshire*. Hughes and Fletcher do touch on the politics of the major towns in their respective county studies, but Fletcher's more systematic overview of government in *Reform in the Provinces* omits civic corporations almost completely.

30. Sacks, "The Corporate Town and the English State," *Widening Gate*; Cust, "Anti-Puritanism and Urban Politics"; J. T. Evans, *Seventeenth-Century Norwich: Politics, Religion, and Government, 1620–1690* (Oxford, 1979).

31. See, for instance, Barry Coward, *The Stuart Age* (Longman, 1980), chaps. 3, 4, 5.

CHAPTER 1: CORPORATIONS AND PATRONAGE

1. NDRO, B1/612 ("An order for choosing a High Steward," 8 November 1637).

2. PRO, PC2/48, pp. 450, 480. The Privy Council referred the matter to the Assize Judges of the Western Circuit.

3. NDRO, B1/3972 (Barnstaple Receiver's Accounts), anno 1642–43.

4. Angel Day, *The English Secretorie: or plaine and direct Method, for the enditing of all manner of epistles or letters, as well Familliar as others* (London, 1595). Books such as Day's fit into the large literature of courtesy books and instruction manuals intended to guide proper behavior.

5. BL, Harl. MS 2103, fol. 10 (copy letter, mayor and corporation of Chester to [William earl of Derby], n.d., but 1612).

6. Hunt. Lib., Ellesmere Collection, EL 1946, fol. 69v.

7. The character of the process of gift exchange has been explicated by Marcel Mauss in his seminal study, *The Gift*. Mauss explored conceptions of gift-exchange in several societies, including Maori, Northwest American Indian, and ancient Roman. In all of these he found that a gift was not simply an object transmitted from one person to another, but symbolized a bond that tied giver to receiver and necessitated reciprocity. In Maori custom, "the obligation attached to a gift itself is not inert. Even when abandoned by the giver, it still forms a part of him. Through it he has a hold over the recipient" (Marcel Mauss, *The Gift: Forms and Functions of Exchange in Archaic Societies*, trans. Ian Cunnison [New York, 1967], p. 9). Ideas of gift in early modern England seem to display some of the same meanings as Mauss discovered in his "archaic" societies.

8. A. Golding's 1578 translation and Thomas Lodge's 1614 translation, enlarged and reprinted in 1620. The ideals of virtue articulated by Seneca and his fellow Roman Cicero were very much a part of the curriculum in grammar schools and universities in this period. See Anthony Esler, *The Aspiring Mind of the Elizabethan Younger Generation* (Durham, NC, 1966), pp. 63, 76.

9. *The Workes of Lucius Annaeus Seneca Newly Inlarged and Corrected,* Thomas Lodge, trans. (London, 1620); *Of Benefits*, Book 1, chap. 1, p. 3, chap. 2, p. 3.

10. Ibid., Book 1, chap. 6, p. 7.

11. Ibid., Book 2, chap. 33, p. 38.

12. For lists of presents to Queen Elizabeth, see John Nicols, *The Progresses . . . of Elizabeth I*, 4 vols. (London, 1828), *passim*; lists of one aristocratic family's New Year's gifts can be found in Hunt. Lib., Hastings Collection, HAF Box 9(8).

13. Linda L. Peck, *Court Patronage and Corruption in Early Stuart England* (London, 1990), pp. 1, 5–9, 152–53, 161–84 *passim*.

14. See e.g., H. E. Salter, ed., *Oxford Council Acts 1585–1626* (Oxford, 1928), pp. 409, 411; NDRO, B1/3972, fols. 176, 188, 189; LRO, BRII/18/9, fol. 34, BRIII/2/75, fol. 43 and *passim*.

15. Based on accounts from Chester, Leicester, and Dover. In each of the three places, accounts were analyzed for four separate years, one from the 1590's, one

from the 1610's, one from the 1620's, and one from the 1630's. KAO, uncataloged Dover records, Dover corporations accounts, 1581–1603, fols. 279, 252, 575, Dover corporation accounts, 1625–60, fol. 141; Ches.CRO, TAR/2/23, 2/26, 3/44, 3/47; LRO, BRIII/2/74, 76, 79, 81.

16. LRO, BRIII/2/76, fol. 20.

17. LRO, BRIII/2/73–76, *passim*. Instructions for the comportment of the civic authorities during the royal visit are laid out in BRII/18/10, fol. 216 (cf. Helen Stocks, ed., *Records of the Borough of Leicester 1603–1688* [Cambridge, 1923], p. 124); BRIII/2/76, fols. 73–77.

18. BL, Add. MS 29,623 (Dover Assembly Minutes), fol. 68. Examples of other towns' preparations for royal visits can be found in W. Hutton, *A History of Derby* (London, 1791), p. 227; C. H. Cooper, ed., *Annals of Cambridge* (Cambridge, 1845), vol. 3, p. 66; W. H. Stevenson, ed., *Records of the Borough of Nottingham* (London, 1889), vol. 4, p. 303; YCA, B.34, fols. 116v, 118, 118v–19.

19. Stocks, ed., *Records of Leicester*, pp. 150, 190; DRO, ECA Receivers' Accounts for 1596–97, 1627; Ches.CRO, TAR/2, treasurers' accounts for 1610–11, 1626–27; HWRO, Worcester corporation records, A.10, Books I and II, *passim*. This list could be multiplied ad infinitum.

20. SRO/I, C9/2(2), fol. 140 (accounts, 1594–1642); Ches.CRO, TAR 2/30 (treasurers' and receivers' accounts).

21. Cooper, ed., *Annals of Cambridge*, vol. 3, pp. 30, 33; Salter, ed., *Oxford Council Acts*, p. 411; SRO/I, C9/2(2), fols. 128, 159v, 175v, 222; J. M. Guilding, ed., *Diary of the Corporation of Reading* (London, 1895), vol. 2, p. 279; HWRO, Worcester corporation records, A.10, e.g., 1589–90, 1593–94, 1623–24; King's Lynn Town Hall, KL/C7/9, fol. 159; DRO, ECA Receiver's Accounts, e.g., 1604–5, 1611–12; Ches.CRO, TAR/2/23–42, *passim* (Treasurers Accounts); Margaret Groombridge, ed., *Calendar of Chester City Council Minutes 1603–1642*, Record Society of Lancashire and Cheshire, vol. 106 (1956), pp. 96, 104; DRO, ECA Chamber Act Book 7, fol. 674.

22. DRO, ECA Receivers' Accounts 1596–97.

23. KAO, uncatalogued Dover records, Accounts 1603–25, fol. 474.

24. SRRC, Shrewsbury corporation records, 3365/2617/158 (Tym Tourneur to Thomas Jones, mayor of Shrewsbury, 3 July 1639) (cf. HMC, *Fifteenth Report*, App. 10 [London, 1895], p. 64); PRO, PC2/48, pp. 369, 390, 407, 631; /50, pp. 86, 435, 440.

25. PRO, PC2/49, pp. 22, 416; SP16/366/48, 386/49; SRRC, Shrewsbury corporation records, 3365/2617/158.

26. KAO, Md/FCa1 (Maidstone Borough Accounts, *passim*).

27. KAO, uncatalogued Dover records, Accounts 1581–1603, fols. 401, 461; BL, Egerton MS 2095, fols. 432–33. The lieutenant of Dover Castle, as the chief officer of the lord warden and someone who had regular concourse with the citizens of Dover, was often well placed to provide assistance to the city's jurats.

28. LRO, BR III/2/75, fol. 63, and BRIII/2, *passim*. See Chap. 6 for an extended discussion of this connection.

29. Stevenson, ed., *Nottingham*, vol. 4, p. 274—Shrewsbury became high steward of Nottingham early in January 1606 (p. 278); HMC, *Rutland (Belvoir Castle)*, vol. 4 (London, 1905), pp. 467, 498, 504.

30. James Bennett, *The History of Tewkesbury* (Tewkesbury, 1830), p. 43; KAO, uncatalogued Dover records, Accounts 1603–25, fol. 376v, 409.

31. KAO, Md/Fcal, 1602–3, 1604–5, 1606–7; LRO, BRIII/2/75, fol. 43, 2/76, fol. 150, 2/73, fol. 204, 2/78, fol. 23; HWRO, Worcester corporation records, A.10, Book II, fols. 27v, 53, 182v.

32. J. W. Horrocks, ed., *Assembly Books of Southampton*, vol. 4 (Southampton, 1925), p. 22; Guilding, ed., *Reading*, vol. 2, p. 415; R. N. Worth, ed., *Calendar of the Plymouth Municipal Records* (Plymouth, 1893), p. 134; and NDRO, B1/3972, e.g., for 1590–91, 1635; HMC, *Rutland*, vol. 4, p. 522.

33. Felicity Heal, *Hospitality in Early Modern England* (Oxford, 1990), pp. 19–20. Heal discusses the uses of hospitality in cities and towns in chapter 8, "Urban Hospitality."

34. Ibid., p. 389.

35. Ches.CRO, TAR/2/30, 33, 35, 39, 42; Salter, ed., *Oxford Council Acts*, p. 411; Worth, ed., *Plymouth Municipal Records*, pp. 130, 134, 135; LRO, BRIII/2/75, fol. 43.

36. Nathaniel Bacon, *Annalls of Ipswiche* (Ipswich, 1654; reprinted Ipswich, 1884), p. 506; John F. Bailey, ed., *Transcription of the Minutes of the Corporation of Boston* (Boston, 1980), vol. 1, p. 720.

37. Salter, ed., *Oxford Council Acts*, pp. 409 (subsidy commission), 411 (Assizes); Cooper, ed., *Annals of Cambridge*, vol. 3, p. 33 (Assizes, muster); KAO, uncataloged Dover records, Accounts 1581–1603, fol. 466v (harbor commission); HWRO, Worcester corporation records, A.10. Book I, *passim* (subsidy commission, Assizes).

38. LRO, BRII/18/15, fols. 542–43 (cf. Stocks, ed., *Records of Leicester*, pp. 218–19); BRIII/2/78, fol. 204.

39. NDRO, B1/3972, e.g., for 1609; LRO, BRIII/2/75, fol. 43; 2/79, fol. 228. Because accounting procedures were not precise, only the minimum can be clearly established.

40. M. E. James, "Ritual, Drama and the Social Body in the Late Medieval English Town," in *Society, Politics and Culture: Studies in Early Modern England* (Cambridge, 1988), pp. 28–29, 35, 35n58.

41. BL, Harl. MS 2125, fol. 60; George Fenwick, *A History of the Ancient City of Chester* (Chester, 1896), p. 185.

42. See Raymond Mentzer, *Blood & Belief: Family Survival and Confessional Identity among the Provincial Huguenot Nobility* (West LaFayette, IN, 1994), pp. 68–70. I would like to thank John Morrill for his insight into the meaning of this episode.

43. Heal, *Hospitality*, p. 302.

44. Ibid., pp. 391–92, 398–401; Peck, *Court Patronage and Corruption*, pp. 210–15.

45. Cov.CRO, BA/H/Q/A79/105 (Henry Sewall to mayor of Coventry, 9 July 1611).

46. Various attempts to categorize English towns have been made, based on population, economic function, prosperity, form of government, etc. See e.g., Sybil Jack, *Towns in Tudor and Stuart Britain* (New York, 1996); Clark and Slack, *English Towns in Transition*; Alan Dyer, *Decline and Growth in English Towns 1400–1640* (Cambridge, 1995).

47. See Graham Mayhew, *Tudor Rye* (Falmer, Sussex, 1987); Pishey Thompson, *The History and Antiquities of Boston* (Boston, 1856).

48. See Stephen K. Roberts, ed., *Evesham Borough Records of the Seventeenth Century*, Worcestershire Historical Society, new ser., vol. 14 (1994); Bromley Challenor, ed., *Selections from the Records of the Borough of Abingdon* (Abingdon, 1898).

49. Members of the Stanley family had regular interaction with Chester, Liverpool, and Preston. See Barry Coward, *The Stanleys, Lords Stanley and Earls of Derby, 1385–1672*, Chetham Society, 3rd ser., vol. 30 (Manchester, 1983), chap. 9.

50. For a general view of the powers of the lord warden over the Cinque Ports, see K. M. E. Murray, *The Constitutional History of the Cinque Ports* (Manchester, 1935); and Ivan Green, *The Book of the Cinque Ports: Their Origin and Development, Heyday and Decline* (Buckingham, 1984). The letterbook registers of Edward Nicholas, secretary to successive lord wardens, provide an important primary source; BL, Add. MS 37,818 (Lord Zouche's Register, 1618–24), Add. MS 37,819 (Duke of Buckingham's Register, 1624–27).

51. KAO, Md/ACml/2, fols. 38v, 52, 96v, 97v; HMC, *Rutland*, vol. 4, pp. 170, 174, 177, 208, 280, 303, 350, 351, 457, 496; LRO, BRII, *passim*.

52. Coward, *The Stanleys*, chap. 9; Bailey, ed., *Minutes of Boston*, vol. 2, pp. 430, 435, 479, 680, 682; W. J. Hardy, ed., *Calendar to the Records of the Borough of Doncaster* (Doncaster, 1899), vol. 4, pp. 12–14, 62–65, 122–24; NDRO, B1/3972, *passim*; HMC, *Rutland*, vol. 4, pp. 170, 174, 177, 208, 280, 303, 350, 351, 457, 496.

53. Andrew Brent, ed., *Doncaster Borough Courtier*, vol. 1 (Doncaster, 1994), p. 111; J. P. Earwaker, *East Cheshire: Past and Present*, vol. 2 (Chester, 1880), pp. 416, 467; John Drakard, *The History of Stamford* (Stamford, 1822), pp. 102, 106.

54. For a full discussion of the relationship between Leicester and the earls of Huntingdon, see below, Chap. 6; Mary Bateson, ed., *Records of the Borough of Leicester*, vol. 3 (Cambridge, 1905) and Stocks, ed., *Records of Leicester, passim*.

55. John Neale, *The Elizabethan House of Commons* (Harmondsworth, 1963), pp. 196, 198; Frederick Willmore, *A History of Walsall* (Walsall, 1887), pp. 185–86; VCH, *Staffordshire* (London, 1976), pp. 214–15.

56. Mervyn James charts this pattern in *Family, Lineage, and Civil Society: A Study of Society, Politics, and Mentality in the Durham Region, 1500–1640* (Oxford, 1974), and *Change and Continuity in the Tudor North: The Rise of Thom-*

as, First Lord Wharton (York, 1965). For a different view, which challenges some of the assumptions about the relationship between the Tudors and the northern lords, see Stephen Ellis, *Tudor Frontiers and Noble Power: The Making of the British State* (Oxford, 1995).

57. NDRO, B1/612; LRO, BRII/18/16, fols. 139, 145, 162, 163; BL, Harl. MS 2105, fols. 100ff.; PRO, CHES 38/58.

58. GEC, q.v. "Banbury earldom;" *DNB*, q.v. "Knollys, William."

59. YCA, B.34, fols. 10–14, 42, 173, B.35, fols. 111, 132v; Robert Davies, *Walks Through the City of York* (Westminster, 1880), pp. 265–73; C. B. Knights, *A History of the City of York* (2nd ed., York, 1944), pp. 406, 442; D. M. Palliser, *Tudor York* (Oxford, 1979), p. 56.

60. SRRC, LB2/1/1, fols. 5v, 21v, 49; Thomas Wright, *History of Ludlow* (Ludlow, 1852), p. 421; Alan Dyer, *The City of Worcester in the Sixteenth Century* (Leicester, 1973), p. 209; HWRO, Worcester corporation records, A.14/1, Book II, fols. 49, 57v, A.10, Book II, fol. 4.

61. Guilding, ed., *Reading*, vol. 3, pp. 418, 419; George May, *History of Evesham* (Evesham, 1834), pp. 175–76; Roberts, ed., *Evesham Borough Records*, p. xiv; L. M. Stanewell, ed., *Calendar of Ancient Deeds, Letters, Miscellaneous Old Documents, etc., in the Archives of the City* (Kingston-upon-Hull, 1951), p. 329.

62. Robert Benson and Henry Hatcher, *Old and New Sarum or Salisbury* (London, 1843), pp. 312, 316; HMC, *Various*, vol. 4 (London, 1907), pp. 234–35; DRO, ECA Law Papers Box 60; ECA Miscellaneous Roll 103; ECA Letters 217–23, 226–32; BL, Harl. MS 2103, fols. 6–10; HWRO, Worcester corporation records, A.14, Book I, fols. 165, 165v, Book II, fols. 36, 200v. See below, Chap. 4, for a more extensive discussion of borough interaction with ecclesiastical lords.

63. John Lyon, *The History of the Town and Port of Dover* (Dover, 1814), pp. 247–48.

64. BL, Egerton MS 2095, fols. 413, 437, 456; BL, Add. MS 37,818, fols. 18, 29, 67. See below, Chap. 4, for an extended discussion of how corporations dealt with larger institutions such as regional courts and jurisdictions.

65. John Latimer, *The Annals of Bristol in the Seventeenth Century* (Bristol, 1900), p. 7; NDRO, B1/566, 612; *The Charters and Letters Patent Granted to the Borough of Colchester* (Colchester, 1904), p. 81; F. A. Keynes, *By-Ways of Cambridge History* (Cambridge, 1947), p. 38; Samuel Rudder, *The History and Antiquities of Gloucester* (Cirencester, 1781), p. 117; NRO, Y/C18/6, fol. 46. Vivienne Hodges, "The Electoral Influence of the Aristocracy 1604–1641," Columbia University, Ph.D. diss., 1977), pp. 202–13 provides a brief discussion of the office.

66. Earwaker, *East Cheshire*, vol. 2, p. 416; Martin Weinbaum, *British Borough Charters 1307–1660* (Cambridge, 1943), p. 52; May, *History of Evesham*, p. 286; Lewis Turner, *History of the Ancient Town and Borough of Hertford* (Hertford, 1830), p. 79; Bennett, *Tewkesbury*, p. 207; PRO, C233/2, fol. 53.

67. NDRO, B1/612; NRO, Y/C19/6, fol. 141v.

68. Alfred Beesley, *The History of Banbury* (London, 1841), p. 255; Turner, *History of Hertford*, p. 79.

69. PRO, SO1/1, fol. 177v.
70. *The Charters and Letters Patent Granted to the Borough of Colchester*, pp. 88–89.
71. NDRO, B1/612; NRO, Y/C19/6, fols. 8v, 141v; SRO/I, C6/3, fol. 112; King's Lynn Town Hall, KL/C7/9, fol. 404v.
72. NDRO, B1/566; PRO, SO1/1, fols. 177–77v.
73. Neale, *House of Commons*, pp. 210, 234–37.
74. E.g., Evesham (1605), Hertford (1605), Tewkesbury (1610), Colchester (1635). Roberts, ed., *Evesham Borough Records*, pp. xii, xiv, 19; May, *History of Evesham*, pp. 175–76; Turner, *History of Hertford*, p. 79; Bennett, *History of Tewkesbury*, p. 207; *The Charters and Letters Patent Granted to the Borough of Colchester*, pp. 81–100. For more on the issue of charters and the high stewardship, see below, Chap. 5.
75. This discussion of high stewards and recorders owes a debt to Hodges, "Electoral Influence," especially Appendix F.
76. Neale, *House of Commons*, pp. 210, 234–37. See Neale, chap. 11, for a detailed discussion of the rivalry between Essex and the Cecils for borough patronage.
77. Cooper, ed., *Annals of Cambridge*, vol. 2, p. 599; PRO, C181, fol. 16; Stanewell, ed., *Kingston upon Hull*, p. 327; King's Lynn Town Hall, KL/C7/9, fol. 6v; Salter, ed., *Oxford Council Acts*, p. 205; A. E. Gibbs, ed., *The Corporation Records of St. Albans* (St. Albans, 1890), p. 63.
78. Bailey, ed., *Minutes of Boston*, vol. 2, p. 678; Cooper, ed., *Annals of Cambridge*, vol. 3, p. 244; T. W. Whitley, *The Parliamentary Representation of Coventry* (Coventry, 1894), p. 78; Roberts, ed., *Evesham Borough Records*, p. 31; VCH *Yorkshire*, East Riding, vol. 1, pp. 101–2; Gibbs, ed., *St. Albans*, pp. 5–6; HWRO, Worcester corporation records, A.14/1, Book II, fol. 101; P. M. Tillott, ed., *A History of Yorkshire: The City of York* [Victoria County History] (London, 1961), p. 182.
79. Latimer, *Annals of Bristol*, p. 35; *The Charters and Letters Patent Granted to the Borough of Colchester*, p. 92; DRO, MS DD61,670; *A Calendar to the Records of the Borough of Doncaster*, vol. 4 (Doncaster, 1902), p. 125; DRO, ECA Act Book 5, fol. 438; N. Salmon, *The History of Hertfordshire* (London, 1728), pp. 36–37; HMC, *Salisbury*, vol. 18, p. 253; R. N. Worth, ed., *Calendar of the Plymouth Municipal Records* (Plymouth, 1893), p. 139; DRO, MS 1579A/7/122 (Totnes borough accounts); W. H. Manchee, *The Westminster City Fathers*, 1585–1601 (London, 1924), p. 21; HRO, Winchester records, W/B1/3, fol. 157; VCH *York*, City of York, p. 182.
80. SRO/I, C6/3, fol. 154, C9/2(2), fol. 154; Latimer, *Annals of Bristol*, pp. 52, 135; DRO, ECA Letters 282 (magistrates of Exeter to William earl of Pembroke, 4 October 1625), 367 (Philip earl of Pembroke to mayor of Exeter, 18 April 1635).
81. Beesley, *Banbury*, p. 255; Guilding, ed., *Reading*, vol. 2, p. 117; HMC, *Eleventh Report*, App. 7, p. 221; Salter, ed., *Oxford Council Acts*, pp. 205, 207; Bromley Challenor, ed., *Selections from the Municipal Chronicles of the Borough*

of Abingdon (Abingdon, 1898), p. 56; John Hedges, The History of Wallingford (London, 1881), vol. 2, p. 121.

82. NRO, Y/C19/6, fol. 142; NDRO, B1/612.

83. The story of Villiers' rise to power is best and most thoroughly told in Roger Lockyer, Buckingham (Oxford, 1981).

84. Hodges, "Electoral Influence," pp. 450, 453; HRO, Winchester corporation records, W/B1/4, fol. 51v.

85. Francis Bacon, The Essays or Counsels, Civill and Moral, of Francis Lord Verulam, Viscount St. Albans (London, 1629), p. 290.

86. John Gruenfelder, "The Lord Wardens and Elections, 1604–1628," Journal of British Studies 16 (Fall 1976), pp. 16–22. Gruenfelder's analysis of these elections has been disputed by Mark Kishlansky in Parliamentary Selection: Social and Political Choice in Early Modern England (Cambridge, 1986), p. 23n.

87. LRO, BRII/18/16, fol. 163.

88. Rudder, Gloucester, pp. 117–18; Richard Johnson, The Ancient Customs of the City of Hereford (London, 1882), p. 229; Hodges, "Electoral Influence," pp. 445–46.

89. E.g., Boston, Grantham, Warwick (Bailey, ed., Minutes of Boston, vol. 2, p. 678; HMC, Rutland, vol. 1, p. 496; Hodges, p. 452).

90. Victor Stater, Noble Government: The Stuart Lord Lieutenancy and the Transformation of English Politics (Athens, GA, and London, 1994), pp. 11–12.

91. Neale, House of Commons, p. 201; see also below, Appendix.

92. Salmon, History of Hertfordshire, p. 37; Lam. Pal., MS 3203, fol. 115; Stevenson, ed., Records of Nottingham, vol. 4, pp. 278, 429.

93. Kevin Sharpe, The Personal Rule of Charles I (New Haven, 1992), pp. 140–45, 742–43, 868; DNB, q.v. "Weston, Richard," "Rich, Henry."

94. Alison Grant, "John Delbridge, Barnstaple Merchant, 1564–1639," in Stephen Fisher, ed., Innovation in Shipping and Trade (Exeter Maritime Studies, no. 6: Exeter, 1989), pp. 94–95; HMC, Salisbury, vol. 18, pp. 213, 221–23, 234–35.

95. NDRO, B1/566 (James I to aldermen and burgesses of Barnstaple, 24 January 1611). Some of the earl's testiness concerning his treatment by the corporation can be seen in HMC, Salisbury, vol. 18, pp. 222–23, 234–35, 304.

96. G.E.C., q.v. "Bath, earldom."

97. NDRO, B1/3972, fols. 228, 229, 234; B1/612.

98. Todd Gray, ed., Devon Household Accounts, 1627–59; Part Two, Henry Fifth Earl of Bath and Rachel, Countess of Bath, of Tawstock and London, 1637–1655, Devon and Cornwall Record Society, new ser., vol. 39 (1996), p. xx; David Smith, "The Fourth Earl of Dorset and the Politics of the Sixteen-Twenties," Historical Research 65 (1992): 37–53.

99. DRO, MS 1579A/5/25.

100. DRO, ECA, Receivers Account Rolls, passim; DRO, MS 1579A/5/25; SRO/I, C9/2 (2), fol. 116; NDRO, B1/3972, fol. 237; HRO, W/B1/1, fol. 221.

101. Salter, ed., Oxford Council Acts, pp. 205, 207.

102. DRO, ECA Letters 160, 332; Cooper, ed., *Annals of Cambridge*, vol. 2, p. 115; SRO/I, C5/14/1, fol. 264v; HRO, W/B1/1, fol. 272; Salter, ed., *Oxford Council Acts*, p. 205; HALS, Off. Acc. 1162/312, fol. 103.

103. HMC, *Various*, vol. 4, p. 229; Shelagh Bond and Norman Evans, "The Process of Granting Charters to English Boroughs, 1547–1649," *English Historical Review* 91 (1976): 105.

104. Benson and Hatcher, *Salisbury*, p. 364.

105. HMC, *Salisbury*, vol. 18, pp. 222–23. For an anthropological perspective on clients' privileges in changing patrons see Wolf, "Kinship, Friendship, and Patron-Client Relations," p. 18.

106. DRO, ECA Chamber Act Book 7, fol. 49; ECA Letter 160; Chamber Act Book 5, fol. 438; Letter 116; Chamber Act Book 7, fol. 176; Letter 167.

107. G.E.C., q.v. "Suffolk, earldom"; *DNB*, q.v. "Howard, Thomas"; *CSPD* 1619–23, pp. 184, 409, 419.

108. SRO/I, C5/14/1, fol. 232.

109. DRO, ECA Letter 217. The city of York, of which Suffolk was also high steward, had similar problems, complaining that the earl was not at the board "to stand for the defense of our rights." The earl agreed to resign his patent in return for a monetary settlement in September 1623. YCA, B.34, fol. 272v.

110. DRO, ECA Letters 205, 238.

111. DRO, ECA Letter 220.

112. DRO, ECA Letter 242. The suit between Exeter and the bishop will be discussed at greater length below in Chap. 4.

113. Menna Prestwich, *Cranfield: Politics and Profits under the Early Stuarts* (Oxford, 1966), chap. 10, "Impeachment and Fall"; DRO, ECA Act Book 7, fol. 624.

114. Latimer, *Annals of Bristol*, pp. 52, 65, 97, 135.

115. John Gruenfelder, *Influence in Early Stuart Elections, 1604–1640* (Columbus, OH, 1981), pp. 6–7, 124; Benson and Hatcher, *Salisbury*, pp. 364, 377; Paul Slack, "Poverty and Politics in Salisbury 1597–1666," in Peter Clark and Paul Slack, eds., *Crisis and Order in English Towns 1500–1700* (London, 1972), pp. 171–87.

116. DRO, MSS 1579A/5/27a, 27b; 16/20, 21, 41; 12/5, 6; 5/33, 34.

117. Thomas Floyd, *The Picture of a Perfit Commonwealth* (London, 1600), pp. 224–25.

118. See Anthony Fletcher, *Reform in the Provinces: The Government of Stuart England* (New Haven, 1986); and T. G. Barnes, *Somerset 1625–1640: A County's Government during the Personal Rule* (London, 1961) for treatments of central authority in the provinces.

119. PRO, C181/2, fols. 16, 71, 112. The volumes in C181 only contain selective commissions for a modest number of towns.

120. Guilding, ed., *Reading*, vol. 2, p. 329; Hedges, *Wallingford*, p. 119; LRO, BRII/1/3, fol. 76.

121. *APC* 1625–26, pp. 217, 314, 315.

122. Guilding, ed., *Reading*, vol. 2, p. 375; Henry Swinden, *The History and Antiquities of the Ancient Burgh of Great Yarmouth* (Norwich, 1772), p. 505n. See below, Chap. 3, for more on Reading and Cambridge.

123. This issue is treated at length below in Chap. 2.

124. *DNB*, q.v. "Talbot, George" and "Talbot, Gilbert"; Lam. Pal., MS 3198 (Talbot Papers), fol. 267 (Dorothy Edmund to earl of Shrewsbury, 8 April [1591]).

125. DRO, ECA Letter 160.

126. Neale, *House of Commons*, p. 225. See Kishlansky, *Parliamentary Selection*, for a thorough discussion of the social meanings of elections and electoral patronage.

127. HMC, *Eleventh Report*, App. 7, p. 221.

128. Hunt. Lib., Hastings Collection, HA5429 (earl of Huntingdon to mayor of Leicester, 11 August 1609).

129. See above, pp. 38–40.

130. Lawrence Stone, *Crisis of the Aristocracy 1558–1641* (Oxford, 1965; reprint 1979), pp. 8–13; NDRO, B1/566; HMC, *Salisbury*, vol. 16, p. 387; LRO, BRII/5/98.

131. Neale, *House of Commons*, p. 209.

132. James, *Society, Politics, and Culture*, pp. 375, 381, 394–95.

CHAPTER 2: PATRONS IN THE LOCALITY

1. HMC, *Eleventh Report*, App. 7 (London, 1888), pp. 221–22.

2. *DNB*, q.v. "Knollys, William, earl of Banbury"; J. M. Guilding, ed., *Diary of the Corporation of Reading* (London, 1895), vol. 2, p. 329; HMC, *Eleventh Report*, App. 7, p. 221; Guilding, ed., *Reading*, vol. 2, pp. 123, 127, 353, 117, 171, 52; HMC, *Eleventh Report*, p. 221; Guilding, ed., *Reading*, vol. 2, pp. 65, 350–51, 473, 8, 10, 168–69, 230–31, 270, 273.

3. HMC, *Eleventh Report*, App. 7, p. 222; Guilding, ed., *Reading*, vol. 3, p. 58.

4. Peter Clark, *English Provincial Society from the Reformation to the Revolution: Religion, Society, and Politics in Kent 1500–1640* (Hassocks, Sussex, 1977), p. 209; see also Joseph Gribble, *Memorials of Barnstaple* (Barnstaple, 1830); Alfred Beesley, *The History of Banbury* (London, 1841); Wallace MacCaffrey, *Exeter, 1540–1640* (Cambridge, MA, 1958); John Gruenfelder, *Influence in Early Stuart Elections* (Columbus, OH, 1981); John Neale, *The Elizabethan House of Commons* (Harmondsworth, 1963).

5. Some more recent work has questioned older arguments. See, for instance, Mark Kishlansky, *Parliamentary Selection* (Cambridge, 1986); David Harris Sacks, *The Widening Gate: Bristol and the Atlantic Economies, 1450–1700* (Berkeley and Los Angeles, 1991); and Robert Tittler, "Elizabethan Towns and the 'Points of Contact': Parliament," *Parliamentary History* 8 (1989): 275–88, and "The End of the Middle Ages in the English County Town," *Sixteenth Century Journal* 18 (1987): 471–87.

6. See Mervyn James, "English Politics and the Concept of Honour, 1485–

1642," in M. E. James, *Society, Politics, and Culture: Studies in Early Modern England* (Cambridge, 1986), pp. 308–414; and Jonathan Powis, *Aristocracy* (Oxford, 1984) for conceptualizations about lordship and its responsibilities in this period.

7. Christopher Haigh, *English Reformations: Religion, Politics, and Society under the Tudors* (Oxford, 1994), pp. 25–39 discusses the types of religious giving English people engaged in on the eve of the Reformation. See also Robert Tittler, *The Reformation and the Towns in England: Politics and Political Culture c. 1540–1640* (Oxford, 1998), which was published too late to be incorporated into the present work.

8. W. K. Jordan, *Philanthropy in England, 1400–1660* (New York, 1959) provides an extensive discussion of how charitable giving in England changed across the period, although some of his specific findings have been questioned. See also James, "English Politics and the Concept of Honour," especially pp. 316–25, which discuss the connection between honor and religion.

9. See Jordan, *Philanthropy*, pp. 279–97.

10. A. E. Gibbs, ed., *The Corporation Records of St. Albans* (St. Albans, 1890), pp. 46–47; Robert Tittler, *Nicholas Bacon: The Making of a Tudor Statesman* (Athens, OH, 1976), pp. 61, 150, 159.

11. Lam. Pal., MS 650, fol. 175. Anthony Bacon was suspected of having Catholic sympathies and spent much of his adult life away from England. It may well be that Stretely's nomination actually came from Anthony's mother, Ann Bacon, who held the firmly Reformed religious principles of her late husband, the lord keeper. For Anthony Bacon's speckled career, see Anthony Esler, *The Aspiring Minds of the Elizabethan Younger Generation* (Durham, NC, 1966), pp. 214–21, and P. W. Hasler, ed., *The House of Commons, 1558–1603* (London, 1981), vol. I, pp. 371–73.

12. Lamb. Pal., MS 651, fol. 96, MS 656, fols. 38, 392.

13. Gibbs, ed., *St. Albans*, pp. 60, 62, 63.

14. LRO, BRIII/2/77, fol. 116; BRII/1/3, fol. 75 (Common Hall, 13 March 1590); BRII/1/3, fol. 123 (28 April 1594).

15. Guilding, ed., *Reading*, vol. 2, pp. 52–53, 136.

16. J. W. Horrocks, ed., *Assembly Books of Southampton* (Southampton, 1917–25), vol. 4, pp. 43, 94n; John Speed, *History and Antiquity of Southampton*, ed. Elinor Aubrey, Southampton Record Society (1909), p. 85, 85n.

17. *A Descriptive and Historical View of Alnwick* (Alnwick, 1822), pp. 323–25. Alnwick was a prescriptive borough rather than an incorporated one, but it was regionally important in sparsely populated Northumberland.

18. Paul Seaver, *The Puritan Lectureships: The Politics of Religious Dissent, 1560–1662* (Stanford, CA, 1970), p. 90; Elsie Toms, *The Story of St. Albans* (St. Albans, 1962), p. 98.

19. J. A. Twemlow, ed., *Liverpool Town Books* (Liverpool, 1935), vol. 2, p. 486. This is an interesting and early case of a "division of the house" being called and a vote being taken in a corporation. As there was a "contrarietie" in the civic Assembly, the mayor sent those who favored James Seddon, the incumbent, down

to the bottom of the hall, and told those who favored James Martyndall, Derby's nominee, to remain up at the front with him, clearly showing his own loyalties. In the final tally, 30 men voted for Martyndall and only 14 for Seddon. The earl's role in this is obscure, since the vote was more a referendum on religious outlooks than on satisfaction of their good lord.

20. Seaver, *Puritan Lectureships*, pp. 105, 108, 102.

21. LRO, BRII/5/25 (earl to corporation, 16 December 1591). The earls of Huntingdon also traditionally had a say in the appointment of the minister of St. Martin's church in Leicester, the largest and most important church in town. (C. W. Foster, ed., *The State of the Church in Lincoln*, Lincoln Record Society, vol. 23 [1926], p. 299; C. W. Foster, ed., *Lincoln Episcopal Records in the Time of Thomas Cooper, Bishop of Lincoln*, Lincoln Record Society, vol. 2 [1912], p. 278.)

22. Mary Bateson, ed., *Records of the Borough of Leicester*, vol. 3 (Cambridge, 1905), pp. 118, 226, 255.

23. For a systematic discussion of the uses of clerical patronage by a particular nobleman, see Barbara Donagan, "The Clerical Patronage of Robert Rich, Second Earl of Warwick, 1619–1642," *Proceedings of the American Philosophical Society* 120 (1976): 388–419.

24. HMC, *Thirteenth Report*, App. 4 (London, 1892), p. 162; *CSPD* 1623–25, pp. 118, 147; HMC, *Thirteenth Report*, App. 4, p. 170.

25. Seaver, *Puritan Lectureships*, p. 98; SRO/I, C6/3, fol. 123r–v (cf. Nathaniel Bacon, *Annalles of Ipswiche* [Ipswich, 1654; reprinted Ipswich, 1884], p. 413).

26. DRO, ECA, Corporation Act Book 5 (1588–1601), fol. 502; Seaver, *Puritan Lectureships*, p. 106. Women are most often associated with artistic, cultural, and religious patronage, where their wealth and influence counted most. Because they could not participate fully in the political nation, women were less likely to be solicited as urban patrons. See below, Chap. 6, for the dowager countess of Devonshire's involvement in Leicester.

27. Hunt. Lib., Hastings Collection, HAF 8(4) (account book of a journey to Harveile, 9 August to 9 October 1619); Cov.CRO, BA/H/C/17/1, fol. 165v.

28. DRO, MS 1579A/7/125.

29. HMC, *Rutland*, vol. 4, p. 454; PRO, PROB 11/1142/207; John F. Bailey, ed., *Transcription of the Minutes of the Corporation of Boston* (Boston, 1980), vol. 2, p. 597.

30. Hunt. Lib., Hastings Collection, HAF 6(4) (account book of the earl of Huntingdon, 23 September 1606 to 12 October 1607).

31. DRO, ECA Letters 325, 353; Exeter Additional Letters 60.B/112; LRO, BRII/18/19, fol. 433 (earl to corporation, 27 March 1633); fol. 431(corporation to earl, 30 March 1633).

32. *History of Guildford* (Guildford, 1801), pp. 11–20.

33. Gerald Hodgett, *Tudor Lincolnshire* (Lincoln, 1975), p. 137.

34. The story of the establishment of Leicester's Hospital in Warwick is told in detail in A. L. Beier, "The Social Problems of an Elizabethan Country Town: Warwick, 1580–90," in P. Clark, ed., *Country Towns in Pre-Industrial England* (Leicester, 1981), pp. 46–85, esp. at pp. 70–71, 75–78.

35. Bateson, ed., *Records of Leicester*, vol. 3, pp. 134, 149, 200, 204, 207, 282–83.

36. Adrienne Rosen, "Winchester in Transition, 1580–1700," in Clark, ed., *Country Towns*, pp. 161–62; Ches.CRO, CR469/542 (William Aldersay's Annals of Chester), anno 1623; Clark, *English Provincial Society*, p. 209. See Peter Borsay, *The English Urban Renaissance: Culture and Society in the Provincial Town 1660–1770* (Oxford, 1989) for the full development of these patterns after the Restoration.

37. MacCaffrey, *Exeter*, p. 183; James Tompson, *The History of Leicester* (Leicester, 1849), p. 256.

38. J. A. Picton, *Memorials of Liverpool, Historical and Topographical* (2nd ed., London, 1875), vol. 1, p. 60; Twemlow, ed., *Liverpool Town Books*, vol. 2, p. 452; [John Seacome], *Memoirs of the Antient and Honourable House of Stanley* (Manchester, 1767), p. 70; Ches.CRO, TAR/2/40 (Rental, 1619–20).

39. Ches.CRO, CAS/11.

40. HMC, *Rutland*, vol. 4, pp. 440–42, 481, 503, 529, 467; LRO, BRIII/3/17, fols. 3–12; Hunt. Lib., Hastings Collection, HAF 14(2) (receipt for cloth from John Smithurst of Leicester, 28 January 1639); HAF 8(26) (bill from William Ive of Leicester for wine, September 1625); HAF 6(4) (account book of the earl of Huntingdon, September 1606 to October 1607).

41. Lawrence Stone, *The Crisis of the Aristocracy 1558–1641* (Oxford, 1965; reprint 1979), pp. 335–36; see also pp. 338–55 for a discussion of peers' participation in the mining industry specifically. Noble patrons might also benefit economically from the participation of urban governors in their entrepreneurial schemes. See DRO, ECA Letters 373, 374.

42. Cov.CRO, BA/H/C/17/1, fols. 338, 339v. The deal ultimately failed. In 1638, the corporation swore out a warrant to seize the coal mines from the earl of Dover, who owed them £450 in back rent. (BA/H/C/17/1, fol. 356v.)

43. Guilding, ed., *Reading*, vol. 2, p. 117; LRO, BRII/18/19, fol. 371 (petition of Mary Floyd, "poor distressed woman," to earl of Huntingdon, 10 November 1632); BRII/18/10, fols. 272, 464 (earl to mayor of Leicester, 5 October 1608, 24 August 1610); BRII/18/11, fol. 143; BRII/18/12, fol. 139.

44. W. J. Hardy, ed., *Calendar to the Records of the Borough of Doncaster* (Doncaster, 1899), vol. 4, p. 64 (Assembly, 5 November 1591).

45. LRO, BRII/18/6, fols. 63, 64 (earl to mayor, 8 March 1603, mayor to earl, 15 March 1603); Cov.CRO, BA/H/Q/A79/97, 102.

46. LRO, BRII/18/8, fols. 488, 615, 616, 493; BRII/1/3, fol. 315.

47. LRO, BRIV/3/36 (earl to mayor, 28 December 1612); BRIV/3/38 (mayor to earl, 6 January 1613).

48. LRO, BRII/1/3, fol. 125; BRII/18/5, fol. 833; BRII/18/9, fols. 248, 250; BRII/18/10, fols. 270, 274.

49. Guilding, ed., *Reading*, vol. 2, pp. 122, 127, 353; H. E. Salter, ed., *Oxford Council Acts 1580–1626* (Oxford, 1928), pp. 212–13; M. G. Hobson and H. E. Salter, eds., *Oxford Council Acts 1626–1665* (Oxford, 1933); John Hedges, *The History of Wallingford* (London, 1881), p. 119.

50. Salter, ed., *Oxford Council Acts 1580–1626*, pp. 282–83, 305, 339.

51. HMC, *Fourteenth Report* (Records of the Corporation of Hertford), pp. 160–61; HALS, Hertford borough records, vol. 33, nos. 2, 3, 4, 6.

52. For instance, Lord Coventry, recorder of Boston in the 1630's, selected Robert Gurdon, esq., as his deputy to serve in his absence. (Bailey, ed., *Minutes of Boston*, vol. 3, pp. 668, 678.)

53. HWRO, Worcester corporation records, A.14/1, Book II, fols. 53, 89, 101, 103v, 107, 109, 141.

54. NDRO, B1/3973 (Barnstaple Sessions Records), unfoliated; Warwick, Stamford, and Grantham also had noble recorders, all of whom appointed deputies to carry out the office. (Hodges, "Electoral Influence," App. F.)

55. Ches.CRO, AB/1, fols. 207, 309v; George Chandler, ed., *Liverpool under James I* (Liverpool, 1960), pp. 175, 209; Robert East, ed., *Extracts from the Records of the Borough of Portsmouth* (Portsmouth, 1891), p. 327; Bromley Challenor, ed., *Selections from the Municipal Chronicles of the Borough of Abingdon from AD 1555 to AD 1897* (Abingdon, 1898), p. 56; Stephen K. Roberts, ed., *Evesham Borough Records of the Seventeenth Century*, Worcester Historical Society, vol. 14 (1994), pp. 10, 22–23; Cov.CRO, BA/H/C/17/1, fol. 188; Herbert Heaton, *The Yorkshire Woollen and Worsted Industries* (Oxford, 1920), p. 223.

56. Barry Coward, *The Stanleys, Lords Stanley and Earls of Derby, 1385 to 1672*, Chetham Society 3rd ser., vol. 30 (Manchester, 1983), chap. 9. Neale, *House of Commons*, also suggests this interpretation.

57. J. T. Evans, *Seventeenth-Century Norwich* (Cambridge, 1979), p. 8.

58. Cov.CRO, BA/H/C/17/1, fols. 175v, 201v.

59. BL, Add. MS 29,625, fol. 56.

60. Horrocks, ed., *Assembly Book of Southampton*, vol. 4, p. 94n.; Cov.CRO, BA/H/C/17/1, fol. 339v; King's Lynn Town Hall, KL/C7/9, fol. 197v; HWRO, Worcester corporation records, A.14/1, Book II, fol. 192; Roberts, ed., *Records of Evesham*, pp. 23, 38; HRO, W/B1/4, fols. 51v, 74; Bailey, ed., *Minutes of Boston*, vol. 2, p. 684; KAO, Md/Acm1/2, fol. 96v (the earl of Hertford in Southampton; the earl of Dover in Coventry; Sir Thomas Southwell, Vice-Admiral of Norfolk, in King's Lynn; Lord Windsor of Bradenham in Worcester; Sir Edward [later Lord] Conwey and Lord Windsor in Evesham; the duke of Buckingham, Lord Conwey, and Lord Cottington in Winchester; the earl of Lindsey in Boston; Sir Francis Fane [son of the earl of Westmorland] in Maidstone).

61. Robert Benson and Henry Hatcher, *Old and New Sarum or Salisbury* (London, 1843), p. 340.

62. George May, *The History of Evesham* (Evesham, 1834), p. 289; Lewis Turner, *History of the Ancient Town and Borough of Hertford* (Hertford, 1830), p. 79.

63. East, ed., *Records of Portsmouth*, p. 137.

64. Ibid., pp. 137–59, 345–53, *passim*.

65. George Chandler, ed., *Liverpool under James I* (Liverpool, 1960), pp. 195, 198.

66. Bailey, ed., *Minutes of Boston*, vol. 2, p. 684.

67. Pishey Thompson, *The History and Antiquities of Boston* (Boston, 1856), pp. 626–29; Bailey, ed., *Minutes of Boston*, vol. 2, p. 695. For more on the politics behind the sewer commissions and fen drainage projects, see Mark Kennedy, "Charles I and Local Government: The Draining of the East and West Fens," *Albion* 15 (1983): 19–31.

68. Hobson and Salter, eds., *Oxford Council Acts*, pp. 90–91. See also Henry Hartopp, *Register of the Freemen of Leicester 1196–1770* (Leicester, 1927), pp. 97–126 *passim*; C. H. Cooper, ed., *Annals of Cambridge*, vol. 3 (Cambridge, 1845), pp. 183–84; Roberts, ed., *Records of Evesham*, p. 22. These examples could be multiplied many times over.

69. HMC, *Fifteenth Report*, App. 10, p. 24 (Assembly order, 21 April 1623).

70. Hobson and Salter, eds., *Oxford Council Acts*, p. 26 (10 August 1630).

71. John Mayhall, *The Annals and History of Leeds* (Leeds, 1860), p. 65; J. P. Earwaker, *East Cheshire: Past and Present* (Chester, 1877–80), vol. 2, pp. 465–67.

72. East, ed., *Records of Portsmouth*, p. 327; Challenor, ed., *Borough of Abingdon*, p. 56; T. Pape, *Newcastle-under-Lyme in Tudor and Early Stuart Times* (Manchester, 1938), p. 51; Roberts, ed., *Evesham Borough Records*, pp. 22–23. Portsmouth chose Charles, Lord Mountjoy as a mayor's assistant (equivalent to an alderman) in 1594 and selected Charles earl of Devonshire for the same position in 1608. In Abingdon, the earl of Banbury was high steward as well as justice of peace in the court of record. Newcastle-under-Lyme, Staffordshire, elected the first earl of Essex as mayor early in Elizabeth's reign, while Evesham made Sir Edward Conwey an alderman and JP.

73. Cov.CRO, BA/H/C/17/1, fol. 188.

74. Picton, *Memorials of Liverpool*, vol. 1, p. 60.

75. Twemlow, ed., *Liverpool Town Books*, vol. 2, pp. 136, 136n., 175, 175n., 180, 181.

76. Twemlow, ed., *Liverpool Town Books*, vol. 1, pp. 446, 581, vol. 2, pp. 155, 487; Chandler, ed., *Liverpool under James I*, p. 105, George Chandler, ed., *Liverpool under Charles I* (Liverpool, 1965), p. 115.

77. HMC, *Salisbury (Cecil)*, vol. 24, p. 3 (Alderman Giles Brooke to Salisbury, [after 4 May 1605]).

78. Chandler, ed., *Liverpool under Charles I*, p. 134; VCH *Lancashire*, vol. 4 (London, 1911), p. 19.

79. Coward, *The Stanleys*, p. 131; Ches.CRO, AB/1, fols. 207, 309v, AB/2, fol. 58.

80. Ches.CRO, ML/6/39 (mayor of Chester to Glaseor and Gamull, March 1610); Ches.CRO, AB/1, fol. 309v.

81. Ches.CRO, AB/1, fols. 210–30, *passim*; ML/1/25, ML/5/91–95, 178–217; ML/5/199.

82. Ches.CRO, AF/10/94; AB/1, fols. 343v–44. See Ches.CRO, Assembly Files (AF/8–20) for attendance lists of many Assembly meeting in the first half of the seventeenth century.

83. Ches.CRO, AF/10/96, CR469/542, anno 1614; BL, Harl. MS 2020, fols. 80v, 81v–82; BL, Stowe MS 812, fols. 12, 32, 63, 68; Ches.CRO, AB/1, fols. 345v, 349v, 350v.

84. Ches.CRO, CR469/542 (William Aldersay's MS annals of Chester), unfoliated; TAR/2/23, 31; AF/8/12, AF/10/94, 95, AF/11, AF/13; CRO, DCH/E/314 (Cholmondley Papers); Ches.CRO, CR60, unfoliated, at anno 1618.

85. See J. S. Morrill, *Cheshire 1630–1660: County Government and Society during the English Revolution* (Oxford, 1974), pp. 7–8, for a brief discussion of Chester's status within the county.

86. Steven Ellis, *Tudor Frontiers and Noble Power: The Making of the British State* (Oxford, 1995), pp. 258, 263.

87. Wallace MacCaffrey, "Place and Patronage in Elizabethan Politics," in S. T. Bindoff, J. Hurstfield, and C. H. Williams, eds., *Elizabethan Government and Society* (London, 1961), pp. 95–126, sets patronage into the context of the early modern polity; see also Linda L. Peck, *Court Patronage and Corruption in Early Stuart England* (New York, 1990).

88. Cooper, ed., *Annals of Cambridge*, vol. 3, p. 169; NRO, Y/C19/5, fol. 88; Hardy, ed., *Doncaster*, vol. 4, p. 121.

89. LRO, BRII/5/67 (earl of Huntingdon to mayor of Leicester, 4 July 1603); BRII/18/6, fol. 145; BRII/18/8, fols. 397, 398, 404, 407; BRIII/8/70.

90. Hardy, ed., *Doncaster*, vol. 4, pp. 13, 14, 62, 63; APC 1590–91, pp. 18–19; Hardy, ed., *Doncaster*, vol. 4, pp. 73, 64.

91. Ches.CRO, AB/1, fol. 291.

92. Ches.CRO, AF/10/116 (n.d., but 1617); AB/1, fol. 260; QSF/49/14.

93. BL, Add. MS. 37,818, fol. 29 (Lord Zouche to mayor of Rye, 30 December 1619).

94. The earl's attempt to get the nomination of the steward and bailiff of the court is discussed at length below, Chap. 6. LRO, BRII/18/8, fol. 308, 18/9, fol. 255, 18/10, fol. 337, 18/11, fol. 115; DRO, MSS 1579A/5/33, 34 (cf. HMC, *Third Report*, Appendix, p. 347). Many other examples could be cited: Philip earl of Pembroke—town clerk of Salisbury; Thomas Lord Coventry—clerk of the pentice of Chester; Lord Keeper Egerton—steward (town clerk) of Coventry; Theophilus earl of Suffolk—town clerk of Cambridge. (Benson and Hatcher, *Salisbury*, p. 384; Ches.CRO, AB/2, fol. 50; BL, Lansdowne MS 87, fol. 51; Cooper, ed., *Annals of Cambridge*, vol. 2, p. 211.)

95. DRO, ECA Letters 149–52. The gentlemen, Sir John Acland and Sir Amyas Bampfylde, had both been named freemen of Exeter in 1606 and remained loyal friends to the city. (Margery Rowe and Andrew Jackson, eds., *Exeter Freemen 1266–1967*, Devon and Cornwall Record Society Publications, Extra Series [Exeter, 1973], p. 113.)

96. Cov.CRO, BA/H/C/17/1, fol. 259; NRO, Y/C19/5, fol. 109. The lords asked for the place for Goodale because he had navigated Arundel's ship safely into harbor during "great storms and tempests" when Arundel returned to England in 1613.

97. Guilding, ed., *Reading*, vol. 2, pp. 350–51; LRO, BRII/18/12, fol. 72;

Ches.CRO, AB/1, fols. 306, 331, 352, AB/2, fols. 7, 27; Coward, *The Stanleys*, p. 132; BL, Add. MS 29,625, fol. 52v; Cov.CRO, BA/H/C/17/1, fol. 306v.

98. W. H. Stevenson, ed., *Records of the Borough of Nottingham* (London, 1889), vol. 4, p. 311; SRO/I, C5/14/1, fols. 169, 178.

99. Salter, ed., *Oxford Council Acts 1583–1626*, p. 117; Ches.CRO, ML/1/22.

100. See for example Twemlow, ed., *Liverpool Town Books*, vol. 2, pp. 160–61, 322.

101. Others who requested this favor for their clients were the earl of Bridgwater, Sir John Savage, Sir Thomas Smith, and Sir Peter Warburton. King Charles himself also made a successful request for the freedom to be given to John Parker, innholder. Ches.CRO, AB/2, fol. 7; ML/2/258a, 258b; ML/6/105; ML/6/172; AB/2, fol. 22.

102. HMC, *Eighth Report*, App. 1, p. 364.

103. Ches.CRO, AB/1, fol. 306v; AF/8/4, 5. The name as it appears in the Assembly Files seems to be Dawes, although in the finished Assembly Book it appears as Vawes.

104. Freedoms are found throughout the Assembly Books and in various Assembly Files and Mayors Letters. The specific cases are: Smith, AB/2, fol. 27; Houghton, AF/10/62; Banckes, AF/10/29.

105. Ches.CRO, AB/1, fol. 352 (Assembly, 29 October 1619). The original petition is in AF/11/35. A similar divergence over the issuing of honorary freedoms has been suggested by Adrienne Rosen for Winchester. (Rosen, "Winchester in Transition," p. 162.)

106. Parliamentary patronage is a subject that has received extensive treatment in the past. See Gruenfelder, *Influence*; Kishlansky, *Parliamentary Selection*; and Vivienne Hodges, "The Electoral Influence of the Aristocracy, 1604–1641" (Ph.D. diss., Columbia University, 1977). Derek Hirst, *The Representative of the People? Voters and Voting in England under the Early Stuarts* (Cambridge, 1975), also discusses the influence of the nobility and the gentry as it affected the borough franchise.

107. Because the elections for the Short and Long Parliaments in 1640 were held under rather different circumstances than earlier ones, and in many cases produced different results, this section focuses primarily on the period 1585–1628.

108. Neale, *House of Commons*, pp. 164, 165–66, 168–69. This language shows clearly the way Neale conceived of the relationship between patrons and boroughs. John Gruenfelder, in his book and many articles on the subject of parliamentary patronage, operates with many of the same assumptions as did Neale.

109. Neale, *House of Commons*, pp. 162, 163, 167.

110. David Dean, "Parliament, Privy Council, and Local Politics in Elizabethan England: The Yarmouth-Lowestoft Fishing Dispute," *Albion* 22 (1990): 39–64; Tittler, "Elizabethan Towns and 'Points of Contact,'" pp. 278, 279.

111. Kishlansky, *Parliamentary Selection*, pp. 31–48.

112. See e.g., SRRC, 3365/2617/155 (earl of Essex to bailiffs of Shrewsbury, 11 March 1594).

113. Stevenson, ed., *Records of Nottingham*, vol. 2, p. 129.
114. NRO, Y/C19/5, fols. 323–23v.
115. PRO, SP16/86/113, 94/191, 95/63.
116. SRRC, LB2/1/1, fol. 131.
117. Cooper, ed., *Annals of Cambridge*, vol. 3, pp. 183–84, 185, 186.
118. Neale, *House of Commons*, p. 164.
119. Cooper, ed., *Annals of Cambridge*, vol. 3, pp. 60–61.
120. Gruenfelder, *Influence*, pp. 65–72; John Gruenfelder, "The Lord Wardens and Elections, 1604–1628," *Journal of British Studies* 16 (Fall 1976): 16–22.
121. LRO, BRII/18/6, fol. 79, 18/7, fol. 289, BRII/13/3, 5; Hunt. Lib., Hastings Collection, HA8519, HA5478, HA9221, HA5506.
122. Coward, *The Stanleys*, p. 129.
123. Guilding, ed., *Reading*, vol. 2, pp. 168–69, 230–31, 270, 273; HMC, *Rutland*, vol. 1, pp. 208, 242, 280; Neale, *House of Commons*, p. 204.
124. Hirst, in *Representative of the People?*, has noted the importance of economic issues in borough franchise disputes and electoral choice. See esp. the case studies in Appendix II, pp. 197–212.
125. VCH *Cheshire*, vol. 2, p. 110. Several of Chester's elections were contentious affairs, reflecting factional fighting in the corporation.
126. J. R. Chanter, *Sketches of the Literary History of Barnstaple* (Barnstaple, 1866), pp. 105, 110, 112 (Philip Wyot's Diary); History of Parliament Trust, unpublished constituency report for Barnstaple, 1604–28. I would like to thank Mr. John Ferris for generously allowing me to use this constituency report before publication.
127. SRO/I, C6/1/3, fol. 165; C6/1/4, fol. 123v; C5/14/1, fols. 320, 328v, 332, 334, 339v.
128. HALS, Off Acc 1162, Box 179, piece 160.
129. SRRC, LB2/1/1, fols. 80v, 81v, 82.
130. Benson and Hatcher, *Salisbury*, pp. 348–49; Paul Slack, "Poverty and Politics in Salisbury 1597–1666," in Peter Clark and Paul Slack, eds., *Crisis and Order in English Towns 1500–1700* (London, 1972), pp. 186–87.
131. NRO, Y/C19/5, fols. 215, 216v, 229, 230.
132. Martin Weinbaum, *The Incorporation of Boroughs* (Manchester, 1937), pp. 97, 107, 123; Hirst, *Representative of the People?*, pp. 45–47.
133. Hunt. Lib., Hastings Correspondence, HA8524 (corporation of Leicester to earl of Huntingdon, 16 January 1624).
134. NRO, Y/C19/6, fols. 450v, 455v, 456.
135. KAO, Sa/Cl, fols. 9v–10 (mayor and jurats of Sandwich to earl of Northumberland, 13 January 1640).
136. Hirst, *Representative of the People?*, pp. 60, 62–64.
137. Kishlansky, *Parliamentary Selection*, Part One.
138. Turner, *History of Hertford*, p. 79; Bennett, *Tewkesbury*, pp. 43, 207; Hardy, ed., *Doncaster*, vol. 4, pp. 62–63; Evangeline de Villiers, "Parliamentary Boroughs Restored by the House of Commons, 1621–41," *English Historical Re-*

view 67 (1952): 175, 177. Tewkesbury acquired the franchise in 1610, Hertford in 1624. Doncaster remained unenfranchised throughout the period.

139. Benson and Hatcher, *Salisbury*, pp. 348–49, 377; Slack, "Poverty and Politics in Salisbury," pp. 186–87; PRO, C233/3, fol. 254v.

140. LRO, BRII/18/7, fols. 115, 116, 118, BRII/1/3, fol. 254.

141. Quoted in Gruenfelder, *Influence*, p. 125.

142. SRRC, Shrewsbury corporation records, 3365/2617/108 (Lord Zouche to bailiffs of Shrewsbury, 7 March 1604).

143. See M. F. Keeler, *The Long Parliament, 1640–1641: A Biographical Study of Its Members,* Memoirs of the American Philosophical Society, vol. 36 (Philadelphia, 1954) for a catalog of the members who sat in this Parliament. See below, Chap. 6, for details of the Short and Long Parliament elections in Leicester.

144. NRO, Y/C19/6, fols. 455v–56, 496v; Henry Hillen, *History of the Borough of King's Lynn,* vol. 1 (Norwich, 1907), pp. 326, 342–43.

145. LA, Grantham corporation records, Minute Book 1633–1704, fols. 71, 83v, 86v; SRO/I, C5/14/3, fol. 302a.

146. William Hunt, *The Puritan Moment* (Cambridge, MA, 1983), p. 210.

CHAPTER 3: PEACEKEEPING AND PATRONS

1. J. T. Evans, "The Decline of Oligarchy in Seventeenth Century Norwich," *Journal of British Studies* 14 (1974): 46–77; Rosemary O'Day, "The Triumph of Civic Oligarchy in Seventeenth Century England," in O'Day et al., *The Traditional Community under Stress* (Milton Keynes, 1977), pp. 103–36.

2. For a discussion of the preservation of urban authority in a slightly earlier period, see Muriel McClendon, " 'Against God's Word': Government, Religion, and the Crisis of Authority in Early Reformation Norwich," *Sixteenth Century Journal* 25 (1994):353–69.

3. Christopher Friedrichs, *The Early Modern City, 1450–1750* (London and New York, 1995), p. 305.

4. Ches.CRO, AB/1, fols. 343v–44, 345v; PRO, CHES 38/48 (Robert Whitby to Edward Whitby, 1 June 1619); Ches.CRO, CR60 (unpaginated). See also A. M. Johnson, "Some Aspects of the Political, Constitutional, Social, and Economic History of the City of Chester, 1550–1662" (D. Phil. diss., Oxford University, 1970), and "Politics in Chester during the Civil Wars and Interregnum," in P. Clark and P. Slack, *Crisis and Order in English Towns, 1500–1700* (London, 1972), pp. 204–36, at pp. 204–8, for more on Chester's conflicts.

5. James VI, *The Trew Lawe of Free Monarchies* (1598).

6. Anthony Fletcher, *Reform in the Provinces: The Government of Stuart England* (New Haven, 1986), pp. 351–52; A. Fletcher and J. Stevenson, eds., *Order and Disorder in Early Modern England* (Cambridge, 1985), pp. 37–38.

7. *APC* June–December 1626, p. 264; *APC* 1627–28, p. 164.

8. Quo warranto offered a serious threat, and a number of corporations did end up in King's Bench trying to prove the validity of their privileges. Nevertheless, it seems unlikely that any borough corporation actually lost its charter at the

end of quo warranto proceedings in this period. The author is currently at work on a full study of quo warranto in this period. See Patterson, "Quo Warranto and Civic Corporations in the Early Seventeenth Century: Royal Enforcement or Local Initiative?" (unpublished paper, North American Conference on British Studies, October 1998).

9. Edith Henderson, *Foundations of English Administrative Law* (Cambridge, MA, 1963), p. 73; *APC* 1613–14, pp. 49–50, 103–4; *APC* 1615–16, pp. 650–54; *APC* 1616–17, pp. 89–90, 121, 144, 303; *APC* 1618–19, pp. 199, 484; and *passim* throughout the volumes of *APC*. For further discussion of franchise issues, see Derek Hirst, *Representative of the People?*(Cambridge, 1975), chap. 3. See below in this chapter, Part V, and Richard Cust, "Anti-Puritanism and Urban Politics: Charles I and Great Yarmouth," *Historical Journal* 35 (1992): 1–26, for more on the Privy Council's treatment of religious difficulties in a borough corporation.

10. Keith Wrightson, *English Society 1580–1680* (London, 1983), p. 154.

11. For more on consensus and consensual procedure, see Mark Kishlansky, *Parliamentary Selection* (Cambridge, 1986).

12. DRO, ECA, Council Act Book 5, e.g., fol. 168. Perez Zagorin has also noted the tendency of corporations to exclude signs of discord from their records. (Perez Zagorin, *The Court and the Country: the Beginning of the English Revolution* [New York, 1970], p. 147.)

13. Ches.CRO, AB/1, fol. 349v; PRO, CHES 38/48 (Robert Whitby to Edward Whitby, 1 June 1619).

14. In his *Architecture and Power: The Town Hall and the English Urban Community c. 1500–1640* (Oxford, 1991), Robert Tittler has shown how civic leaders used the built environment to display their authority and prosperity to the surrounding community and to reinforce their own importance to themselves. See especially pp. 105–22 for a discussion of the symbolic power of civic trappings: buildings, maces and swords, chairs and benches, clothing, etc.

15. Cov.CRO, BA/H/C/17/1, fol. 206v ("An order for the preservation of the peace of this House," 24 January 1615).

16. Craig Muldrew, "Credit and the Courts: Debt Litigation in a Seventeenth-Century Urban Community," *Economic History Review* 46 (1993): 26. In King's Lynn in the second half of the seventeenth century, the Guildhall Court heard an average of over 1,000 suits per year.

17. Sidney Webb and Beatrice Webb, *English Local Government from the Revolution to the Municipal Corporations Act*, vol. 2, *The Manor and the Borough* (London, 1908), Pt. 1, p. 338.

18. Martin Ingram, *Church Courts, Sex, and Marriage in England 1570–1640* (Cambridge, 1987), p. 28; J. A. Sharpe, " 'Such Disagreement betwyx Neighbors': Litigation and Human Relations in Early Modern England," in J. Bossy, ed., *Disputes and Settlements: Law and Human Relations in the West* (Cambridge, 1983), pp. 168, 170; C. W. Brooks, "Interpersonal Conflict and Social Tension: Civil Litigation in England 1640–1830," in A. Beier, D. Cannadine, and J. Rosenheim, eds., *The First Modern Society* (Cambridge, 1989), p. 360.

19. E.g., PRO, KB21/3/65; 4/50; 5A/12; 6/31v; 8/27; 10/115; 12/166. Thirty-four such writs of restitution have been found for the period 1606 to 1640.

20. Cov.CRO, BA/H/C/17/1, fols. 222, 222v, 223, 226, 228, 234v; HWRO, Worcester corporation records, A.14/1, Book II, fols. 61v, 63v, 64, 91, 99.

21. Muldrew, "Credit and the Courts," p. 27.

22. Sharpe, " 'Such Disagreement betwyx Neighbors,' " pp. 177–78.

23. Brooks, "Interpersonal Conflict," p. 387.

24. HMC, *Fourteenth Report*, App. 8 (London, 1895), p. 85; J. S. Cockburn, ed., *Western Circuit Assize Orders, 1629–1648: A Calendar*, Camden Society 4th ser., vol. 17 (1976), p. 9; SRO/I, C6/3, fol. 141v; Ches.CRO, AB/2, fol. 21. See also HWRO, Worcester corporation records, A.14/1 Book II, fol. 99.

25. LRO, BRIII/2/73, 74, 75; DRO, ECA, Receivers' Account Rolls, e.g., 1604–5, 1611–12, 1627–28; King's Lynn Town Hall, KL/C7/9. fol. 159; C. H. Cooper, ed., *Annals of Cambridge*, vol. 2 (Cambridge, 1843), p. 33; HWRO, Worcester corporation records, A.10, e.g., 1589–90, 1593–94, 1623–24, 1625–26.

26. John Bailey, ed., *Transcription of the Minutes of the Corporation of Boston* (Boston, 1980), vol. 2, p. 430; LRO, BRIV/9/13, 17, BRII/5/21, 29; Lam. Pal., MS 3203 (Talbot Papers), fols. 108, 115, MS 702 (Shrewsbury Papers), fol. 31; Ches.CRO, AB/2, fols. 28, 35v–36; BL, Harl. MS 2083, p. 597, MS 2104, p. 438.

27. For instance, East Retford, Chester, Exeter, Reading, Leicester, and Ipswich. HMC, *Report of the Manuscripts of the Duke of Rutland at Belvoir Castle* (London, 1905), vol. 4, p. 303; Ches.CRO, AB/2, fol. 12v; DRO, ECA Letters 273, 274; APC 1623–25, pp. 452, 480; J. M. Guilding, ed., *Diary of the Corporation of Reading* (London, 1895), vol. 2, p. 136; LRO, BRII/18/13, fol. 411, /16, fol. 65; SRO/I, C6/1/4, fols. 8v, 13v, 67v, 75v.

28. J. R. Chanter, *Sketches of the Literary History of Barnstaple* (Barnstaple, 1866), pp. 107–8 (Philip Wyot's Diary).

29. HMC, *Rutland*, vol. 1, pp. 350–51; H. W. Saunders, ed., *The Official Papers of Nathaniel Bacon of Stiffkey, 1580–1620*, Camden Society, 3rd ser., vol. 26 (1915), pp. 16–17. Unfortunately, in neither of these cases is the outcome of the dispute known. In East Retford, the earl of Rutland handed the matter over to two local deputy lieutenants for their attention and resolution. John Manners, the earl's uncle, was a JP as well as DL, and also was serving as sheriff that year. John Thornagh the elder was the earl's "cousin" and steward of some of his estates; townsmen had asked Thornagh to assist in civic matters in the past. The earl was at this time a young man of 22, and was apparently in London when the townsmen asked him to intervene. Rutland may have taken less interest in the matter than the townsmen had hoped, or he may have thought the two gentlemen, who had regular dealings with the townsmen through their deputy lieutenancies, were better prepared to make a fair settlement. (HMC, *Rutland*, vol. 1, pp. 351, 350, 339, 303.)

30. C. H. Cooper, ed., *Annals of Cambridge* (Cambridge, 1845), vol. 3, pp. 42–43.

31. Ches.CRO, AB/1, fol. 355; H. E. Salter, ed., *Oxford Council Acts 1583–1626*, Oxford Historical Society Publications, vol. 87 (Oxford, 1928), p. 297; Guilding, ed., *Reading*, vol. 2, pp. 220, 221.

32. Ellesmere became recorder in 1596, then high steward in 1600; Coventry became high steward in 1626. Cooper, ed., *Annals of Cambridge*, vol. 2, pp. 556, 599; vol. 3, pp. 42, 115, 185, 200, 218. Ellesmere was also asked to give his approval to a contested set of orders for tippling and alehouses in St. Albans, where he held the high stewardship. (HALS, Off Acc 1162/312, fol. 90.)

33. The offenders were labeled "recusants" not because they were Roman Catholic, but simply because they refused to take the freeman's oath of the town, thus recusing themselves from citizenship.

34. Chanter, *Barnstaple*, p. 107; History of Parliament Trust, unpublished 1604–29 constituency report for Barnstaple (with thanks to Mr. John Ferris and the History of Parliament Trust for allowing me to use this report before publication).

35. Chanter, *Barnstaple*, p. 107.

36. Ibid., p. 108; *APC* 1599–1600, p. 63.

37. BL, Egerton MS 2584, fols. 305–6.

38. Ibid., fol. 307; *DNB*, q.v. "Zouche, Edward." The precise nature of his intervention could not be determined, although the outcome is clear.

39. Other instances of patron involvement in religious questions can be found in Lincoln, Rye, and Great Yarmouth. J. W. Hill, *Tudor and Stuart Lincoln* (Cambridge, 1956), pp. 111–12; HMC, *Thirteenth Report*, App. 4, pp. 162, 170; *CSPD* 1623–25, pp. 118, 147; Henry Swinden, *History and Antiquities of the Burgh of Great Yarmouth* (Norwich, 1772), pp. 505n, 506–7n; NRO, Y/C18/6, fols. 256, 256v, 257.

40. Ches.CRO, AB/1, fols. 291, 293. See also above, Chap. 2.

41. Derby: Ches.CRO, AB/1, fols. 309v, 318v; John Seacombe, *Memoirs of the Ancient and Honourable House of Stanley* (Manchester, 1767), p. 70; Ches.CRO, TAR/2/40; AB/2, fol. 8; Warburton: *DNB*, q.v. "Sir Peter Warburton"; Ches.CRO, AB/1, fols. 247v, 297v, 355; TAR/2/23; CAS/5, 6; AF/10/96; Savage: PRO, SP16/53/18; Ches.CRO, AB/1, fols. 288, 303v, 345v; AB/2, fol. 12v, 13v.

42. Ches.CRO, AB/1, fols. 272, 294v, 319, 320v, 326v; BL, Harl. MS 2103, fols. 6, 8v, 10 (mayor and corporation of Chester to [earl of Derby], n.d., [but 1612–13]). See also Johnson, "Politics in Chester," pp. 204–8.

43. See Johnson, "Some Aspects . . . of Chester," for a detailed discussion of the rival groups and the background of the factional fighting, which long predated the seventeenth century.

44. Ches.CRO, AB/1, fols. 343v–44; CR60 (unpaginated, at 1617).

45. Ches.CRO, AB/1, fols. 343v–44, 345v.

46. PRO, CHES 38/48 (Robert Whitby to Edward Whitby, 1 June 1619); Ches.CRO, AB/1, fol. 349v.

47. It is not clear whether the earl of Derby attended the meeting.

48. Ches.CRO, CR60 (unpaginated, at 1619).

49. The depositions are in the Huntington Library, Ellesmere Collection EL 1946 ("The behavior and carriage of Thomas Harris late Alderman of the city of Oxford in his late Mayoralty and since for which he was displaced") and EL 1945 ("The answer of Thomas Harris unto the Articles objected against him").

50. VCH *Oxford*, vol. 4: *The City of Oxford* (London, 1979), pp. 74, 122.

51. Salter, ed., *Oxford Council Acts*, pp. 205, 206–7; G.E.C., q.v. "Banbury earldom"; *DNB*, q.v. "Knollys, William."

52. Salter, ed., *Oxford Council Acts*, p. 207.

53. Hunt. Lib., EL 1946, fol. 68; EL 1945, fol. 66.

54. Hunt. Lib., EL 1946, fols. 68v, 69.

55. Salter, ed., *Oxford Council Acts*, p. 208.

56. Ibid., pp. 209–11.

57. Hunt. Lib., EL 1946, fol. 69.

58. Ibid.; VCH *Oxford*, vol. 4, p. 147.

59. See Salter, ed., *Oxford Council Acts*, p. 69; M. G. Hobson and H. E. Salter, eds., *Oxford Council Acts 1626–1665* (Oxford, 1933), p. 4; VCH *Oxford*, vol. 4, p. 147.

60. Salter, ed., *Oxford Council Acts*, pp. 212–13.

61. Hunt. Lib., EL 1946, fol. 69v; Salter, ed., *Oxford Council Acts*, p. 213. There is no way of knowing whether the council reached a unanimous decision or not.

62. Hunt. Lib., EL 1945.

63. Hunt. Lib., EL 1946, fol. 69v.

64. Salter, ed., *Oxford Council Acts*, pp. 221–22.

65. Ibid., p. 255. Harris was ejected from the corporation again in November 1626 for having abused the mayor in words and for showing contempt toward his fellow city councilors. (Hobson and Salter, eds., *Oxford Council Acts 1626–1665*, p. 4.)

66. Stephen K. Roberts, ed., *Evesham Borough Records of the Seventeenth Century*, Worcestershire Historical Society Publications, vol. 14 (1994), pp. xiv, 3, 7.

67. W. J. Hardy, ed., *A Calendar to the Records of the Borough of Doncaster*, vol. 4 (Doncaster, 1902), p. 64; *APC* 1590–91, pp. 86–87.

68. Andrew Brent, ed., *Doncaster Borough Courtier*, vol. 1 (Doncaster, 1994), p. 109.

69. Ibid., p. 111; Lam. Pal., MS 3199, fol. 123.

70. *APC* 1590–91, pp. 18–19; Lam. Pal., MS 3200, fol. 90.

71. Brent, ed., *Doncaster Borough Courtier*, p. 111; Hardy, ed., *Doncaster*, vol. 4, pp. 13–14; *APC* 1590–91, p. 19. The Privy Council confirmed Shrewsbury's privileges over the office of recorder.

72. Lam. Pal., MS 3200, fols. 85, 90, 98.

73. 18 November 1590. (G.E.C., q.v. "Shrewsbury earldom.")

74. Hardy, ed., *Doncaster*, vol. 4, p. 124; *APC* 1590–91, pp. 128–29.

75. *APC* 1590–91, pp. 261–64.

76. Brent, ed., *Doncaster Borough Courtier*, p. 113; Hardy, ed., *Doncaster*, vol. 4, p. 64; Lam Pal., MS 3199, fol. 123.

77. Hardy, ed., *Doncaster*, vol. 4, p. 124 (Hunsdon to corporation of Doncaster, 3 July 1592).

78. Ibid.

79. Brent, ed., *Doncaster Borough Courtier*, p. 118.

80. Hardy, ed., *Doncaster*, vol. 4, p. 124 (Hunsdon to corporation of Doncaster, 6 November 1592). Gilbert earl of Shrewsbury seems to have been particularly sensitive about his honor. In 1603, the bailiffs of Derby asked him to settle a dispute in the town concerning enclosures. He first agreed, then asked two neighboring gentlemen to do it because "it would be some touch to me, in case I should hear the cause at large and not be able to make an end thereof." Lam. Pal., MS 702, fol. 31 (earl of Shrewsbury to Sir John Harpur and Sir John Willoughby, 20 September 1603).

81. Hardy, ed., Doncaster, vol. 4, p. 124 (Hunsdon to corporation of Doncaster, 6 November 1592).

82. Guilding, ed., *Reading*, vol. 2, pp. 106, 108.

83. *DNB*, q.v. "Knollys, William"; G.E.C., q.v. "Banbury earldom." Sir Francis Knollys became Baron Knollys in 1603, Viscount Wallingford in 1616, and earl of Banbury in 1626.

84. Guilding, ed., *Reading*, vol. 2, p. 8.

85. Ibid., pp. 115, 116, 117. The exact contents of the earl's letters are unfortunately not disclosed in the Corporation Diary.

86. *APC 1621–23*, p. 444.

87. *APC 1621–23*, pp. 460, 466, 467.

88. Ibid., p. 468.

89. Guilding, ed., *Reading*, vol. 2, pp. 122, 127.

90. *APC 1621–23*, pp. 516–17.

91. *APC 1623–25*, p. 16; Guilding, ed., *Reading*, vol. 2, p. 134.

92. Cooper, ed., *Annals of Cambridge*, vol. 3, pp. 218–19 ("Orders for the better government and quiet of the town," 14 August 1629).

93. Ibid., p. 254 (Coventry to mayor of Cambridge, 23 July 1632).

94. Ibid., pp. 260–61 (Coventry to mayor of Cambridge, 13 August 1633).

95. NRO, Y/C19/6, fols. 122v–23, 126, 127; Swinden, *Great Yarmouth*, pp. 501, 502n, 503–4, 505n; Cust, "Anti-Puritanism and Urban Politics," pp. 12–13. Cust's article admirably dissects the religious issues involved in this episode.

96. NRO, Y/C19/6, fols. 141v–42.

97. NRO, Y/C19/6, fol. 155. The king's referees consisted of Lord Keeper Coventry, Lord Treasurer Weston, the earl of Dorset, Viscount Dorchester, and the bishop of London.

98. NRO, Y/C18/6, fol. 256; Swinden, *Great Yarmouth*, pp. 502–3, 505n, 506n.

99. Richard Cust identifies Alderman Cooper's friends at Court as Attorney General Robert Heath and Viscount Dorchester. (Cust, "Anti-Puritanism and Urban Politics," p. 13.) The archbishop of York, Samuel Harsnett, also favored the new scheme. He had previously been bishop of Norwich; his stringent en-

forcement of conformity during his episcopacy there at times put him at odds with the corporators of Yarmouth. (NRO, Y/C19/6, fol. 155, Y/C18/6, fols. 212, 215, 238; Swinden, *Great Yarmouth*, p. 504.)

100. NRO, Y/C18/6, fol. 256; Swinden, *Great Yarmouth*, p. 505n.

101. NRO, Y/C18/6, fol. 254v.

102. Ibid., fol. 256.

103. Ibid., fol. 257v; Swinden, *Great Yarmouth*, pp. 509n–13n, 514n; *APC* 1630–31, p. 384.

104. NRO, Y/C19/6, fol. 199v; Swinden, *Great Yarmouth*, p. 515n.

105. NRO, Y/C19/6, fol. 200.

106. NRO, Y/C19/6, fol. 263v.

107. A recent monograph on Great Yarmouth—Perry Gauci, *Politics and Society in Great Yarmouth 1660–1772* (Oxford, 1996)—indicates that after the Restoration, this corporation continued to establish links with important figures beyond city boundaries. "The corporation recognized that the maintenance of its legal and natural advantages relied heavily on the preservation of a dialogue between itself and outsiders, and thus it attempted to formalize the channels of influence which led to the authorities most regularly involved in Yarmouth's affairs" (Gauci, pp. 48–49).

108. Ches.CRO, CR60.

CHAPTER 4: CORPORATIONS AND COMPETING AUTHORITIES

1. See Joseph Strayer, *The Medieval Origins of the Modern State* (Princeton, NJ, 1970); Philip Corrigan and Derek Sayer, *The Great Arch: English State Formation as Cultural Revolution* (Oxford, 1985); J. Shennan, *Origins of the Modern European State, 1450–1725* (London, 1974); Thomas Ertman, *Birth of Leviathan: Building States and Regimes in Medieval and Early Modern Europe* (Cambridge, 1997). For a discussion of the development of government in the seventeenth century specifically, see Michael Braddick, "State Formation and Social Change in Early Modern England: A Problem Stated and Approaches Suggested," *Social History* 16 (January 1991): 1–17; Anthony Fletcher, *Reform in the Provinces: The Government of Stuart England* (New Haven and London, 1986).

2. For further discussion of the many parts of the state and the way they interacted, see Braddick, "State Formation and Social Change," pp. 2–5; and Michael Braddick, *Parliamentary Taxation in Seventeenth-Century England* (Woodbridge, Suffolk, 1994), pp. 13–16.

3. G. R. Elton, in his *Tudor Revolution in Government* (Cambridge, 1953) and *England under the Tudors* (Cambridge, 1961), offers arguments for the increasing strength and consistency of the Tudor state, particularly as crafted by Thomas Cromwell; the view from the localities, however, suggests a much less organized structure than Elton allowed.

4. G. E. Aylmer, *The King's Servants: The Civil Service of Charles I 1625–*

1642 (New York, 1961) describes in detail just how complex and confusing early modern bureaucracy and government could be.

5. Peter Clark, *English Provincial Society from the Reformation to the Revolution: Religion, Politics and Society in Kent 1500–1640* (Hassocks, Sussex, 1977), pp. 142, 143.

6. Robert Tittler, "The Incorporation of Boroughs, 1540–1558," *History* 62 (1977): 22–42; Martin Weinbaum, *The Incorporation of Boroughs* (Manchester, 1937); Martin Weinbaum, *British Borough Charters, 1307–1660* (Cambridge, 1943).

7. John Lyon, *History of the Town and Port of Dover* (Dover, 1813); P. Williams, *The Council of the Marches of Wales under Elizabeth* (Cardiff, 1958); J. B. Blakeway and H. Owen, *A History of Shrewsbury* (London, 1825); D. M. Palliser, *Tudor York* (Oxford, 1979); R. Somerville, *History of the Duchy of Lancaster* (London, 1953); VCH *Cheshire*, vol. 2, pp. 36–39.

8. Felix Hull, *A Calendar of the White and Black Books of the Cinque Ports, 1432–1955* (London, 1966), pp. xxv–xxvii, xxxv–xxxvi. See also K. M. E. Murray, *The Constitutional History of the Cinque Ports* (Manchester, 1935).

9. S. P. Statham, *Dover Charters and Other Documents* (London, 1902), *passim*; Lyon, *History of the Town and Port of Dover*, pp. 194–214.

10. Murray, *Cinque Ports*, pp. 77–101, 205–25.

11. Peter Clark suggests that as the privileges of the Cinque Ports as a liberty decayed in the later sixteenth century, individual towns in the liberty had to "fall back on a second line of defense—their own municipal liberties" (*English Provincial Society*, p. 112). It is debatable whether most of the ports saw their corporate privileges as a second rather than a first line of defense.

12. BL, Add. MS 29,623, fol. 106.

13. This idea of "manifest" versus "latent" duties and responsibilities of early modern office-holders comes from Victor Morgan, "Some Types of Patronage, Mainly in Sixteenth and Seventeenth Century England," in *Klientelsysteme in Europa der Frühen Neuzeit*, ed. Antoni Mączak (Munich, 1988), p. 104.

14. Linda Levy Peck's *Northampton: Patronage and Policy at the Court of James I* (London, 1982) provides an excellent picture of one lord warden's manifold responsibilities.

15. Peck, *Northampton*, pp. 60–62.

16. BL, Egerton MS 2584, fols. 57, 65, 118, 240, 246.

17. BL, Add. MS 37,818 (Nicholas Papers, Lord Zouche's Register), fols. 24v, 33, 34v.

18. VCH *Cheshire*, vol. 2, p. 111.

19. Ibid., p. 36ff. For more on the Palatine Court in the Tudor period, see E. W. Ives, "Court and County Palatine in the Reign of Henry VIII: The Career of William Brereton of Malpas," *Transactions of the Historical Society of Lancashire and Cheshire* 123 (1972).

20. CRO, MS D4360/3, "Book of Alexander Brayne, Gent.," unfoliated; BL, Harl. MS 2125, fol. 213. Earls of Derby held the office of chancellor from 1559 to 1565 and from 1596 to 1647. In the intervening 30 years, the queen gave the of-

fice to Court figures, Robert earl of Leicester (1565–88) and Sir Thomas Egerton (1594–96). (VCH *Cheshire*, vol. 2, pp. 38–40.)

21. VCH *Cheshire*, vol. 2, p. 111.

22. HWRO, Worcester corporation records, A.14, Box 1, Book 1, fols. 155v, 191; Book 2, fols. 49, 57v, 76v, 106, 117. For more on the council, see John Guy, *Tudor England* (Oxford, 1988), pp. 173–76; Glanmor Williams, *Renewal and Reformation: Wales c. 1415–1642* (Oxford, 1993), pp. 242, 253–54. 336–39.

23. SRRC, LB2/1/1, fols. 5v, 10v.

24. Alan Dyer, *The City of Worcester in the Sixteenth Century* (Leicester, 1973), p. 209; HWRO, Worcester corporation records, A.6, Box 5, fols. 76v, 107, 169, 256; A.14, Box 1, Book 1, fols. 155v, 191; see also Worcester Account Books, *passim*, throughout the 1590's to the 1630's.

25. YCA, B.34, fols. 77, 77v, 79v, 81; B.35, fols. 17v–18, 111, 185.

26. D. M. Palliser, *Tudor York* (Oxford, 1979), p. 56.

27. YCA, B.34, fols. 5v, 10–13, 14–15.

28. YCA, B.34, fols. 42, 68, 173, B.35, fols. 87v, 132v.

29. YCA, B.36, fol. 59v; Palliser, *Tudor York*, p. 56.

30. John Hedges, *The History of Wallingford* (Wallingford, 1881), pp. 94, 105–6, 121.

31. Robert East, ed., *Extracts from the Records of the Borough of Portsmouth* (Portsmouth, 1891), pp. 137–39, 141, 143, 145, 327.

32. Barry Coward, *The Stanleys, Lords Stanley and Earls of Derby, 1385–1672*, Chetham Society, 3rd ser., vol. 30 (Manchester, 1983); Claire Cross, *The Puritan Earl* (New York, 1966); G.E.C., q.v. "Derby," "Huntingdon," "Banbury."

33. VCH *Cheshire*, vol. 2, p. 38; Ches.CRO, ML/5/32; AB/1, fol. 218; TAR/2/27, 31, 35. It should be remembered, however, that the city reserved the right not to gratify the chamberlain, as the Assembly refused to grant the earl of Leicester's request to have a client of his made a freeman of the city (HMC, *Eighth Report*, App. I, p. 364).

34. See e.g., LRO, BRIII/2/73, fol. 203, /75, fols. 27, 137.

35. Robert Somerville, *Duchy of Lancaster Officeholders* (Chichester, 1972), p. 1; P. W. Hasler, ed., *The History of Parliament: The House of Commons 1558–1603* (London, 1981), vol. 2, p. 210.

36. LRO, BRII/18/15, fols. 576, 581, 582; BRII/18/16, fol. 123 (mayor of Leicester to Sir Humphrey May, 16 June 1626); BRII/18/17, fol. 293 (same to same, 4 June 1628).

37. Robert Benson and Henry Hatcher, *Old and New Sarum or Salisbury* (London, 1843), pp. 43–44; Margaret Bonney, *Lordship and the Urban Community: Durham and its Overlords 1250–1540* (Cambridge, 1990), pp. 27, 29, 46; Weinbaum, *British Borough Charters*, pp. 122, 34; VCH *Durham*, vol. 6, pp. 33–40.

38. See Stanford Lehmberg, *The Reformation of Cathedrals* (Princeton, NJ, 1988) for a discussion of English cathedrals throughout the sixteenth century. See also Robert Tittler, *The Reformation and the Towns in England: Politics and Po-*

litical Culture, c. 1540–1640 (Oxford, 1998) for the impact of the Reformation on towns in general.

39. Lehmberg, *Reformation of Cathedrals*, pp. 271–75 provides some discussion of the place of the cathedral in city life.

40. Claire Cross, in "'Dens of loitering lubbers': Protest Against Cathedral Foundations, 1540–1640," in *Studies in Church History* 9 (1972), pp. 231–37, discusses the threat cathedral establishments found themselves under after the Reformation.

41. William Collins, *Historical Landmarks of Hereford* (Hereford, 1915), pp. 32, 33.

42. Thomas Harwood, *The History and Antiquities of the City of Lichfield* (Lichfield, 1806), pp. 339, 347; Dyer, *Worcester*, p. 232. As will be seen below, conflict between corporation and cathedral did not end in 1516. See also Bonney, *Lordship and the Urban Community*, p. 234; VCH *Durham*, vol. 6, pp. 33–40.

43. Benson and Hatcher, *Salisbury*, p. 298; *DNB*, q.v. "Coldwell, John"; Fanny Street, "The Relations of the Bishop and Citizens of Salisbury between 1225 and 1612," *Wiltshire Archaeological and Natural History Magazine* 39 (1915–17): 332, 345, 351.

44. HMC, *Report on the Records of the City of Exeter* (London, 1916), pp. 1–8.

45. DRO, ECA Law Papers, Box 60, nos. 1–6 (petitions and counterpetitions on behalf of the corporation, bishop, and dean of Exeter). For an overview of relations between the city and cathedral in Exeter, see Muriel Curtis, *Some Disputes between the City and the Cathedral Authorities of Exeter* (Manchester, 1932).

46. DRO, ECA Miscellaneous Roll 103, "A Particular of some wrongs and encroachments of the citizens of Exeter upon the liberties of the Bishop, Dean, and Chapter" and "An Answer to the Bishop's Articles." See also Curtis, *Some Disputes*, pp. 50–54.

47. DRO, ECA Letters 138, 139 (petitions from corporation of Exeter to the master of requests and Sir Henry Hobart, attorney general, respectively).

48. DRO, ECA Law Papers, Box 60, nos. 1, 2, 5.

49. Documented cases of conflict over civic regalia exist for Winchester, Chichester, London, Lichfield, Salisbury, and York, as well as Chester. (PRO, SO1/3, fol. 41, PC2/48, p. 26; PC2/46, p. 245; PC2/43, p. 13; VCH *Staffordshire*, vol. 14, p. 84; VCH *Wiltshire*, vol. 6, p. 105; CRO, EDA3/1 [Bishop Bridgeman's Register], fol. 469.)

50. Ches.CRO, AB/1, fol. 297 (Assembly, 30 January 1607).

51. BL, Harl. MS 1944, fol. 92 (Catalog of the Mayors of Chester, for 1606–7). Egerton hailed from Cheshire and also owned Brewer's Hall in the city of Chester, which he purchased in 1592 (Hunt. Lib., Ellesmere Collection, EL 573, 579, 209).

52. In retribution for the decision about the sword, the prebends of the cathedral refused to celebrate the funeral of the swordbearer Nicholas Mercer, who died soon after the dispute. While the mayor and his brethren entered the minster with the sword borne before them, some of the prebends shut the west door,

leaving the corpse sitting unceremoniously outside. (R. V. H. Burne, *Chester Cathedral* [London, 1958], p. 88.)

53. BL, Harl. MS 2103, fol. 7.

54. Ibid., fol. 6. The bishop, too, preached sermons against the corporation. See BL, Harl. MS 2103, fol. 8v–9.

55. Ibid., fol. 7; Ibid., fol. 10r–v.

56. Ibid. No record of Derby's response has been found, but it seems to have favored the corporation, as mention of the conflict abruptly halts.

57. For another discussion of this incident, see Wallace MacCaffrey, *Exeter 1540–1640* (Cambridge, MA, 1958), pp. 218–20.

58. PRO, C181/2, fols. 21v, 71, 137v, 169v, 179.

59. DRO, ECA Letter 217 (William Prowse to John Prowse, 4 May 1622).

60. Benbow is referred to as "clerk of the crown of the Chancery"; it was he who first tipped the city off to the bishop's attempt to become JP. DRO, ECA Chamber Act Book 7, fol. 432; ECA Letter 217.

61. DRO, ECA Letter 218 (W. Prowse to J. Prowse, 7 May 1622); ECA Letter 219 (W. Prowse to J. Prowse, 18 May 1622); ECA Letter 232.

62. DRO, ECA Letter 220 (W. Prowse to J. Prowse, 25 May 1622).

63. DRO, ECA Letter 222 (W. Prowse to J. Prowse, 29 May 1622).

64. There is no direct positive evidence to prove that the bishop was or was not placed on the commission. But had he been made a JP, it is almost certain that some evidence of it would exist in the city's records. All discussion of the issue simply disappears after 1623. The corporation did, however, protect itself from further threats of this sort when they renewed their charter in 1627.

65. DRO, ECA Letters 219, 220, 227, 229.

66. Ches.CRO, TAR/2/33, TAR/3/42; DRO, ECA Receivers Accounts 1627–28, ECA Chamber Act Book 7, fol. 80; SRO/I, C6/1/3, fol. 177v; Benson and Hatcher, *Salisbury*, p. 312; YCA, B.33, fol. 181, B.35, fols. 71v, 206, 249v, 290v–91.

67. See Robert Tittler, "The Incorporation of Boroughs," pp. 24–42; "Incorporation and Politics in Sixteenth-Century Thaxted," *Essex Archaeology and History* 8 (1976): 224–33.

68. LRO, BRIII/2/76, fol. 205 (Chamberlain's Accounts, 1614–15).

69. According to Peter Clark, "The administrative corollary of county centralisation was a still further abridgement of urban independence." Clark, *English Provincial Society*, p. 312. See also W. G. Hoskins, *Provincial England: Essays in Social and Economic History* (London, 1963); and Dyer, *Worcester*.

70. Frederic W. Willmore, *A History of Walsall* (Walsall, 1887), pp. 185–86; VCH *Staffordshire*, vol. 17, pp. 214–15.

71. Quoted in Ann Hughes, *Politics, Society, and Civil War in Warwickshire, 1620–1660* (Cambridge, 1987), p. 18.

72. J. R. Chanter, *Sketches of the Literary History of Barnstaple* (Barnstaple, 1866), pp. 115–17 (Philip Wyot's Diary, for 1607).

73. HWRO, Worcester corporation records, A.14, Box 1, Book 1, fol. 189v, Book 2, fol. 75. The city of Worcester went even further in the seventeenth cen-

tury, procuring a charter that erected the city into a county of itself in 1621, one of very few towns to achieve this status in the early Stuart period. (Weinbaum, *British Borough Charters*, p. 124.)

74. Anthony Fletcher, *A County Community in Peace and War: Sussex 1600–1660* (London, 1975), pp. 234–35.

75. Much of the evidence of this suit and its outcome is found in BL, Stowe MS 812, *passim*; see also Ches.CRO, AB/2, fols. 20, 21, 22, 23.

76. Fletcher, *Reform in the Provinces*, details the concerns of the county gentry and the crown on the critical issue of order, but makes little mention of civic leaders in his analysis.

77. Rosemary Horrox, "Urban Patronage and Patrons in the Fifteenth Century," in Ralph Griffiths, ed., *Patronage, the Crown, and the Provinces in Later Medieval England* (Atlantic Highlands, NJ, 1981), pp. 155–56.

78. John F. Bailey, ed., *Transcription of the Minutes of the Corporation of Boston* (Boston, 1980), vol. 2, p. 702.

79. M. G. Hobson and H. E. Salter, eds., *Oxford Council Acts 1626–1665*, Oxford Historical Society Publications, vol. 95 (Oxford, 1933), p. 25; Stephen K. Roberts, ed., *Evesham Borough Records of the Seventeenth Century*, Worcester Historical Society Publications, vol. 14 (1994), pp. 10, 15, 23, 32, 38.

80. Ches.CRO, CR60 (anno 1618); W. Hutton, *A History of Derby* (London, 1791), p. 121; George Chandler, ed., *Liverpool under James I* (Liverpool, 1960), p. 238; *APC* 1613–14, p. 265.

81. Thomas G. Barnes, *Somerset 1625–1640: A County's Government during the Personal Rule* (Cambridge, MA, 1961), p. 46.

82. PRO, C181/2, fols. 16, 71, 112, 127.

83. H. E. Salter, ed., *Oxford Council Acts 1583–1626*, Oxford Historical Society Publications, vol. 87 (Oxford, 1928), p. 316.

84. LA, L1/1/1/4, fols. 149, 150, 151v, 170v, 260; J. F. W. Hill, *Tudor and Stuart Lincoln* (Cambridge, 1956), pp. 130–33.

85. LRO, BRIV/9/81/9 (gentlemen of Leicester to the earl of Dorset, 4 June 1607).

86. L. M. Stanewell, ed., *Kingston upon Hull: Calendar of the Ancient Deeds, Letters, etc., in the Archives of the Corporation* (Hull, 1951), pp. 194–95 (corporation documents L.281, L.284, L.285).

87. The earl fostered the same cooperative effort when King Charles came to Leicester in 1634. LRO, BRII/5/122 (mayor of Leicester to earl of Huntingdon, 30 December 1613); BRII/18/19, fol. 610 (earl to mayor, 18 July 1634); BRIII/2/80 (Chamberlain's Accounts, 1633–34).

88. LRO, BRII/18/8, fol. 532 (Lord Grey to mayor, 27 September 1604); BRIII/2/76, fol. 154 (Chamberlain's Accounts, 1613–14).

89. Dyer, *Worcester*, p. 212.

90. LRO, BRII/18/11, fols. 12, 59, 63; BRIII/2/76 (Chamberlain's Accounts, 1614–15).

91. DRO, ECA Letters 150, 151, 152; MacCaffrey, *Exeter*, pp. 212–16; Ches.CRO, AB/1, fols. 332, 350v, CR60 (anno 1614), TAR/2/31; G. C. M.

Smith, *The Family of Withipoll* (Walthamstowe, 1936); SRO/I, C6/4, fol. 56, C6/5, fol. 100; KAO, Md/ACm1/2 (Maidstone Burghmote Book), fols. 38v, 52, 96v; HRO, W/B1/3, fol. 168.

92. *DNB*, q.v. Savage, Thomas; VCH *Cheshire*, vol. 2, p. 111. For Savage, see especially BL, Harl. MS 2105, fols. 100–290, a series of letters between Viscount Savage and members of Chester corporation that show clearly the warm and cordial relations between the parties and the affection that Savage retained for the city; also PRO, SP16/53/18, 39. PRO, CHES 38/58 contains numerous letters between Savage and members of the Whitby family, discussing both personal and civic matters.

93. Salter, ed., *Oxford Council Acts*, pp. 64, 108, 110, 226; Hasler, ed., *House of Commons*, vol. 1, pp. 530–31.

94. LRO, BRII/18/5, fol. 731; BRII/5/30 (R. Parkins to Sir Edward Hastings, 12 December 1591); see LRO, BRIII/2/73, *passim*, for gifts to Sir Edward.

95. Pishey Thompson, *The History and Antiquities of Boston* (Boston, 1856), pp. 392–93.

96. Hasler, ed., *House of Commons*, vol. 1, pp. 603–4; HMC, *Salisbury*, vol. 15, pp. 19, 95; LRO, BRII/18/7, fol. 153, /8, fol. 605, /14, fol. 76.

97. Hughes, *Warwickshire*, pp. 17–18; Cov.CRO, BA/H/C/17/1, fols. 175v, 188v.

98. See below, Chap. 5, section III; Hunt. Lib., Hastings Collection HAM 53 (6), *Leicestershire and Rutland Lieutenancy Book*, fols. 181v, 182, 187v, 190, 195; PRO, SP16/53/18 (Viscount Savage to duke of Buckingham, 4 February 1627); Hughes, *Warwickshire*, pp. 59, 98–99.

99. The stresses on local government caused by Caroline policy have been analyzed in a number of county studies, most notably Thomas Barnes, *Somerset 1625–1640: A County's Government during the "Personal Rule"* (Oxford, 1961); and Fletcher, *Sussex*.

100. PRO, PC2/45, pp. 46, 107, 122, 111, 112, 132, 156, 161, 233; PC2/46, pp. 177, 191.

101. PRO, PC2/45, pp. 108, 140, 200; Cov.CRO, BA/H/Q/A79/155; Hughes, *Warwickshire*, pp. 105–6.

102. PRO, PC2/45, pp. 175, 335, 372; Fletcher, *Sussex*, pp. 235–36.

103. King's Lynn Town Hall, KL/C7/9, fols. 399, 404v, 412, 414v; PRO, PC2/45, p. 46. The townsmen did eventually manage to have their rate lowered, but not until mid-1637. (KL/C7/9, fols. 457v, 466v.)

104. BL, Add. MS 29,623, fol. 105; YCA, B.35, fols. 279, 289v, 292v.

105. PRO, PC2/45, p. 147; PC2/46, p. 79; Ches.CRO, AB/2, fols. 40, 40v, CL/111, fols. a, b; BL, Harl. MS 2093, *passim*; Peter Lake, "The Collection of Ship Money in Cheshire during the Sixteen-Thirties: A Case Study of Relations between Central and Local Government," *Northern History* 17 (1981): 45–47, 52.

106. Lake, "The Collection of Ship Money," pp. 50, 68–70.

107. See below, Chap. 6, for a discussion of the earl of Huntingdon's problems as a patron when he lost his standing with the king during the Forced Loan controversy.

108. York's corporation agreed in 1634 to petition the king to be "dismissed absolutely" from the Ship Money charge; if a dismissal could not be obtained, only then would they ask for a reduction in rate. A group of mayors of towns in Norfolk agreed to petition the king and devise reasons "for avoiding or for lessening" Ship Money. (YCA, B.35, fol. 259v; NRO, Y/C18/6, fol. 148v.)

109. See Julian Davies, *The Caroline Captivity of the Church: Charles I and the Remoulding of Anglicanism 1625–1641* (Oxford, 1992), and Nicholas Tyacke, *Anti-Calvinists: The Rise of English Arminianism* (Oxford, 1987), esp. chap. 8.

110. Patrick Collinson, *The Religion of Protestants: The Church in English Society, 1559–1625* (Oxford, 1982), p. 170; Peter Clark and Paul Slack, *English Towns in Transition, 1500–1700* (Oxford, 1976), pp. 150–51.

111. PRO, PC2/44, p. 348, PC2/45, pp. 201, 335, PC2/47, p. 238, PC2/49, p. 221; VCH *York*, p. 174; PC2/46, p. 247, PC2/48, p. 340, PC2/46, p. 245, PC2/48, pp. 466–67. For Winchester, see also W. R. Stephens and F. T. Madge, eds., *Documents Relating to the History of the Cathedral and Church of Winchester in the Seventeenth Century* (London and Winchester, 1897), pp. 1–18.

112. PRO, PC2/46, p. 247; PC2/47, pp. 380, 432–33.

113. PRO, PC2/44, p. 348, PC2/45, p. 335.

114. PRO, PC2/48, p. 466–67.

115. PRO, PC2/45, p. 201.

116. PRO, PC2/46, pp. 245, 246, 247, PC2/48, pp. 26, 340.

117. YCA, B.35, fols. 218, 220v, 221.

118. YCA, B.35, fols. 221, 224v, 225d-v, 230, 230v, 249v, 279, 290v–91, 293.

119. YCA, B.35, fols. 257, 259v, 279, 289v, 292v, 294.

120. PRO, PC2/46, p. 247; Anthony Fletcher, "Factionalism in Town and Country: The Significance of Puritanism and Arminianism," *Studies in Church History* 16 (1979): 291–300; Claire Cross, "Achieving the Millennium: The Church in York during the Commonwealth," *Studies in Church History* 4 (1967): 279; *CSPD* 1635–36, p. 539.

121. *CSPD* 1637, p. 277; PC2/46, p. 247; YCA, B.35, fols. 335v–36; VCH *York*, p. 350.

122. CRO, EDA 3/1 (Bishop Bridgeman's Register), fol. 469.

123. BL, Harl. MS 1944, fol. 92; PRO, PC2/47, p. 404. See also Paul Slack, "Religious Protest and Urban Authority: The Case of Henry Sherfield, Iconoclast, 1633," *Studies in Church History* 9 (1972): 297–98.

124. PRO, SO1/2, fol. 250, SO1/3, fols. 29v, 41.

125. For an opposing view, see Alan Dyer, *Worcester*, p. 211. Dyer argues that sixteenth-century Worcester fought "a continuing battle for complete independence." In a similar vein, Wallace MacCaffrey says of Exeter, "For most inhabitants, this little world embraced the whole range of their hopes and cares. Almost all the important events of their lives transpired within it. . . . Exeter was . . . a semiautonomous community, with its own corporate life and own special interests" (MacCaf-

frey, *Exeter*, p. 203). Peter Clark, speaking of Kentish towns, states, "the rise of centralised town administrations responsive to Crown wishes, of potentially unpopular urban oligarchies and of outward-facing municipal bureaucracies made them especially vulnerable to external pressure—not least from the rapidly expanding county government" (Clark, *English Provincial Society*, p. 142).

126. See Linda L. Peck, *Court Patronage and Corruption in Early Stuart England* (New York, 1990), chap. 4, for a detailed discussion of how country gentry fit themselves into patronage networks at the early Stuart Court. These were the networks on which townsmen, too, relied.

CHAPTER 5: CORPORATIONS AND THE CROWN

1. D. M. Dean, "Parliament and Locality," in D. M. Dean and N. L. Jones, eds., *The Parliaments of Elizabethan England* (London, 1990), p. 162. See also Robert Tittler, "Elizabethan Towns and 'Points of Contact': Parliament," *Parliamentary History* 8 (1989): 275–88.

2. A. Fletcher and J. Stevenson, eds., *Order and Disorder in Early Modern England* (Cambridge, 1985), pp. 37–38.

3. Many examples of both Privy Council orders and commissions for hearing causes are apparent throughout all the volumes of the *Acts of the Privy Council* and the *Calendar of State Papers, Domestic* for this period. See for example several orders and commissions from the Privy Council to or concerning corporations in the summer of 1630: *APC* June 1630–June 1631, pp. 14, 22, 39, 47.

4. Henry Swinden, *The History and Antiquities of the Ancient Burgh of Great Yarmouth* (Norwich, 1772), p. 505n; BL, Stowe MS 812, fols. 58, 62, 66; PRO, SP16/53/18.

5. Wallace MacCaffrey, "Place and Patronage in Elizabethan Politics," in S. T. Bindoff, J. Hurstfield, and C. Williams, eds., *Elizabethan Government and Society* (London, 1961), p. 98. MacCaffrey clearly lays out the crown's problem and the usefulness of patronage in the early modern state.

6. LRO, BRII/18/8, fol. 627 (Thomas Chettell to mayor of Leicester, 19 February 1605); DRO, ECA Letters 290, 290A (Giles Carpenter to Ignatius Jurdain, 6 February 1627).

7. Thomas Milles, *Catalogue of Honour or Treasury of the True Nobility Peculiar and Proper to the Isle of Great Britain* (London, 1610), p. 18; HMC, *Ninth Report*, Part I, Appendix, p. 251.

8. DRO, MSS 1579A/16/31 (mayor of Totnes to earl of Salisbury, 1 June 1609), 1579A/16/32 (mayor of Totnes to earl of Northampton, 14 September 1613), 1579A/16/35 (mayor of Totnes to earl of Pembroke, n.d. [1622?]); DRO, MS DD61,851 (mayor and masters of Dartmouth to earl of Bath, 3 September 1613). Dartmouth Receivers Accounts for 1612–13 show members of the corporation riding to see the earl of Bath on at least two occasions about the "French charter," at the expense of over £4 (DRO, MS DD61,838).

9. DRO, MS 1579A/16/45/1. See also HMC, *Salisbury*, vol. 17, p. 20, vol. 18, pp. 253, 513, for similar appeals to the earl of Salisbury.

10. BL, Egerton MS 2095, fols. 437, 474v–75, MS 2096, fol. 4v; BL, Add. MS 28,036, fols. 8, 14; Add. MS 29,623, fols. 40–42, 78–79; Add. MS 29,621, fol. 528; *CSPD 1625–26*, pp. 408, 476.

11. John Latimer, *The Annals of Bristol in the Seventeenth Century* (Bristol, 1900), p. 123.

12. DRO, ECA Letter 159 (mayor of Exeter to [earl of Northampton], 16 February 1614).

13. LRO, BRII/5/126, 128 (mayor of Leicester to Sir Thomas Parry and earl of Huntingdon, both 16 April 1614); HMC, *Salisbury*, vol. 17, p. 169 (mayor of Boston to Viscount Cranborne, 2 May 1605).

14. PRO, SO1/1, fol. 177v.

15. HMC, *Salisbury*, vol. 17, p. 167.

16. NRO, Y/C19/6, fols. 252, 253v, 273v; Y/C18/6, fol. 138; Swinden, *Great Yarmouth*, p. 472n.

17. BL, Harl. MS 2020, fols. 52, 53, 53v, 54, 54v.

18. LRO, BRII/18/12, fol. 161 (George Wadland to Mayor Thomas Eyricke, 6 May 1617).

19. LRO, BRII/18/12, fols. 193, 203, 146; PRO, IND1/6745 (Docket Book), February 1618.

20. LRO, BRII/18/12, fol. 285 (George Wadland to George Hawfield, 9 May 1618).

21. John Nichols, *History and Antiquities of the County of Leicester* (London, 1795; reprint Wakesfield, Yorks., 1971), vol. 1, p. 340 (mayor of Leicester to Sir William Heyrick, 17 November 1613); ibid. (same to same, 23 January 1614); ibid., p. 341 (Robert Heyrick to Sir William Heyrick, 10 May 1614); ibid. (same to same, 24 May 1614).

22. Ibid., p. 342 (mayor to Sir William Heyrick, 23 June 1614); Bodl. Lib., MS Eng. hist. c. 475, fol. 55 (Thomas Sacheverell to Sir William Heyrick, 19 July 1614); Nichols, *Leicester*, vol. 1, p. 342 (mayor to Sir William, 2 August 1614); Bodl. Lib., MS Eng. hist. c. 475, fol. 58 (Thomas Sacheverell to Sir William Heyrick, 9 August 1614); Nichols, *Leicester*, p. 342 (Robert Heyrick to Sir William Heyrick, 7 November 1614); S. H. Skillington, *The Trinity Hospital, Leicester* (Leicester, 1931), p. 31; Bodl. Lib., MS Eng. hist. c. 477, fol. 189. The poem is an acrostic on Heyrick's name and is addressed "To the most venerable and honorably minded knight Sir William Heyrick: all joys be multiplied in this and the world to come," by John Howe:

> W:elcome good knight unto your native town
> I:f ever any man were welcome here
> L:eicester is bound to sett forth your renown
> L:oe your good deedes thereto do make appeare
> I:even I have heard more of your worth
> A:nd more a great deal then I can declare
> M:ight I by written volumes set it forth.

> H:e lives not now that ere did half that good
> E:ven aged Beadsmen shew itt night and day
> Y:et this is not enough, the poore that want their food
> R:unne after you, and for your coming pray
> I:n every church the bells do sweetly ringe
> C:anticles for your sake the people singe
> K:yrie Elison: this from your heart doth spring.

23. Guide books for appropriate use of this language became popular in this period, for instance Angel Day, *The English Secretorie: or plaine and direct Method, for the enditing of all manner of Epistles or letters, as well Familliar as others* (London, 1595).

24. For instance, when involved in an Exchequer suit, the city of Exeter gave £20 in plate to the earl of Dorset and £10 in plate to the earl of Manchester because the two noblemen "have of late showed themselves very respective about the business of this city." DRO, ECA Chamber Act Book 7, fol. 781 (21 April 1631).

25. DRO, ECA Chamber Act Book 7, fols. 859, 863.

26. References to "fees" and "giftures" can be found in myriad places, e.g., DRO, ECA Letters 217, 218, 219; LRO, BRIII/2/75, fols. 106, 108.

27. DRO, ECA Letter 134 (Sir George Smyth and Mr. John Prowse to mayor of Exeter, 25 February 1610). February 1610 saw the initial negotiations in Parliament over the Great Contract, which may have been the source of the king's ire. (Roger Lockyer, *The Early Stuarts* [London, 1989], pp. 173–74.)

28. See Linda L. Peck, *Court Patronage and Corruption in Early Stuart England* (Boston, 1990) and " 'For a King Not to Be Bountiful Were a Fault': Perspectives on Court Patronage in Early Stuart England," *Journal of British Studies* 25 (1986): 31–61 for discussion of the limits and impact of patronage and corruption in the early Stuart Court. Peck suggests that patronage tended more toward corruption as the seventeenth century advanced.

29. Martin Weinbaum, *British Borough Charters 1307–1660* (Cambridge, 1943). The best work on the details of charter procurement at the center is Shelagh Bond and Norman Evans, "The Process of Granting Charters to English Boroughs, 1547–1649," *English Historical Review* 91 (1976): 101–20.

30. See Weinbaum, *British Borough Charters*, for a summary of the main contents of borough charters.

31. Rosemary O'Day, "The Triumph of Civic Oligarchy in Seventeenth Century England," in *The Traditional Community under Stress*, ed. O'Day et al. (Milton Keynes, 1977), pp. 103–36. For an alternative view, see J. T. Evans, "The Decline of Oligarchy in Seventeenth-Century Norwich," *Journal of British Studies* 14 (1974): 46–76.

32. Peter Clark and Paul Slack, eds., *Crisis and Order in English Towns 1500–1700* (London, 1972), pp. 22–23.

33. Bromley Challenor, ed., *Selections from the Municipal Chronicles of the*

Borough of Abingdon from AD 1555 to AD 1897 (Abingdon, 1898), p. 56; VCH *Berkshire*, vol. 3, p. 227; George May, *History of Evesham* (Evesham, 1834), p. 308.

34. James Bennett, *The History of Tewkesbury* (Tewkesbury, 1830), pp. 383, 43.

35. William James, *The Charters and Other Documents Relating to the King's Parish and Town of Maidstone* (London, 1825), p. 102.

36. Sidney Webb and Beatrice Webb, *English Local Government from the Revolution to the Municipal Corporations Act: The Manor and the Borough* (London, 1908); Martin Weinbaum, *The Incorporation of Boroughs* (Manchester, 1937), *British Borough Charters.*

37. Robert Tittler, "The Incorporation of Boroughs 1540–1558," *History* 62 (1977): 24–42, "Incorporation and Politics in Sixteenth-Century Thaxted," *Essex Archaeology and History* 8 (1976): 224–33; see also Tittler, "The Emergence of Urban Policy," in J. Loach and R. Tittler, eds., *The Mid-Tudor Polity* (London, 1980), pp. 74–93.

38. See, for instance, Joseph Gribble, *Memorials of Barnstaple* (Barnstaple, 1830) and Alfred Beesley, *The History of Banbury* (London, 1841).

39. According to Peter Clark, "Not only did the weakness of many towns make them vulnerable to outside influence, it even led them to welcome intervention." (*English Provincial Society from the Reformation to the Revolution: Religion, Politics and Society in Kent 1500–1640* [Hassocks, 1977], p. 143). While elite participation was important, the present work suggests a more positive interpretation of it.

40. John Tomlinson, *Doncaster from the Roman Occupation to the Present Time* (Doncaster, 1887), p. 79; Robert Benson and Henry Hatcher, *Old and New Sarum or Salisbury* (London, 1843), p. 298; VCH *Durham*, vol. 6, pp. 33–40; Catherine Patterson, "Leicester and Lord Huntingdon: Urban Patronage in Early Modern England," *Midland History* 16 (1991): 51–58.

41. Bond and Evans, "The Process of Granting Charters," *passim.* Charters were granted under the Great Seal by the lord keeper for the monarch, but in fact it was often the attorney general or solicitor general who had the most to do with its passage or failure. Petitions were referred to their legal officials for evaluation before any further steps would be taken. A request for a charter would have to go through several more layers of reports, warrants, and bills before letters patent were finally drawn up and enrolled. The process could take months or even years.

42. HWRO, Worcester corporation records, A.14/1, Book II, fols. 67, 72; NRO, Y/C19/6, fol. 153; LRO, BRII/18/8, fol. 627, /9, fol. 26; George Chandler, ed., *Liverpool under James I* (Liverpool, 1960), p. 195; DRO, ECA Letters 164, 219.

43. Cov.CRO, Microfilm 1124/1 (Humphrey Burton's Book), fol. 151; Cov.CRO, BA/H/Q/A79/106; SRO/I, C9/2/2, fols. 370, 370v, 378, 392, 392v.

44. LA, L1/1/1/4, fol. 224v (cf. J. F. W. Hill, *Tudor and Stuart Lincoln* [Cambridge, 1956], p. 120); Chandler, ed., *Liverpool under James I*, pp. 198–201. Worcester corporation became indebted for £200 in pursuing their charter in

1621; they agreed to take the sum out of "Mr. Honton's money," a charity, which they promised to repay. (HWRO, Worcester corporation records, A.14/1, Book II, fol. 76.)

45. LRO, BRI/2/46/10.

46. LRO, BRIII/2/75, fols. 29, 108.

47. Cov.CRO, BA/H/Q/A79/105, BA/H/C/17/1, fol. 188, BA/F/A/13/1, 6; NRO, Y/C19/6, fol. 155; DRO, ECA Letters 229, 230. There is some evidence suggesting that pursuing charters was getting costlier and required greater "gratifications" to Court officials. See Cov.CRO, BA/H/Q/A79/105.

48. DRO, ECA Letter 164.

49. Ibid. (drafts of both letters were written on one sheet).

50. Mary Bateson, ed., *Records of the Borough of Leicester*, vol. 3 (Cambridge, 1905), pp. 239, 240, 247; Swinden, *Great Yarmouth*, pp. 705–6; Thomas Harwood, *The History and Antiquities of the City of Lichfield* (Lichfield, 1806), pp. 339, 344–45; Robert East, ed., *Extracts from the Records of the Borough of Portsmouth* (Portsmouth, 1891), pp. 578–84; Latimer, *Annals of Bristol*, p. 90; Benson and Hatcher, *Salisbury*, p. 377; Barry Coward, *The Stanleys, Lords Stanley and Earls of Derby, 1385–1672*, Chetham Society, 3rd ser., vol. 30 (Manchester, 1983), p. 134; John Lyon, *History of the Town and Port of Dover* (Dover, 1813), pp. 194–214.

51. DRO, ECA Letter 218 (William Prowse to mayor of Exeter, 7 May 1622).

52. Linda L. Peck, "'For a King Not to Be Bountiful,'" pp. 31–61, *Court Patronage and Corruption in Early Stuart England* (Boston, 1990), pp. 40, 44. Buckingham, though, was never an important urban patron.

53. A recent historian of London's government has shown that even the lord mayor of London required patronage to accomplish business at Court. James C. Robertson, "London 1580–1642: The View from Whitehall, the View from Guildhall" (Ph.D. diss., Washington University St. Louis, 1993), pp. 260, 261, 264.

54. Stephen K. Roberts, ed., *Evesham Borough Records of the Seventeenth Century*, Worcestershire Historical Society Publications, new ser., vol. 14 (1994), pp. xiii–xiv. According to Roberts, there is no direct evidence that Prince Henry's connection to Evesham came through Baylie, but he seems the most likely suspect. See also May, *History of Evesham*, pp. 289, 175, 175n., 176.

55. Challenor, ed., *Municipal Chronicles of Abingdon*, p. 56; C. A. Markham and J. C. Cox, eds., *The Records of the Borough of Northampton* (Northampton, 1897), vol. 2, p. 127; C. H. Cooper, ed., *Annals of Cambridge* (Cambridge, 1843), vol. 2, p. 17; John Mayhall, *Annals and History of Leeds* (Leeds, 1860), pp. 65–66; PRO, C233/3, fol. 254v, C233/4, fol. 192v. The incorporation of Welsh boroughs seems to have occurred similarly. Cardiff received its incorporation in 1608 at the suit of the earl of Pembroke. PRO, IND1/6744 (Privy Seal Docket Book).

56. John Drakard, *The History of Stamford* (Stamford, 1822), p. 102 (Exeter was actually Stamford's recorder, but his role was effectively that of high steward); Swinden, *Great Yarmouth*, pp. 705–6; Benson and Hatcher, *Salisbury*, p. 377.

57. H. E. Salter, ed., *Oxford Council Acts 1583–1626*, Oxford Historical Society Publications, vol. 87 (Oxford, 1928), p. 277.

58. James Bennett, *The History of Tewkesbury* (Tewkesbury, 1830), p. 43; T. Pape, *Newcastle-under-Lyme in Tudor and Early Stuart Times* (Manchester, 1938), p. 46; Charles Ferrers Palmer, *History of the Town and Castle of Tamworth* (Tamworth, 1845), p. 112; J. P. Earwaker, *East Cheshire: Past and Present*, vol. 2 (Chester, 1880), p. 416.

59. Many examples could be cited, including Hereford, 1597 (Weinbaum, *British Borough Charters*, p. 52); Evesham, 1604 (May, *History of Evesham*, p. 286); Hertford, 1605 (Lewis Turner, *History of the Ancient Town and Borough of Hertford* [Hertford, 1830], p. 79); Banbury, 1608 (Beesley, *History of Banbury*, p. 255); Tewkesbury, 1610 (Bennett, *Tewkesbury*, p. 207); Wokingham, 1612 (Weinbaum, *British Borough Charters*, p. 12); St. Albans, 1633 (A. E. Gibbs, ed., *The Corporation Records of St. Albans* [St. Albans, 1890], p. 506).

60. See DRO, ECA Letters 205, 220, 238.

61. DRO, ECA Chamber Act Book 7, fols. 687, 681.

62. Weinbaum, *British Borough Charters*, p. 25; *CSPD 1627–28*, p. 426.

63. Cov.CRO, BA/H/Q/A79/105, 106, 107.

64. John Roberts, "Parliamentary Representation of Devon and Dorset, 1559–1601" (MA thesis, University of London, 1958), pp. 224–26, 238–39; Edward Windeatt, "The Muniments of the Corporation of Totnes, Part I," *Transactions of the Devonshire Association* 32 (1900), 403. The quo warranto proceedings themselves can be followed in PRO, KB21/2, fols. 59, 75, 77, 101.

65. Roberts, "Devon and Dorset," p. 233.

66. For a concise summary of the argument concerning crown support of urban oligarchies, see Clark and Slack, eds., *Crisis and Order*, pp. 22–23.

67. PRO, SP16/146/40; LRO, BRI/2/45/2–3 (recorder's accounts, 1629); LRO, BRIII/2/79, fol. 242; PRO, PC2/42, pp. 14–16.

68. John Sydenham, *The History of the Town and County of Poole* (Poole, 1839; reprint Poole, 1986), pp. 184–86.

69. Benson and Hatcher, *Salisbury*, pp. 43, 296, 298; Fanny Street, "The Relations of the Bishops and Citizens of Salisbury between 1225 and 1612," *Wiltshire Archaeological and Natural History Magazine* 39 (1915–17): 331–32.

70. Benson and Hatcher, *Salisbury*, p. 296; HMC, *Various*, vol. 4, p. 229.

71. Benson and Hatcher, *Salisbury*, p. 312; HMC, *Various*, vol. 4, pp. 234–35.

72. Benson and Hatcher, *Salisbury*, p. 316; Street, "Relations," pp. 350–51.

73. Benson and Hatcher, *Salisbury*, pp. 317–18 ([?] to Richard Godfrey, 18 May 1610).

74. Ibid., p. 773; Weinbaum, *British Borough Charters*, p. 122.

75. Bennett, *Tewkesbury*, p. 43.

76. W. H. Stevenson, ed., *The Records of the Borough of Nottingham*, vol. 4 (London, 1890), pp. 274, 278.

77. Latimer, *Annals of Bristol*, pp. 91, 97.

78. HMC, *Salisbury*, vol. 18, pp. 213, 221–23, 234–35; NDRO B1/203; B1/3972 (receiver's accounts), for 1610–11; J. R. Chanter, *Sketches of the Literary History of Barnstaple* (Barnstaple, 1866), pp. 117–18 (Philip Wyot's Diary); HMC, *Salisbury*, vol. 18, p. 253. See also Alison Grant, "John Delbridge, Barnstaple Merchant, 1564–1639," in Stephen Fisher, ed., *Innovation in Shipping and Trade* (Exeter Maritime Studies no. 6: Exeter, 1989), pp. 91–109.

79. NDRO, B1/3972, receiver's accounts for, e.g., 1605–6, 1611, 1612; Chanter, ed., *Literary History of Barnstaple*, p. 114 (Philip Wyot's Diary).

80. NDRO, B1/566.

81. J. R. Chanter and Thomas Wainwright, eds., *Reprint of the Barnstaple Records* (Barnstaple, 1900), p. 223.

82. *The Charters and Letters Patent Granted to the Borough of Colchester* (Colchester, 1904).

83. PRO, SO1/1, fols. 123, 177. In the event, Doncaster selected Ayr and their charter remained unchanged.

84. It is difficult to make any systematic count; quo warranto could come out of different courts, it proceeded in different ways, and it seems sometimes to have been threatened rather than carried through. See Catherine Patterson, "Borough Corporations and Quo Warranto, 1590–1640: Keeping Local Order in the Central Courts" (unpublished paper, delivered at the American Society for Legal History, October 1998).

85. NRO, Y/C19/6, fols. 122v, 126, 155; Y/C18/6, fols. 251, 257v. It also seems that a quo warranto was issued against Coventry's corporation specifically in retaliation for their alleged assistance to Burton and Prynne when the two passed through town in 1637 (Cov.CRO, BA/F/A/17/1).

86. The literature on this subject is large. See Michael Braddick, *Parliamentary Taxation in Seventeenth Century England* (Woodbridge, Suffolk, 1994) and *The Nerves of State: Taxation and the Financing of the English State, 1558–1714* (Manchester and New York, 1996); Lindsay Boynton, *The Elizabethan Militia 1558–1638* (Newton Abbott, 1971); Richard Cust, *The Forced Loan and English Politics 1626–1628* (Oxford, 1987); A. A. M. Gill, "Ship Money during the Personal Rule of Charles I: Politics, Ideology, and the Law 1634 to 1640" (Ph.D. diss., Sheffield, 1990).

87. The lord lieutenancy is analyzed in Victor Stater, *Noble Government: The Stuart Lord Lieutenancy and the Transformation of English Politics* (Athens, GA, and London, 1994).

88. For a systematic discussion of the militia and the difficulties surrounding it throughout England, see Boynton, *The Elizabethan Militia*; Anthony Fletcher, *Reform in the Provinces: The Government of Stuart England* (New Haven and London, 1986), chap. 9; and Stater, *Noble Government*. Stater's dissertation, "The Lord Lieutenancy in Stuart England" (Ph.D. diss., University of Chicago, 1988), upon which his book is based, deals with the militia itself at greater length than does the book.

89. NRO, Y/C19/6, fol. 22; Y/C18/6, fol. 158v.

90. LRO, BRIII/2/27, fol. 196.

91. DRO, ECA Letter 142 (DLs of Exeter to William earl of Bath, November 1611).

92. Ches.CRO, AB/1, fol. 215v.

93. Ches.CRO, ML/5/210 ([mayor of Chester] to [secretary of the earl of Derby], 14 January 1590). The earl asked the city to name a servant of his as muster master for the city's forces again in 1596 (Ches.CRO, MF/30/196, 10 February 1596).

94. W. Murphy, ed., *The Earl of Hertford's Lieutenancy Papers, 1603–1612*, Wiltshire Record Society Publications, vol. 23 (Devizes, 1969), pp. 51–53, 127.

95. BL, Add. MS 39,245 (Wodehouse Papers, vol. 28, Suffolk Lieutenancy Letter Book, 1608–40), fols. 8v, 9v, 10v, 11, 17, 26v, 27; Nathaniel Bacon, *Annalles of Ipswiche* (Ipswich, 1654; reprint 1884), p. 520; SRO/I, C6/5, fols. 78, 86, 71v. For similar relations between the town of Barnstaple and the earl of Bedford, Lord Lieutenant in the 1620's and 1630's, see NDRO, B1/46/332 (Francis earl of Bedford to corporation of Barnstaple, 4 July 1631); PRO, SP14/266/21 (mayor of Barnstaple to earl of Bedford, 12 April 1634); NDRO, B1/46/853.

96. DRO, MS DD61,858 (mayor of Dartmouth to earl of Northampton, 20 April 1613); *APC* 1613–14, pp. 47–48 (Privy Council to earl of Bath, 25 May 1613); PRO, SP14/78/4 (earl of Bath to Privy Council, 3 October 1614).

97. LRO, BRII/18/15, fol. 567 (earl of Huntingdon to corporation of Leicester, 12 May 1625); Hunt. Lib., HAM 53 (6), *Leicestershire and Rutland Lieutenancy Book* (hereafter *LRLB*), fol. 123r (corporation to earl, 5 June 1625); BRII/18/15, fol. 580 (earl to corporation, 14 June 1625). Lutterworth was about eight miles away from Leicester, so privilege as much as cost was most likely the real issue.

98. LRO, BRII/18/15, fol. 578 (corporation to earl, 19 June 1625).

99. Ibid., fol. 576 (corporation to Sir Humphrey May, 16 June 1625), fol. 557 (Common Hall, 3 May 1625), fol. 581 (Sir Humphrey May and Edward Moseley [attorney of the duchy] to earl, 18 June 1625), fol. 582 (corporation to Sir Humphrey May, 22 June 1625). The corporation had apparently also written to the muster master, Francis Staresmore (an appointee of the earl) on this behalf, as the earl received a letter from Staresmore asking that the town militia be mustered at home (*LRLB*, fol. 125v, 18 June 1625). For an extensive discussion of the problems of the earl of Huntingdon with the militia rates of the 1620's, see Thomas Cogswell, *Home Divisions: Aristocracy, the State, and Provincial Conflict* (Manchester, 1998).

100. LRO, BRII/18/21, fol. 594a (corporation of Leicester to Henry Hastings, 27 April 1640), fol. 594b (corporation to earl of Huntingdon, 30 April 1640), fol. 594 (corporation to Lord Newburgh, n.d.), fol. 596 (Newburgh to corporation, n.d.)

101. Cov.CRO, BA/H/Q/A79/126.

102. LRO, BRII/5/53 (Henry earl of Huntingdon to Sir George Hastings and Thomas Cave, esq., 22 October 1595); BRII/1/3, fol. 206 (meeting of the aldermen, 14 February 1600); BRIII/2/75.

103. *LRLB*, fol. 181v (mayor of Leicester to earl of Huntingdon, 15 August 1626), fol. 182 (earl to town clerk, n.d.), fol. 187v (earl to mayor, 26 February 1627), fol. 190 (mayor to earl, 6 March 1627), fol. 195 (mayor to earl, 13 March 1627), fols. 197v–98v (earl to mayor, 14 March 1627).

104. Ches.CRO, ML/6/158 (earl of Derby to Sir George Boothe and Sir William Brereton, 24 November 1621), 159 (Sir George Boothe to mayor of Chester, n.d.), 160 (mayor of Chester to earl of Derby, 10 December 1621).

105. A broader view of the Forced Loan, including the reactions of borough corporations to it, is provided by Richard Cust, *The Forced Loan and English Politics, 1626–1828* (Oxford, 1987). For the effects of the loan, as well as militia issues, on a single county see Gary Owens, "Norfolk, 1620–1641: Local Government and Central Authority in an East Anglian County" (Ph.D. diss., University of Wisconsin-Madison, 1970). On Ship Money, see Gill, "Ship Money."

106. Braddick, *Parliamentary Taxation, passim.*

107. Thomas Cogswell, *The Blessed Revolution* (Cambridge, 1989), analyzes this problem at length.

108. Conrad Russell, *Parliaments and English Politics, 1621–1629* (Oxford, 1979).

109. SRO/I, C6/4, fol. 69v (Ipswich Assembly, 5 February 1612); LRO, BRII/1/3, fol. 76; BRII/5/18; BRII/18/14, fol. 42 (corporation to Sir William Heyrick, n.d. [spring 1621?]); BRII/18/15, fol. 348 (corporation to Sir Humphrey May, n.d. [1624]).

110. BL, Egerton MS 2095, fol. 414.

111. Lam. Pal., MS 3199 (Talbot Papers), fol. 261 (bailiffs of Derby to earl of Shrewsbury, 17 March 1591); DRO, ECA Letter 142 (mayor and other DLs of Exeter to earl of Bath, November 1611); Bodl. Lib., MS Eng. hist. c. 475, fol. 13 (Robert Heyrick to Sir William Heyrick, 22 November 1611); DRO, ECA Letter 142; LRO, BRII/18/18, fol. 140.

112. NRO, Y/C19/5, fol. 93v.

113. Hobson and Salter, eds., *Oxford Council Acts*, p. 5.

114. YCA, B.35, fol. 34v.

115. YCA, B.35, fol. 20.

116. YCA, B.35, fols. 25v, 33v, 34v, 38v.

117. Cust, *Forced Loan*, pp. 127–32.

118. LRO, BRII/18/18, fols. 37 (earl of Huntingdon, Sir Wolstan Dixie, and Sir John Skeffington to corporation of Leicester, 5 November 1630), 38 (same to same, 13 November 1630), 140 (Common Hall, 28 April 1631).

119. John Bailey, ed., *Transcription of Minutes of the Corporation of Boston* (Boston, 1980), vol. 2, pp. 704, 738.

120. J. M. Guilding, ed., *Diary of the Corporation of Reading* (London, 1895), vol. 3, p. 343.

121. LRO, BRII/18/21, fols. 496, 509 (Common Halls, 18 March, 10 July, 1639).

CHAPTER 6: URBAN PATRONAGE AT WORK

1. LRO, BRII/5/105/1, 3, 4, 7. All MS refs. are to LRO unless otherwise noted.

2. See Michael Braddick, "State Formation and Social Change in Early Modern England: A Problem Stated and Approaches Suggested," *Social History* 16 (1991): 1–17.

3. VCH *Leicester*, vol. 4, *The City of Leicester*, p. 1; Mary Bateson, ed., *The Records of the Borough of Leicester*, vol. 3 (Leicester, 1905) (hereafter *RBL* 3), p. 247; Henry Hartopp, ed., *Register of the Freemen of Leicester, 1196–1770* (Leicester, 1927), *passim*.

4. *RBL* 3, pp. 291–97, 233. The corporation petitioned for charters in 1588–89, 1599, 1605–9, and 1629–32.

5. G.E.C., q.v. "Huntingdon, earldom," "Hastings, barony."

6. Ibid.

7. *RBL* 3, p. 58 (Francis earl of Huntingdon to corporation of Leicester, 14 November 1549); *RBL* 3, p. 60 (same to same, 25 November 1549).

8. The evidence for gift giving can be found throughout the annual Chamberlain's Accounts under the section headed "Gifts of wine, sugar, etc." These accounts are in BRIII/2.

9. Claire Cross, *The Puritan Earl: The Life of Henry Hastings, Third Earl of Huntingdon 1536–1595* (London and New York, 1966), pp. 3, 16–17. As his biographer suggests, he was referred to as the Puritan Earl.

10. *RBL* 3, pp. 118, 134, 149, 152, 200, 226, 255, 282, 299. See also BRII/1/3, fol. 75, and BRII/5/25. One of those who may have remained Catholic was his brother and heir, Sir George Hastings.

11. *RBL* 3, pp. 148, 272.

12. Ibid., p. 2.

13. Ibid., pp. 296, 297, 219, 221, 252. Mr. Tusser, the attorney of the duchy, wanted to prosecute the townsmen, but they wished to compose. The mayor asked the earl to call Tusser before him and persuade the attorney to compromise. Although it ultimately required many trips to the duchy court to petition and to the earl of Huntingdon to ask advice, the borough finally settled with Tusser and got the desired lease.

14. Ibid., pp. 239, 240, 247.

15. Ibid., pp. 111, 182, 209, 220.

16. Paul Hasler, ed., *The House of Commons, 1559–1603* (London, 1981), vol. 1, p. 193; BRII/5/53; *RBL* 3, pp. 299, 301, 318, 321, 328. See also John Gruenfelder, "Electoral Influence of the Earls of Huntingdon," *Transactions of the Leicestershire Archaeological and Historical Society* 50 (1974–75): 18.

17. See Cross, *The Puritan Earl*, chap. 4, for details of some of this earl's dealings with the town of Leicester. The portrait of the earl still hangs in the Leicester Guildhall. It would be interesting to know the specific circumstances around the creation of this portrait. In 1623 the third earl had been dead 28 years and his great-nephew Henry carried the family mantle. The latter Henry had an intense and not always tranquil relationship with the townsmen of Leicester, as shall be seen.

18. See Cross, *The Puritan Earl*, esp. chap. 3, for a discussion of the third earl's financial difficulties and the impact on his heirs.

19. *RBL* 3, p. 385–86, 412–14. Unfortunately for the town, Sir John Grey could not be kept off the commission, but Sir Edward Hastings, the town's great friend, was added to the commission to balance out Sir John's antipathy. See also *RBL* 3, pp. 340, 346, 356, 359, 399, 422–23, 427–28.

20. BRII/18/6, fol. 145 (mayor of Leicester to earl of Huntingdon, 15 July 1603).

21. BRII/18/8, fols. 397, 398, 404, 407.

22. *RBL* 3, pp. 336–37; BRII/18/7, fol. 115 (earl of Huntingdon to mayor of Leicester, 30 September 1601); BRII/18/7, fol. 116 (same to same, 15 October 1601); *RBL* 3, p. 435; BRII/18/7, fol. 118 (earl to mayor, 26 October 1601). For two different retellings of the incident with Belgrave, see Mark Kishlansky, *Parliamentary Selection* (Cambridge, 1986), p. 70 and John Neale, *The Elizabethan House of Commons* (London, 1949), pp. 174–76.

23. BRII/18/8, fol. 431 (earl of Huntingdon to mayor, [?] January 1604).

24. Theophilus, the seventh earl, claimed that Earl Henry had tried to live in a way suitable to "that station which his great uncle [the third earl] held there." (Bodl. Lib., MS Carte 78, fol. 411.)

25. G.E.C., q.v. "Huntingdon earldom." He was born in 1587.

26. G.E.C., q.v. "Grey barony."

27. HMC, *Salisbury*, vol. 16, p. 387, vol. 17, p. 603; Hunt. Lib., Hastings Collection, HAP Box 15 (7). Earl George had specifically commended his young grandson to the care of Sir Robert Cecil for the period of his minority (HMC, *Salisbury*, vol. 10, p. 314). See also Richard Cust, "Purveyance and Politics in Jacobean Leicestershire" (unpublished paper), p. 9; my thanks to Dr. Cust for allowing me to read and use this paper.

28. Many of the fifth earl's papers exemplify his concern for his honor and his ongoing financial struggles. The bulk are in the Hastings Collection in the Huntington Library, San Marino, California; the Hastings Correspondence has been microfilmed by Harvester Microforms—*The Aristocracy, the State, and the Local Community: The Hastings Collection of Manuscripts from the Huntington Library in California, Part One: The Hastings Correspondence* (Brighton, 1986). See also Bodleian Library, MSS Carte 77 and 78. Professor Victor Stater confirms that the fifth earl of Huntingdon used his local offices to bolster his prestige in the absence of financial strength. See Stater, *Noble Government: The Stuart Lord Lieutenancy and the Transformation of English Politics* (Athens, GA, and London, 1994), pp. 8–11.

29. For more on the charter dispute, see Catherine Patterson, "Leicester and Lord Huntingdon: Urban Patronage in early Modern England," *Midland History* 16 (1991): 45–62.

30. *RBL* 3, pp. xvii, xx.

31. Numerous contemporary lists of the earl's objections and the town's answers still exist; see esp. BRI/2/35–46.

32. BRII/5/98 (Henry earl of Huntingdon to Sir John Brograve, 8 February

1605); BRI/2/36/4 (petition of Sir Henry Harrington to the lord chancellor of England).

33. BRII/5/98.

34. BRIV/9/69/7a; BRI/2/46/13. The castle was specifically a parcel of the duchy and was not under the jurisdiction of the corporation.

35. BRI/2/35/3 (petition of the corporation of Leicester to Lord Chancellor Ellesmere, [?] 1605); BRII/18/8 fol. 627 (Thomas Chettell to corporation of Leicester, 19 February 1605). Chettell complained that Mr. William Morton, a member of the corporation, stirred up the earl of Huntingdon to cause trouble for the town (BRII/18/9, fol. 26; BRI/2/40/1).

36. BRII/18/9, fol. 18 (Robert Pilkington to [mayor of Leicester], [November 1606?]); BRIII/2/75, fol. 43 (Chamberlain's Accounts, 1606–7); BRII/18/9, fol. 34 (Augustine Nicholls to mayor of Leicester, 17 January 1607).

37. BRII/18/9, fol. 34 (Nicholls to mayor, 17 January 1607).

38. BRIII/2/75, fol. 39 (Chamberlain's Accounts, 1606–7); Hunt. Lib., Hastings Collection, HA4814 (countess of Huntingdon to earl of Huntingdon, [date illegible, but 1607]); HA4815 (same to same, c. January 1607). This resort to the countess marks an interesting tactic on the part of the town and reveals as much about husband-wife relations as about patronage ties. The corporation probably took full advantage of the fact that the countess was a very young woman whose sympathies might be played upon readily. Had the townsmen been able to oblige the countess through their gift, the obligation would have devolved upon her husband as well. Hence the earl urged her so adamantly to refuse the gelding, having no desire to be bound in this way until the townsmen atoned for their lack of deference. Countess Elizabeth obeyed her husband, but the corporators gained her sympathies if not her full participation in their plan.

39. BRII/18/9, fol. 71 (Hugh Hunter to Mr. Chatwyn, 30 March 1607); BRII/18/9, fol. 71 appended note (Chatwyn to Hunter, 1 April 1607); BRII/18/9, fol. 70 ("My Remembrance to Mr. Recorder," [n.d., but March 1607]); BRIII/2/75, fol. 39 (Chamberlain's Accounts 1606–7).

40. For a full recounting of events in Leicester during this very dramatic period, see Patterson, "Leicester and Lord Huntingdon," pp. 53–55.

41. BRIII/2/75, fol. 40; BRII/18/9, fol. 189.

42. BRII/18/9, fols. 195, 197, 207. See Patterson, "Leicester and Lord Huntingdon," pp. 55–57, for a more detailed discussion of this period of the charter negotiations.

43. BRII/18/9, fols. 207, 248, 267, /10, fols. 270, 274; BRI/1/61/1. A full translation of the charter appears in Helen Stocks, ed., *Records of the Borough of Leicester, 1603–1688* (Cambridge, 1923), pp. 79–89.

44. BRII/18/10, fol. 362 (earl of Huntingdon to mayor of Leicester, 7 June 1609); BRII/18/10, fol. 369 (mayor to earl, 13 June 1609).

45. Hunt. Lib., Hastings Collection, HA5429 (earl to mayor of Leicester, 11 August 1609).

46. Because of Ellesmere's close family connection to Huntingdon, it almost certainly involved not just crown privilege but personal politics.

47. For instance, Lord Darcy wrote to Huntingdon to prefer a man to be lecturer at Leicester, as Huntingdon was "potent amongst that people." (Hunt. Lib., Hastings Collection, HA1906.)

48. New Year's gifts to the earl and countess are listed for every year of the fifth earl's life in the town chamberlains' accounts, BRIII/2/73–82. The value of the gift was usually in the range of £5 to £7, depending on the year. In 1610, because of the ravages of the plague, the corporation agreed to send a smaller than normal gift, valued at £4 4s. 11d. (BRII/18/11, fol. 31; BRIII/2/76, fol. 64.)

49. BRIII/2/76, fols. 65, 148, /78, fols. 23, 106a, /77, fols. 28, 70.

50. BRIII/2/75, fol. 43, /76, fol. 150.

51. Thomas North, ed., *The Accounts of the Churchwardens of St. Martin's, Leicester* (Leicester, 1884), pp. 161, 163, 171, 172, 173, 177, 192; ibid., pp. 156, 162.

52. BRII/18/13, fol. 411; BRIII/2/77, fol. 113. A member of the corporation rode to see the earl at least once a year, and often four or five times. Ashby was a day's ride away from Leicester, so the emissary usually had to stay over night. In contrast, Bradgate, the home of the Grey family, was just outside of Leicester, but very rarely did the corporation send delegations to speak to Lord Grey.

53. BRII/18/11, fol. 143 (earl to corporation, 25 February 1612); BRIV/3/38 (mayor to earl, 6 January 1613); BRII/18/12, fol. 139 (earl to mayor, 17 March 1617); BRII/18/12, fol. 140 (mayor to earl, 22 March 1617); BRII/18/12, fol. 120 (Common Hall, 15 January 1617); BRII/18/11, fol. 147 (earl to corporation, 2 March 1612); BRII/18/12, fol. 6 (earl to corporation, 2 October 1615); BRII/18/12, fol. 159 (earl to mayor, 9 May 1617); BRII/18/12, fol. 158 (mayor to earl, 14 May 1617); BRII/18/11, fol. 72 (earl to corporation, 3 July 1616).

54. BRII/18/11, fol. 12 (mayor to earl, [1610 or 1611]); ibid., fol. 204 (mayor to earl, 22 June 1612); BRII/18/12, fol. 293 (mayor to earl, 18 June 1618). He aided them in getting the county to contribute to plague relief during the serious outbreak of 1610–11 and in getting assistance from the county for road repairs when the king came on progress in 1612. He also helped them to obtain their desired candidate for schoolmaster, Mr. Wallys.

55. BRII/18/9, fol. 255 (Renell Payne to mayor, 31 August 1608), fol. 250 (Common Hall, 9 September 1608); BRII/6/13 (earl to mayor, 22 May 1614), /14 (earl to mayor, 12 July 1614), /15 (Edmund Loe to mayor, 13 July 1614). According to Loe, "his Honor hath procured me that favor with the Dean of Westminster and others which will benefit me more than that place [in Leicester] can do." The earl clearly had his own network of clients, offices, and favor that he had to balance in order to retain his status as patron.

56. BRII/5/136 (corporation to earl, 6 August 1614).

57. BRII/18/10, fols. 442 (earl to corporation, 3 May 1610), 439 (corporation to earl, 7 May 1610), 437 (earl to corporation, 9 May 1610); the election indentures are at fols. 475–76.

58. BRII/13/3 (Sir Thomas Parry to corporation, 21 February 1614), /5 (earl to corporation, 4 March 1614); John Nichols, *The History and Antiquities of the County of Leicester* (London, 1795; reprint Wakesfield,

1971), vol. 1, pt. 2, p. 341 (Robert Heyrick to Sir William Heyrick, 22 February 1614).

59. BRII/13/4 (Sir William Heyrick to corporation, 26 February 1614).

60. Nichols, *Leicestershire*, vol. 1, pt. 2, p. 341 (Robert Heyrick to Sir William Heyrick, 26 February 1614); BRII/13/7, 8 (Sir Francis Harvey to mayor, 11 March 1614, corporation to Chancellor Parry, [?] March 1614); Nichols, *Leicestershire*, p. 341 (Robert Heyrick to Sir William Heyrick, 14 March 1614); BRII/13/8 (corporation to earl, 14 March 1614); Nichols, *Leicestershire*, p. 341 (Robert Heyrick to Sir William Heyrick, 22 March 1614). I would like to thank Mr. John Ferris of the History of Parliament Trust for allowing me to see the unpublished constituency report for Leicester, 1604–28.

61. BRII/2/69 (Common Hall, 2 April 1614); BRII/13/11. Although the choice of Rich and Leigh may have been in the town's best interest, the corporators remained concerned that the two knights knew too little about Leicester and its problems. The mayor and aldermen wrote a letter to the two, asking them to take special care of their corporation and others, particularly on the issues of depopulation and decay of tillage and of the brewing of strong ale and beer. "And so for any other good motion which shall be made in the Parliament House for good of the Church, Commonwealth, and Corporations we earnestly desire you to show yourselves forward to the effecting thereof" (BRII/5/130).

62. It is a mark of Heyrick's care for the town, and a testament to the flexibility of patronage, that Sir William continued to broker the hospital business for Leicester despite this disappointment.

63. For instance, helping the corporation buy a large property outside the borough (BRII/5/120 [earl to Sir William Smyth, 20 December 1613]); BRIII/2/76, fol. 164; Bodl. Lib., MS Eng. hist. c. 475, fol. 55 (Thomas Sacheverell to Sir William Heyrick, 19 July 1614); consulting about local business such as the schoolmaster and the almshouses (BRII/18/12, fols. 193, 274, 293, 492); and choosing local officers (BRII/18/12, fols. 238, 244, 248).

64. Thomas Cogswell explores in detail the place of the fifth earl of Huntingdon in county politics and his serious difficulties in maintaining his position in *Home Divisions: Aristocracy, the State, and Provincial Conflict* (Manchester, 1998). I would like to thank Prof. Cogswell for kindly allowing me to read the manuscript of his book prior to publication.

65. For a general discussion of the position of the lord lieutenancy in the early modern state, see Stater, *Noble Government*. See also T. G. Barnes, *Somerset 1625–40: A County's Government during the "Personal Rule"* (Oxford, 1961), and Anthony Fletcher, *Reform in the Provinces* (New Haven, 1986), for more on this general theme.

66. BRII/18/15, fol. 581; Hunt. Lib., Hastings Collection, HAM Box 53 (6), *Leicestershire and Rutland Lieutenancy Book* (hereafter *LRLB*), fols. 197v–98r.

67. *RBL* 3, pp. 340, 400.

68. Hunt. Lib., Hastings Collection, HA8519, HA5458, HA8520; BRII/18/14, fols. 7, 8, 17, 20, 21.

69. Hunt. Lib., Hastings Collection, HA9221, HA5478, HA387, HA5479,

HA1725, HA5481, HA8524, HA9222; BRII/18/14, fol. 279. Sir William Heyrick by this time had offended the duke of Buckingham over the monopoly of gold and silver thread, and his position in the political wilderness may partly explain why he did not stand again. It may also be more simply explained as a gracious act on his part, deferring to his brother-in-law Chancellor May. Unfortunately, the earl's response to the town's "sleight of hand" is not recorded. But his brother Sir George did serve for Leicester in the succeeding two parliaments.

70. BRII/18/15, fols. 451, 462, 502, 531.

71. BRII/18/15, fol. 235; Hunt. Lib., Hastings Collection, HA8522, HA8523; BRII/18/15, fols. 446, 448, 449.

72. For more on Huntingdon during this difficult period, see Cogswell, *Home Divisions*.

73. Hunt. Lib., Hastings Collection, *LRLB*, fols. 92–93, 54, 149. See also Stater, *Noble Government*, pp. 8–11.

74. Hunt. Lib., Hastings Collection, HA5514 (earl of Huntingdon to earl of Marlborough, 22 January 1627).

75. Hunt. Lib., Hastings Collection, HAF 8(32). The earl and his wife took this trip from 28 August to 28 September 1626, during which they spent £500. I would like to thank Tom Cogswell for pointing out the significance of Huntingdon's trip at this time.

76. Hunt. Lib., Hastings Collection, HAF 8(6).

77. Hunt. Lib., Hastings Collection, HA3148 (Sir William Fawnt to Sir Wolstan Dixie, 15 November 1626), HA2294 (Sir Wolstan Dixie to Sir William Fawnt, [November 1626]), HA5519 (Huntingdon to Mr. Leeving, 27 February 1628); *LRLB*, fols. 118v, 207v, 212. The earl was eventually cleared of the accusations and those who made them were punished by the Privy Council. The lords of the council did, however, concede that "perhaps by the directions you had, the country were put to some more charges than the occasions of service since require" (HA4240, Privy Council to Huntingdon, 27 December 1627).

78. BRII/18/15, fols. 567, 575, 576, 578, 580, 581, /16, fols. 125, 131, 135.

79. *CSPD* 1625–26, p. 195.

80. BRII/18/16, fol. 139.

81. BRII/18/16, fols. 162, 145.

82. BRII/18/16, fol. 179.

83. BRII/18/16, fol. 163.

84. BRII/18/16, fol. 249; /17, fol. 285. This offer gives some credence to Linda Peck's suggestion that money and the market intruded themselves more fully into government and the Court in the early Stuart period. Linda L. Peck, *Court Patronage and Corruption in Early Stuart England* (Boston, 1990), pp. 38, 211–13.

85. James Thompson, *The History of Leicester* (Leicester, 1849), p. 353.

86. Hunt. Lib., Hastings Collection, HA5530. Huntingdon's suit dragged on for years. His wife, Elizabeth, who had many connections at Court, spent a considerable amount of time in the early 1630's pursuing her husband's suit in London. She in fact died in London in 1633 at the home of the earl of Bridgewater

while pursuing this suit. The earl finally received some satisfaction in 1640; in return for a "free gift" of £3000 from King Charles, he relinquished all of his rights as forester of Leicester Forest to the crown. (HA4846-HA4854; Hunt. Lib., EL 6839, 6840; BL, Harl. MS 3881, fol. 65v; *CSPD* 1639, p. 617.)

87. Hunt. Lib., *LRLB*, fol. 209r.

88. BRII/18/16, fol. 243; Hunt. Lib., Hastings Collection, HA8526. Stanhope was also a Forced Loan refuser.

89. BRII/18/18, fols. 37, 38; Bodl. Lib., MS Carte 78, fol. 92; BRII/18/18, fol. 140; Bodl. Lib., MS Carte 78, fol. 95v. According to the composition list maintained in the earl of Huntingdon's papers, nine men in Leicester were eligible for knighthood, and each of these composed for £10, with the wealthiest, Mr. William Ive, paying £20.

90. Hunt. Lib., Hastings Collection, HA5515.

91. See Hunt. Lib., Hastings Collection, HA5541, HA2296, HA5542, HA5543, HA3149, HA3150; HAL Box 5 (12).

92. BRI/2/45/1; PRO, SP16/146/40, 41; BRI/2/45/2, 3; BRII/18/17, fols. 469, 507, 522, /18, fol. 8.

93. BRII/18/18, fol. 269; Stocks, ed., *Records of Leicester*, p. 261.

94. Stocks, ed., *Records of Leicester*, p. 264; PRO, PC2/42, pp. 14–16.

95. G.E.C., q.v. "Grey, barony," "Stamford, earldom."

96. BRII/18/19, fols. 488, 610, 614, 641.

97. PRO, SP16/233/60; BRII/18/19, fols. 425–26, 440; BRII/18/20, fols. 210, 211, 222.

98. BRII/18/19, fol. 441.

99. BRII/18/19, fols. 442, 449, 457.

100. BRIII/2/80, fol. 216, /81, fols. 69, 98. In March 1638, the Common Hall ordered that a distress be taken against 31 men for their Ship Money assessments. Many of those distrained came from families who actively participated in civic government, and several individuals can be identified as current or future members of the corporation. Six of the men were members of the corporation in 1640. Mr. William Speechley, who headed the list for distraints, was a member of the 24 by 1640, served as coroner in 1640–41, steward of the fair in 1646–47, and mayor in 1649–50. It is likely that he was one of the 24 in 1638, when he refused to pay the levy. Three of those named—Alexander Cotes, Thomas Overing, and William Callis—were listed as members of the corporation both in November 1660 and in October 1662, after the Corporation Act had been enforced in Leicester. (BRII/18/20, fol. 210, /21, fol. 642; Stocks, ed., *Records of Leicester*, pp. 598–607.)

101. BRII/18/21, fols. 522, 508. Unfortunately, the original letter from the earl to the mayor is no longer extant. Unlike the records from the earlier part of the century, those from the 1630's and onward are woefully skimpy.

102. BRII/18/21, fols. 593, 596. Again, the original letter from the earl to the corporation no longer exists.

103. BRII/18/21, fol. 599.

104. BRII/18/22, fol. 14 (cf. Hunt. Lib., Hastings Collection, HA8527). Presumably, the rate in question was to pay for the muster ordered by King Charles

in response to the Bishop's War; the order to Huntingdon and his son Ferdinando is dated 3 September 1640. (BRII/18/22, fol. 1.)

105. Hunt. Lib., Hastings Collection, HA5557, fol. 2.

106. BRII/18/21, fols. 548, 550, 551, 552; Hunt. Lib., Hastings Collection, HA5551; BRII/18/21, fol. 549.

107. BRII/18/21, fols. 578, 579, 584.

108. Probably in recognition of the earl's advanced age (he was 53), the king issued the commission to the earl and his eldest son, Ferdinando Lord Hastings, as joint lieutenants. (Hunt. Lib., HAM 58A [11].)

109. BRII/18/22, fols. 3, 8, 10. Huntingdon's candidates lost in both the spring and autumn elections for knights of the shire. (John Gruenfelder, *Influence in Early Stuart Elections* [Columbus, OH, 1981], p. 192.)

110. Nichols, *Leicester*, vol. 1, pt. 2, p. 456; Hunt. Lib., Hastings Collection, HA5549.

111. Huntingdon had long supported the rights of parliament and by no means advocated absolutism, but he clung firmly to his loyalty to the king. He appears to have believed in what David Smith identifies as constitutional royalism. See David L. Smith, *Constitutional Royalism and the Search for Settlement, c. 1640–1649* (Cambridge, 1994).

112. For a systematic discussion of this transition, see Stater, *Noble Government.*

113. BRII/18/22, fols. 21, 128, 217, 299.

114. BRII/18/22, fols. 289, 294, 305, /24, fol. 20.

115. The Leicester records, as those of many towns, are sketchy and uneven for the 1640's and 1650's, so clear information about events in the town is hard to come by. The Royalists sacked the town in 1645, destroying many of the archival records and stealing the town's charters. Two items in the Chamberlain's Accounts make this apparent: "Item, paid to the Town Clerk for writing the rental after the town was taken, the former Rental being part lost and the rest torn and spoiled by the Cavaliers. Item, paid to [blank] to redeem the town Charters being seized when the King's forces came to town" (BRIII/2/82, fol. 146). After the Battle of Naseby in June 1645, the town surrendered to General Fairfax. Much of the information on the town's interaction with the earl of Huntingdon and the earl of Stamford can only be gleaned from passing references in the accounts. See BRIII/2/82 (Chamberlain's Accounts, 1640–45), *passim*; BRII/18/23, fols. 542, 552, /24, fol. 457, /25, fol. 607.

116. Bodl. Lib., MS Carte 78, fol. 84; BRII/18/30, fols. 16, 19, 49, 50, 69.

117. Paul Halliday discusses the relationship in the 1670's and 1680's between the corporation of Leicester and the seventh earl of Huntingdon, Theophilus, in *Dismembering the Body Politic: Partisan Politics in England's Towns, 1650–1730* (Cambridge, 1998), pp. 189–91, 235.

CONCLUSION

1. HMC, *Rutland*, vol. 1, p. 281 (Sir George Chaworth to Elizabeth countess of Rutland, 22 February 1590; same to bailiffs and brethren of the corporation of

Retford, 22 February 1590; same to David Wadson and William Wadson, 22 February 1590).

2. See G. E. Aylmer, *The State's Servants: The Civil Service of the English Republic 1649–1660* (London, 1973).

3. This transition can be seen in Mark Kishlansky, "The Emergence of Adversary Politics in the Long Parliament," *Journal of Modern History* 49 (1977): 617–40, and *Parliamentary Selection*, esp. chap. 5.

4. The Corporation Act, 13 Charles II st. II c. 1 (1661).

5. Paul Halliday, *Dismembering the Body Politic: Partisan Politics in England's Towns, 1650–1730* (Cambridge, 1998). The book provides a systematic analysis of partisan conflict in towns and its consequences for politics and governance in England as a whole in the later Stuart period.

6. Halliday, *Dismembering*, pp. 189–91.

Bibliography

MANUSCRIPTS

British Library, London
  Additional Manuscripts
     15,084 Suffolk Lieutenancy Book
     28,036, 29,623 Dover Corporation Records
     37,818, 37,819 Nicholas Papers
     39,254 Wodehouse Papers (Suffolk Lieutenancy Book)
  Egerton Manuscripts
     2087, 2095, 2096, 2109, 2111 Dover Corporation Records
     2584 Correspondence of the Lord Wardens of the Cinque Ports
  Harleian Manuscripts
     1929, 1944, 2020, 2054, 2057, 2103, 2105, 2125, 2150 Randle Holmes
       Collections
  Lansdowne Manuscripts
     87 Various Manuscripts
  Stowe Manuscripts
     812 Randle Holmes Collections
Public Record Office, London
  C181 Chancery Crown Office commission books
  C233 Chancery Patent Office Great Seal dockets
  CHES Chester Exchequer records
  KB21 King's Bench Crown Side Order Books
  KB29 King's Bench Controlment Rolls
  PC2 Privy Council Registers, Charles I
  PROB Archdiocese of Canterbury probate records
  SO1 Signet Office Registers
  SP14 State Papers, James I
  SP16 State Papers, Charles I
Bodleian Library, Oxford
  Carte Manuscripts (MSS Carte 77, 78)
  English History Manuscripts (MS Eng. hist.)
Canterbury Cathedral Archives, Canterbury
  Canterbury burghmote book (AC4)

Cheshire Record Office, Chester
    Bishop Bridgeman's Register (EDA3)
    Cholmondley Papers (DCH/E)
Chester City Record Office, Chester
    Assembly books (AB)
    Assembly files (AF)
    Mayor's books (MB)
    Mayor's files (MF)
    Miscellaneous Chester records (CR)
    Treasurer's accounts (TAR)
    Subsidy records (CAS)
    The Diary of Thomas Whitby of Boughton, April–December 1619
Coventry City Record Office, Coventry
    City Correspondence and Loose Papers (BA/H/Q/A79)
    City Council Minute Book (BA/H/C/17/1)
    Humphrey Burton's Book (Microfilm 1124/1)
Devon Record Office, Exeter
    Dartmouth borough records (DD)
    Exeter city archives (ECA)
    Totnes borough records
Hampshire Record Office, Winchester
    Winchester City Ordinance Books (W/B1/1–4)
Hereford and Worcester Record Office, Hereford
    Hereford borough records (O/U 123, 124, 126)
Hereford and Worcester Record Office, Worcester (St. Helen's Branch)
    Worcester Chamber Order Act Books (A.14/1)
    Worcester City Account Books (A.10)   ·
Henry E. Huntington Library, San Marino, California
    Ellesmere Collection (EL)
    Hastings Collection (HA)
Hertfordshire Archives and Local Studies, Hertford
    Hertford corporation records (Off Acc 216)
    St. Albans borough records (Off Acc 1162)
Kent Archives Office, Maidstone (now Centre for Kentish Studies)
    Cinque Ports records (CP)
    Dover corporation records (uncatalogued)
    Maidstone borough records (Md)
King's Lynn Town Hall
    King's Lynn Hall Book (KL/C7/9)
Lambeth Palace Library, London
    Bacon Papers (MSS 649, 650, 651, 656)
    Shrewsbury Papers (MSS 701, 702)
    Talbot Papers (MSS 3198, 3199, 3200, 3203)
Leicestershire Record Office, Leicester
    Duchy of Lancaster records (DL)

Leicester borough records (BR)
Lincolnshire Archives, Lincoln
    Grantham corporation records
    Lincoln corporation records (L1)
Norfolk Record Office, Norwich
    Great Yarmouth Assembly Books (Y/C19/5, Y/C19/6)
    Great Yarmouth Borough Memorandum Book (Y/C18/6)
    The Book of Francis Parlett (MF/RO 396/13)
North Devon Record Office, Barnstaple
    Barnstaple borough records (B1)
Shropshire Records and Research Centre, Shrewsbury
    Ludlow borough records (LB2)
    Shrewsbury corporation records (SSR3365)
Suffolk Record Office, Bury St. Edmunds
    Bury St. Edmunds borough records (EE 500)
    Sudbury borough records (EE 501)
Suffolk Record Office, Ipswich
    Ipswich borough records (C1, C2, C5, C6, C7, C8, C9, C11, HD)
York City Archives, York
    York Assembly Books (B.33, B.34, B.35, B.36)

PRINTED PRIMARY SOURCES

Acts of the Privy Council of England. New Series, 32 vols. London, 1890–1907.

B., R. *Lachrymae Musarum.* London, 1649.

Bacon, Francis. *The Essays or Counsels, Civill and Morall, of Francis Lord Verulam, Viscount St. Albans.* London, 1629.

Bacon, Nathaniel. *The Annalls of Ipswiche.* Ipswich, 1654. Reprinted Ipswich, 1884.

Bailey, John, ed. *Transcription of the Minutes of the Corporation of Boston.* 4 vols. Boston, 1980–90.

Bateson, Mary, ed. *Records of the Borough of Leicester,* vol. 3. Cambridge, 1905.

Bennett, J. H., and J. C. Dewhurst, eds. *Quarter Sessions Records for the County Palatine of Chester 1559–1760.* Record Society of Lancashire and Cheshire Publications, vol. 94. Chester, 1940.

Birch, Walter, ed. *The Royal Charters of the City of Lincoln, Henry II to William III.* Cambridge, 1911.

Bond, Shelagh, ed., *The Chamber Order Book of Worcester, 1602–1650.* Worcestershire Historical Society, New Series, vol. 8 (1974).

Brathwaite, Richard. *The English Gentleman.* London, 1641.

Brent, Andrew, ed. *Doncaster Borough Courtier,* vol. 1. Doncaster, 1994.

Calendar of State Papers, Domestic Series, of the Reign of Elizabeth I. 10 vols. London, 1858–97.

Calendar of State Papers, Domestic Series, of the Reign of James I. 20 vols. London, 1860.

Calendar of State Papers, Domestic Series, of the Reign of Charles I. 12 vols. London, 1858–97.

Challenor, Bromley, ed. *Selections from the Records of the Borough of Abingdon.* Abingdon, 1898.

Chandler, George, ed. *Liverpool under James I.* Liverpool, 1960.

———. *Liverpool under Charles I.* Liverpool, 1965.

Chanter, J. R., and Thomas Wainwright, eds. *Reprint of the Barnstaple Records.* 2 vols. Barnstaple, 1900.

Clark, Peter, and Jennifer Clark, eds. *The Boston Assembly Minutes 1545–1575.* Lincoln Record Society Publications, vol. 77. Lincoln, 1987.

Cleland, James. *Propaideia, or the Institution of a Young Noble Man.* Oxford, 1607.

Cockburn, J. S. *Western Circuit Assize Orders, 1629–1648: A Calendar.* Camden Society, Fourth Series, vol. 17 (1976).

Colchester. *The Charters and Letters Patent Granted to the Borough.* Colchester, 1904.

Cooper, C. H., ed. *Annals of Cambridge.* 4 vols. Cambridge, 1843–45.

Cooper, Thomas. *The Art of Giving: Describing the True Nature and Right Use of Liberality.* London, 1615.

Crie of the Poore for the Death of the Right Honorable the Earl of Huntingdon, The. London, 1596.

Day, Angel. *The English Secretorie: or plaine and direct Method, for the enditing of all manner of Epistles.* London, 1595.

Dibben, A. A., ed. *Coventry City Charters.* Coventry, 1969.

East, Robert, ed. *Extracts from the Records of the Borough of Portsmouth.* Portsmouth, 1891.

F., I. *A Sermon Preached at Ashby de la Zouche at the Funerall of Elizabeth Countess of Huntingdon.* London, 1635.

Ferguson, R. S., ed. *Royal Charters of the City of Carlisle.* Carlisle, 1894.

Ferguson, R. S., and W. Nanson, eds. *Some Municipal Records of the City of Carlisle.* Carlisle, 1887.

Floyd, Thomas. *The Picture of a Perfit Commonwealth.* London, 1600.

Foster, C. W., ed. *Lincoln Episcopal Records in the Time of Thomas Cooper, Bishop of Lincoln.* Lincoln Record Society Publications, vol. 2. Lincoln, 1912.

———. *The State of the Church . . . in the Diocese of Lincoln.* Lincoln Record Society Publications, vol. 23. Horncastle, 1926.

Gibbs, A. E., ed. *The Corporation Records of St. Albans.* St. Albans, 1890.

Gibson, J. S. W., and E. R. Brinkworth, eds. *Banbury Corporation Records: Tudor and Stuart.* Banbury Historical Society Publications, vol. 15. Banbury, 1977.

Giles, William, ed. *Catalogue of the Charters, Housebooks, . . . and Old Documents Belonging to the Corporation of York.* York, 1908.

Gray, Todd, ed. *Devon Household Accounts, 1627–59.* Part II, *Henry, Fifth Earl of Bath and Rachel, Countess of Bath, 1637–1655.* Devon and Cornwall Record Society, new ser., vol. 39. Exeter, 1996.

Groombridge, Margaret, ed. *Calendar of Chester City Council Minutes 1603–*

1642. Record Society of Lancanshire and Cheshire Publications, vol. 106. Chester, 1956.

Guilding, J. M., ed. *Diary of the Corporation of Reading*, 4 vols. London, 1895.

Hardy, W. J., ed. *Calendar to the Records of the Borough of Doncaster*. 4 vols. Doncaster, 1899.

Historical Manuscripts Commission. *Eighth Report*, Appendix 1 (Manuscripts of the Corporations of Chester and Leicester). London, 1881.

———. *Ninth Report*, Appendix 1 (Manuscripts of the Corporations of Ipswich, Canterbury, and Barnstaple). London, 1883.

———. *Eleventh Report*, Appendix 7 (Manuscripts of the Corporation of Reading). London, 1888.

———. *Thirteenth Report*, Appendix 4 (Manuscripts of the Corporation of Rye). London, 1892.

———. *Fourteenth Report*, Appendix 7 (Manuscripts of the Corporations of Lincoln, Bury St. Edmunds, and Hertford). London, 1895.

———. *Fifteenth Report*, Appendix 10 (Manuscripts of the Corporations of Shrewsbury and Coventry). London, 1899.

———. *Report on the Manuscripts in Various Collections*. 8 vols. London, 1901–14. Vol. 1, *Report on the Manuscripts of the Corporation of Berwick-upon-Tweed; Burford; and Lostwithiel*; Vol. 4, *Report on the Manuscripts of the Corporation of Aldborough; Orford; and Salisbury*; Vol. 7, *Report on the Manuscripts of the Corporation of Beccles; Southwold; Thetford; and the Dissolved Corporation of Dunwich*.

———. *Report on the Manuscripts of the Duke of Rutland at Belvoir Castle*. 4 vols. London, 1888–1905.

———. *Report on the Manuscripts of the Marquess of Salisbury*. 24 vols. London, 1883–1981.

———. *Report on the Manuscripts of Reginald Rawdon-Hastings*. 4 vols. London, 1928–47.

Hobson, M. G., and H. E. Salter, eds., *Oxford Council Acts 1626–1665*. Oxford Historical Society Publications, vol. 95. Oxford, 1933.

Hoker, John Vowell alias. *The Description of the City of Exeter*. Transcribed by Walter Harte et al. 2 vols. Exeter, 1919.

Horrocks, J. W., ed. *The Assembly Books of Southampton*. 4 vols. Southampton, 1917–25.

Hull, Felix. *A Calendar of the White and Black Books of the Cinque Ports, 1432–1955*. London, 1955.

James, William, ed. *The Charters and Other Documents Relating to the King's Town and Parish of Maidstone*. London, 1925.

Jones, John Bavington, ed. *The Records of Dover*. Dover, 1920.

Kettle, Ann, ed. "Matthew Cradocke's Book of Remembrance 1614–15." In *Collections for a History of Staffordshire*. Staffordshire Record Society, Fourth Series, vol. 16 (1994): 67–169.

Lodge, Thomas, trans. *The Workes of Lucius Annaeus Seneca, Newly Inlarged and Corrected*. London, 1620.

Mabbs, A. W., ed. *Guild Steward's Book of the Borough of Calne.* Wiltshire Archaeological and Natural History Society Publications, vol. 7. Devizes, 1953.

Markham, C. A., and J. C. Cox, eds. *The Records of the Borough of Northampton.* 2 vols. Northampton, 1897.

Martin, G. H., ed. *The Royal Charters of Grantham.* Leicester, 1963.

Martin, K. S., ed. *Records of Maidstone.* Maidstone, 1926.

Maslen, Marjorie, ed. *Woodstock Chamberlain's Accounts, 1609–50.* Oxfordshire Record Society, vol. 58. Oxford, 1993.

Mayo, C. H., ed. *Municipal Records of Dorchester, Dorset.* Exeter, 1908.

Milles, Thomas. *The Catalogue of Honour, or Treasury of True Nobility Peculiar and Proper to the Isle of Great Britain.* London, 1610.

Murphy, W. P., ed. *The Earl of Hertford's Lieutenancy Papers, 1603–1612.* Wiltshire Record Society Publications, vol. 23. Devizes, 1969.

North, Thomas, ed. *The Accounts of the Churchwardens of St. Martin's, Leicester.* Leicester, 1884.

Roberts, Stephen K., ed. *Evesham Borough Records of the Seventeenth Century.* Worcestershire Historical Society, vol. 14 (1994).

Salter, H. E., ed. *Oxford Council Acts 1583–1626.* Oxford Historical Society Publications, vol. 87. Oxford, 1928.

Savage, Richard, ed. *Minutes and Accounts of the Corporation of Stratford-upon-Avon and other Records, 1553–1620,* vol. 4. Dugdale Society Publications, vol. 10. London, 1929.

Slack, Paul, ed. *Poverty in Early-Stuart Salisbury.* Wiltshire Record Society Publications, vol. 31. Devizes, 1975.

Smith, William, and William Webb. *The Vale-Royall of England, or the County Palatine of Chester Illustrated.* London, 1656.

Stanewell, L. M., ed., *Calendar of the Ancient Deeds, Letters, Miscellaneous Documents, etc., in the Archive of the Corporation of Kingston-upon-Hull.* Kingston-upon-Hull, 1951.

Steer, Francis. *Chichester City Charters.* Chichester, 1956. (The Chichester Papers, No. 3.)

Stephens, W. R., and F. T. Madge, eds. *Documents Relating to the History of the Cathedral Church of Winchester in the Seventeenth Century.* London and Winchester, 1897.

Stevenson, W. H., ed. *The Records of the Borough of Nottingham,* vols. 4 and 5. London, 1889–1900.

Stocks, Helen, and W. H. Stevenson, eds. *Records of the Borough of Leicester 1603–1688.* Cambridge, 1923.

Twemlow, J. A., ed. *Liverpool Town Books.* Liverpool, 1935.

Worth, R. N., ed. *Calendar of the Plymouth Municipal Records.* Plymouth, 1893.

Worthy, Charles, ed. *Devonshire Wills.* London, 1896.

SECONDARY WORKS

Adams, Simon. "Officeholders of the Borough of Denbigh and the Stewards of the Lordships of Denbighshire in the Reign of Elizabeth I." *Transactions of the Denbighshire Historical Society* 25 (1976): 92–113.

Adey, K. R. "Seventeenth-Century Stafford: A County Town in Decline." *Midland History* 2 (1973–74): 152–67.

Amussen, Susan. *An Ordered Society: Gender and Class in Early Modern England.* New York, 1988.

Aylmer, G. E. *The King's Servants: The Civil Service of Charles I, 1625–1642.* New York, 1961.

Barnes, T. G. *Somerset 1625–40: A County's Government during the "Personal Rule."* Oxford, 1961.

Bean, J. M. W. *From Lord to Patron: Lordship in Late Medieval England.* Manchester, 1989.

Beesley, Alfred. *The History of Banbury.* London, 1841.

Beier, A. L. "The Social Problems of an Elizabethan Country Town: Warwick, 1580–90." In *Country Towns in Pre-Industrial England*, ed. P. Clark. Leicester, 1981: 46–85.

Beik, William. *Absolutism and Society in Seventeenth-Century France: State Power and Provincial Aristocracy in Languedoc.* New York, 1985.

Bennett, Frank. *Chester Cathedral.* Chester, 1925.

Bennett, James. *The History of Tewkesbury.* Tewkesbury, 1830.

Benson, Robert, and Henry Hatcher. *Old and New Sarum or Salisbury.* Vol. 6 of the *History of Modern Wiltshire* by Sir Richard Hoare. London, 1843.

Blakeway, J. B., and H. Owen. *A History of Shrewsbury.* London, 1825.

Boissevain, Jeremy. *Friends of Friends: Networks, Manipulators, and Coalitions.* New York, 1974.

Bond, Shelagh, and Norman Evans. "The Process of Granting Charters to English Boroughs, 1547–1649." *English Historical Review* 91 (1976): 101–20.

Bonney, Margaret. *Lordship and the Urban Community: Durham and Its Overlords 1250–1540.* Cambridge, 1990.

Boynton, Lindsay. *The Elizabethan Militia 1558–1638.* Newton Abbot, 1971.

Braddick, Michael. *Parliamentary Taxation in Seventeenth-Century England.* Woodbridge, Suffolk, 1994.

———. "State Formation and Social Change in Early Modern England: A Problem Stated and Approaches Suggested." *Social History* 16 (1991): 1–17.

Brooks, C. W. "Interpersonal Conflict and Social Tension: Civil Litigation in England 1640–1830." In *The First Modern Society*, ed. A. Beier, D. Cannadine, and J. Rosenheim. Cambridge, 1989.

Brown, Keith. "Burgh, Lords and Feuds in Jacobean Scotland." In *The Early Modern Town in Scotland*, ed. Michael Lynch. London, 1987: 102–24.

Chanter, J. R. *Sketches of the Literary History of Barnstaple, including a Transcript of the Diary of Philip Wyot.* Barnstaple, 1866.

————. *Sketches of Some Striking Incidents in the History of Barnstaple.* Barnstaple, 1865.

Clark, Peter, and Paul Slack, eds. *Crisis and Order in English Towns 1500–1700.* London, 1972.

————. *English Towns in Transition 1500–1700.* Oxford, 1976.

Clark, Peter. *English Provincial Society from the Reformation to the Revolution: Religion, Politics and Society in Kent 1500–1640.* Hassocks, 1977.

————. "'The Ramoth-Gilead of the Good': Urban Change and Political Radicalism at Gloucester, 1540–1640." In *The English Commonwealth 1547–1640: Essays in Politics and Society Presented to Joel Hurstfield,* ed. P. Clark, A. G. R. Smith, and N. Tyacke. Leicester, 1979: 167–87.

Clarke, G. R. *History and Description of the Town and Borough of Ipswich.* Ipswich. 1830.

Cogswell, Thomas. *Home Divisions: Aristocracy, the State, and Provincial Conflict.* Manchester, 1998.

Cokayne, G. E. *The Complete Peerage of England, Scotland, Ireland, Great Britain and the United Kingdom by G.E.C.* 10 vols. London, 1926.

Collins, William. *Historical Landmarks of Hereford.* Hereford, 1915.

Collinson, Patrick. *The Religion of Protestants: The Church in English Society, 1559–1625.* Oxford, 1982.

Corrigan, Philip, and Derek Sayer. *The Great Arch: English State Formation as Cultural Revolution.* Oxford, 1985.

Cotton, William, and Henry Woollcombe. *Gleanings from the Municipal and Cathedral Records Relative to the History of the City of Exeter.* Exeter, 1877.

Coward, Barry. "A 'Crisis of the Aristocracy' in the Sixteenth and Seventeenth Centuries? The Case of the Stanleys, Earls of Derby 1504–1642." *Northern History* 18 (1982): 54–77.

————. *The Stanleys, Lords Stanley and Earls of Derby, 1385–1672.* Chetham Society, Third Series, vol. 30. Manchester, 1983.

Cross, Claire. "Achieving the Millenium: The Church in York during the Commonwealth." *Studies in Church History* 4 (1967): 122–42.

————. *The Puritan Earl.* New York, 1966.

————. "The Third Earl of Huntingdon and Elizabethan Leicestershire." *Transactions of the Leicestershire Archaeological and Historical Society* 36 (1969): 6–21.

Cunnington, B. H. *Some Annals of the Borough of Devizes.* Devizes, 1925.

Curtis, Muriel. *Some Disputes between the City and the Cathedral Authorities of Exeter.* History of Exeter Research Group Monograph No. 5. Manchester, 1932.

Cust, Richard. "Anti-Puritanism and Urban Politics: Charles I and Great Yarmouth." *Historical Journal* 35 (1992): 1–26.

————. *The Forced Loan and English Politics, 1626–1628.* Oxford, 1987.

————. "Purveyance and Politics in Jacobean Leicestershire." Unpublished paper, 1990.

Davies, Robert. *Walks through the City of York.* Westminster, 1880.

de Villiers, Evangeline. "Parliamentary Boroughs Restored by the House of Commons 1621–41." *English Historical Review* 67 (1952): 175–202.

Dean, David. "Parliament and Locality." In *The Parliaments of Elizabethan England*, ed. David Dean and Norman Jones. London, 1990.

———. "Parliament, Privy Council, and Local Politics in Elizabethan England: The Yarmouth-Lowestoft Fishing Dispute." *Albion* 22 (1990): 39–64.

Descriptive and Historical View of Alnwick, A. Alnwick, 1822.

Donagan, Barbara. "The Clerical Patronage of Robert Rich, Second Earl of Warwick, 1619–1642." *Proceedings of the American Philosophical Society* 120, 5 (1976): 388–419.

Drakard, John. *The History of Stamford.* Stamford, 1822.

Dyer, Alan. *The City of Worcester in the Sixteenth Century.* Leicester, 1973.

Earwaker, J. P. *East Cheshire: Past and Present.* 2 vols. Chester, 1877–80.

Eisenstadt, S. N., and Louis Roniger. "Patron-Client Relations as a Model of Structuring Social Exchange." *Comparative Studies in Society and History* 22 (January 1980): 42–77.

Ellis, Steven. *Tudor Frontiers and Noble Power: The Making of the British State.* Oxford, 1995.

Elton, G. R. *The Tudor Revolution in Government.* Cambridge, 1953.

Ertman, Thomas. *Birth of the Leviathan: Building States and Regimes in Medieval and Early Modern Europe.* Cambridge, 1997.

Esler, Anthony. *The Aspiring Minds of the Elizabethan Younger Generation.* Durham, NC, 1966.

Evans, J. T. "The Decline of Oligarchy in Seventeenth-Century Norwich." *Journal of British Studies* 14 (1974): 46–76.

———. *Seventeenth-Century Norwich.* Cambridge, 1979.

Everitt, Alan. "Country, County, and Town: Patterns of Regional Evolution in England." *Transactions of the Royal Historical Society*, Fifth Series, 29 (1979): 79–108.

Fleming, David. "Faction and Civil War in Leicestershire." *Transactions of the Leicestershire Archaeological and Historical Society* 57 (1981–82): 26–36.

Fletcher, Anthony. *A County Community in Peace and War: Sussex 1600–1660.* London, 1975.

———. "Factionalism in Town and Country: The Significance of Puritanism and Arminianism." *Studies in Church History* 16 (1979): 291–300.

———. *Reform in the Provinces: The Government of Stuart England.* New Haven, CT, 1986.

Fletcher, Anthony, and John Stevenson, eds. *Order and Disorder in Early Modern England.* Cambridge, 1985.

Fogle, French, and Louis Knafla. *Patronage in Renaissance England.* Los Angeles, 1983.

Foster, Andrew. "Church Policies of the 1630s." In *Conflict in Early Stuart England*, ed. R. Cust and A. Hughes. London, 1989: 193–223.

Foster, Elizabeth. *The House of Lords, 1603–1649.* Chapel Hill, NC, 1983.

Fox, Levi, and Percy Russell. *Leicester Forest.* Leicester, 1948.

Freeman, Ray. *Dartmouth: A New History of the Port and Its People*. Dartmouth, 1983.

Freidrichs, Christopher. *The Early Modern City, 1450–1750*. London and New York, 1995.

Gellner, Ernest, and John Waterbury, eds. *Patrons and Clients in Mediterranean Society*. London, 1977.

Gill, A. A. M. "Ship Money during the Personal Rule of Charles I." Ph.D. diss., University of Sheffield, 1990.

Grant, Alison. "John Delbridge, Barnstaple Merchant, 1564–1639." In *Innovation in Shipping and Trade*, ed. Stephen Fisher. Exeter Maritime Studies No. 6. Exeter, 1989.

Gribble, Joseph. *Memorials of Barnstaple*. Barnstaple, 1830.

Groombridge, Margaret. "Calendar of the Council Minutes of Chester 1603–1642." M.A. thesis, University of London, 1951.

———. "Introduction to the Records of the City of Chester." *Cheshire Historian* 2 (1952): 34–40.

Gruenfelder, John. "Boston's Early Stuart Elections, 1604–1640." *Lincolnshire History and Archaeology* 13 (1978): 47–50.

———. "Electoral Influence of the Earls of Huntingdon, 1603–1640." *Transactions of the Leicestershire Archaeological and Historical Society* 50 (1974–75): 17–29.

———. *Influence in Early Stuart Elections*. Columbus, OH, 1981.

———. "The Lord Wardens and Elections, 1604–1628." *Journal of British Studies* 16 (Fall 1976): 16–22.

———. "The Parliamentary Election for Shrewsbury, 1604." *Transactions of the Shropshire Archaeological Society* 59 (1973–74): 272–77.

———. "Yorkshire Borough Elections, 1603–1640." *Yorkshire Archaeological Journal* 49 (1977): 101–14.

Halliday, Paul. *Dismembering the Body Politic: Partisan Politics in England's Towns 1650–1730*. Cambridge, 1998.

Hamilton, A. H. "The Justices of the Peace for the County of Devon in the Year 1592." *Transactions of the Devonshire Association* 8 (1876): 517–25.

Harwood, Thomas. *The History and Antiquities of the City of Lichfield*. Lichfield, 1806.

Hasler, P. W., ed. *The History of Parliament: The House of Commons, 1558–1603*. 3 vols. London, 1981.

Hay, Alexander. *The History of Chichester*. Chichester, 1804.

Heal, Felicity. *Hospitality in Early Modern England*. Oxford, 1990.

Heaton, Herbert. *The Yorkshire Woollen and Worsted Industries*. Oxford, 1920.

Hedges, John. *The History of Wallingford*. London, 1881.

Hemingway, Joseph. *History of the City of Chester*. 2 vols. Chester, 1831.

Henderson, Edith. *Foundations of English Administrative Law*. Cambridge, 1963.

Henning, B. D., ed. *The History of Parliament: The Commons 1660–1690*. 3 vols. London, 1983.

Hill, J. W. F. *Tudor and Stuart Lincoln.* Cambridge, 1956.

Hill, Lamar. "Continuity and Discontinuity: Professor Neale and the Two Worlds of Elizabethan Government." *Albion* 9 (1977): 343–58.

Hillen, Henry J. *The History of the Borough of King's Lynn.* Norwich, 1907; repr. Wakefield, Yorks., 1978.

Hirst, Derek. *The Representative of the People? Voters and Voting in England under the Early Stuarts.* Cambridge, 1975.

Historical Manuscripts Commission Guide to the Reports on Collections of Manuscripts. London, 1914.

History of Guildford, The. Guildford, 1801.

Hodges, Vivienne. "The Electoral Influence of the Aristocracy, 1604–1641." Ph.D. diss., Columbia University, 1977.

Hodgett, Gerald. *Tudor Lincolnshire.* Lincoln, 1975.

Holmes, Clive. "The County Community in Stuart Historiography." *Journal of British Studies* 19 (1980): 54–73.

Horrox, Rosemary. "The Urban Gentry in the Fifteenth Century." In *Towns and Townspeople in the Fifteenth Century*, ed. John Thomson. Gloucester, 1988: 22–44.

———. "Urban Patronage and Patrons in the Fifteenth Century." In *Patronage, the Crown, and the Provinces in Later Medieval England*, ed. Ralph Griffiths. Atlantic Highlands, NJ, 1981: 145–66.

Hoskins, W. G. "The Elizabethan Merchants of Exeter." In *Elizabethan Government and Society*, ed. S. T. Bindoff, J. Hurstfield, and C. H. Williams. London, 1961: 163–87.

———. "An Elizabethan Provincial Town: Leicester." In *Provincial England*, ed. W. G. Hoskins. London, 1963: 86–114.

Hughes, Ann. *Politics, Society and Civil War in Warwickshire 1620–1660.* Cambridge, 1987.

Hunt, William. *The Puritan Moment: The Coming of Revolution in an English County.* Cambridge, MA, 1983.

Hurstfield, Joel. *Freedom, Corruption, and Government in Elizabethan England.* London, 1973.

Hutchison, John. "The Administration of the Borough of Ipswich under Elizabeth I and James I." Ph.D. diss., Special School of History, 1952.

Hutton, W. *A History of Derby.* London, 1791.

Jack, Sybil. *Towns in Tudor and Stuart Britain.* New York, 1996.

James, Mervyn. *English Politics and the Concept of Honour, 1485–1642.* Past and Present Supplement 3. Oxford, 1978.

———. *Society, Politics and Culture: Studies in Early Modern England.* Cambridge, 1988.

James, William. *The Charters and Other Documents Relating to the King's Parish and Town of Maidstone.* London, 1825.

Johnson, A. M. "Politics in Chester during the Civil War and Interregnum, 1640–62." In *Crisis and Order in English Towns, 1500–1700*, ed. Peter Clark and Paul Slack. Leicester, 1979: 204–36.

————. "Some Aspects of the Political, Constitutional, Social, and Economic History of the City of Exeter." D.Phil. diss., Oxford, 1970.

Johnson, Richard. *The Ancient Customs of the City of Hereford.* London, 1882.

Jones, John Bavington. *Annals of Dover.* Dover, 1916.

Jordan, W. K. *Philanthropy in England 1400–1660.* New York, 1959.

Keeler, Mary Frear. *The Long Parliament, 1640–1641: A Biographical Study of Its Members.* Memoirs of the American Philosophical Society, vol. 36 Philadelphia, 1954.

Kennedy, Mark. "Charles I and Local Government: The Draining of the East and West Fens." *Albion* 15 (1983): 19–31.

Kettering, Sharon. "Gift-Giving and Patronage in Early Modern France." *French History* 2 (June 1988): 131–51.

————. *Patrons, Brokers, and Clients in Seventeenth-Century France.* Oxford, 1986.

Keynes, F. A. *By-Ways of Cambridge History.* Cambridge, 1947.

Kishlansky, Mark. *Parliamentary Selection: Social and Political Choice in Early Modern England.* Cambridge, 1986.

Knafla, Louis. *Law and Politics in Jacobean England: The Tracts of Lord Chancellor Ellesmere.* Cambridge, 1977.

Knights, C. B. *A History of the City of York.* 2nd ed. York, 1944.

Lake, Peter. "The Collection of Ship Money in Cheshire during the Sixteen-Thirties: A Case Study of Relations between Central and Local Government." *Northern History* 17 (1981): 44–71.

Latimer, John. *The Annals of Bristol in the Seventeenth Century.* Bristol, 1900.

Lehmberg, Stanford. *The Reformation of Cathedrals.* Princeton, NJ, 1988.

List and Index Society. *The Henry E. Huntington Library Hastings Manuscripts.* L.I.S. Special Services, vol. 22. London, 1987.

Lyon, John. *History of the Port and Town of Dover.* Dover, 1813.

Lytle, Guy, and Stephen Orgel, eds. *Patronage in the Renaissance.* Princeton, NJ, 1981.

MacCaffrey, Wallace. *Exeter, 1540–1640.* Cambridge, MA, 1958.

————. "Place and Patronage in Elizabethan Politics." In *Elizabethan Government and Society,* ed. S. T. Bindoff et al. London, 1961: 95–126.

Mączak, A., and E. Müller-Luckner, eds. *Klientelsysteme in Europa der Frühen Neuzeit.* Munich, 1988. (Schriften des Historischen Kollegs, Kolloquien 9).

Major, Kathleen. "The Lincoln Diocesan Records." *Transactions of the Royal Historical Society,* Fourth Series, 22 (1940): 39–66.

Mauss, Marcel. *The Gift: Forms and Functions of Exchange in Archaic Societies.* Trans. Ian Cunnison. London, 1954.

May, George. *The History of Evesham.* Evesham, 1834.

Mayhall, John. *The Annals and History of Leeds.* Leeds, 1860.

McClendon, Muriel. "'Against God's Word': Government, Religion, and the Crisis of Authority in Early Reformation Norwich." *Sixteenth-Century Journal* 25 (1994): 353–69.

McFarlane, K. B. *The Nobility of Later Medieval England.* Oxford, 1973.

Mentzer, Raymond. *Blood & Belief: Family Survival and Confessional Identity among the Provincial Huguenot Nobility.* West LaFayette, IN, 1994.

Miller, Edward. *The History and Antiquities of Doncaster.* Doncaster, n.d.

Miller, John. "The Crown and the Borough Charters in the Reign of Charles II." *English Historical Review* 100 (1985): 53–84.

Milner, John. *The History and Survey of the Antiquities of Winchester.* 2 vols. Winchester, 1839.

Molyneaux, John. "Clientage Groups in the English Parliaments of the 1620's." Ph.D. diss., University of Virginia, 1968.

[Morant, Philip]. *The History and Antiquities of Colchester.* Colchester, 1789.

Morgan, Victor. "Some Types of Patronage, Mainly in Sixteenth and Seventeenth Century England." In *Klientelsysteme in Europa der Frühen Neuzeit,* ed. Antoni Maczak. Munich, 1988: 91–115.

Morrill, J. S. *Cheshire 1630–1660: County Government and Society during the English Revolution.* Oxford, 1974.

Morris, Rupert. *Chester in the Plantagenet and Tudor Reigns.* Chester, n.d.

Muldrew, Craig. "Credit and the Courts: Debt Litigation in a Seventeenth-Century Urban Community." *Economic History Review* 46 (1993).

Murray, K. M. E. *The Constitutional History of the Cinque Ports.* Manchester, 1935.

Neale, John. *The Elizabethan House of Commons.* London, 1949.

Nichols, John. *The History and Antiquities of the County of Leicester.* London, 1795, reprinted Wakesfield, Yorkshire, 1971.

Nichols, John Gough. "The Heyricke Letters." *Transactions of the Leicestershire Architectural and Archaeological Society* 2 (1870): 11–20.

Noonkester, Myron. "Kings of Their Counties: The Shrievalty in England from Elizabeth I to Charles I." Ph.D. diss., University of Chicago, 1984.

O'Day, Rosemary. "The Triumph of Civic Oligarchy in Seventeenth Century England." In *The Traditional Community under Stress,* ed. Rosemary O'Day et al. Milton Keynes, 1977: 103–36.

Oliver, George. *The History and Antiquities of the Town and Minster of Beverley.* Beverley, 1829.

Ormerod, George. *The History of the County Palatine and City of Chester.* Chester, 1819.

Owens, G. L. "Norfolk 1620–1641: Local Government and Central Authority in an East Anglian County." Ph.D. diss., University of Wisconsin, 1970.

Palliser, David. *Tudor York.* Oxford, 1979.

Palmer, Charles. *History of the Town and Castle of Tamworth.* Tamworth, 1845.

Palmer, Marilyn, ed. "The Aristocratic Estate: The Hastings in Leicestershire and South Derbyshire." Unpublished conference papers, Leicester University, 1982.

Pape, T. *Newcastle-under-Lyme in Tudor and Early Stuart Times.* Manchester, 1938.

Parker, L. A. "The Agrarian Revolution at Cotesbach, 1501–1612." *Transactions of the Leicestershire Archaeological and Historical Society* 24.

[Parkins, C.] *The History of Great Yarmouth*. Lynn, 1776.

Peck, Linda L. "The British Case: Corruption and Political Development in the Early Modern State." In *Before Watergate: Problems of Corruption in American Society*, ed. S. N. Eisenstadt et al. New York, 1979: 35–48.

———. "Corruption and the Court of James I: The Undermining of Legitimacy." In *After the Reformation: Essays in Honor of J. H. Hexter*, ed. Barbara Malament. Philadelphia, 1980: 75–94.

———. *Court Patronage and Corruption in Early Stuart England*. New York, 1990.

———. "'For a King Not to Be Bountiful Were a Fault': Perspectives on Court Patronage in Early Stuart England." *Journal of British Studies* 25 (1986): 31–61.

———. *Northampton: Patronage and Policy at the Court of James I*. London, 1982.

Perry, H. L. *The Founding of Exeter School*. Exeter, 1913.

Picton, J. A. *Memorials of Liverpool, Historical and Topographical*. 2nd ed., London, 1875.

Poole, Benjamin. *Coventry: Its History and Antiquities*. London and Coventry, 1870.

Prestwich, Menna. *Cranfield: Politics and Profits under the Early Stuarts*. Oxford, 1966.

Prince, John. *Danmonii Orientales Illustres, or the Worthies of Devon*. Exeter, 1701.

Reed, Michael. "Ipswich in the Seventeenth Century." Ph.D. diss., Leicester University, 1973.

Richards, J. "The Greys of Bradgate in the English Civil War: A Study of Henry Grey, First Earl of Stamford and His Son and Heir Thomas, Lord Grey of Groby." *Transactions of the Leicestershire Archaeological and Historical Society* 62 (1988): 32–52.

Roberts, John. "The Armada Lieutenant: His Family and Career, Part I." *Transactions of the Devonshire Association* 102 (1970): 71–85. "Part II." *TDA* 103 (1971): 103–22.

———. "Parliamentary Representation of Devon and Dorset 1559–1601." M.A. thesis, University of London, 1958.

Robertson, James C. "London 1580–1642: The View from Whitehall, the View from Guildhall." Ph.D. diss., Washington University, St. Louis, 1993.

Rosen, Adrienne. "Winchester in Transition, 1580–1700." In *Country Towns in Pre-Industrial England*, ed. P. Clark. London, 1981: 144–95.

Ross, Charles, ed. *Patronage, Pedigree, and Power in Later Medieval England*. Gloucester, 1979.

Rowe, Margery, and Andrew Jackson. *Exeter Freemen 1266–1967*. Devon and Cornwall Record Society Publications, Extra Series. Exeter, 1973.

Rowe, Violet. "The Influence of the Earls of Pembroke on Parliamentary Elections, 1625–41." *English Historical Review* 50 (1935): 242–56.

Rudder, Samuel. *The History and Antiquities of Gloucester*. Cirencester, 1781.

Russell, J. M. *The History of Maidstone*. Maidstone, 1881, reprinted Rochester, Kent, 1978.

Russell, Percy. *The Good Town of Totnes*. Exeter, 1964.

Sacks, David Harris. "The Corporate Town and the English State: Bristol's 'Little Businesses' 1625–1641." *Past and Present* No. 110 (February 1986): 69–105.

———. *The Widening Gate: Bristol and the Atlantic Economy, 1450–1700*. Berkeley and Los Angeles, 1991.

Salmon, N. *The History of Hertfordshire*. London, 1728.

Schochet, G. J. *Patriarchalism in Political Thought*. London, 1975.

Seacombe, John. *Memoirs of the Ancient and Honourable House of Stanley*. Manchester, 1767.

Seaver, Paul. *The Puritan Lectureships: The Politics of Religious Dissent, 1560–1662*. Stanford, CA, 1970.

Sharpe, J. A. "'Such Disagreement betwyx Neighbors': Litigation and Human Relations in Early Modern England." In *Disputes and Settlements: Law and Human Relations in the West*, ed. John Bossy. Cambridge, 1983: 167–88.

Sharpe, Kevin. *The Personal Rule of Charles I*. New Haven, CT, 1992.

Simpson, Robert. *The History and Antiquities of Derby*. Derby, 1826.

Skillington, S. H. *A History of Leicester*. Leicester, 1923.

Slack, Paul. "Poverty and Politics in Salisbury 1597–1666." In *Crisis and Order in English Towns 1500–1700*, ed. P. Clark and P. Slack. London, 1972: 164–203.

———. "Religious Protest and Urban Authority: The Case of Henry Sherfield, Iconoclast, 1633." *Studies in Church History* 9 (1972): 295–302.

Smith, A. Hassell. "Militia Rates and Militia Statutes 1558–1663." In *The English Commonwealth 1547–1640*, ed. P. Clark, A. G. R. Smith, N. Tyacke. Leicester, 1979: 95–110.

Smith, David. "The Fourth Earl of Dorset and the Politics of the Sixteen-Twenties." *Historical Research* 65 (1992): 37–53.

Smith, G. C. M. *The Family of Withypoll, with Special Reference to the Manor of Christchurch, Ipswich*. Ipswich, 1936.

Smith-Dampier, J. L. *East Anglian Worthies*. Oxford, 1949.

Snow, Vernon. "John Hooker's Circle: Evidence from His New Year's Gift List of 1584." *Devon and Cornwall Notes and Queries* 33 (Spring 1977): 273–77.

Somerville, Robert. *History of the Duchy of Lancaster*. London, 1953.

———. *Office-holders in the Duchy and County Palatine of Lancaster from 1603*. Chichester, 1972.

Speed, John. *History and Antiquities of Southampton*, ed. Elinor Aubrey. Southampton Record Society, 1909.

Stater, Victor. *Noble Government: The Stuart Lord Lieutenancy and the Transformation of English Politics*. Athens, GA and London, 1994.

Stone, Lawrence. *The Crisis of the Aristocracy*. Oxford, 1965.

———. "The Electoral Influence of the Second Earl of Salisbury, 1614–68." *English Historical Review* 71 (1956): 384–400.

————. *Family and Fortune: Studies in Aristocratic Finance in the Sixteenth and Seventeenth Centuries.* Oxford, 1973.

Street, Fanny. "The Relations of the Bishop and Citizens of Salisbury between 1225 and 1612." *Wiltshire Archaeological and Natural History Magazine* 39 (1915–17): 319–68.

Swinden, Henry. *The History and Antiquities of the Ancient Burgh of Great Yarmouth.* Norwich, 1772.

Sydenham, John. *The History of the Town and County of Poole.* Poole, 1839, reprinted Poole, 1986.

Tait, James. "The Common Council of the Borough." *English Historical Review* 46 (1931): 1–29.

Thompson, James. *An Account of Leicester Castle.* Leicester, 1859.

————. *The History of Leicester.* Leicester, 1849.

Thompson, Pishey. *The History and Antiquities of Boston.* Boston, 1856.

Thomson, John, ed. *Towns and Townspeople in the Fifteenth Century.* Gloucester, 1988.

Tittler, Robert. *Architecture and Power: The Town Hall and the English Urban Community c. 1500–1640.* Oxford, 1991.

————. "Elizabethan Towns and 'Points of Contact': Parliament." *Parliamentary History* 8 (1989): 275–88.

————. "The Emergence of Urban Policy." In *The Mid-Tudor Polity*, ed. Jennifer Loach and Robert Tittler. London, 1980: 74–93.

————. "The End of the Middle Ages in the English County Town." *Sixteenth-Century Journal* 18 (Winter 1987): 471–87.

————. "Incorporation and Politics in Sixteenth-Century Thaxted." *Essex Archaeology and History* 8 (1976): 224–33.

————. "The Incorporation of Boroughs 1540–1558." *History* 62 (1977): 24–42.

————. *Nicholas Bacon: The Making of a Tudor Statesman.* Athens, OH, 1976.

Tomlinson, John. *Doncaster from the Roman Occupation to the Present Time.* Doncaster, 1887.

Toms, Elsie. *The Story of St. Albans.* St. Albans, 1962.

Turner, Lewis. *The History of the Ancient Town and Borough of Hertford.* Hertford, 1830.

Underdown, David. *Fire from Heaven: Life in an English Town in the Seventeenth Century.* New Haven and London, 1992.

Victoria County History of Berkshire, The. London, 1972.

Victoria County History of Cambridgeshire, The. Vol. 3, *The City and University of Cambridge.* London, 1959.

Victoria County History of Chester, The. Vol. 2. London, 1979.

Victoria County History of Durham, The. London, 1968.

Victoria County History of Leicestershire, The. Vol. 4, *The City of Leicester.* London, 1958.

Victoria County History of Stafford, The. London, 1976.

Victoria County History of Sussex, The. Vol. 3, ed. L. F. Salzman. London, 1935.

Victoria County History of Wiltshire, The. Vols. 5 and 6. London, 1957–62.

Watson, I. G. "Career and Community: A Study of the Officeholders of the Town Council in Leicester 1485–1535." M.A. thesis, Leicester University, 1988.

Webb, Sydney, and Beatrice Webb. *English Local Government from the Revolution to the Municipal Corporations Act: The Manor and the Borough.* 2 parts. London, 1908.

Weinbaum, Martin. *British Borough Charters, 1307–1660.* Cambridge, 1943.

———. *The Incorporation of Boroughs.* Manchester, 1937.

Williams, P. *The Council of the Marches of Wales under Elizabeth.* Cardiff, 1958.

Willmore, Frederic. *A History of Walsall.* Walsall, 1887.

Windeatt, Edward. "Totnes: Its Mayors and Mayoralties 1627–76." *Transactions of the Devonshire Association* 32 (1900): 111–41.

Wolf, Eric. "Kinship, Friendship, and Patron-Client Relations in Complex Societies." In *The Social Anthropology of Complex Societies*, ed. Michael Barton. London, 1969: 1–20.

Wright, Thomas. *History of Ludlow.* Ludlow, 1852.

Youings, Joyce. "Tudor Barnstaple: New Life for an Ancient Borough." *Transactions of the Devonshire Association* 121 (1989): 1–14.

Index

In this index an "f" after a number indicates a separate reference on the next page, and an "ff" indicates separate references on the next two pages. A continuous discussion over two or more pages is indicated by a span of page numbers, e.g., "57–59." *Passim* is used for a cluster of references in close but not consecutive sequence.

Library of Congress Cataloging-in-Publication Data

Patterson, Catherine F.
  Urban patronage in early modern England : corporate boroughs, the
landed elite, and the crown, 1580–1640 / Catherine F. Patterson.
      p.   cm.
  Includes bibliographical references and index.
  ISBN 0-8047-3587-5 (alk. paper)
      1. Boroughs—England—History.   2. Municipal corporations—
England—History.   3. Patronage, political—England—History.
I. Title.

JS3265.P37   1999
306.2'0942'09032—DC21   99-35537
                                                                        CIP

This book is printed on acid-free, archival-quality paper.

Original printing 1999
Last figure below indicates year of this printing:
08   07   06   05   04   03   02   01   00   99

Designed and typeset by John Feneron in 10/12.5 Sabon